The Principal N
Voyages, Traff
Discoveries of the English
Nation — Volume 03

Richard Hakluyt

Alpha Editions

This edition published in 2024

ISBN 9789362510112

Design and Setting By
Alpha Editions
www.alphaedis.com
Email - info@alphaedis.com

Contents

VOL. III

NORTH-EASTERN EUROPE AND ADJACENT COUNTRIES PART II

THE MUSCOVY COMPANY AND THE NORTH-EASTERN PASSAGE

Navigations, Voyages, Traffiques, and Discoveries
IN NORTH-EASTERN EUROPE.

A briefe Treatise of the great Duke of Moscouia his genealogie, being taken
  out of the Moscouites manuscript Chronicles written by a Polacke.

It hath almost euer bene the custome of nations, in searching out the
infancie and first beginnings of their estate, to ascribe the same vnto such
authors as liued among men in great honour and endued mankinde with
some one or other excellent benefite. Nowe, this inbred desire of all nations
to blaze and set foorth their owne petigree hath so much preuayled with the
greater part, that leauing the vndoubted trueth, they haue betaken
themselues vnto meere fables and fictions. Yea and the Chronicles of many
nations written in diuers and sundrie ages doe testifie the same. Euen so the
Grecians boasted that they were either Autocthones, that is earthbredde, or
els lineally descended from the Gods. And the Romans affirme that Mars
was father vnto their first founder Romulus. Right well therefore and
iudicially sayth Titus Liuius: Neither meane I to auouch (quoth he) ne to
disable or confute those thinges which before the building and foundation
of the Citie haue beene reported, being more adorned and fraught with
Poeticall fables then with incorrupt and sacred monuments of trueth:
antiquitie is it to be pardoned in this behalfe, namely in ioyning together
matters historicall and poeticall, to make the beginnings of cities to seeme
the more honourable. For sith antiquity it selfe is accompted such a notable
argument of true nobility, euen priuate men in all ages haue contended
thereabout. Wherefore citizens of Rome being desirous to make
demonstration of their Gentrie, vse to haue their auncestors armes painted
along the walles of their houses: in which regarde they were so puffed vp,
that oftentimes they would arrogantly disdaine those men, which by their
owne vertue had attained vnto honour. In like sorte Poets, when the
originall of their woorthies and braue champions was either vtterly
vnknowen or somewhat obscure, would ofte referre it vnto their Gods
themselues. So in these our dayes (to lette passe others) the Turkish
Emperour with great presumption boasteth himselfe to bee descended of
the Troian blood. Likewise the great duke of Moscouie, to make himselfe
and his predecessours seeme the more souereigne, deriueth the beginnings
of his parentage from the Romane Emperours, yea euen from Augustus
Caesar. Albeit therefore no man is so fonde as to accept of this report for
trueth, yet will wee briefly set downe what the Moscouites haue written in
their Chronicles as touching this matter.

Augustus (beleeue it who listeth) had certaine brethren or kinsfolkes which were appoynted gouenours ouer diuers prouinces. Amongst the rest one Prussus (of whome Prussia was named) had his place of gouernment assigned vnto him vpon the shore of the eastern or Balthick Sea, and vpon the famous riuer of Wixel. This mans graund children or nephewes of the fourth generation were Rurek, Sinaus, and Truuor, who likewise inhabited in the very same places. Whereas therefore, at the very same time the Russians or the Moscquites without any ciuill regiment possessed large and spacious territories towards the north, the foresayd three brethren, vpon the perswasion of one Gostomislius the chiefe citizen of Nouogrod, in the yeare since the worldes creation (acording to the computation of the Greekes) 6370, which was in the yeare of our Lord 572, were sent for, to beare rule. And so ioyning their kinsman Olechus vnto them, and diuiding these huge countreys among themselues, they laboured to reduce the barbarous and sauage people vnto a ciuill kinde of life.

Sinaus and Truuor deceasing without issue, Rurek succeeded and left a sonne behinde him named Igor; who not being of sufficient yeres to beare rule, was committed vnto the protection of his kinsman Olechus. The sayde Igor begate of Olha daughter vnto a citizen of Plesco (who, after her husbande was slaine by his enemies, taking her iourney to Constantinople, was there baptized by the name of Helena) a sonne called Stoslaus, who fought many battels with the neighbour countreys. Howbeit at length Stoslaus was slayne by his foe, who making a drinking cup of his skull, engraued therupon in golden letters this sentence: Seeking after other mens he lost his owne. He left behind him three sonnes, namely Teropolchus, Olega, and Vulodimir. The which Vulodimir hauing slaine his two brethren, became sole gouernour of Russia, or (as the Moscouites call it) Rosseia, his owne selfe. This man beginning at length to loath and mislike the ethnik religion, and the multitude of false gods, applyed his minde vnto the religion of Christ, and hauing taken to wife Anna sister vnto Basilius and Constantinus Emperours of Constantinople, was together with his whole nation, in the yeare of Christ 988. baptized, and imbraced the Christian religion, with the rites and ceremonies of the Greeke Church, and his name being changed, he was called Basilius.

Howbeit Zonoras reporteth that before the time of Vulodimir, Basilius Emperour of Constantinople sent a bishop vnto the Russians, by whose meanes they were conuerted vnto the Christian faith. He reporteth moreouer that they would not be perswaded vnlesse they might see a miracle: whereupon the said bishop hauing made his prayers vnto almighty God, threwe the booke of the Euangelists into the fire, which remained there vnconsumed. And that by this miracle they were moued to giue credits vnto the doctrine of Christ, and to conforme themselues thereunto.

The sonnes of Vulodimir were Vuiseslaus, Isoslaus, Iaroslaus, Suatopolcus, Borissus, Glebus, Stoslaus, Vulzeuolodus, Stanislaus, Sudislaus, and Podius who died in his childhood. Amongst the residue all Russia was diuided by their father, who not being contented with their portions, but inuading each other, were most of them slaine by their mutuall contentions. Borissus and Glebus in regard of their holy conuersation were registred for Saints, whose feasts are euery yeere celebrated with great solemnitie vpon the twelfth of Nouember.

At length Iaroslaus only got the Souereigne authoritie into his owne hands, and left behind him foure sonnes, Vvlodimir, Isoslauus, Weceslauus, and Vuszeuolodus.

The foresaid Vulodimir sonne of Iaroslaus kept his residence at the ancient citie of Kiow standing vpon the riuer of Boristhenes, and after diuers conflicts with his kinsmen, hauing subdued all the prouinces vnto himselfe, was called Monomachos, that is, the onely champion. This man (for I thinke it not amisse to report those things which their owne Manuscript Chronicles make mention of) waged warre against Constantine the Emperour of Constantinople, when he had wasted and ouerrun Thracia, being returned home with great and rich spoyles, and making preparation for new wars, Constantine sent Neophytus the Metropolitane of Ephesus and two Bishops, with the gouernour of Antiochia, and Eustaphius the Abbat of Ierusalem, to present rich and magnificent gifts vnto him; as namely, part of the crosse of Sauiour Christ, a crowne of gold, a drinking cup curiously made of Sardonyx stone, a cloake set all ouer with precious stones, and a golden chaine; commaunded them to salute him by the name of Czar (which name, as it may be prooued by many arguments, signifieth a king, and not an Emperour) and concluded a most inuiolable league of amity and friendship with him.

The foresayd Vulodimir begate Vuszeuolodus the second. This Vuszeuolodus
lefte eight sonnes behind him, Miscislaus, Isoslaus, Stoslaus, Teropolcus, Weceslaus, Romanus, Georgius, and Andrew. The sonnes of George were Roseslaus, Andrew, Basilius, and Demetrius.

Demetrius begat George, in the yeere 1237. was slaine by one Bathy, a Tartarian duke, which Bathy wasted Moscouia, and subdued the same vnto himselfe. Since which time the Russians were tributary to the Tartars, and were gouerned by such dukes as they pleased to set ouer them. Howbeit the Tartars so greatly abused that authoritie, that when they sent their ambassadours vnto the prince of Moscouie, he was constrained to goe forth and meete with them, and (as Herbortus Fulstinius in his Polonian historie reporteth) to offer them a bason full of mares milke, and if they had spilt any whit thereof vpon their horses maines, to licke it off with his toung, and hauing conducted them into his princely court, to stand bareheaded before them while they sate downe, and with all reuerence to giue eare and attendance vnto them. But by what meanes they shooke off at the length this yoake of seruitude, I will forthwith declare.

About the same time almost all Polonia, and the dukedome of Silesia were ouerrun by the Tartars with fire and sword. Who hauing burnt Presla the chiefe citie of Silesia, and being come before the citie of Legnitz, they fought there a most cruel and bloody field, wherin was slain Duke Henrie himselfe being sonne vnto the most holy and deuout lady Heduice, with many others, whose monuments and graues be as yet extant in sundry places, and with an infinite multitude of common souldiers, insomuch that the Tartars filled nine great sackes with the eares of them which they had slaine. The Tartars to the end they might obtaine the victorie, presented vnto the view of our souldiers the portrature of a mans head placed by arte magique vpon a banner, wherein the letter X. was painted, which being shaken and mooued vp and downe breathed foorth a most loathsome stench, and strooke such a terrour into the hearts of our men, that being as it were astonished with the snaky visage of Medusa, they were vtterly daunted and dismayed.

From thence Bathy and his company with the same bloodthirstie intent marched into Hungarie, and had almost slaine king Bela the fourth, who together with his sonne escaping by flight did scarcely ridde themselues out of the enemies hand. And when the whole world almost was exceedingly terrified at the cruel inuasions of this most barbarous nation, at length Pope Innocentius the fourth sending ambassadours [Marginal note: These ambassadours were Iohan. de Plano Carpini and Frier Benedict a Polonian.] vnto Bathy obtained peace for fiue yeeres: but to forsake his heathenish superstitions and to become a Christian, he would by no meanes bee perswaded. For he was by the instigation of the Saracens infected with deuilish opinions of Mahomet, as being more agreeable vnto his barbarous rudenes, which euen vnto this day the Tartars do maintaine, like as the prophane Turkes also.

This Bathy had a sonne called Tamerlan, whome the Mosoouites call Temirkutla, who likewise, as it is recorded in histories, attained vnto great renoume. For he caried about with him in a cage Baiazet the Turkish Emperour being fettered in golden chaines, and made him a laughing stocke vnto all men.

Let vs now retume vnto the Russians. George being slaine, Iaroslaus his brother succeeded in his room, and left behinde him three sonnes, Theodorus, Alexander, and Andreas. Daniel the sonne of Alexander first established his royal seat in the citie of Mosco, and magnificently building the Castle which before time had been obscure, he tooke vpon him the title of the great Duke of Russia. He had fiue sonnes, namely, George, Alexander, Borissus, Ophonias, and Iohn. This Iohn succeeded his father, and because he continually caried a scrippe about with him to bestow almes, he was sirnamed Kaleta, which word signifieth a scrippe. His sonnes were, Simeon, Iohn, and Andrew. He gaue vnto his sonne Simeon the prouinces of Vvlodimiria and Moscouia: which Simeon deceasing without issue his brother Iohn succeeded, who begate a son called Demetrius. This Demetrius had seuen sonnes, namely, Daniel, Basilius, George, Andrew, Peter, Iohn, and Constantine. Basilius reigned after his fathers death. This man disinheriting his sonne whiche was called after his owne name; because he suspected his mother of adulterie, at his death surrendred his Dukedome vnto his brother George, who kept his nephewe a long time in prison. Howbeit at his death, though himselfe had two sonnes namely Andrew and Demetrius, yet being stricken perhaps with remorse of conscience, he bestowed the Dukedome vpon his nephew Basilius. Against whom his two cousins bearing a grudge waged warre, and at length hauing taken him by a wyly stratageme they put out his eyes. Notwithstanding the Boiarens (for so the Moscouites call their nobles) continued their duetifull alleageance vnto this their blinde Duke, whom for his blindnes they called Cziemnox, that is to, say, darke or darkened. He left a sonne behind him called Iuan Vasilowich who brought the Russian common wealth, being before his time but obscure, vnto great excellencie and renowme. Who that he might the better get all the superiority into his owne hands put to death so many sonnes and nephewes of the former Dukes as he could lay hold on, and began to take vpon him the title of the great Duke of Vvlodimiria, Moscouia, and Nouogardia, and to cail himself the Monarch or Czar of all Russia. He brought vnder his subiection two principall cities, namely Plesco being the only walled citie in all Moscouie, and Mouogrod [Transcriber's note: sic.], both of them being in regard of traffike most riche and flourishing cities, and hauing bin subiect vnto the Lithuanians for the space of 50. yeeres before. The treasure of Nouogrod was so exceeding, that the great Duke is reported to haue carried home from thence 300. carts laden with gold and siluer.

He also was the first man that waged warre against the Polonians and the Liuonians: against Polonia he pretended a quarell alleaging that his daughter Helena (whome hee had married vnto Alexander the great Duke of Lithuania, which was afterward king of Polonia) was euil intreated, and was withdrawen from the Greekish religion vnto the ceremonies of the Church of Rome. But against the Liuonians for none other cause, but onely for an incredible desire of enlarging his dominions. Howbeit what impulsiue causes of litle or no moment happened in the mean season, we will in another place more plainely declare. Notwithstanding he was very often and in diuers battels vanquished by Plettebergius the great master of the Dutch knights: but it is not to the purpose to stand any longer vpon this discourse.

He was married first vnto Marie the Duke of Tyuersky his daughter, and of her hee begate Iohn, vnto whom in his life time he surrendred his Dukedome, and married him vnto the daughter of Stephan the Palatine of Moldauia: which Iohn, after he had begotten his sonne Demetrius, deceased before his father.

Afterward Iuan Vasilowich aforesaide married a wife called Sophia being daughter vnto Thomas Palælogus, which is reported to haue had her dowry out of the Popes treasury, because the Moscouite had promised to conforme himselfe vnto the Romish Church. This Sophia being a woman of a princely and aspiring minde, and often complaining that she was married vnto the Tartars vassal, at length by her instant intreatie and continual perswasions, and by a notable stratageme she cast off that slauish yoke very much vnbeseeming so mighty a prince. For whereas the Tartarian Duke had his procuratours and agents in the Moscouites court, who dwelt in their owne houses built within the very castle of Mosco, and were eye witnesses of all affaires which were there performed: Sophia said she was admonished from heauen to builde a Temple in the selfe same place where the Tartars house stoode, and to consecrate it vnto Saint Nicholas. Being therfore deliuered of a sonne she inuited the Tartarian Duke vnto the solemne baptizing of him, and beeing come, shee requested him to giue her his house, and obtained it at his hands. Which house being razed and those Tartarians espials beeing excluded, the Tartars at length were quite bereaued and vtterly dispossessed of their authoritie which they had exercised ouer the Russians for many yeres, and could neuer yet recouer it; albeit they haue giuen sundry attempts. Of his wife Sophia he begate six children, namely, a daughter called Helena, and fiue sonnes, that is to say, Gabriel, Demetrius, George, Simeon, and Andrew.

The Dukedome of right appertayned vnto Demetrius the sonne of Iohn, which was the sonne of Vasilowich by his first marriage. Howbeit Sophia preuailed so with her husband, that neglecting his graund-childe Demetrius, hee bestowed his Dukedome vpon Gabriel his sonne.

Andrew the younger had a sonne called Vvlodmir, of whom Mary was borne, which in the yeere of Christ 1573, was maried vnto Magnus the Duke of Holst.

Gabriel hauing obtained the great dukedome of Russia, changed his name calling himselfe Basilius, and applied his minde to the atchieuing of high and great enterprises. For hee reduced a great part of the dukedome of Moscouie, which Vitoldus the great Duke of Lithuania helde in possession, vnder his owne iurisdiction, and wonne vpon the riuer of Boristhenes (which the Russians call Neiper) many cities and especially Smolensco, in the yeere of our Lord 1514. Hauing diuorced his first wife, hee begate of Helena daughter vnto Duke Glinskie, Iuan Vasilowich, which now this present 1580. reigneth as great Duke. He was borne in the yeere of our Lorde 1528. the 25. of August, sixe houres after the rising of the sonne. The great dukedome of Russia fell vnto the said Iuan Vasilowich in the fifth yeere of his age, hauing his vncle George for his great protector; being 25. yeeres of age, and being of a strong body and of a courageous mind he subdued the Tartars of Cazan and Astracan vpon the riuer of Volgha, carrying their Dukes and chieftaines into captiuitie.

But by what wayes and meanes (after the league which by the intercession of the most sacred Roman Emperour, continued from the yeere 1503. for the space of fifty yeeres, was expired) hauing renewed warres against Liuonia, hee brought that most flourishing prouince into extreame miserie, vsing for the same purpose a new pretense, and alleadging that it belonged vnto him by right of inheritance, I tremble to recount: and it requireth a large historie, which perhaps in time and place conuenient some more learned then my selfe will take vpon them to addresse.

He is exceedingly addicted vnto piety and deuotion, and doth oftentimes obserue very strict fastings and abstinence with his monks: and whereas the Russes in doing reuerence and adoration vnto God doe beate their foreheads against the ground, this Iuan Vasilowich with performing of the same ceremonie causeth his forehead to be ful of boines and swellings, and sometimes to be black and blew, and very often to bleed. He is much delighted with building of Churches and spareth no cost for that purpose. Whether therfore by nature, or (which hee pretendeth to bee the cause) by reason of his subiects malice and treacherie, he be so addicted vnto all rigour and cruelty, I dare not determine, especially sithens he hath not an illiberal or mishapen countenance, as Attila is reported, to haue had. Of his first wife which was sister vnto Mikita Romanowich, beeing nowe great steward of his houshold, he begate two sonnes, namely Iuan and Theodore. And albeit he was fiue times married, yet had he not one childe more.

Whereas this Iuan Vasilowich vpon certaine friuolous reasons calleth himselfe the naturall lord of Liuonia, I thought it not amisse to adde an Epistle hereunto, which was written by a certaine honourable man concerning the same matter.

S. All we which inhabite this Prouince with all seemely reuerence and submission of mind, do offer most humble thanks vnto the Emperors most sacred and peerelesse maiesty our most gracious lord, in that according to his fatherly affection which he beareth towards all Christendome, and for the good and commodity of this our distressed and afflicted countrey, which these many yeres hath bin in stead of a bulwarke against the inuasion of barbarous nations, he hath sent his ambassadors vnto the great duke of Moscouia. In regard of which his fatherly loue and great benefite vouchsafed on vs, wee are ready when occasion shall serue, to aduenture our liues and goods; praying in the meane season vnto Almightie God, who is the onely establisher and confounder of common wealths, to bring this excellent woorke, the foundation whereof is already laide vnto a prosperous conclusion. But as touching the title which the Moscouite maketh to this prouince, to say the very trueth, we greatly wondred and were astonished at the declaration thereof. For it is most apparent, not onely out of all ancient and credible histories, but euen from the experience and state of these regions, that the said title and allegations are fabulous and fained. For out of all auncient monuments, by what names soeuer they bee called (whereof there are diuers extant among vs) it cannot be proued by any mention, nor yet by any likelihoode or coniecture, that those things which the Moscouite affirmeth concerning the people which were gouernors of these regions in times past, and concerning the right and title of his ancestors vnto this prouince, are grounded vpon truth.

For it is not vnknowen by what meanes this prouince, partly through the industry of marchants, and partly by the benefite of nauigation, was first discouered: neither is it vnknowen howe the inhabitants thereof beeing wholly addicted vnto heathenish superstitions and idolatrie, were by the croised [Footnote: *Croised*: wearing the cross, Crusaders,] knights (who drew other knights professing the same order in Prussia to aide and accompanie them in this their enterprise) and that with great labour and difficultie, conuerted vnto the Christian faith: when as at the same time the Liuonians had no knowledge at all of the iurisdiction, religion, maners, or language of Moscouie: who had not onely no conuersation nor dealings with the Moscouites, but were estranged also from all other nations whatsoeuer: for leading a miserable, poore, barbarous, and heathenish life, in sauage maner among wilde beastes, and in the desert and solitary woods, they were vtterly ignorant of God and destitute of ciuil magistrates. Howbeit this kind of gouernment was peculiar vnto them, namely that all of one familie and society vsed a kinde of reuerence vnto their elders more then to any other, whom also, that their authoritie might be the greater, they called by the name of kings, and (albeit one of their families consisted of a 100 persons) they obeyed them in al respects, and after their rude and barbarous maner did them loyal seruice. At the very same time the Moscouites had receiued the religion, and the Ecclesiasticall ceremonies of the Greeke and Easterne Church, which religion they published and dispersed throughout all prouinces subiect to their dominion, vsing their owne proper letters and characters for the same purpose. Of all which things the Liuonians which very barbarously inhabited a lande beeing enuironed with Russia, Lithuania, Samogitia, Prussia, and the Balthic Sea, neuer heard any report at all. It is moreouer to be noted that neuer at any time heretofore either within the earth, or in other places of Liuonia, there haue bene found any monuments at all of the antiquitie or letters of the Russes: which verily must needs haue come to passe, if the Moscouites, Russes, or any other nations which vse the foresaid particulars, had borne rule and authority ouer the Liuonians: yea there had beene left some remainder and token, either of their religion and diuine worship, or of their lawes and customes, or at the least of their maners, language, and letters. This indeed we can in no wise deny, that euen in Liuonia it selfe, there haue bin in times past and at this present are many and diuers languages spoken by the people. Howbeit no one language of them all hath any affinity either with the Moscouian tongue, or with the tongues of any other nations. But whereas the Moscouite pretendeth that there hath been visually paide a pension or tribute vnto himselfe and his predecessours out of the whole prouince, it is as incredible as the former.

About the beginning of this tragicall warre, the Moscouite, to cloke his tyranny and ambition vnder some faire pretense amongst other of his demaunds, made mention also of a tribute which should be due vnto him out of the bishop of Dorpat his iurisdiction, whereof notwithstanding hee could neither bring any iust account, nor affirm any certainty: howbeit there is no man liuing to be found which either can tell of his owne remembrance, or from the relation of others, that any such tribute was euer paid vnto the Moscouite. What time therefore he referred al this negotiation vnto the master of the Liuonian order, and commanded him to get what knowledge hee could therof from the men of Dorpat, and vrged the tribute, saying if it were worth but one haire, that he would not remit it: at length it was found recorded in the ancient Chronicles of Dorpat, that beyond the memory of man, when the territory of Plesco contained nothing but woods and forrests for wilde beastes, that the peasaunts of the liberty of Dorpat called Neuhus, by the consent of the Russian borderers, enioyed Bee hiues in the said woods, and paid euery yeere in lieu thereof vnto the Russian gouernours, sixe shillings of Liuonian coine. But so soone as the Russians had felled the woods and had built townes and villages in their place, the saide pension ceased together with the trees which were cut downe. Wherefore the saide sixe shillings were neuer since that time either demanded by the Russes or paid by the Liuonians. These things which I knew concerning the causes of the Liuonian warres I thought good to signifie vnto you. Giuen the 22. of May, in the yeere of our Lord 1576.

* * * * *

Ordinances, instructions, and aduertisements of and for the direction of the intended voyage for Cathay, compiled, made, and deliuered by the right worshipfull M. Sebastian Cabota Esquier, gouernour of the mysterie and companie of the Marchants aduenturers for the discouerie of Regiones, Dominions, Islands and places vnknowen, the 9. day of May, in the yere of our Lord God, 1553. and in the 7. yeere of the reign of our most dread soueraigne Lord Edward the 6. by the grace of God, king of England, Fraunce, and Ireland, defender of the faith, and of the Church of England and Ireland, in earth supreame head. [Footnote: "Some of these Instructions now indeed appear rather childish, but others might still be used as rules for any well-ordered exploratory expedition."— Nordenskiöld, *Voyage of the Vega*, vol. I, p. 58.]

First the Captaine general, with the pilot maior, the masters, marchants and other officers, to be so knit and accorded in vnitie, loue, conformitie, and obedience in euery degree on all sides, that no dissention, variance, or contention may rise or spring betwixt them and the mariners of this companie, to the damage or hinderance of the voyage: for that dissention (by many experiences) hath ouerthrown many notable intended and likely enterprises and exploits.

2. Item, for as much as euery person hath giuen an othe to be true, faithfull, and loial subiects, and liege men to the kings most excellent Maiestie, his heires and successors, and for the obseruation of all lawes and statutes, made for the preseruation of his most excellent Maiestie, and his crown Imperiall of his realmes of England and Ireland, and to serue his grace, the Realme, and this present voyage truely, and not to giue vp, intermit, or leaue off the said voyage and enterprise vntill it shalbe accomplished, so farre forth as possibilitie and the life of man may serue or extend: Therfore it behoueth euery person in his degree, as well for conscience, as for dueties sake to remember his said charge, and the accomplishment thereof.

3. Item, where furthermore euery mariner or passenger in his ship hath giuen like othe to bee obedient to the Captaine generall, and to euery Captaine and master in his ship, for the obseruation of these present orders contained in this booke, and all other which hereafter shalbe made by the 12. counsailers in this present book named, or the most part of them, for the better conduction, and preseruation of the fleete, and atchieuing of the voyage, and to be prompt, ready and obedient in all acts and feates of honesty, reason, and duetie to be ministred, shewed and executed, in aduancement and preferment of the voyage and exploit: therfore it is conuenient that this present booke shall once euery weeke (by the discretion of the Captaine) be read to the said companie, to the intent that euery man may the better remember his othe, conscience, duetie and charge.

4. Item, euery person by vertue of his othe, to doe effectually and with good wil (as farre forth as him shall complie) all and euery such act and acts, deede and deeds, as shalbe to him or them from time to time commanded, committed and enioyned (during the voyage) by the Captain generall, with the assent of the Counsell and assistants, as well in and during the whole Nauigation and voyage, as also in discouering and landing, as cases and occasions shall require.

5. Item, all courses in Nauigation to be set and kept, by the aduice of the Captaine, Pilot maior, masters, and masters mates, with the assents of the counsailers and the most number of them, and in voyces vniformely agreeing in one to preuaile, and take place, so that the Captaine generall, shall in all counsailes and assemblies haue a double voyce.

6. Item, that the fleete shal keep together, and not separate themselues asunder, as much as by winde and weather may be done or permitted, and that the Captaines, Pilots and masters shall speedily come aboord the Admiral, when and as often as he shall seeme to haue iust cause to assemble them for counsaile or consultation to be had concerning the affaires of the fleete and voyage.

7. Item, that the merchants, and other skillful persons in writing, shal daily write, describe, and put in memorie the Nauigation of euery day and night, with the points, and obseruation of the lands, tides, elements, altitude of the sunne, course of the moon and starres, and the same so noted by the order of the Master and pilot of euery ship to be put in writing, the captaine generall assembling the masters together once euery weeke (if winde and weather shal serue) to conferre all the obseruations, and notes of the said ships, to the intent it may appeare wherein the notes do agree, and wherein they dissent and vpon good debatement, deliberation, and conclusion determined, to put the same into a common leger, to remain of record for the company: the like order to be kept in proportioning of the Cardes, Astrolabes, and, other instruments prepared for the voyage, at the charge of the companie.

8. Item, that all enterprises and exploits of discouering or landing to search Iles, regions, and such like, to be searched, attempted, and enterprised by good deliberation, and common assent, determined aduisedly. And that in all enterprises, notable ambassages, suites, requests, or presentment of giftes, or presents to Princes, to be done and executed by the captaine generall in person, or by such other, as he by common assent shall appoint or assigne to doe or cause to be done in the same.

9. Item, the steward and cooke of euery ship, and their associats, to giue and render to the captaine and other head officers of their shippe weekely (or oftner,) if it shall seeme requisite, a iust or plaine and perfect accompt of

expenses of the victuals, as wel flesh, fish, bisket, meate, or bread, as also of beere, wine, oyle, or vinegar, and all other kinde of victualling vnder their charge, and they, and euery of them so to order and dispende the same, that no waste or vnprofitable excesse be made otherwise then reason and necessitie shall command.

10. Item, when any inferiour or meane officer of what degree or condition he shalbe, shalbe tried vntrue, remisse, negligent, or vnprofitable in or about his office in the voyage, or not to vse himselfe in his charge accordingly, then euery such officer to be punished or remoued at the discretion of the captaine and assistants, or the most part of them, and the person so remoued not to be reputed, accepted, or taken from the time of his remoue, any more for an officer, but to remaine in such condition and place, as hee shall be assigned vnto, and none of the companie, to resist such chastisement or worthie punishment, as shalbe ministred vnto him moderately, according to the fault or desert of his offence, after the lawes and common customes of the seas, in such cases heretofore vsed and obserued.

11. Item, if any Mariner or officer inferiour shalbe found by his labour not meete nor worthie the place that he is presently shipped for, such person may bee vnshipped and put on lande at any place within the kings Maiesties realme and dominion, and one other person more able and worthy to be put in his place, at the discretion of the captaine and masters, and order to be taken that the partie dismissed shalbe allowed proportionably the value of that he shall haue deserued to the time of his dismission or discharge, and he to giue order with sureties, pawn, or other assurance, to repay the ouerplus of that he shall haue receiued, which he shall not haue deserued, and such wages to be made with the partie newly placed as shalbe thought reasonable, and he to haue the furniture of all such necessaries as were prepared for the partie dismissed, according to right and conscience.

12. Item, that no blaspheming of God, or detestable swearing be vsed in any ship, nor communication of ribaldrie, filthy tales, or vngodly talke to be suffred in the company of any ship, neither dicing, carding, tabling, nor other diuelish games to be frequented, whereby ensueth not onely pouertie to the players, but also strife, variance, brauling, fighting, and oftentimes murther to the vtter destruction of the parties, and prouoking of Gods most iust wrath, and sworde of vengeance. These and all such like pestilences, and contagions of vices, and sinnes to bee eschewed, and the offenders once monished, and not reforming, to bee punished at the discretion of the captaine and master, as appertaineth.

13. Item, that morning and euening prayer, with other common seruices appointed by the kings Maiestie, and lawes of this Realme to be read and

saide in euery ship daily by the minister in the Admirall, and the marchant or some other person learned in other ships, and the Bible or paraphrases to be read deuoutly and Christianly to Gods honour, and for his grace to be obtained, and had by humble and heartie praier of the Nauigants accordingly.

14. Item, that euery officer is to be charged by Inuentorie with the particulars of his charge, and to render a perfect accompt of the diffraying of the same together with modest and temperate dispending of powder, shot, and vse of all kinde of artillery, which is not to be misused, but diligently to be preserued for the necessary defence of the fleete and voyage, together with due keeping of all instruments of your Nauigation, and other requisites.

15. Item, no liquor to be spilt on the balast, nor filthiness to be left within boord: the cook room, and all other places to be kept cleane for the better health of the companie, the gromals and pages to bee brought vp according to the laudable order and vse of the Sea, as well in learning of Nauigation, as in exercising of that which to them appertaineth.

16. Item, the liueries in apparel giuen to the mariners be to be kept by the marchants, and not to be worne, but by the order of the captaine, when he shall see cause to muster or shewe them in good aray, for the aduancement and honour of the voyage, and the liueries to bee redeliuered to the keeping of the marchants, vntill it shal be thought conuenient for euery person to haue the ful vse of his garment.

17. Item, when any mariner or any other passenger shal haue neede of any necessarie furniture of apparell for his body, and conseruation of his health, the same shall bee deliuered him by the Marchant, at the assignement of the captaine and Master of that shippe, wherein such needie person shall be, at such reasonable price as the same cost, without any gaine to be exacted by the marchants, the value therof to be entred by the marchant in his booke, and the same to be discounted off the parties wages, that so shal receiue, and weare the same.

18. Item, the sicke, diseased, weake, and visited person within boord, to be tendred, relieued, comforted, and holpen in the time of his infirmitie, and euery maner of person, without respect, to beare anothers burden, and no man to refuse such labour as shall be put to him, for the most benefite, and publike wealth of the voyage, and enterprise, to be atchieued exactly.

19. Item, if any person shal fortune to die, or miscary in the voyage, such apparell, and other goods, as he shall haue at the time of his death, is to be kept by the order of the captaine and Master of the shippe, and an inuentorie to be made of it, and conserued to the vse of his wife, and

children, or otherwise according to his mind, and wil, and the day of his death to be entred in the Marchants and Stewards Bookes: to the intent it may be knowen what wages he shall haue deserued, to his death, and what shall rest due to him.

20. Item, that the Marchants appointed for this present voyage, shall not make any shew or sale of any kind of marchandizes, or open their commodities to any forrein princes, or any of their subiects, without the consent, priuitie, or agreement of the Captaines, the cape Marchants and the assistants, or foure of them, whereof the captaine generall, the Pilot Maior, and cape marchant to be three, and euery of the pettie marchants to shewe his reckoning to the cape marchant, when they, or any of them shall be required: and no commutation or trucke to be made by any of the petie marchants, without the assent abouesaid: and all wares, and commodities trucked, bought or giuen to the companie, by way of marchandise, trucke, or any other respect, to be booked by the marchants, and to be wel ordred, packed, and conserued in one masse entirely, and not to be broken or altered, vntil the shippes shall returne to the right discharges, and inuentorie of al goods, wares, and merchandises so trucked, bought, or otherwise dispended, to be presented to the Gouernor, Consuls, and Assistants in London, [Marginal note: King Edward's Corporation.] in good order, to the intent the Kings Maiestie may be truly answered of that which to his grace by his grant of corporation is limited, according to our most bound dueties, and the whole companie also to haue that which by right vnto them appertaineth, and no embezelment shall be vsed, but the truth of the whole voyage to bee opened, to the common wealth and benefite of the whole companie, and mysterie, as appertaineth, without guile, fraude, or male engine.

21. Item, no particular person, to hinder or preiudicate the common stocke of the company, in sale or preferment of his own proper wares, and things, and no particular emergent or purchase to be employed to any seuerall profite, vntill the common stocke of the companie shall be furnished, and no person to hinder the common benefite in such purchases or contingents, as shal fortune to any one of them, by his owne proper policie, industrie, or chance, nor no contention to rise in that behalfe, by any occasion of iewel, stone, pearles, precious mettals, or other things of the region, where it shall chance the same to rise, or to be found bought, trucked, permuted, or giuen: but euery person to be bounden in such case, and vpon such occasion, by order, and direction, as the generall captaine, and the Councell shall establish and determine, to whose order and discretion the same is left: for that of things vncertaine, no certaine rules may or can be giuen.

22. Item not to disclose to any nation the state of our religion, but to passe it ouer in silence, without any declaration of it, seeming to beare with such lawes, and rites, as the place hath, where you shall arriue.

23. Item for as much as our people, and shippes may appeare vnto them strange and wonderous, and theirs also to ours: it is to be considered, how they may be vsed, learning much of their natures and dispositions, by some one such person, as you may first either allure, or take to be brought aboord your ships, and there to learne as you may, without violence or force, and no woman to be tempted, or intreated to incontinencie, or dishonestie.

24. Item the person so taken, to be well entertained, vsed, and apparelled, to be set on land, to the intent that he or she may allure other to draw nigh to shewe the commodities: and if the person taken may be made drunke with your beere, or wine, you shal know the secrets of his heart.

25. Item our people may not passe further into a land, then that they may be able to recouer their pinnesses, or ships, and not to credit the faire words of the strange people, which be many times tried subtile, and false, nor to be drawen into perill of losse, for the desire of golde, siluer, or riches, and esteeme your owne commodities aboue al other, and in countenance shew not much to desire the forren commodities: neuertheless take them as for friendship, or by way of permutation.

26. Item euery nation and region is to be considered aduisedly, and not to prouoke them by any disdaine, laughing, contempt, or such like, but to vse them with prudent circumspection, with al gentlenes, and curtesie, and not to tary long in one place, vntill you shall haue attained the most worthy place that nay be found, in such sort, as you may returne with victuals sufficient prosperously.

27. Item the names of the people of euery Island, are to be taken in writing, with the commodities, and incommodities of the same, their natures, qualities, and dispositions, the site of the same, and what things they are most desirous of, and what commodities they wil most willingly depart with, and what mettals they haue in hils, mountaines, streames, or riuers, in, or vnder the earth.

28. Item if people shal appeare gathering of stones, gold, mettall, or other like, on the sand, your pinnesses may drawe nigh, marking what things they gather, vsing or playing vpon the drumme, or such other instruments, as may allure them to harkening, to fantasie, or desire to see, and heare your instruments and voyces, but keepe you out of danger, and shewe to them no poynt or signe of rigour and hostilitie.

29. Item if you shall be inuited into any Lords or Rulers house, to dinner, or other parliance, goe in such order of strength, that you may be stronger then they, and be warie of woods and ambushes, and that your weapons be not out of your possessions.

30. Item if you shall see them weare Lyons or Beares skinnes, hauing long bowes, and arrowes, be not afraid of that sight: for such be worne oftentimes more to feare strangers, then for any other cause.

31. Item there are people that can swimme in the sea, hauens, and riuers, naked, hauing bowes and shafts, coueting to draw nigh your ships, which if they shal finde not wel watched, or warded, they wil assault, desirous of the bodies of men, which they couet for meate: if you resist them, they diue, and so will flee, and therefore diligent watch is to be kept both day and night, in some Islands.

32. Item if occasion shal serue, that you may giue aduertisements of your proceedings in such things as may correspond to the expectation of the company, and likelihood of successe in the voyage, passing such dangers of the seas, perils of ice, intolerable coldes, and other impediments, which by sundry authors and writers, haue ministred matter of suspition in some heads, that this voyage could not succede for the extremitie of the North pole, lacke of passage, and such like, which haue caused wauering minds, and doubtful heads, not onely to withdraw themselues from the aduenture of this voyage, but also disswaded others from the same, the certaintie whereof, when you shall haue tried by experience, (most certaine Master of all worldly knowledge) then for declaration of the trueth, which you shall haue experted, you may by common assent of counsell, sende either by lande, or otherwaies, such two or one person, to bring the same by credite, as you shal think may passe in safetie: which sending is not be done, but vpon vrgent causes, in likely successe of the voyage, in finding of passage, in towardlines of beneficiall traffike, or such other like, whereby the company being aduertised of your estates and proceedings, may further prouide, foresee, and determine that which may seeme most good and beneficiall for the publike wealth of the same: either prouiding before hand such things, as shall bee requisite for the continuance of the voyage, or else otherwise to dispose as occasion shall serue: in which things your wisedomes and discretions are to be vsed, and shewed, and the contents of this capitule, by you much to be pondred, for that you be not ignorant, how many persons, as well the kings Maiestie, the Lords of his honorable Counsel, this whole companie, as also your wiues, children, kinsfolkes, allies, friends and familiars, be replenished in their hearts with ardent desire to learne and know your estates, conditions, and welfares, and in what likelihood you be in, to obtain this notable enterprise, which is hoped no lesse to succeed to you, then the Orient or Occident Indias haue to the high

benefite of the Emperour, and kings of Portingal, whose subiects industries, and trauailes by sea, haue inriched them, by those lands and Islands, which were to all Cosmographers, and other writers both vnknowne, and also by apparances of reason voide of experience thought and reputed vnhabitable for extremities of heates, and colds, and yet indeed tried most rich, peopled, temperate, and so commodious, as all Europe hath not the like.

33. Item no conspiracies, parttakings, factions, false tales, vntrue reports, which be the very seedes, and fruits of contention, discord, and confusion, by euill tongues to be suffered, but the same, and all other vngodlines to be chastened charitably with brotherly loue, and alwaies obedience to be vsed and practised by al persons in their degrees, not only for duetie and conscience sake towards God, vnder whose mercifull hand nauigants aboue all other creatures naturally bee most nigh, and vicine, but also for prudent and worldly pollicie, and publike weale, considering and alwaies hauing present in your mindes that you be all one most royall kings subiects, and naturals, with daily remembrance of the great importance of the voyage, the honour, glorie, praise, and benefite that depend of, and vpon the same, toward the common wealth of this noble Realme, the aduancement of you the trauailers therein, your wiues, and children, and so to endeuour your selues as that you may satisfie the expectation of them, who at their great costs, charges, and expenses, haue so furnished you in good sort, and plentie of all necessaries, as the like was neuer in any realme seene, vsed, or knowen requisite and needful for such an exploit, which is most likely to be atchieued, and brought to good effect, if euery person in his vocation shall endeauour himselfe according to his charge, and most bounden duetie: praying the liuing God, to giue you his grace, to accomplish your charge to his glorie, whose merciful hand shal prosper your voyage, and preserue you from all dangers.

In witnes whereof I Sebastian Cabota, Gouernour aforesaide, to these present ordinances, haue subscribed my name, and put my seale, the day and yeere aboue written.

The names of the twelue Counsellors appointed in this voyage.

1. Sir Hugh Willoughby, Knight, Captaine generall. 2. Richard Chancelour Captaine of the Edward Bonauenture, and Pilot generall of the fleete. 3. George Burton Cape marchant. 4. Master Richard Stafford Minister. 5. Thomas Langlie Marchant. 6. Iames Dalabere Gentleman. 7. William Gefferson Master of the Bona Speranza Admirall. 8. Stephen Borrough Master of the Edward Bonauenture. 9. Cornelius Durfurth Master of the Confidentia. 10. Roger Wilson. | 11. Iohn Buckland. + Masters mates 12. Richard Ingram. |

* * * * *

Exemplar Epistolæ seu literarum Missiuarum, quas illustrissimus Princeps Eduardus eius nominis Sextus, Angliæ, Franciæ, et Hiberniæ Rex, misit ad Principes Septentrionalem, ac Orientalem mundi plagam inhabitantes iuxta mare glaciale, nec non Indiam Orientalem; Anno Domini 1553 Regni sui anno septimo, et vltimo.

Eduardus sextus, Angliæ, Franciæ, et Hiberniæ Rex, etc. Omnibus Regibus et principibus ac dominis, et cunctis Iudicibus terræ, et ducibus eius, quibuscunque est excellens aliqua dignitas in ea, cunctis in locis quæ sunt sub vniuerso coelo: Pax, tranquillitas, et honor vobis, terris, et regionibus vestris quæ imperio vestro subiacent, cuique vestrum quemadmodum conuenit ei. Proptereà quòd indidit Deus Opt. Max. hominibus præ cunctis alijs viuentibus; cor et desiderium tale, vt appetat quisque cum alijs societatem inire, amare, et vicissim amari, beneficijs afficere, et mutua accipere beneficia studeat, ideò cuique pro facultate sua hoc desiderium in omnibus quidem hominibus beneficijs fouere et conseruare conuenit, in illis autem maximè, qui hoc desiderio adducti, à remotis etiam regionibus ad eos veniunt. Quo enim longius iter eius rei gratia ingressi sunt, eò ardentius in eis hoc desiderium fuisse declararunt. Insuper etiam ad hoc, nos patrum maiorúmque nostrorum exempla inuitant, qui semper humanissimè susceperunt et benignissimè tractauerunt illos, qui tum à locis propinquis, tum à remotis, eos amicè adibant, eorum se protectioni commendantes. Quod si omnibus id præstare æquum est, certè mercatoribus imprimis præstari debet, qui per vniuersum orbem discurrunt, mare circumlustrantes et aridam, vt res bonas et vtiles, quæ Dei beneficio in regione eorum inueniuntur, ad remotissimas regiones et regna adferant, atque inde vicissim referant, quòd suæ regioni vtile ibi repeterint: vt et populi ad quos eunt, non destituantur commodis quæ non profert illis terra eorum, et ipsi sint participes rerum quibus illi abundant. Nam Deus cæli et terræ, humano generi maximè consulens, noluit vt omnia in quauis regione inuenirentur, quò regio ope alterius regionis indigeret, et gens ab alia gente commodum aliquod expectaret, ac ita stabiliretur amicitia inter omnes, singulíque omnibus benefacere quærerent. Hoc itaque ineundæ ac stabiliendæ amicitiæ desiderio moti viri quidam regni nostri, iter in remotas maritimas regiones instituerunt, vt inter nostros et illos populos, viam mercibus inferendis et efferendis aperirent nòsque rogauerunt et vt id illis concederemus. Qui petitioni illorum annuentes, concessimus viro honorabili et forti, Hugoni Wilibeo, et alijs qui cum eo sunt seruis nostris fidis et charis, vt pro sua voluntate, in regiones eis priùs incognitas eant, quæsituri ea quibus nos caremus, et adducant illis ex nostris terris id quo illi carent. Atque ita illis et nobis commodum inde accedat, sítque amicitia perpetua, et foedus indissoluble inter illos et nos, dum permittent illi nos accipere de rebus, quibus superabundant in regnis suis, et nos concedemus illis ex regnis nostris res, quibus destituuntur. Rogamus itaque vos Reges et Principes, et omnes quibus aliqua est potestas in terra, vt viris istis nostris, transitum permittatis per regiones vestras. Non enim tangent quicquam ex rebus vestris inuitis vobis. Cogitate quòd homines et ipsi sunt. Et si qua re caruerint, oramus pro vestra beneficentia, eam vos illis tribuatis, accipientes vicissim ab eis quod poterunt rependere vobis. Ita vos gerite erga eos, quemadmodum cuperetis vt nos, et subditi nostri, nos gereremus erga seruos vestros, si quando transierint per regiones nostras. Atque promittimus vobis per Deum omnium quæ cælo, terra et mari continentur, pérque vitam nostram, et tranquillitatem regnorum nostrorum, nos pari benignitate seruos vestros accepturos, si ad regna nostra aliquando venerint. Atque à nobis et subditis nostris, ac si nati fuissent in regnis nostris ita benignè tractabuntur, vt rependamus vobis benignitatem, quam nostris exhibueritis. Postquam vos Reges, Principes, etc. rogauimus, vt humanitate et beneficentia omni prosequamini seruos nostros nobis charos, oramus omnipotentem Deum nostrum, vt vobis diuturnam vitam largiatur, et pacem quæ nullam habeat finem. Scriptum Londini, quæ ciuitas est primaria regni nostri, Anno 5515. à creato mundo, mense Iair, 14. die mensis, anno septimo regni nostri.

The same in English.

The copie of the letters missiue, which the right noble Prince Edward the sixt sent to the Kings, Princes, and other Potentates, inhabiting the Northeast partes of the worlde, toward the mighty Empire of Cathay, at such time as Sir Hugh Willoughby knight, and Richard Chancelor, with their company attempted their voyage thither in the yeere of Christ 1553. and the seuenth and last yeere of his raigne.

Edward the sixt, by the grace of God, King of England, France, and Ireland, &c. To all Kings, Princes, Rulers, Iudges, and gouernours of the earth, and all other hauing any excellent dignitie on the same, in all places vnder the vniuersall heauen: peace, tranquillitie, and honour be vnto you, and your lands and regions, which are vnder your dominions, and to euery of you, as is conuenient.

Forasmuch as the great and Almightie God hath giuen vnto mankinde, aboue all other liuing creatures, such an heart and desire, that euery man desireth to ioine friendship with other, to loue, and be loued, also to giue and receiue mutuall benefites: it is therefore the duety of all men, according to their power, to maintaine and increase this desire in euery man, with well deseruing to all men, and especially to shew this good affection to such, as beeing moued with this desire, come vnto them from farre countreis. For how much the longer voyage they haue attempted for this intent, so much the more doe they thereby declare that this desire hath bene ardent in them. Furthermore also, the examples of our fathers and predecessors doe inuite vs hereunto, forasmuch as they haue euer gently and louingly intreated such as of friendly mind came to them, aswell from Countries neare hand, as farre remote, commending themselues to their protection. And if it be right and equity, to shew such humanitie toward all men, doubtlesse the same ought chiefly to be shewed to marchants, who wandering about the world, search both the land and the sea, to carry such good and profitable things, as are found in their Countries, to remote regions and kingdomes, and againe to bring from the same, such things as they find there commodious for their owne Countries: both aswell that the people, to whom they goe, may not be destitute of such commodities as their Countries bring not foorth to them, as that also they may be partakers of such things, whereof they abound. For the God of heauen and earth greatly prouiding for mankinde, would not that all things should be found in one region, to the ende that one should haue neede of another, that by this meanes friendship might be established among all men, and euery one seeke to gratifie all. For the establishing and furtherance of which vniuersall amitie, certaine men of our Realme, mooued heereunto by the said desire, haue instituted and taken vpon them a voyage by sea into farre Countries, to the intent that betweene our people and them, a way may bee opened to bring in, and cary out marchandises, desiring vs to further their enterprise. Who assenting to their petition, haue licensed the right valiant and worthy Sir Hugh Willoughby, knight, and other our trusty and faithfull seruants, which are with him, according to their desire, to goe to countries to them heeretofore vnknowen, aswell to seeke such things as we lacke, as also to cary vnto them from our regions, such things as they lacke. So that hereby not onely commoditie may ensue both to them and vs, but also an indissoluble and perpetuall league of friendship be established betweene vs both, while they permit vs to take of their things, such whereof they haue abundance in their regions, and we againe grant them such things of ours, whereof they are destitute. We therefore desire you kings and princes, and al other, to whom there is any power on the earth, to permit vnto these our seruants free passage by your regions and dominions: for they shall not touch any thing of yours unwilling vnto you. Consider you that they also are men. If therefore they shall stand in neede of any thing, we desire you of all humanitie, and for the nobilities which is in you, to ayde and helpe them with such things as they lacke, receiuing againe of them such things as they shall be able to giue you in recompense. Shew your selues so towards them, as you would that we and our subiects should shewe ourselues towards your seruants, if at any time they shall passe by our regions.

Thus doing, we promise you by the God of all things that are contained in heauen, earth, and the Sea, and by the life and tranquillitie of our kingdomes, that we will with like humanitie accept your seruants, if at any time they shall come to our kingdomes, where they shall as friendly and gently bee entertained, as if they were borne in our Dominions, that wee may hereby recompence the fauour and benignitie which you haue shewed to our men. Thus after we haue desired you Kings and princes, &c. with all humanity and fauour, to entertaine our welbeloued seruants, we will pray our Almighty God, to graunt you long life, and peace, which neuer shall haue ende. Written in London, which is the chiefe citie of our kingdome, in the yeere from the creation of the world 5515. in the month of Iair, [Marginal note: Iair, I would reade Mair, that is, in the Sarasen language, mixt of Turkish and Aegyptian, Februarie, interpreted by them the moneth to set ships to the sea.] the fourteenth day of the moneth, and seuenth yeere of our reigne.

This letter was written also in Greeke, and diuers others languages.

* * * * *

The true copie of a note found wrltten in one of the two ships, to wit, the Speranza, which wintered in Lappia, Where sir Hugh Willoughby and all his companie died, being frozen to death. Anno 1553.

The voiage intended for the discouerie of Cathay, and diuers other regions, dominions, Islands, and places vnknowen, set forth by the right worshipful, master Sebastian Cabota Esquire, and Gouernour of the mysterie and company of the Marchants Aduenturers of the citie of London: which fleete being furnished, did set forth the tenth day of May, 1553. and in the seuenth yeere of our most dread Soueraigne Lord, and King, Edward the sixt.

The names of the shippes of the fleete and of their burden, together with the names of the Captaines, and Counsellors, Pilot Maior, Masters of the ships, Marchants, with other officers, and Mariners, as hereafter followeth.

THE FIRST SHIP: The Bona Esperanza, Admirall of the fleete, of 120. tunnes, hauing with her a pinnesse, and a boate.

Sir Hugh Willoughby, knight, Captaine generall of the fleete.

William Gefferson, Master of the shippe.

Roger Wilson, his Mate.

William Gittons, Charles Barret, Gabriel Willoughby, Iohn Andrews, Alexander Woodfoord, Ralph Chatterton, Marchants.

Mariners and officers, according to the custome, and vse of the Seas,

Iohn Brooke, Master Gunner.

Nicholas Anthony, Boateswaine.

Iohn Web, his Mate.

Christopher Banbrucke, Thomas Dauison, Robert Rosse, Thomas Simpson, quarter Masters.

William White, Iames Smith, Thomas Painter, Iohn Smith, their Mates.

Richard Gwinne, George Goiswine, Carpenters.

Robert Gwinne, Purser.

Laurence Edwards, his Mate, and Couper.

Richard Morgan, Cooke.

Thomas Nashe, his Mate.

William Light, Iohn Brande, Cutbert Chelsie, George Blage, Thomas Walker,
Thomas Allen, Edward Smith, Edward Hunt, Iohn Fawkner, Rowland Brooke.

Alexander Gardiner, Richard Molton, Surgeons, which two were taken in at Harwich.

Discharged at Harwich, by reason of sicknes, George Blake, [Footnote: The "George Blage" mentioned above.] Nicholas Anthony.

For pickerie ducked at the yards arme, and so discharged Thomas Nash.

THE SECOND SHIP: The Edward Bonauenture, of 160. tunnes, with her a pinnesse, and a boate.

Richard Chancelor, Captaine, and Pilot maior of the fleete.

Stephen Borowgh, Master of the ship.

Iohn Buckland, his Mate.

George Burton, Arthur Edwards, Marchants.

Iohn Stafford, Minister.

Iames Dallaber, Nicholas Newborrow, Iohn Sedgswike, Thomas Francis, Iohn
Hasse, Richard Iohnson, William Kempe.

Mariners and officers, according to the custome and vse of the Seas.

Robert Stanton, Master Gunner.

Iohn Walker, his Mate.

Iames Long, Iohn Cocks, Gunners.

Thomas Walter, Surgeon.

Peter Palmer, Boateswaine.

Richard Strowde, his Mate.

Iohn Robinson, Iohn Carowe, Thomas Stone, Roger Lishbie, quarter Masters.

Iohn Austen, Steward: Patricke Steuens, his Mate.

Austen Iacks, Cooke.

William Euery, Cowper.

Griffin Wagham, Carpenter.

Thomas Steltson, Thomas Townes, Iohn Robinson, Iohn White, William Laurence, Miles Butter, Iohn Browne, William Morren, William Watson, Thomas
Handcocks, Edward Pacie, Thomas Browne, Arthur Pet, George Phibarie, Edward
Patterson, William Beare, Iohn Potter, Nicholas Lawrence, William Burrough
[Marginal note: Nowe comptroller of Her Maiesties (Queen Elizabeth) Nauie.], Roger Welford, Iohn Williams.

THE THIRD SHIP: The Bona Confidentia of 90. tunnes, hauing with her a pinnesse, and a boate.

Cornelias Durfoorth, Master of the shippe.

Richard Ingram, his Mate.

Thomas Langlie, Edward Kener, Henrie Dorset, Marchants.

Mariners and officers, according to the vse and custome of the Sea.

Henrie Tailer, Master Gunner.

George Thurland, his Mate.

William Hamane, Boateswaine.

Iohn Edwards, his Mate.

Thomas Kirbie, Henrie Dickenson, Iohn Haye, William Shepwash, quarter Masters.

Iohn Reyne, Steward.

Thomas Hante, Cooke. William Lassie, his Mate.

Nicholas Knight, Carpenter.

Peter Lewike, Nicholas Wiggleworth, Iohn Moore, William Chapman, Brian Chester, William Barrie, Richard Wood, Clement Gibson, Iohn Clarocke, Erasmus Bently, Iohn Duriforth.

The Iurameutum, or othe, ministred to the Captaine.

You shall sweare to be a faithful, true, and loyal subiect in all points, and duties, that to a subiect appertaineth, to our soueraigne Lord the kings Maiestie, his heires, and successors: and that you shall wel and truely to the vttermost of your capacitie, wit, and knowledge, serue this present voiage, committed to your charge, and not to giue vp nor sooner intermit the same, vntil you shall haue atchieued the same, so farre foorth, as you may without danger of your life, and losse of the fleete: you shall giue good, true and faithful counsell to the said societie, and to such as shal haue the charge with or vnder you, and not to disclose the secrets, or priuities of the same to any person by any maner of meane, to the preiudice, hurt, or damage of it. You shal minister iustice to all men vnder your charge, without respect of person, or any affection, that might moue you to decline from the true ministration of iustice. And further, you shal obserue, and cause to be obserued, as much as in you lieth, all and singular rules, articles, prouisions hitherto made, or heereafter to be made for the preseruation or safeconduct of the fleete and voyage, and benefit of the company. You shall not permit nor suffer the stocke or goods of the company to be wasted, imbezeled, or consumed, but shall conserue the same whole and entire, without diminishment, vntill you shall haue deliuered, or cause to be deliuered the same, to the vse of the companie. And finally you shall vse your selfe in all points, sorts, and conditions, as to a faithfull captaine, and brother of this companie shall belong and appertaine: So helpe you God, &c.

The othe ministred to the Maister of the ship, &c.

You shall sweare by the holy contents in that booke, that you according and to the vttermost of your knowledge and good vnderstanding in mariners science and craft, shall in your vocation doe your best to conduct the good shippe called the N. &c. whereof you nowe are Maister vnder God, both vnto and from the portes of your discouerie, and so vse your indeauour and faithfull diligence, in charging, discharging, lading againe, and roomaging of the same shippe, as may be most for the benefite and profite of this right woorshipfull fellowship: and you shall not priuately bargein, buy, sell, exchange, barter, or distribute any goods, wares, merchandise, or things whatsoeuer (necessary tackles and victuals for the shippe onely excepted) to or for your owne lucre, gaine or profit, neither to nor for the priuate lucre, gaine, or profit of any other person or persons whatsoeuer. And further, If you shall know any boatswaine, mariner, or any other person or persons whatsoeuer, to buy, sell, barter, trucke, or exchange any goods, wares, merchandises, or things for priuate account, reckoning, or behalfe, you shall doe your best to withstand and let the same: and if you cannot commodiously so doe, that then before the discharge of such goods bought for priuat account, you shall giue knowledge therof to the cape marchant of this said fellowship for the time being. And you shall not receiue nor take, nor suffer to be receiued or taken into your said ship during this voyage any maner person or persons whatsoeuer, going or returning, but onely those mariners which without fraud or guile shall be hired to be of your company, and to serue in mariners craft and science onely: so helpe you God, &c.

These foresaid shippes being fully furnished with their pinnesses and boates, well appointed with al maner of artillerie, and other things necessary for their defence with al the men aforesaid, departed from Ratcliffe, and valed vnto Detford, the 10. day of May, 1553.

The 11. day about two of the clocke, we departed from Detford, passing by Greenwhich, saluting the kings Maiesty then being there, shooting off our ordinance, and so valed vnto Blackwall, and there remained vntil the 17. day, and that day in the morning we went from Blackwall, and came to Woolwhich by nine of the clocke, and there remained one tide, and so the same night vnto Heyreth.

The 18. day from Heyreth vnto Grauesend, and there remained vntil the twentieth day: that day being Saterday, from Grauesend vnto Tilberie hope, remayning there vntill the two and twentieth day.

The 22. day from Tilbury Hope to Hollie Hauen.

The 23. day from Hollie Hauen, till we came against Lee, and there remained that night, by reason that the winde was contrary to vs.

The 24. day the winde being in the Southwest in the morning, we sailed along the coast ouer the Spits, vntill we came against S. Osyth, about sixe of the clocke at night, and there came to anker, and abode there all that night.

The 25. day about tenne of the clocke we departed from S. Osyth, and so sailed forward vnto the Nase, and there abode that night for winde and tide.

The 26. day at fiue of the clock in the morning, we weyed our anker, and sailed ouer the Nase, the winde being at the Southwest, vntill wee came to Orwell wands, and there came to an anker, and abode there vntill the 28. day.

The same day being Trinitie Sunday about 7. of the clocke before noone we weyed our ankers, and sailed til we came athwart Walsursye, and there came to an anker.

The 29. day from thence to Holmehead, where we stayed that day, where we consulted which way, and what courses were best to be holden for the discouerie of our voyage, and there agreed.

The 30. day of May at fiue of the clocke in the morning wee set saile, and came against Yermouth about three leagues into the sea, riding there at anker all that night.

The last of May into the sea six leagues Northeast, and there taried that night, where the winde blew very sore.

The first of Iune the winde being at North contrary to vs, wee came backe againe to Orwell, and remained there vntill the 15. day tarying for the winde, for all this time the winde was contrary to our purpose.

The 15 day being at Orwel in the latitude of 52 degrees, in the morning wee weyed our ankers, and went forth into the wands about two miles from the towne, and lay there that night.

The 16 day at eight of the clocke we set forward, and sayled vntill we came athwart Alburrough, and there stayed that night.

The 17 day about fiue of the clocke before noone we went backe unto Orfordnesse, and there remained vntill the 19 day.

The 19 day at eight of the clocke in the morning we went backe to Orwel, and abode there three dayes tarying for the winde.

The 23 day of Iune the wind being faire in the Southwest we hailed into the seas to Orfordnesse, and from thence into the seas ten leagues Northeast: then being past the sands, we changed our course sixe leagues Northnortheast: about midnight we changed our course againe, and went due North, continuing in the same vnto the 27 day.

The 27 day about seuen of the clocke Northnorthwest 42 leagues to the ende to fall with Shotland: then the wind veared to the West, so that we could lie but North and by West, continuing in the same course 40 leagues, whereby we could not fetch Shotland: then we sayled North 16 leagues by estimation, after that North and by West, and Northnorthwest, then Southeast, with diuers other courses, trauersing and tracing the seas, by reason of sundry and manifolde contrary windes, vntill the 14 day of Iuly: and then the sunne entring into Leo, we discouered land Eastward of vs, vnto the which we sayled that night as much as we might: and after wee went on shore with our Pinnesse, and found little houses to the number of 30, where we knew that it was inhabited, but the people were fled away, as we iudged, for feare of vs.

The land was all full of little Islands, and that innumerable, which were called (as we learned afterwards) Ægeland and Halgeland [Marginal note: In this land dwelt Octher, as it seemeth.][Footnote: See Vol I., p. 51 of this Edition.], which lieth from Orfordnesse North and by East, being in the latitude of 66 degrees. The distance betweene Orfordnesse and Ægeland 250 leagues. Then we sailed from thence 12 leagues Northwest, and found many other Islandes, and there came to anker the 19 day, and manned our Pinnesse, and went on shore to the Islands, and found people mowing and making of hay, which came to the shore and welcomed vs. In which place were an innumerable sort of Islands, which were called the Isles of Rost, being vnder the dominion of the king of Denmarke: which place was in latitude 66 degrees, and 30 minutes. The winde being contrary, we remayned there three dayes, and there was an innumerable sort of foules of diuers kindes, of which we tooke very many.

The 22 day the winde coming fayre, we departed from Rost, sailing Northnortheast, keeping the sea vntil the 27 day, and then we drew neere vnto the land, which was still East of vs: then went forth our Pinnesse to seeke harborow, and found many good harbours, of the which we entred into one with our shippes, which was called Stanfew [Footnote: Steenfjord, on the West of Lofoden.], and the land being Islands, were called Lewfoot, or Lofoot, which were plentifully inhabited, and very gentle people, being also vnder the king of Denmarke: but we could not learne how farre it was from the maine land: and we remained there vntill the 30 day, being in latitude 68 degrees, and from the foresaid Rost about 30 leagues Northnortheast.

The 30 day of Iuly about noone we weyed our ankers, and went into the Seas, and sayled along these Islands Northnortheast, keeping the land still in sight vntill the second day of August: then hailing in close aboord the land, to the entent to knowe what land it was, there came a skiffe of the island aboord of vs, of whom we asked many questions, who shewed vnto us, that the Island was called Seynam, which is the latitude of seuenty degrees, and from Stanfew thirtie leagues, being also vnder the king of Demarke, and that there was no merchandise there, but onely dryed fish; and traine oyle. Then we being purposed to goe vnto Finmarke, inquired of him, if we might haue a pilot to bring vs vnto Finmarke, and he said, that if we could beare in, we should haue a good harbour, and on the next day a pilot to bring vs vnto Finmarke, vnto the wardhouse, [Footnote: Vardoe.] which is the strongest holde in Finmarke, and most resorted to by report. But when wee would haue entred into an harbour, the land being very high on euery side, there came such flawes of winde and terrible whirlewinds, that we were not able to beare in, but by violence were constrained to take the sea agayne, our Pinnesse being vnshipt: we sailed North and by East, the wind increasing so sore that we were not able to beare any saile, but tooke them in, and lay a drift, to the end to let the storme ouer passe. And that night by violence of winde, and thickenesse of mists, we were not able to keepe together within sight, and then about midnight we lost our pinnesse, which was a discomfort vnto vs. Assoone as it was day, and the fogge ouerpast, we looked about, and at the last we descried one of our shippes to Leeward of vs: then we spred an hullocke of our foresaile, and bare roome with her, which was the Confidence, but the Edward we could not see. [Footnote: This vessel's successful voyage is related further on.] Then the flaw something abating, we and the Confidence hoysed vp our sailes the fourth day, sayling Northeast and by North, to the end to fall with the Wardhouse, as we did consult to doe before, in case we should part company. Thus running Northeast and by North, and Northeast fiftie leagues, then we sounded, and had 160 fadomes, whereby we thought to be farre from land, and perceiued that the land lay not as the Globe made mention. Wherfore we changed our course the sixt day, and sailed Southeast and by South eight and fortie leagues, thinking thereby to find the Wardhouse.

The eight day much winde arising at the Westnorthwest, we not knowing how the coast lay, strook our sayles, and lay a drift, where we sounded and found 160 fadomes as afore.

The ninth day, the wind vearing to the South Southeast, we sailed Northeast 25 leagues.

The tenth day we sounded, and could get no ground, neither yet could see any land, wherat we wondered: then the wind comming at the Northeast, we ran Southeast about 48 leagues.

The 11 day, the winde being at South, we sounded, and found 40 fadoms, and faire sand.

The 12 day the winde being at South and by East, we lay with our saile East, and East and by North 30 leagues.

[Sidenote: Willoughbie his land in 72 degrees.] The 14 day early in the morning we descried land, which land we bare with all, hoising out our boat to discouer what land it might be: but the boat could not come to land the water was so shoale, where was very much ice also, but there was no similitude of habitation, and this land lyeth from Seynam East and by North, 160 leagues, being in latitude 72 degrees. Then we plyed to the Northward the 15, 16 and 17 day. [Footnote: In *Purchas*, III., p. 462, Thomas Edge, a captain in the service of the Muscovy Company, endeavoured to show that this land was Spitzbergen. This being proved incorrect, others have supposed that the land Willoughby saw was

Gooseland. or Novaya Zemlya. Nordenskiöld supposes it to be Kolgujev Island. This, he says, would make its latitude two degrees less than stated, but such errors are not impossible in the determination of the oldest explorers.]

The 18 day, the winde comming at the Northeast, and the Confidence being troubled with bilge water, and stocked, we thought it good to seeke harbour for her redresse: then we bare roome the 18 day Southsoutheast, about 70 leagues.

The 21 day we sounded, and found 10 fadome, after that we sounded againe, and found but 7 fadome, so shoalder and shoalder water, and yet could see no land, where we marueiled greatly: to auoide this danger, we bare roomer into the sea all that night Northwest and by the West.

The next day we sounded, and had 20. fadoms, then shaped our course, and ran West Southwest vntill the 23. day: then we descried Low land, vnto which we bare as nigh as we could, and it appeared vnto vs vnhabitable. Then we plyed Westward along by that lande, which lyeth West Southwest, and East Northeast, and much winde blowing at the West, we haled into the sea North and by East 30. leagues. Then the winde comming about at the Northeast, we sailed West Northwest: after that, the winde bearing to the Northwest, we lay with our sailes West southwest, about 14. leagues, and then descried land, and bare in with it, being the 28 day, finding shoale water, and bare in till we came to 3. fadome, then perceiuing it to be shoale water, and also seeing drie sands, we haled out againe Northeast along that land vntill we came to the point therof. That land turning to the Westwarde, we ran along 16. leagues Northwest: then comming into a faire bay, we went on land with our boat, which place was vnhabited, but yet it appeared vnto vs that the people had bin there, by crosses, and other signes: from thence we went all along the coast Westward.

The fourth day of September we lost sight of land, by reason of contrary winds, and the eight day we descried land againe. Within two dayes after we lost the sight of it: then running West and by South about 30. leagues, we gat the sight of land againe, and bare in with it vntill night: then perceiuing it to be a lee shore, we gat vs into the sea, to the end to haue sea roome.

The 12. of September we hailed to shoareward againe, hauing then indifferent wind and weather: then beeing neere vnto the shoare, and the tide almost spent, we came to an anker in 30 fadoms water.

The 13. day we came along the coast, which lay Northwest and by West, and
Southeast and by East.

The 14. day we came to an anker within two leagues of the shoare, hauing 60. fadoms.

There we went a shore with our boat, and found two or three good harboroughs, the land being rocky, and high, but as for people could we see none. The 15 day we ran still along the coast vntill the 17 day: then the winde being contrary vnto vs, we thought it best to returne vnto the harbor which we had found before, and so we bare roomer with the same, howbeit we could not accomplish our desire that day. The next day being the 18 of September, we entred into the Hauen, and there came to an anker at 6 fadoms. This hauen runneth into the maine, about two leagues, and is in bredth halfe a league, wherein were very many seale fishes, and other great fishes, and vpon the maine we saw beares, great deere, foxes, with diuers strange beasts, as guloines, [Marginal note: Or, Ellons.] and such other which were to vs vnknowen, and also wonderfull. Thus remaining in this hauen the space of a weeke, seeing the yeare farre spent, and also very euill wether, as frost, snow, and haile, as though it had beene the deepe of winter, we thought best to winter there. Wherefore we sent out three men Southsouthwest, to search if they could find people who went three dayes iourney, but could figd none: after that, we sent other three Westward foure daies iourney, which also returned without finding any people. Then sent we three men Southeast three dayes three dayes iourney, who in like sorte returned without finding of people, or any similitude of habitation.

Here endeth Sir Hugh Willoughbie his note, which was written with his owne hand.

These two notes following were written vpon the outside of this Pamphlet, or Booke.

1. The proceedings of Sir Hugh Willoughby after he was separated from the Edward Bonauenture.

2. Our shippe being at an anker in the harbour called Sterfier in the Island Lofoote. [Footnote: The object of Willoughby's voyage was to discover a new route to Asia, inaccessible to the armadas of Spain and Portugal, a feat only performed in 1878-9 by Professor Nordenskiöld. It was the first maritime expedition on a large scale sent out by England. The above narrative, written by Willoughby himself, is all we know of that unfortunate navigator's proceedings after his separation from the *Edward Bonaventure* in August 1553. The following year some Russian fishermen found, at the ship's winter station, the bodies of those who had perished, probably of scurvy, with the above journal and a will, referred to in the note on page 40. The two ships, with Willoughby's corpse, were sent to England in 1555 by George Killingworth.]

The riuer or hauen wherein Sir Hugh Willoughbie with the companie of his two ships perished for cold, is called Arzina in Lapland, neere vnto Kegor. [Footnote: "With regard to the position of Arzina, it appears from a statement in Anthony Jenkinson's first voyage [*see post*] that it took seven days to go from Vardoehus to Swjatoinos, and that on the sixth he passed the mouth of the river where Sir Hugh Willoughby wintered. At a distance from Vardoehus of about six-sevenths of the way Between that town and Swjatoinos, there debouches into the Arctic Ocean, in 68 deg. 20 min. N. L. and 38 deg. 30 min. E. L. from Greenwich, a river, which in recent maps is called the Varzina. It was doubtless at the mouth of this river that the two vessels of the first North-East Passage Expedition wintered, with so unfortunate an issue for the officers and men."—NORDENSKIÖLD, *Voyage of the Vega*, Vol. I., p. 63.] But it appeared by a Will found in the ship that Sir Hugh Willoughbie and most of the company were aliue in January 1554. [Footnote: The testator was Gabriel Willoughby, and Sir Hugh was a witness.]

* * * * *

The booke of the great and mighty Emperor of Russia, and Duke of Muscouia, and of the dominions orders and commodities thereunto belonging: drawen by Richard Chancelour.

Forasmuch as it is meete and necessary for all those that minde to take in hande the trauell into farre or strange countreys, to endeuour themselues not onely to vngerstande the orders, commodities, and fruitfulnesse thereof, but also to applie them to the setting foorth of the same, whereby it may incourage others to the like trauaile: therefore haue I nowe thought good to make a briefe rehearsall of the orders of this my trauaile in Russia and Moscouia, and other countreys thereunto adioyning; because it was my chaunce to fall with the North partes of Russia before I came towards Moscouia, I will partly declare my knowledge therein. Russia is very plentifull both of land and people, and also wealthy for such commodities as they haue. They be very great fishers for Salmons and small Coddes: they haue much oyle which wee call treine oyle, the most whereof is made by a riuer called Duina. They make it in other places, but not so much as there. They haue also a great trade in seething of salte water. To the North parte of that countrey are the places where they haue their Furres, as Sables, marterns, greese Beuers, Foxes white, blacke, and redde, Minkes, Ermines, Miniuer, and Harts. There are also a fishes teeth, which fish is called a Morsse. The takers thereof dwell in a place called Postesora, [Footnote: Query, Petschora?] which bring them vpon Hartes to Lampas to sell, and from Lampas carie them to a place called Colmogro, [Footnote: Cholmogori, near Archangel.] where the hie market is holden on Saint Nicholas day. To the West of Colmogra there is a place called Gratanowe, in our language Nouogorode, where much fine flaxe and Hempe groweth, and also much, waxe and honie. The Dutch marchants haue a Staplehouse there. There is also great store of hides, and at a place called Plesco: [Footnote: Ploska, on the Dwina.] and thereabout is great store of Flaxe, Hempe, Waxe, Honie; and that towne is from Colmogro 120 miles.

There is a place called Vologda; the commodities whereof are Tallowe, Waxe, and Flaxe: but not so great plenty as is in Gratanowe. From Vologda to Colmogro there runneth a riuer called Duyna, and from thence it falleth into the sea. Colmogro serueth Gratonowe, Vologda and the Mosco with all the countrey thereabout with salte and saltfish. From Vologda to Ieraslaue is two hundreth miles: [Footnote: Rather less; about 160 miles.] which towne is very great. The commodities thereof are hides, and talowe, and come in great plenty, and some Waxe, but not so plentifull as in other places.

The Mosco is from Ieraslaue two hundreth miles. The countrey betwixt them is very well replenished with small Villages, which are so well filled with people, that it is wonder to see them: the ground is well stored with corne which they carie to the citie of Mosco in such abundance that it is wonder to see it. You shall meete in a morning seuen or eight hundred sleds comming or going thither, that carie corne, and some carie fish. You shall haue some that carie corne to the Mosco, and some that fetch corne from thence, that at the least dwell a thousand miles off; and all their cariage is on sleds. Those which come so farre dwell in the North partes of the Dukes dominions, where the cold will suffer no corne to grow, it is so extreme. They bring thither fishes, furres, and beastes skinnes. In those partes they haue but small store of cattell.

The Mosco it selfe is great: I take the whole towne to bee greater then London with the suburbes: but it is very rude, and standeth without all order. Their houses are all of timber very dangerous for fire. There is a faire Castle, the walles whereof are of bricke, and very high: they say they are eighteene foote thicke, but I doe not beleeue it, it doth not so seeme, notwithstanding I doe not certainely know it: for no stranger may come to viewe it. The one side is ditched, and on the other side runneth a riuer called Moscua which runneth into Tartarie and so into the sea called Mare Caspium: and on the North side there is a base towne, the which hath also a bricke wall about it, and so it ioyneth with the Castle wall. The Emperour lieth in the castle, wherein are nine fayre Churches, and therein are religious men. Also there is a Metropolitane with diuers Bishops. I will not stande in description of their buildinges nor of the strength thereof because we haue better in all points in England. They be well furnished with ordinance of all sortes.

The Emperours or Dukes house neither in building nor in the outward shew, nor yet within the house is so sumptuous as I haue seene. It is very lowe built in eight square, much like the olde building of England, with small windowes, and so in other poynts.

Now to declare my comming before his Maiestie; [Footnote: Ivan Vasilovitsch.] After I had remained twelue daies, the Secretary which hath the hearing of strangers did send for me, aduertising me that the Dukes pleasure was to haue me to come before his Ma. with the kings my masters letters: whereof I was right glad, and so I gaue mine attendance. And when the Duke was in his place appointed, the interpretour came for me into the vtter chamber, where sate one hundred or moe gentlemen, all in cloth of golde very sumptuous, and from thence I came into the Counsaile chamber, where sate the Duke himselfe with his nobles, which were a faire company: they sate round about the chamber on high, yet so that he himselfe sate much higher then any of his nobles in a chaire gilt, and in a long garment of beaten golde, with an emperial crowne vpon his head and a stafle of Cristall and golde in his right hand, and his other hand halfe leaning on his chaire. The Chancelour stoode vp with the Secretary before the Duke. After my dutie done and my letter deliuered, he bade me welcome, and enquired of me the health of the King my master, and I answered that he was in good health at my departure from his court, and that my trust was that he was now in the same. Vpon the which he bade me to dinner. The chancelour presented my present vnto his Grace bareheaded (for before they were all couered) and When his Grace had receiued my letter, I was required to depart: for I had charge not to speake to the Duke, but when he spake to me. So I departed vnto the Secretaries chamber, where I remayned two houres, and then I was sent for agayne vnto another palace which is called the golden palace, but I saw no cause why it should be so called; for I haue seene many fayrer then it in all poynts: and so I came into the hall, which was small and not great as is the Kings Maiesties of England, and the table was couered with a tablecloth; and the Marshall sate at the ende of the table with a little white rod in his hand, which boorde was fall of vessell of golde: and on the other side of the hall did stand a faire cupborde of plate. From thence I came into the dining chamber, where the Duke himselfe sate at his table without cloth of estate, in a gowne of siluer, with a crowne emperiall vpon his head, he sate in a chaire somewhat hie: There sate none near him by a great way. There were long tables set round about the chamber, which were full set with such as the Duke had at dinner: they were all in white. Also the places where the tables stoode were higher by two steppes than the rest of the house. In the middest of the chamber stoode a table or cupbord to set plate on; which stoode full of cuppes of golde: and amongst all the rest there stoode foure marueilous great pottes or crudences as they call them, of golde and siluer: I think they were a good yarde and a halfe hie. By the cupborde stoode two gentlemen with napkins on their shoulders, and in their handes each of them had a cuppe of gold set with pearles and precious stones, which were the Dukes owne drinking cups; when he was disposed, he drunke them off at a draught. And for his seruice at meate it came in without order, yet it was very rich seruice, for all were serued in gold, not onely he himselfe, but also all the rest of vs, and it was very massie: the cups also were of golde and very massie. The number that dined there that day was two hundred persons, and all were serued in golden vessell. The gentlemen that waited were all in cloth of gold, and they serued him with their caps on their heads. Before the seruice came in, the Duke sent to euery man a great shiuer of bread, and the bearer called the party so sent to by his name aloude, and sayd, John Basiliuich Emperour of Russia and great Duke of Moscouia doth reward thee with bread: then must all men stand vp, and doe at all times when those words are spoken. And then last of all he giueth the Marshall bread, whereof he eateth before the Dukes Grace, and so doth reuerence and departeth. Then commeth the Dukes seruice of the Swannes all in pieces, and euery one in a seuerall dish: the which the Duke sendeth as he did the bread, and the bearer sayth the same wordes as he sayd before. As I sayd before, the seruice of his meate is in no order, but commeth in dish by dish: and then after that the Duke sendeth drinke, with the like saying as before is tolde. Also before dinner hee changed his crowne, and in dinner time two crownes; so that I saw three seuerall crownes vpon his head in one day. And thus when his seruice was all come in he gaue to euery one of his gentlemen waiters meate with his owne hand, and so likewise drinke. His intent thereby is, as I haue heard, that euery man shall know perfectly his seruants. Thus when dinner is done hee calleth his nobles before him name by name, that it is wonder to heare howe he could name them, hauing so many as he hath. Thus when dinner was done I departed to my lodging, which was an hower within night. I will leaue this, and speake no more of him nor his houshold: but I will somewhat declare of his land and people, with their nature and power in the wars. This Duke is Lord and Emperour of many countries, and his power is marueilous great. For he is able to bring into the field two or three hundred thousand men: he neuer goeth into, the field himselfe with vnder two hundred thousand men: And when he goeth himselfe he furnisheth his borders all with men of warre, which are no small number. He leaueth on the borders of Liefland fortie thousand men, and vpon the borders of Letto 60 thousand men, and towarde the Nagayan Tartars sixtie thousand, which is wonder to heare of: yet doeth hee neuer take to his warres neither husbandman nor marchant. All his men are horsemen: he vseth no footmen, but such as goe with the ordinance and labourers, which are thirtie thousand. The horsemen are all archers, with such bowes as the Turkes haue, and they ride short as doe the Turkes. Their armour is a coate of plate, with a skull, on their heads. Some of their coates are couered with veluet or cloth of gold: their desire is to be sumptuous in the field, and especially the nobles and gentlemen: as I haue heard their trimming is very costly, and partly I haue seene it, or else I would scarcely haue beleeued it: but the Duke himselfe is richly attired aboue all measure: his pauilion is couered either with cloth of gold or siluer, and so set with stones that it is wonderfull to see it. I haue seene the Kings Maiesties of England and the French Kings pauilions, which are fayre, yet not like vnto his. And when they bee sent into farre or strange countreys, or that strangers come to them, they be very gorgious. Els the Duke himselfe goeth but meanly in apparell: and when he goeth betwixt one place and another hee is but reasonably apparelled ouer other times. In the while that I was in Mosco the Duke sent two Ambassadours to the King of Poleland, which had at the lest fiue hundred horses; their sumptuousnes was aboue measure, not onely in them selues, but also in their horses, as veluet, cloth of golde, and cloth of siluer set with pearles and not scant. What shall I farther say? I neuer heard of nor saw men so sumptuous: but it is no dayly guise, for when they haue not occasion, as I sayd before, all their doing is but meane. And now to the effect of their warres: They are men without al order in the field. For they runne hurling on heapes, and for the most part they neuer giue battell to their enemies: but that which they doe, they doe it all by stelth. But I beleeue they be such men for hard liuing as are not vnder the sun: for no cold wil hurt them. Yea and though they lie in the field two moneths, at such time as it shall freese more then a yard thicke, the common souldier hath neither tent nor any thing else ouer his head: the most defence they haue against the wether is a felte, which is set against the winde and weather, and when Snowe commeth hee doth cast it off, and maketh him a fire, and laieth him down thereby. Thus doe the most of all his men, except they bee gentlemen which haue other prouision of their owne. Their lying in the fielde is not so strange as is their hardnes: for euery man must carie and make prouision for himselfe and his horse for a moneth or two, which is very wonderful. For he himselfe shall liue vpon water and otemeale mingled together cold, and drinke water therto, his horse shall eat green wood, and such like baggage, and shall stand open in the cold field without couert, and yet wil he labour and serue him right wel. I pray you amongst all our boasting warriours how many should we find to endure the field with them but one moneth. I know no such region about vs that beareth that name for man and beast. Now what might be made of these men if they were trained and broken to order and knowledge of ciuill wars? If this Prince had within his countreys such men as could make them to vnderstand the things aforesaid, I do beleeue that 2 of the best or greatest princes in Christendome were not wel able to match with him, considering the greatnes of his power and the hardnes of his people and straite liuing both of people and horse, and the small charges which his warres stand him in: for he giueth no wages, except to strangers. They haue a yerely stipend and not much. As for his own countrey men euery one serueth of his owne proper costes and charges, sauing that he giueth to his Harcubisiers certaine allowance for powder and shot: or else no man in all his countrey hath one pennie wages. But if any man hath done very good seruice he giueth him a ferme or a piece of lande; for the which hee is bound at all times to be readie with so many men as the Duke shall appoynt: who considereth in his mind what that lande or ferme is well able to finde: and so many shall he bee bound to furnish at all and euery such time as warres are holden in any of the Dukes dominions. For there is no man of liuing, but hee is bound likewise, whether the Duke call for either souldier or labourer, to furnish them with all such necessaries as to them belong.

Also, if any gentleman or man of liuing do die without issue male, immediately after his death the Duke entreth his land, notwithstanding he haue neuer so many daughters, and peraduenture giueth it foorthwith to another man, except a small portion that he spareth to marrie the daughters with all. Also if there be a rich man, a fermour, or man of liuing, which is stricken in age or by chance is maimed, and be not able to doe the Duke seruice, some other gentleman that is not able to liue and more able to doe seruice, will come to the Duke and complayne, saying, your Grace hath such an one, which is vnmeete to doe seruice to your Highnes, who hath great abundance of welth, and likewise your Grace hath many gentlemen which are poore and lacke liuing, and we that lacke are well able to doe good seruice, your grace might doe well to looke vpon him, and make him to helpe those that want. Immediately the Duke sendeth forth to inquire of his wealth: and if it be so proued, he shall be called before the Duke, and it shall bee sayd vnto him, friend, you haue too much liuing, and are vnseruiceable to your prince, lesse will serue you, and the rest will serue other men that are more able to serue, whereupon immediately his liuing shall be taken away from him, sauing a little to find himselfe and his wife on, and he may not once repine thereat: but for answere he will say, that he hath nothing, but it is Gods and the Dukes Graces, and cannot say, as we the common people in England say, if wee haue any thing; that is God's and our owne. Men may say, that these men are in wonderfull great awe, and obedience, that thus one must giue and grant his goods which he hath bene scraping and scratching for all his life to be at his Princes pleasure and commandement. Oh that our sturdie rebels were had in the like subiection to knowe their duety towarde their Princes. They may not say as some snudges in England say, I would find the Queene a man to serue in my place, or make his friends tarrie at home if money, haue the vpper hand. No, no, it is not so in this countrey: for hee shall make humble sute to serue the Duke. And whom he sendeth most to the warres he thinketh he is most in his fauour: and yet as I before haue sayde, hee giueth no wages. If they knewe their strength no man were able to make match with them: nor they that dwel neere them should haue any rest of them. But I thinke it is not Gods will: for I may compare them to a young horse that knoweth not his strength: whome a little childe ruleth and guideth with a bridle, for all his great strength: for if he did, neither childe nor man could rule him. Their warres are holden against the Crimme Tartarians and the Nagaians.

I will stand no longer in the rehearsall of their power and warres. For it were too tedious to the reader. But I will in part declare their lawes, and punishments, and the execution of iustice. And first I will begin with the commons of the countrey, which the gentlemen haue rule on: And that is, that euery gentleman hath rule and iustice vpon his owne tenants. And if it so fall out that two gentlemens seruants and tenaunts doe disagree, the two gentlemen examine the matter, and haue the parties before them, and soe giue the sentence. And yet cannot they make the ende betwixt them of the controuersie, but either of the gentlemen must bring his seruant or tenant before the high iudge or iustice of that countrey, and there present them, and declare the matter and case. The plaintife sayth, I require the law: which is graunted: then commeth an officer and arresteth the party defendant, and vseth him contrarie to the lawes of England. For when they attach any man they beate him about the legges, vntill such time as he findeth sureties to answere the matter: And if not, his handes and necke are bound together, and he is led about the towne and beaten aboute the legges, with other extreme punishments till he come to his answere: And the Iustice demaundeth if it be for debt, and sayth: Owest thou this man any such debt? He will perhaps say nay. Then sayth the Iudge: art thou able to denie it? Let vs heare how? By othe sayth the defendant. Then he commandeth to leaue beating him till further triall be had.

Their order in one point is commendable. They haue no man of Lawe to plead their causes in any court: but euery man pleadeth his owne cause, and giueth bill and answere in writing: contrarie to the order in England. The complaint is in maner of a supplication, and made to the Dukes grace, and deliuered him into his owne hand, requiring to haue iustice as in his complaint is alleadged.

The Duke giueth sentence himselfe vpon all matters in the Law. Which is very commendable, that such a Prince wil take paines to see ministration of iustice. Yet nowithstanding it is wonderfully abused: and thereby the Duke is much deceiued. But if it fall out that the officers be espied in cloking the trueth, they haue most condigne punishment. And if the plaintife can nothing prooue, then the defendant must take his oth vpon the crucifixe whether he be in the right or no. Then is demanded if the plaintife be any thing able further to make proof: if hee bee not; then sometimes he will say,

I am able to prooue it by my body and hands, or by my champions body, so requiring the Campe. After the other hath his othe, it is graunted aswell to the one as to the other. So when they goe to the field, they sweare vpon the Crucifixe, that they be both in the right, and that the one shall make the other to confesse the trueth before they depart foorth of the field: and so they goe both to the battell armed with such weapons as they vse in that countrey: they fight all on foote, and seldome the parties themselues do fight, except they be Gentlemen, for they stand much vpon their reputation, for they wil not fight, but with such as are come of as good an house as themselues. So that if either partie require the combate, it is granted vnto them, and no champion is to serue in their room: wherein is no deceit: but otherwise by champions there is. For although they take great othes vpon them to doe the battell truely, yet is the contrarie often seene: because the common champions haue none other liuing. And assoone as the one partie hath gotten the victorie, he demandeth the debt, and the other is carried to prison, and there is shamefully vsed till he take order. There is also another order in the lawe, that the plaintife may sweare in some causes of debt. And if the partie defendant be poore, he shalbe set vnder the Crucifixe, and the partie plaintife must sweare ouer his head, and when hee hath taken his othe, the Duke taketh the partie defendant home to his house, and vseth him as his bond-man, and putteth him to labour, or letteth him for hier to any such as neede him, vntill such time as his friends make prousion for his redemption: or else hee remaineth in bondage all the dayes of his life. Againe there are many that will sell themselues to Gentlemen or Marchants to bee their bond-men, to haue during their life meate, drinke and cloth, and at their comming to haue a piece of mony, yea and some will sell their wiues and children to be bawdes and drudges to the byer. Also they haue a Lawe for Fellons and Pickers contrary to the Lawes of England. For by their law they can hang no man for his first offence; but may keepe him long in prison, and oftentimes beate him with whips and other punishment: and there he shall remaine vntill his friends be able to bayle him. If he be a picker or a cut-purse, as there be very many, the second time he is taken, he hath a piece of his nose cut off, and is burned in the forehead, and kept in prison till hee finde sureties for his good behauiour. And, if he be taken the third time, he is hanged. And at the first time he is extremely punished and not released, except hee haue very good friends, or that some Gentleman require to haue him to the warres: And in so doing, he shall enter into great bonds for him: by which meanes the countrey is brought into good quietnesse. But they be naturally giuen to great deceit, except extreme beating did bridle them. They be naturally giuen to hard liuing aswell in fare as in lodging. I heard a Russian say, that it was a great deale merrier liuing in prison then foorth, but for the great beating. For they haue meate and drinke without any labour, and get the charitie of well disposed people: But being at libertie they get nothing. The poore is very innumerable, and liue most miserably: for I haue seene them eate the pickle of Hearring and other stinking fish: nor the fish cannot be so stinking nor rotten, but they will eate it and praise it to be more wholesome then other fish or fresh meate. In mine opinion there be no such people vnder the sunne for their hardnesse of liuing. Well, I will leaue them in this poynt, and will in part declare their Religion. They doe obserue the lawe of the Greekes with such excesse of superstition, as the like hath not bene heard of. They haue no grauen images in their Churches, but all painted, to the intent they will not breake the commandement: but to their painted images they vse such idolatrie, that the like was neuer heard of in England. They will neither worship nor honour any image that is made forth of their owne countrey. For their owne images (say they) haue pictures to declare what they be, and howe they be of God, and so be not ours: They say, Looke how the Painter or Caruer hath made them, so we doe worship them, and they worship none before they be Christened. They say we be but halfe Christians: because we obserue not part of the olde Law with the Turks. Therefore they call themselues more holy then vs. They haue none other learning but their mother tongue, nor will suffer no other in their countrey among them. All their seruice in Churches is in their mother tongue. They haue the olde and newe Testament, which are daily read among them: and yet their superstition is no lesse. For when the Priests doe reade, they haue such tricks in their reading, that no man can vnderstand them, nor no man giueth eare to them. For all the while the Priest readeth, the people sit downe and one talke with another. But when the Priest is at seruice no man sitteth, but gagle and ducke like so many Geese. And as for their prayers they haue but little skill, but vse to say *As bodi pomele*: As much to say, Lord haue mercy vpon me. For the tenth man within the land cannot say the Pater noster. And as for the Creede, no man may be so bolde as to meddle therewith but in the Church: for they say it shoulde not bee spoken of, but in the Churches. Speake to them of the Commandements, and they will say they were giuen to Moses in the law, which Christ hath now abrogated by his precious death and passion: therefore, (say they) we obserue little or none thereof. And I doe beleeue them. For if they were examined of their Lawe and Commaundements together, they shoulde agree but in fewe poynts. They haue the Sacrament of the Lords Supper in both kindes, and more ceremonies then wee haue. They present them in a dish in both kindes together, and carrie them rounde about the Church vpon the Priestes head, and so doe minister at all such times as any shall require. They be great offerers of Candles, and sometimes of money, which wee call in England, Soule pense, with more ceremonies then I am able to declare. They haue foure Lents in the yeere, whereof our Lent is the greatest. Looke as we doe begin on the Wednesday, so they doe on the Munday before: And the weeke before that they call The Butter weeke: And in that weeke they eate nothing but Butter and milke. Howbeit I beleeue there bee in no other countrey the like people for drunkennesse. The next Lent is called Saint Peters Lent, and beginneth alwayes the Munday next after Trinitie sunday, and endeth on Saint Peters euen. If they should breake that fast, their beliefe is, that they should not come in at heauen gates. And when any of them die, they haue a testimoniall with them in the Coffin, that when the soule commeth to heauen gates it may deliuer the same to Saint Peter, which declareth that the partie is a true and holy Russian. The third Lent beginneth fifteene dayes before the later Lady day, and endeth on our Lady Eeuen. The fourth Lent beginneth on Saint Martin's day, and endeth on Christmas Eeuen: which Lent is fasted for Saint Philip, Saint Peter, Saint Nicholas, and Saint Clement. For they foure be the principall arid greatest Saints in that Countrey. In these Lents they eate neither Butter, Egges, Milke, or Cheese; but they are very straitely kept with Fish, Cabbages, and Rootes. And out of their Lents, they obserue truely the Wednesdayes and Fridayes throughout the yeere: and on the Saturday they doe eate flesh. Furthermore they haue a great number of Religious men: which are blacke Monks, and they eate no flesh throughout the yeere, but fish, milke and Butter. By their order they should eate no fresh-fish, and in their Lents they eate nothing but Coleworts, Cabbages, salt Cowcumbers, with other rootes, as Radish and such like. Their drinke is like our peny Ale, and is called Quass. They haue seruice daily in their Churches; and vse to goe to seruice two houres before day, and that is ended by day light. At nine of the clocke they goe to Masse: that ended, to dinner: and after that to seruice againe: and then to supper. You shall vnderstand that at euery dinner and supper they haue declared the exposition of the Gospel of that day: but howe they wrest and twine the Scripture and that together by report it is wonderfull. As for whoredome and drunkennesse there be none such liuing: and for extortion, they be the most abhominable under the sunne. Nowe iudge of their holinesse. They haue twise as much land as the Duke himselfe hath: but yet he is reasonable eeuen with them, as thus: When they take bribes of any of the poore and simple, he hath it by an order. When the Abbot of any of their houses dieth, then the Duke hath all his goods moueable and vnmoueable: so that the successour buieth all at the Dukes hands: and by this meane they be the best Fermers the Duke hath. Thus with their Religion I make an ende, trusting hereafter to know it better.

To the right worshipful and my singular good Vncle, Master Christopher Frothingham, giue these.

Sir, Reade and correct;
For great is the defect.

* * * * *

The Testimonie of M. Richard Eden in his decades, concerning the Booke following.

And whereas (saith he) I haue before made mention howe Moscouie was in our time discouered by Richard Chanceler in his voyage toward Cathay, by the direction and information of M. Sebastian Cabota, who long before had this secret in his minde: I shall not neede here to describe that voyage, forasmuch as the same is largely and faithfully written in the Latine tongue, by that learned yong man Clement Adams, schoolemaster to the Queenes henshmen, as he receiued it at the mouth of the said Richard Chanceler.

* * * * *

The newe Nauigation and discouerie of the kingdome of Moscouia, by the
  Northeast, in the yeere 1553: Enterprised by Sir Hugh Willoughbie knight,
  and perfourmed by Richard Chancelor Pilot maior of the voyage: Written in
  Latine by Clement Adams.

At what time our Marchants perceiued the commodities and wares of England to bee in small request with the countreys and people about vs, and neere vnto vs, and that those Marchandizes which strangers in the time and memorie of our auncesters did earnestly seeke and desire, were nowe neglected, and the price thereof abated, although by vs carried to their owne portes, and all forreine Marchandises in great accompt, and their prises wonderfully raised: certaine graue Citizens of London, and men of great wisedome, and carefull for the good of their Countrey, began to thinke with themselues, howe this mischiefe might bee remedied. Neither was a remedie (as it then appeared) wanting to their desires, for the auoyding of so great an inconuenience: for seeing that the wealth of the Spaniards and Portingales, by the discouerie and search of newe trades and Countreys was marueilously increased, supposing the same to be a course and meane for them also to obteine the like, they thereupon resolued vpon a newe and strange Nauigation. And whereas at the same time one Sebastian Cabota, a man in those dayes very renowmed, happened to bee in London, they began first of all to deale and consult diligently with him, and after much speech and conference together, it was at last concluded that three shippes should bee prepared and furnished out, for the search and discouerie of the Northerne part of the world, to open a way and passage to our men for trauaile to newe and vnknowen kingdomes.

And whereas many things seemed necessary to bee regarded in this so hard and difficult a matter, they first make choyse of certaine graue and wise persons in maner of a Senate or companie, which should lay their heads together, and giue their iudgments, and prouide things requisite and profitable for all occasions: by this companie it was thought expedient, that a certaine summe of money should publiquely bee collected to serue for the furnishing of so many shippes. And lest any priuate man should bee too much oppressed and charged, a course was taken that euery man willing to be of the societie, should disburse the portion of twentie and fiue pounds a piece: so that in short time by this meanes the summe of sixe thousand pounds being gathered, the three shippes were bought, the most part whereof they prouided to be newly built and trimmed. But in this action, I wote not whether I may more admire the care of the Marchants, or the diligence of the Shipwrights: for the Marchants, they get very strong and well seasoned plankes for the building, the Shippewrights, they with daily trauaile, and their greatest skill doe fitte them for the dispatch of the shippes: they calke them, pitch them, and among the rest, they make one most stanch and firme, by an excellent and ingenious inuention. For they had heard that in certaine parts of the Ocean, a kinde of wormes is bredde, which many times pearceth and eateth through the strongest oake that is: and therfore that the Mariners, and the rest to bee imployed in this voyage might bee free and safe from this danger, they couer a piece of the keele of the shippe with thinne sheetes of leade: and hauing thus built the ships, and furnished them with armour and artillerie, then followed a second care no lesse troublesome and necessarie then the former, namely, the prouision of victuals, which was to be made according to the time and length of the voyage. And whereas they afore determined to haue the East part of the world sayled vnto, and yet that the sea towards the same was not open, except they kept the Northern tract, whereas yet it was doubtfull whether there were any passage yea or no, they resolued to victuall the ships for eighteene moneths, which they did for this reason. For our men being to passe that huge and colde part of the world, they wisely foreseeing it, allowe them sixe moneths victuall to saile to the place, so much more to remaine there if the extremitie of the winter hindered their returne, and so much more also for the time of their comming home.

Nowe this prouision being made and caried aboord, with armour and munition of all sorts, sufficient Captaines and gouenours of so great an enterprise were as yet wanting: to which office and place, although many men, (and some voyde of experience) offered themselues, yet one Sir Hugh Willoughbie a most valiant Gentleman, and well borne, very earnestly requested to haue that care and charge committed vnto him: of whom before all others, both by reason of his goodly personage (for he was of a tall stature) as also for his singular skill in the seruices of warre, the company of the Marchants made greatest accompt: so that at the last they concluded and made choyce of him for the Generall of this voyage, and appoynted him to the Admirall with authortie and command ouer all the rest. And for the gouernement of other ships although diuers men seemed willing, and made offers of themselues thereunto, yet by a common consent one Richard Chanceler, a man of great estimation for many good partes of wit in him, was elected, in whom alone great hope for the performance of this businesse rested. This man was brought vp by one Master Henry Sidney, a noble young Gentleman and very much beloued of King Edward, who at this time comming to the place where the Marchants were gathered together, beganne a very eloquent speech or Oration, and spake to them after this maner following.

My very worshipfull friends, I cannot but greatly commend your present godly and vertuous intention, in the serious enterprising (for the singular loue you beare to your Countrey) a matter, which (I hope) will prooue profitable for this nation, and honourable to this our land. Which intention of yours wee also of the Nobilitie are ready to our power to helpe and further: neither doe wee holde any thing so deare and precious vnto vs, which wee will not willingly forgoe, and lay out in so commendable a cause. But principally I reioyce in my selfe, that I haue nourished and maintained that witte, which is like by some meanes and in some measure, to profile and steede you in this worthy action. But yet I would not haue you ignorant of this one thing, that I doe now part with Chanceler, not because I make little reckoning of the man, or that his maintenance is burdenous and chargeable vnto mee, but that you might conceiue and vnderstand my good will and promptitude for the furtherance of this businesse, and that the authoritie and estimation which hee deserueth may be giuen him. You know the man by report, I by experience, you by wordes, I by deedes, you by speech and companie, but I by the daily triall of his life haue a full and perfect knowledge of him. And you are also to remember, into howe many perils for your sakes, and his countreys loue, he is nowe to runne: whereof it is requisite that wee be not vnmindefull, if it please God to send him good successe. Wee commit a little money to the chaunce and hazard of Fortune: He commits his life (a thing to a man of all things most deare) to the raging Sea, and the vncertainties of many dangers. We shall here liue and rest at home quietly with our friends, and acquaintance: but hee in the meane time labouring to keepe the ignorant and vnruly Mariners in good order and obedience, with howe many cares shall hee trouble and vexe himselfe? with how many troubles shall he breake himselfe? and howe many disquietings shall hee bee forced to sustaine? We shall keepe our owne coastes and countrey: Hee shall seeke strange and vnknowen kingdomes. He shall commit his safetie to barbarous and cruell people, and shall hazard his life amongst the monstrous and terrible beastes of the Sea. Wherefore in respect of the greatnesse of the dangers, and the excellencie of his charge, you are to fauour and loue the man thus departing from vs:

and if it fall so happily out that hee returne againe, it is your part and duetie also, liberally to reward him.

After that this noble yong Getleman had deliuered this or some such like speech, much more eloquently then I can possiblie report it, the companie then present beganne one to looke vpon another, one to question and conferre with another: and some (to whom the vertue and sufficiencie of the man was knowen) began secretly to reioyce with themselues, and to conceiue a speciall hope, that the man would prooue in time very rare and excellent, and that his vertues already appearing and shining to the world woulde growe to the great honour and aduancement of this kingdome.

After all this, the companie growing to some silence, it seemed good to them that were of greatest grauity amongst them, to inquire, search and seeke what might be learned and knowen, concerning the Easterly part or tract of the world. For which cause two Tartarians, which were then of the kings Stable, were sent for, and an interpreter was gotten to be present, by whom they were demaunded touching their Countrey and the maners of their nation. But they were able to answere nothing to the purpose: being in deede more acquainted (as one there merily and openly said) to tosse pottes, then to learne the states and dispositions of people. But after much adoe and many things passed about this matter, they grew at last to this issue, to set downe and appoynt a time for the departure of the shippes: because diuers were of opinion, that a great part of the best time of the yeere was already spent, and if the delay grewe longer, the way would bee stopt and bard by the force of the Ice, and the colde climate: and therefore it was thought best by the opinion of them all, that by the twentieth day of May, [Marginal note: They departed from Ratcliffe, the 20. of May, 1553.] the Captaines and Mariners should take shipping, and depart from Radcliffe vpon the ebbe, if it pleased God. They hauing saluted their acquaintance, one his wife, another his children, another his kinsfolkes, and another his friends deerer then his kinsfolkes, were present and ready at the day appoynted: and hauing wayed ancre, they departed with the turning of the water, and sailing easily, came first to Greenewich. The greater shippes are towed downe with boates, and oares, and the mariners being all apparelled in Watchet or skie coloured cloth, rowed amaine, and made way with diligence. And being come neere to Greenewich, (where the Court then lay) presently vpon the newes therof, the Courtiers came running out, and the common people flockt together, standing very thicke vpon the shoare: the priuie Counsel, they lookt out at the windowes of the Court, and the rest ranne vp to the toppes of the towers: the shippes hereupon discharge their Ordinance, and shoot off their pieces after the maner of warre, and of the sea, insomuch that the tops of the hilles sounded therewith, the valleys and the waters gaue an Eccho, and the Mariners, they shouted in such sort, that the skie rang againe with the noyse thereof. One stoode in the poope of the ship, and by his gesture bids farewell to his friendes in the best maner hee could. Another walkes vpon the hatches, another climbes the shrowds, another stands vpon the maine yard, and another in the top of the shippe. To be short, it was a very triumph (after a sort) in all respects to the beholders. But (alas) the good King Edward (in respect of whom principally all this was prepared) hee onely by reason of his sickenesse was absent from this shewe, and not long after the departure of these ships, the lamentable and most sorrowfull accident of his death followed.

But to proceede in the matter.

The shippes going downe with the tyde came at last to Woolwich, where they stayed and cast ancre, with purpose to depart therehence againe, as soone as the turning of the water, and a better winde should draw them to set saile. After this they departed and came to Harwich, in which porte they stayed long, not without great losse and consuming of time: yet at the last with a good winde they hoysed vp saile, and committed themselues to the sea, giuing their last adieu to their natiue Countrey, which they knewe not whether they should euer returne to see againe or not. Many of them looked oftentimes back, and could not refraine from teares, considering into what hazards they were to fall, and what vncertainties of the sea they were to make triall of.

Amongst the rest, Richard Chanceler the Captaine of the Edward Bonauenture, was not a little grieued with the feare of wanting victuals, part whereof was found to be corrupt and putrified at Harwich, and the hoggesheads of wine also leaked, and were not stanch: his naturall and fatherly affection also somewhat troubled him, for he left behinde him his two little sonnes, which were in the case of Orphanes if he spedde not well: the estate also of his companie mooued him to care, being in the former respects after a sort vnhappie, and were to abide with himselfe euery good or badde accident: but in the meane time while his minde was thus tormented with the multiplicitie of sorrows and cares, after many dayes sayling, they kenned land afarre off, whereunto the Pilots directed the ships: and being come to it, they land, and find it to be Rost Island, where they stayed certaine dayes, and afterwards set saile againe, and proceeding towards the North, they espied certaine other Islands, which were called the Crosse of Islands. From which places when they were a little departed, Sir Hugh Willoughby the General, a man of good foresight and prouidence in all his actions, erected and set out his flagge, by which hee called together the chiefest men of the other shippes, that by the helpe and assistance of their counsels, the order of the gouernement, and conduction of the shippes in the whole voyage might bee the better: who being come together accordingly, they conclude and agree, that if any great tempest should arise at any time, and happen to disperse and scatter them, euery shippe should indeuour his best to goe to Wardhouse, a hauen, or castell of some name in the kingdome of Norway, and that they that arriued there first in safetie should stay and expect the comming of the rest.

The very same day in the afternoone, about foure of the clocke, so great a tempest suddenly arose, and the Seas were so outrageous, that the ships could not keepe their intended course, but some were perforce driuen one way, and some another way, to their great perill and hazard: The generall with his lowdest voyce cried out to Richard Chanceler, and earnestly requested him not to goe farre from him: but hee neither would nor could keepe companie with him, if he sailed still so fast: for the Admirall was of better saile then his shippe. But the said Admirall (I knowe not by what meanes) bearing all his sailes, was caried away with so great force and swiftnesse, that not long after hee was quite out of sight, and the third ship also with the same storme and like rage was dispersed and lost vs.

The shippe boate of the Admirall (striking against the shippe,) was ouerwhelmed in the sight and viewe of the Mariners of the Bonauenture: and as for them that are already returned and arriued, they know nothing of the rest of the ships what was become of them.

But if it be so, that any miserable mishap haue ouertaken them, If the rage and furie of the Sea haue deuoured those good men, or if as yet they liue, and wander vp and downe in strange Countreys, I must needs say they were men worthy of better fortune, and if they be liuing, let vs wish them safetie and a good returne: but if the crueltie of death hath taken holde of them, God send them a Christian graue and Sepulchre.

Nowe Richard Chanceler with his shippe and company being thus left alone, and become very pensiue, heauie, and sorrowfull, by this dispersion of the Fleete, hee (according to the order before taken,) shapeth his course for Wardhouse in Norway, there to expect and abide the arriuall of the rest of the shippes. And being come thither, and hauing stayed there the space of 7 dayes, and looked in vaine for their comming, hee determined at length to proceede alone in the purposed voyage. And as hee was preparing himselfe to depart, it happened that hee fell in company and speech with certaine Scottish men: who hauing vnderstanding of his intention, and wishing well to his actions, beganne earnestly to disswade him from the further prosecution of the discouerie, by amplifying the dangers which hee was to fall into, and omitted no reason that might serue to that purpose. But hee holding nothing so ignominious and reproachfull, as inconstancie and leuitie of minde, and perswading himselfe that a man of valour coulde not commit a more dishonourable part then for feare of danger to auoyde and shunne great attempts, was nothing at all changed or discouraged with the speeches and words of the Scots, remaining stedfast and immutable in his first resolution: determining either to bring that to passe which was intended, or els to die the death.

And as for them which were with Master Chanceler in his shippe, although they had great cause of discomfort by the losse of their companie (whom the foresaid tempest had separated from them,) and were not a little troubled with cogitations and pertubations of minde, in respect of their doubtfull course: yet notwithstanding, they were of such consent and agreement of minde with Master Chanceler, that they were resolute, and prepared vnder his direction and gouernment, to make proofe and triall of all aduentures, without all feare or mistrust of future dangers. Which constancie of minde in all the companie did exceedingly increase their Captaines carefulnesse: for hee being swallowed vp with like good will and loue towards them, feared lest through any errour of his, the safetie of the companie should bee indangered. To conclude, when they sawe their desire and hope of the arriuall of the rest of the shippes to be euery day more and more frustrated, they prouided to sea againe, and Master Chanceler held on his course towards that vnknowen part of the world, and sailed so farre, that hee came at last to the place where he found no night at all, but a continual light and brightnesse of the Sunne shining clearely vpon the huge and mightie Sea. [Sidenote: They arriue in the Bay of Saint Nicholas.] And hauing the benefite of this perpetuall light for certaine dayes, at the length it pleased God to bring them into a certaine great Bay, which was of one hundreth miles or thereabout ouer. Whereinto they entred, and somewhat farre within it cast ancre, and looking euery way about them, it happened that they espied a farre off a certaine fisher boate, which Master Chanceler, accompanied with a fewe of his men, went towards to common with the fishermen that were in it, and to knowe of them what Countrey it was, and what people, and of what maner of liuing they were: but they beeing amazed with the strange greatnesse of his shippe, (for in those partes before that time they had neuer seene the like) beganne presently to auoyde and to flee: but hee still following them at last ouertooke them, and being come to them, they (being in great feare, as men halfe dead) prostrated themselues before him, offering to kisse his feete: but hee (according to his great and singular courtesie,) looked pleasantly vpon them, comforting them by signes and gestures, refusing those dueties and reuerences of theirs, and taking them vp in all louing sort from the ground. And it is strange to consider howe much fauour afterwards in that place, this humanitie of his did purchase to himselfe. For they being dismissed spread by and by a report abroad of the arriuall of a strange nation, of a singular gentlenesse and courtesie: whereupon the common people came together offering to these newe-come ghests victuals freely, and not refusing to traffique with them, except they had bene bound by a certaine religious vse and custome, not to buy any forreine commodities, without the knowledge and consent of the king.

By this time our men had learned that this Countrey was called Russia, or Moscouie, and that Iuan Vasiliwich (which was at that time their Kings name) ruled and gouerned farre and wide in those places. And the barbarous Russes asked likewise of our men whence they were, and what they came for: whereunto answere was made, that they were Englishmen sent into those coastes, from the most excellent King Edward the sixt, hauing from him in commandement certaine things to deliuer to their King, and seeking nothing els but his amitie and friendship, and traffique with his people, whereby they doubted not, but that great commoditie and profit would grow to the subiects of both kingdomes.

The Barbarians heard these things very gladly, and promised their aide and furtherance to acquaint their king out of hand with so honest and a reasonable request.

In the meane time Master Chanceler intreated victuals for his money of the gouernour of that place (who together with others came aboord him) and required hostages of them likewise for the more assurance of safetie to himselfe and his company. To whom the gouernours answered, that they knewe not in that case the will of their king, but yet were willing in such things as they might lawfully doe, to pleasure him: which was as then to affoord him the benefit of victuals.

Nowe while these things were a doing, they secretly sent a messenger vnto the Emperour, to certifie him of the arriuall of a strange nation, and withall to knowe his pleasure concerning them. Which message was very welcome vnto him, insomuch that voluntarily he inuited them to come to his Court. But if by reason of the tediousnesse of so long a iourney, they thought it not best so to doe, then hee graunted libertie to his subiects to bargaine, and to traffique with them: and further promised, that if it would please then to come to him, hee himselfe would beare the whole charges of poste horses. In the meane time the gouernours of the place differred the matter from day to day, pretending diuers excuses, and saying one while that the consent of all the gouernours, and another while, that the great and waightie affaires of the kingdome compelled them to differ their answere: and this they did of purpose, so long to protract the time, vntill the messenger (sent before to the king) did returne with relation of his will and pleasure.

But Master Chanceler, (seeing himselfe held in this suspense with long and vaine expectation, and thinking that of intention to delude him, they posted the matter off so often,) was very instant with them to performe their promise: Which if they would not doe, hee tolde them that hee would depart and proceede in his voyage. So that the Moscouites (although as yet they knew not the minde of their king) yet fearing the departure in deede of our men who had such wares and commodities as they greatly desired, they at last resolued to furnish our people with all things necessarie, and to conduct them by land to the presence of their king. And so Master Chanceler beganne his iourney, which was very long and most troublesome, wherein hee had the vse of certaine sleds, and all their carriages are in the same sort, the people almost not knowing any other maner of carriage, the cause whereof is the exceeding hardnesse of the ground congealed in the winter time by the force of the colde, which in those places is very extreme and horrible, whereof hereafter we will say something.

But nowe they hauing passed the greater part of their iourney, mette at last with the Sleddeman (of whom I spake before) sent to the king secretly from the Iustices or gouernours, who by some ill happe had lost his way, and had gone to the Sea side, which is neere to the Countrey of the Tartars thinking there to haue found our ship. But hauing long erred and wandered out of his way, at the last in his direct returne, hee met (as hee was coming) our Captaine on the way. To whom hee by and by deliuered the Emperours letters, which were written to him with all courtesie and in the most louing maner that could be: wherein expresse commandement was giuen, that post horses should bee gotten for him and the rest of his company without any money. Which thing was of all the Russes in the rest of their iourney so willingly done, that they began to quarrell, yea, and to fight also in striuing and contending which of them should put their post horses to the sledde: so that after much adoe and great paines taken in this long and wearie iourney, (for they had trauelled very neere fifteene hundred miles) Master Chanceler came at last to Mosco the chiefe citie of the kingdome, and the seate of the king: of which citie, and of the Emperour himselfe, and of the principall cities of Moscouie, wee will speake immediately more at large in this discourse.

Of Moscouie, which is also called Russia.

Moscouie, which hath the name also of Russia the white, is a very large and spacious Countrey, euery way bounded with diuers nations. Towards the South and the East, it is compassed with Tartaria: the Northren side of it stretcheth to the Scytian Ocean: vpon the West part border the Lappians, a rude and sauage nation, liuing in woods, whose language is not knowen to any other people: next vnto these, more towards the South, is Swecia, then Finlandia, then Liuonia, and last of all Lituania. This Countrey of Moscouie, hath also very many and great riuers in it, and is marish ground, in many places: and as for the riuers, the greatest and most famous amongst, all the rest, is that, which the Russes in their owne tongue call Volga, but others know it by the name of Rha. Next vnto it in fame is Tanais, which they call

Don, and the third Boristhenes which at this day they call Neper. Two of these, to wit, Rha, and Boristhenes yssuing both out of one fountaine, runne very farre through the land: Rha receiuing many other pleasant riuers into it, and running from the very head or spring of it towards the East, after many crooked turnings and windings, dischargeth it selfe, and all the other waters and riuers that fall into it by diuers passages into the Caspian Sea. Tanais springing from a fountaine of great name in those partes, and growing great neere to his head, spreds it selfe at length very largely, and makes a great lake: and then growing narrowe againe, doth so runne for certaine miles, vntill it fall into another lake, which they call Iuan: and therehence fetching a very crooked course, comes very neere to the riuer Volga: but disdaining as it were the company of any other riuer, doth there turne it selfe againe from Volga, and runnes toward the South, and fals at last into the Lake of Moeotis. Boristhenes, which comes from the same head that Rha doth, (as wee sayde before) carieth both it selfe, and other waters that are neere vnto it, towards the South, not refusing the mixture of other small riuers: and running by many great and large Countreys fals at last into Pontius Euxinus. Besides these riuers, are also in Muscouie certaine lakes, and pooles, the lakes breede fish by the celestiall influence: and amongst them all, the chiefest and most principall is called Bealozera, which is very famous by reason of a very strong towre built in it, wherein the kings of Muscouie reserue and repose their treasure in all times of warre and danger.

Touching the Riphean mountaines, whereupon the snow lieth continually, and where hence in times past it was thought that Tanais the riuer did spring, and that the rest of the wonders of nature, which the Grecians fained and inuented of olde, were there to be seene: our men which lately came from thence, neither sawe them, not yet haue brought home any perfect relation of them, although they remained there for the space of three moneths, and had gotten in that time some intelligence of the language of Moscouie. The whole Countrey is plaine and champion, and few hils in it: and towards the North it hath very large and spacious woods, wherein is great store of Firre trees, a wood very necessarie, and fit for the building of houses: there are also wilde beastes bred in those woods, as Buffes, Beares, and blacke Wolues, and another kinde of beast vnknowen to vs, but called by them Rossomakka: and the nature of the same is very rare and wonderfull: for when it is great with yong, and ready to bring foorth, it seeketh out some narrow place betweene two stakes, and so going through them, presseth it selfe, and by that meanes is eased of her burden, which otherwise could not be done. They hunt their buffes for the most part a horsebacke, but their Beares a foot, with wodden forkes. The north parts of the Countrey are reported to be so cold, that the very ice or water which distilleth out of the moist wood which they lay upon the fire is presently congealed and frozen: the diuersitie growing suddenly to be so great, that in one and the selfe same firebrand, a man shall see both fire and ice. When the winter doth once begin there it doth still more and more increase by a perpetuitie of cold: neither doth that colde slake, vntill the force of the Sunne beames doth dissolue the cold, and make glad the earth, returning to it againe. Our mariners which we left in the ship in the meane time to keepe it, in their going vp onely from their cabbins to the hatches, had their breath oftentimes so suddenly taken away, that they eftsoones fell downe as men very neere dead, so great is the sharpenesse of that colde climate: but as for the South parts of the Countrey, they are somewhat more temperate.

Of Mosco the chiefe Citie of the kingdome, and of the Emperour thereof.

It remaineth that a larger discourse be made of Mosco, the principall City of that Countrey, and of the Prince also, as before we haue promised. The Empire and gouernment of the king is very large, and his wealth at this time exceeding great. And because the citie of Mosco is the chiefest of al the rest, it seemeth of it selfe to challenge the first place in this discourse. Our men say, that in bignesse it is as great as the Citie of London, with the suburbes thereof. There are many and great buildings in it, but for beautie and fairenesse, nothing comparable to ours. There are many Townes and Villages also, but built out of order, and with no hansomnesse: their streets and wayes are not paued with stone as ours are: the walles of their houses are of wood: the roofes for the most part are couered with shingle boords. There is hard by the Citie a very faire Castle, strong, and furnished with artillerie, whereunto the Citie is ioyned directly towards the North, with a bricke wall: the walles also of the Castle are built with bricke, and are in breadth or thickenesse eighteene foote. This Castle hath on the one side a drie ditch, on the other side the riuer Moscua, whereby it is made almost inexpugnable. The same Moscua trending towards the East doth admit into it the companie of the riuer Occa.

In the Castle aforesaide, there are in number nine Churches, or Chappells, not altogether vnhansome, which are vsed and kept by certaine religious men, ouer whom there is after a sort, a Patriarke, or Gouernour, and with him other reuerend Fathers all which for the greater part, dwell within the Castle. As for the kings Court and Palace, it is not of the neatest, onely in forme it is foure square, and of low building, much surpassed and excelled by the beautie and elegancie of the houses of the kings of England. The windowes are very narrowly built, and some of them by glasse, some other by lettisses admit the light: and whereas the Palaces of our Princes are decked, and adorned with hangings of cloth of gold, there is none such there: they build and ioyne to all their wals benches, and that not onely in the Court of the Emperour, but in all priuate mens houses.

Nowe after that they had remained about twelue dayes in the Citie there was then a Messenger sent vnto them, to bring them to the Kings house: and they being after a sort wearied with their long stay, were very ready, and willing so to doe: and being entred within the gates of the Court, there sate a very honorable companie of Courtiers, to the number of one hundred, all apparelled in cloth of golde, downe to their ankles: and there hence being conducted into the chamber of presence, our men beganne to wonder at the Maiestie of the Emperour: his seate was aloft, in a very royall throne, hauing on his head a Diademe, or Crowne of golde, apparalled with a robe all of Goldsmiths worke, and in his hand hee held a Scepter garnished, and beset with precious stones: and besides all other notes and apparances of honour, there was a Maiestie in his countenance proportionable with the excellencie of his estate: on the one side of him stood his chiefe Secretaire, on the other side, the great Commander of silence, both of them arayed also in cloth of gold: and then there sate the Counsel of one hundred and fiftie in number, all in like sort arayed, and of great State. This so honorable an assemblie, so great a Maiestie of the Emperour, and of the place might very well haue amazed our men, and haue dasht them out of countenance: but notwithstanding Master Chanceler being therewithall nothing dismaied saluted, and did his duetie to the Emperour, after the maner of England, and withall, deliuered vnto him the letters of our king, Edward the sixt. The Emperour hauing taken, and read the letters, began a litle to question with them, and to aske them of the welfare of our king: whereunto our men answered him directly, and in few words: hereupon our men presented some thing to the Emperour, by the chiefe Secretary, which at the deliuery of it, put of his hat, being before all the time couered: and so the Emperour hauing inuited them to dinner, dismissed them from his presence: and going into the chamber of him that was Master of the Requests to the Emperour, and hauing stayed there the space of two howres, at the last, the Messenger commeth, and calleth them to dinner: they goe, and being conducted into the golden Court, (for so they call it, although not very faire) they finde the Emperour sitting vpon an high and stately seate, apparelled with a robe of siluer, and with another Diademe on his head: our men being placed ouer against him, sit downe: in the middes of the roome stoode a mightie Cupboord vpon a square foote, whereupon stoode also a round boord, in manner of a Diamond, broade beneath, and towardes the toppe narrowe, and euery steppe rose vp more narrowe then another. Vpon this Cupboorde was placed the Emperours plate, which was so much, that the very Cupboord it selfe was scant able to sustaine the waight of it: the better part of all the vessels, and goblets, was made of very fine gold: and amongst the rest, there were foure pots of very large bignesse, which did adorne the rest of the plate in great measure: for they were so high, that they thought them at the least fiue foote long. There were also vpon this

Cupbord certaine siluer caskes, not much differing from the quantitie of our Fyrkins, wherein was reserued the Emperours drinke: on each side of the Hall stood foure Tables, each of them layde and couered with very cleane table clothes, whereunto the company ascended by three steps or degrees: all which were filled with the assemblie present: the ghests were all apparelled with linnen without, and with rich skinnes within, and so did notably set out this royall feast The Emperour, when hee takes any bread or knife in his hand, doth first of all crosse himselfe vpon his forehead: they that are in special fauour with the Emperour sit vpon the same bench with him, but somewhat farre from him: and before the comming in of the meate, the Emperour himselfe, according to an ancient custome of the kings of Moscouy, doth first bestow a piece of bread vpon euery one of his ghests, with a loud pronunciation of his title, and honour, in this manner: The great Duke of Moscouie, and chiefe Emperour of Russia, Iohn Basiliwich (and then the officer nameth the ghest) doth giue thee bread. Whereupon al the ghests rise vp, and by and by sit downe againe. This done, the Gentleman Vsher of the Hall comes in, with a notable company of seruants, carying the dishes, and hauing done his reuerence to the Emperour, puts a yong Swanne in a golden platter vpon the table, and immediately takes it thence againe, deliuering it to the Caruer, and seuen other of his fellowes, to be cut up: which being perfourmed, the meate is then distributed to the ghests, with the like pompe, and ceremonies. In the meane time, the Gentleman Vsher receiues his bread, and tasteth to the Emperour, and afterward, hauing done his reuerence, he departeth. Touching the rest of the dishes, because they were brought in out of order, our men can report no certaintie: but this is true, that all the furniture of dishes, and drinking vessels, which were then for the vse of a hundred ghests, was all of pure golde, and the tables were so laden with vessels of gold, that there was no roome for some to stand vpon them.

We may not forget, that there were 140. seruitors arayed in cloth of gold, that in the dinner time, changed thrise their habit and apparell, which seruitors are in like sort serued with bread from the Emperour, as the rest of the ghests. Last of all, dinner being ended, and candles brought in, (for by this time night was come) the Emperour calleth all his ghests and Noble Men by their names, in such sort, that it seemes miraculous, that a Prince, otherwise occupied in great matters of estate, should so well remember so many and sundry particular names. The Russes tolde our men, that the reason thereof, as also of the bestowing of bread in that maner, was to the ende that the Emperour might keepe the knowledge of his owne houshold: and withal, that such as are vnder his displeasure, might by this meanes be knowen.

Of the discipline of warre among the Russes.

Whensoeuer the iniuries of their neighbours doe call the King foorth to battell, hee neuer armeth a lesse number against the enemie, then 300. thousand soldiers, 100. thousand whereof hee carieth out into the field with him, and leaueth the rest in garison in some fit places, for the better safetie of his Empire. He presseth no husbandman, nor Marchant: for the Countrey is so populous, that these being left at home, the youth of the Realme is sufficient for all his wars. As many as goe out to warfare doe prouide all things of their owne cost: they fight not on foote, but altogether on horsebacke: their armour is a coate of maile, and a helmet: the coate of maile without is gilded, or els adorned with silke, although it pertaine to a common soldier: they haue a great pride in shewing their wealth: they vse bowes, and arrowes, as the Turks do: they cary lances also into the field. They ride with a short stirrop, after the maner of the Turks: They are a kinde of people most sparing in diet, and most patient in extremitie of cold, aboue all others. For when the ground is couered with snowe, and is growen terrible and hard with the frost, this Russe hangs vp his mantle, or souldiers coate, against that part from whence the winde and Snowe driues, and so making a little fire, lieth downe with his backe towards the weather: this mantle of his serues him for his bed, wall, house and all: his drinke is colde water of the riuer, mingled with oatemeale, and this is all his good cheere, and he thinketh himselfe well, and daintily fedde therewith, and so sitteth downe by his fire, and vpon the hard ground, rosteth as it were his wearie sides thus daintily stuffed: the hard ground is his feather bed, and some blocke or stone his pillow: and as for his horse, he is as it were a chamberfellow with his master, faring both alike. How iustly may this barbarous, and rude Russe condemne the daintinesse and nicenesse of our Captaines, who liuing in a soile and aire much more temperate, yet commonly vse furred boots, and clokes? But thus much of the furniture of their common souldiers. But those that are of higher degrees come into the field a little better prouided. As for the furniture of the Emperour himselfe, it is then aboue all other times, most notable. The couerings of his tent for the most part, are all of gold, adorned with stones of great price, and with the curious workemanship of plumasiers. As often as they are to skirmish with the enemie, they goe forth without any order at all: they make no wings, nor militarie diuisions of their men, as we doe, but lying for the most part, in ambush, doe suddenly set vpon the enemie. Their horses can well abstaine two whole daies from any meate. They feede vpon the barkes of trees, and the most tender branches, in all the time of warre. And this scant and miserable maner of liuing, both the horse and his Master can well endure, sometimes for the space of two moneths, lustie, and in good state of body. If any man behaue himselfe valiantly in the fielde, to the contentation of the Emperour, he bestoweth vpon him in recompense of his seruice, some farme, or so much ground as he and his may liue vpon, which notwithstanding after his death, returneth againe to the Emperour, if he die without a male issue. For although his daughters be neuer so many, yet no part of that inheritance comes to them, except peraduenture the Emperour of his goodnesse, giue some portion of the land amongst them, to bestowe them withall. As for the man, whosoeuer he be, that is in this sort rewarded by the Emperours liberalitie, hee is bound in a great summe, to maintaine so many souldiers for the warre, when need shall require, as that land, in the opinion of the Emperour, is able to maintaine. And all those, to whom any land fals by inheritance, are in no better condition: for if they die without any male issue, all their lands fall into the hands of the Emperour. And moreouer, if there be any rich man amongst them, who in his owne person is vnfit for the warres, and yet hath such wealth, that thereby many Noble men and warriours might be maintained, if any of the Courtiers present his name to the Emperour, the vnhappy man is by and by sent for, and in that instant, depriued of all his riches, which with great paines and trauell all his life time he had gotten together: except perhaps some small portion thereof be left him, to maintaine his wife, children and familie. But all this is done of all the people so willingly at the Emperours commandement, that a man would thinke, they rather make restitution of other mens goods, then giue that which is their owne to other men. Nowe the Emperour hauing taken these goods into his hands, bestoweth them among his Courtiers, according to their deserts: and the oftener that a man is sent to the warres, the more fauour he thinketh is borne to him by the Emperour, although he goe vpon his owne charge, as I said before. So great is the obedience of all men generally to their Prince.

Of the Ambassadours of the Emperour of Moscouie.

The Moscouite, with no lesse pompe, and magnificence, then that which we haue spoken of, sends his Ambassadors to forrein Princes, in the affaires of estate. For while our men were abiding in the Citie of Mosco, there were two Ambassadors sent to the King of Poland, accompanied with 500. notable horses, and the greater part of the men were arrayed in cloth of gold, and of silke, and the worst apparell was of garments of blewe colour, to speake nothing of the trappings of the horses, which were adorned with gold and siluer, and very curiously embrodered: they had also with them one hundred white and faire spare horses, to vse them at such times, as any wearinesse came vpon them. But now the time requireth me to speake briefly of other Cities of the Moscouites, and of the wares and commodities that the Countrey yeeldeth.

Nouogorode.

Next vnto Mosco, the Citie of Nouogorode is reputed the chiefest of Russia: for although it be in Maiestie inferior to it, yet in greatnesse it goeth beyond it. It is the chiefest and greatest Marte Towne of all Moscouie: and albeit the Emperour's seate is not there, but at Mosco, yet the commodiousness of the riuer, falling into the gulfe, which is called Sinus Finnicus, whereby it is well frequented by Marchants, makes it more famous then Mosco it selfe. This towne excels all the rest in the commodities of flaxe and hempe: It yeeldes also hides, honie, and waxe. The Flemings there sometimes had a house of Marchandize, but by reason that they vsed the like ill dealing there, which they did with vs, they lost their priuileges, a restitution whereof they earnestly sued for at the time that our men were there. But those Flemings hearing of the arriuall of our men in those parts, wrote their letters to the Emperour against them, accusing them for pirats and rouers, wishing him to detaine, and imprison them. Which things when they were knowen of our men, they conceiued feare, that they should neuer haue returned home. But the Emperour beleeuing rather the Kings letters, which our men brought, then the lying and false suggestions of the Flemings, vsed no ill intreatie towards them.

Yeraslaue.

Yeraslaue also is a Towne of some good fame, for the commodities of hides, tallow, and corne, which it yeeldes in great abundance. Cakes of waxe are there also to bee solde, although other places haue greater store: This Yeraslaue is distant from Mosco, about two hundred miles: and betwixt them are many populous villages. Their fields yeeld such store of corne, that in conuaying it towards Mosco, sometimes in a forenoone, a man shall see seuen hundred or eight hundred sleds, going and comming, laden with corne and salt fish: the people come a thousand miles to Mosco, to buy that corne, and then cary it away vpon sleds: and these are those people that dwell in the North parts, where the colde is so terrible, that no corne doth growe there, or if it spring vp it neuer comes to ripenesse. The commodities that they bring with them, are salt fish, skinnes, and hides.

Vologda.

Vologda being from Mosco, 550. miles yeeldes the commodities of Hempe and
Flaxe also: although the greatest store of Flaxe is solde at Nouogrode.

Plesco.

The Towne of Plesco, is frequented of Marchants for the good store of Honie and Waxe that it yeeldeth.

Colmagro.

The North parts of Russia yeelde very rare and precious skinnes: and amongst the rest, those principally, which we call Sables, worne about the neckes of our Noble women and Ladies: it hath also Martins skinnes, white, blacke, and red Foxe skinnes, skinnes of Hares, and Ermyns, and others, which they call and terme barbarously, as Beuers, Minxes, and Miniuers. The sea adioyning, breedes a certaine beast, which they call the Mors, which seeketh his foode vpon the rockes, climing vp with the helpe of his teeth. The Russes vse to take them, for the great vertue that is in their teeth, whereof they make as great accompt, as we doe of the Elephants tooth. These commodities they cary vpon Deeres backes to the towne of Lampas: and from thence to Colmagro, and there in the winter time, are kept great Faires for the sale of them. This Citie of Colmagro, serues all the Countrey about it with salt, and salt fish. The Russians also of the North parts, send thither oyle, which they call traine, which they make in a riuer called Vna, [Marginal note: Or Dwina.] although it be also made elsewhere: and here they vse to boile the water of the sea, whereof they make very great store of salt.

Of controuersies in Lawe, and how they are ended.

Hauing hitherto spoken so much of the chiefest Cities of Russia, as the matter required: it remaineth that we speake somewhat of the lawes, that the Moscouits doe vse, as farre foorth as the same are come to our knowledge. If any controuersie arise among them, they first make their Landlords Iudges in the matter, and if they cannot end it, then they preferre it to the Magistrate. The plaintif craueth of the said Magistrate, that he may haue leaue to enter law against his aduesarie: and hauing obtained it, the officer fetcheth the defendant, and beateth him on the legges, till he bring forth a suretie for him: but if he be not of such credite, as to procure a surety, then are his hands by an officer tied to his necke, and he is beaten all the way, till he come before the Iudge. The Iudge then asketh him (as for example in the matter of debt) whether he oweth any thing to the plaintife. If he denies it, then saith the Iudge, How canst thou deny it? the defendant answereth, By an othe: thereupon the officer is commaunded to cease from beating of him, vntill the matter be further tried. They haue no Lawyers, but euery man is his owne Aduocate, and both the complaint of the accuser, and the answere of the defendant, are in maner of petition deliuered to the Emperour, intreating iustice at his hands. The Emperour himselfe heareth euery great controuersie, and vpon the hearing of it, giueth iudgement, and that with great equitie, which I take to be a thing worthy of speciall commendation, in the Maiestie of a Prince. But although he doe this with a good purpose of mind, yet the corrupt Magistrates do wonderfully peruert the same: but if the Emperour take them in any fault, he doeth punish them most seuerely. Now at the last, when ech partie hath defended his cause with his best reasons, the Iudge demandeth of the accuser, whether he hath any more to say for himselfe: he answereth, that he will trie the matter in fight by his Champion, or else intreateth, that in fight betwixt themselues the matter may be ended: which being graunted, they both fight it out: or if both of them, or either of them seeme vnfit for that kinde of triall, then they haue publike Champions to be hired, which liue by ending of quarrels. These Champions are armed with yron axes, and speares, and fight on foote, and he whose Champion is ouercome, is by and by taken, and imprisoned, and terribly handled, vntill he agree with his aduersarie. But if either of them be of any good calling, and degree, and doe challenge one another to fight, the Iudge granteth it: in which case they may not vse publike Champions. And he that is of any good birth, doth contemne the other, if he be basely borne, and wil not fight with him. If a poore man happen to grow in debt, his Creditor takes him, and maketh him pay the debt, in working either to himselfe, or to some other man, whose wages he taketh vp. And there are some among them, that vse willingly to make themselues, their wiues, and children, bondslaues vnto rich men, to haue a little money at the first into their hands, and so for euer after content themselues with meate and drinke: so little accompt doe they make of libertie.

Of punishments vpon theeues.

If any man be taken vpon committing of theft, he is imprisoned, and often beaten, but not hanged for the first offence, as the manner is with vs: and this they call the lawe of mercie. He that offendeth the second time hath his nose cut off, and is burnt in the forehead with a hot yron. The third time, he is hanged. There are many cutpurses among them, and if the rigour of the Prince did not cut them off they could not be auoyded.

Of their religion.

They maintaine the opinions of the Greeke Church: they suffer no grauen images of saints in their Churches, but their pictures painted in tables they haue in great abundance, which they do adore and offer vnto, and burne waxe candles before them, and cast holy water vpon them, without other honour. They say that our images which are set vp in Churches, and carued, haue no diuinitie in them. In their priuate houses they haue images for their household saints, and for the most part, they are put in the darkest place of the house: hee that comes into his neighbours house doth first salute his saints, although he see them not. If any foorme or stoole stand in his way, hee oftentimes beateth his browe vpon the same, and often ducking downe with his head, and body, worshippeth the chiefe Image. The habite, and attire of the Priests, and of the Lay men, doth nothing at all differ: as for marriage, it is forbidden to no man: onely this is receiued and held amongst them for a rule, and custome, that if a Priests wife doe die, he may not marry againe, nor take a second wife: and therefore they of secular Priests, as they call them, are made Monkes, to whom then chastitie for euer is commanded. Their diuine seruice is all done and said in their owne language, that euery man may vnderstand it: they receiue the Lords Supper with leauened bread, and after the consecration, they carry it about the Church in a saucer, and prohibite no man from receiuing and taking of it, that is willing so to doe. They vse both the Olde and the Newe Testament, and read both in their owne language, but so confusedly, that they themselues that doe reade, vnderstand not what themselues doe say: and while any part of either Testament is read, there is liberty giuen by custome to prattle, talke, and make a noise: but in the time of the rest of the seruice they vse very great silence and reuerence and behaue themselues very modestly, and in good sort. As touching the Lords praier, the tenth man amongst them knowes it not: and for the articles of our faith, and the ten commandements, no man, or at the least very fewe of them doe either know them or can say them: their opinion is, that such secrete and holy things as they are should not rashly and imprudently be communicated with the common people. They holde for a maxime amongst them, that the olde Lawe, and the commandements also are abolished by the death and blood of Christ: all studies and letters of humanitie they vtterly refuse: concerning the Latine, Greeke, and Hebrew tongues, they are altogether ignorant in them.

Euery yeere they celebrate foure seuerall fastes, which they call according to the names of the Saints: the first beginnes with them, at the time that our Lent beginnes. The second is called amongst them the fast of S. Peter. The third is taken from the day of the Virgin Marie. And the fourth and last begins vpon S. Philips day. But as we begin our Lent vpon Wednesday, so they begin theirs vpon the Sunday. Vpon the Saturday they eate flesh: whensoeuer any of those fasting feastes doe drawe neere, looke what weeke doth immediately goe before them, the same weeke they liue altogether vpon white meates, and in their common language they call those weekes, the fast of Butter.

In the time of their fasts, the neighbours euery where goe from one to another, and visite one another, and kisse one another with kisses of peace, in token of their mutuall loue and Christian concord: and then also they doe more often then at any other time goe to the holy Communion. When seuen dayes are past, from the beginning of the fast, then they doe often either goe to their Churches, or keepe themselues at home, and vse often prayer: and for that seuennight they eate nothing but hearbes: but after that seuennights fast is once past, then they returne to their old intemperancie of drinking, for they are notable tospots. As for the keeping of their fasting dayes, they doe it very streightly, neither doe they eate any thing besides hearbes, and salt fish, as long as those fasting dayes doe endure: but vpon euery Wednesday and Friday, in euery weeke thoughout the yeere, they fast.

There are very many Monasteries of the order of S. Benedict, amongst them, to which many great liuings, for their maintenance, doe belong: for the Friers and the Monkes doe at the least possesse the third part of the liuings, throughout the whole Moscouite Empire. To those Monkes that are of this Order, there is amongst them a perpetuall prohibition, that they may eate no flesh: and therefore their meate is onely salt fish, milke, and butter: neither is it permitted them by the lawes, and customes of their religion, to eate any fresh fish at all: and at those foure fasting times, whereof we spake before, they eate no fish at all: onely they liue with hearbes, and cucumbers, which they doe continually for that purpose cause and take order to grow and spring, for their vse and diet.

As for their drinke, it is very weake, and small. For the discharge of their office, they do euery day say seruice, and that early in the mornings before day: and they doe in such sort, and with such obseruation begin their seruice, that they will be sure to make an ende of it, before day: and about nine of the clocke in the morning they celebrate the Communion. When they haue so done, they goe to dinner, and after dinner they goe againe to seruice, and the like also after supper: and in the meane time while they are at dinner there is some exposition or interpretation of the Gospel vsed.

Whensoeuer any Abbot of any monasterie dieth, the Emperour taketh all his housholde stuffe, beastes, flockes of sheepe, golde, siluer, and all that he hath: or els hee that is to succeede him in his place and dignitie doth redeeme all those things, and buyeth them of the Emperour for money.

Their churches are built of timber, and the towers of their churches for the most part are centered with shingle boordes. At the doores of their churches, they vsually build some entrance or porch as we doe, and in their churchyardes they erect a certain house of woode, wherein they set vp their bels, wherein sometimes they haue but one, in some two, and in some also three.

There is one vse and custome amongst them, which is strange and rare, but yet it is very ridiculous, and that is this: when any man dyeth amongst them, they take the dead body and put it in a coffine or chest, and in the hand of the corps they put a little scroule, and in the same there are these wordes written, that the same man died a Russe of Russes, hauing receiued the faith, and died in the same. This writing or letter they say they send to S. Peter, who receiuing it (as they affirme) reades it, and by and by admits him into heauen, and that his glory and place is higher and greater than the glory of the Christians of the Latine church, reputing themselues to be followers of a more sincere faith and religion than they: they hold opinion that we are but halfe Christians, and themselues onely to be the true and perfect church: these are the foolish and childish dotages of such ignorant Barbarians.

Of the Moscouites that are Idolaters, dwelling neere to Tartaria.

There is a certaine part of Moscouie bordering vpon the countreys of the Tartars, wherein those Moscouites that dwell are very great idolaters: they haue one famous idole amongst them, which they call the Golden old wife: and they haue a custome that whensoeuer any plague or any calamity doth afflict the country, as hunger, warre, or such like, then they goe to consult with their idol, which they do after this manner: they fall down prostrate before the idol, and pray vnto it, and put in the presence of the same, a cymbal: and about the same certaine persons stand, which are chosen amongst them by lot: vpon their cymball they place a siluer tode, and sound the cymball, and to whomsoeuer of those lotted persons that tode goeth, he is taken, and by and by slaine: and immediately, I know not by what illusions of the deuill or idole, he is againe restored to life, and then doth reueale and deliuer the causes of the present calamitie. And by this meanes knowing how to pacifie the idole, they are deliuered from the imminent danger.

Of the forme of their priuate houses, and of the apparell of the people.

The common houses of the countrey are euery where built of beames of Firre tree: the lower beames doe so receiue the round hollownesse of the vppermost, that by the meanes of the building thereupon, they resist, and expell all winds that blow, and where the timber is ioined together, there they stop the chinks with mosse. The forme and fashion of their houses in al places is foure square, with streit and narrow windoes, whereby with a transparent casement made or couered with skinne like to parchment, they receiue the light The roofes of their houses are made of boords couered without with ye barke of trees: within their houses they haue benches or griezes hard by their wals, which commonly they sleepe vpon, for the common people knowe not the vse of beds: they haue stoues wherein in the morning they make a fire, and the same fire doth either moderately warme, or make very hote the whole house.

The apparell of the people for the most part is made of wooll, their caps are picked like vnto a rike or diamond, broad beneath, and sharpe vpward. In the maner of making whereof, there is a signe and representation of nobilitie: for the loftier or higher their caps are, the greater is their birth supposed to be, and the greater reuerence is giuen them by the common people.

The conclusion to Queen Marie.

These are the things most excellent Queene, which your Subiects newly returned from Russia haue brought home concerning the state of that countrey: wherfore if your maiestie shall be fauourable, and grant a continuance of the trauell, there is no doubt but that the honour and renowne of your name will be spred amongst those nations, whereunto three onely noble personages from the verie creation haue had accesse, to whom no man hath bene comparable.

* * * * *

The copie of the Duke of Moscouie and Emperour of Russia his letters, sent to King Edward the sixt, by the hands of Richard Chancelour.

The Almighty power of God, and the incomprehensible holy Trinitie, rightfull Christian beliefe, &c. We great Duke Iuan Vasiliuich, [Marginal note: Iuan Vasiluich, that is to say, Iohn the sonne of Basilius.] by the grace of God great lord and Emperor of all Russia, great Duke of Volodemer, Mosco, and Nouograd, King of Kazan, King of Astracan, lord of Plesko, and great duke of Smolensko, of Twerria, Ioughoria, Permia, Vadska, Bulghoria, and others, lord and great duke of Nouograd in the Low countrey of Chernigo, Resan, Polotskoy, Rostoue, Yaruslaueley, Bealozera, Liefland, Oudoria, Obdoria, and Condensa, Commander of all Siberia, and of the North parts, and lord of many other countries, greeting. Before all, right great and worthy of honour Edward King of England &c. according to our most hearty and good zeale with good intent and friendly desire, and according to our holy Christian faith, and great gouernance, and being in the light of great vnderstanding, our answere by this our honourable writing vnto your kingly gouernance, at the request of your faithfull seruant Richard Chancelour, with his company, as they shall let you wisely know, is this. In the strength of the twentieth yeere of our gouernance, be it knowen that at our sea coastes arriued a shippe, with one Richard, and his companie, and sayd, that hee was desirous to come into our dominions, and according to his request, hath seene our Maiestie, and our eyes: [Marginal note: That is, come into our presence.] and hath declared vnto vs your Maiesties desire, as that we should grant vnto your subiects, to goe and come, and in our dominions, and among our subiects, to frequent free Marts, with all sortes of marchandizes, and vpon the same to haue wares for their returne. And they haue also deliuered vs your letters, which declare the same request. And hereupon we haue giuen order, that wheresoeuer your faithful seruant Hugh Willoughbie land or touch in our dominions, to be wel entertained, who as yet is not arriued, as your seruant Richard can declare.

And we with Christian beliefe and faithfulnes, and according to your honourable request, and my honourable commandement will not leaue it vndone: and are furthermore willing that you send vnto vs your ships and vessels, when and as often as they may haue passage, with good assurance on our part to see them harmlesse. And if you send one of your maiesties counsel to treate with vs whereby your countrey marchants may with all kinds of wares, and where they wil make their market in our dominions, they shall haue their free Marte with all free liberties through my whole dominions with all kinde of wares to come and goe at their pleasure, without any let, damage or impediment, according to this our letter, our word and our seale which we haue commaunded to be vnder sealed. Written in our dominion, in our citie and our palace in the castle of Mosco, in the yeare 7060, the second moneth of February.

[This letter was written in the Moscouian tongue, in letters much like to the Greeke letters, very faire written in paper, with a broad seale hanging at the same, sealed in paper vpon waxe. This seale was much like the broad seale of England, hauing on the one side the image of a man on horseback in compleate harnesse fighting with a dragon. Vnder this letter was another paper written in the Dutch tongue, which was the interpretation of the other written in the Moscouian letters. These letters were sent the next yere after the date of king Edwards letters, 1554.]

* * * * *

The letters of king Philip and Queene Marie to Iuan Vasiliuich the Emperour of Russia written the first of April 1555 and in the second voyage.

Philip and Marie by the grace of God, King and Queene of England, France, Naples, Ierusalem, and Ireland, defenders of the faith, Princes of Spaine and Sicilie, Archdukes of Austrich, Dukes of Burgundie, Millaine, and Brabant, Counties of Haspurge, Flanders, and Tiroll: To the right High, right Mightie, and right excellent Prince, garnished with all gifts of nature, by Gods grace Iohn Vasiliuich Emperour of all Russia, great Duke of Volodemer, Mosco, and Nouogrod, King of Cazan, King of Astracan, Lord of Plesco, and great Duke of Smolensko, of Tueria, Ioughoria, Permia, Vadska, Bulghoria, and others, Lorde and great Duke of Nouogrod of the lowe Countrey, of Chernigo, Rezan, Polotskay, Rostoue, Yeraslaue, Bealozera, Liefland. Oudoria, Obdoria, and Condensa, Commander of all Siberia, and of the North partes, and lord of many other countreys, greeting. Whereas by the consent and license of our most deare and entirely beloued late brother, King Edward the sixt, whose soule God pardon, sundrie of our subiects marchants of the citie of London within this our realme of England did at their owne proper costs and aduenture furnish three shippes to discouer, serch and find lands, Islands, regions, and territories before this aduenture not knowen, ne commonly haunted and frequented by seas. The one of the which three shippes, named the Edward Bonauenture, (whereof our right welbeloued Richard Chancelour was then gouernour and great Captaine) chanced by the grace of God, and the good conduct of the sayd Chancelour to arriue and winter in the North part of your Empire of Russia. Forasmuch as we be credibly informed by the report of our trustie and welbeloued subiect, that your Maiestie did not onely call him and certaine of his company to your emperiall presence and speech, entertayned and banqueted them with all humanitie and gentlenes but also being thereunto requested partly by the letters of our said brother, and partly by request of the sayd Richard Chancelour haue by your letters patents vnder your seale among other things granted: That all such marchants as shall come forth of anie of our realms of England or Ireland with al maner of wares, if they wil trauel or occupie within your dominions, the same marchants with their marchandises in al your lordship may freely, and at their libertie trauaile out and in without hindrance or any maner of losse: And of your farther ample goodnesse haue promised that our ambassadours, if wee send any, shall with free good will passe to and from you without any hindrance or losse, with such message as shall come vnto you, and to returne the same to our kingdomes well answered, as by the same your letters, written in your lordly Palace and Castle of Mosco in the yeere 7063 [Footnote: Should be 7060.] the moneth of Februarie, more at large appeareth. Like as wee cannot but much commend your princely fauour and goodnesse, and in like manner thank you for the abundant grace, extended to the sayd Richard Chancelour, and others our subiects marchants: Euen so these are to pray and request you to continue the same beneuolence toward them, and other our marchants and subiects, which doe or heereafter shall resorte to your countrey: And for the more assurance and incouragement to trade and exercise the feate of marchandise with your subiects and all other marchants within your dominions, that it may please you at this our contemplation to assigne and authorise such Commissaries as you shall thinke meete to trade and conferre with our welbeloued subiects and marchants, the sayd Richard Chancelour, George Killingworth, and Richard Graie, bearers of these our letters: who are by vs authorised for that purpose: and to confirme and graunt such other liberties and priuiledges vnto the Gouernour, Consuls, Assistants, and Communaltie of the fellowship of the saide Marchants, as the said bearers in their name propone and require by you to be granted for their safe conduct, good gouernment, and order to bee erected and continued among them in your saide dominions; And this with such your clemencie and expedition, as we, vpon the next arriuall of the saide Richard Chancelour may bee enformed of your gracious disposition and answere. Which your beneuolences so to bee extended, wee bee minded to requite towards any your subiects Marchants, that shal frequent this our realme at your contemplation therefore to be made. Thus right high, right Excellent, and right mightie, Almightie God the Father, the Sonne and the holy Ghost haue you in his blessed keeping. Giuen vnder our seale at our Palace of Westminster, the first of April, in the yeere from the blessed incarnation of our Sauiour Iesus Christ, 1555. and in the first and second yeeres of our reignes.

* * * * *

Articles conceiued and determined for the Commission of the Merchants of this company residant in Russia, and at the Wardhouse, for the second voyage, 1555. the first of May, as followeth.

First, the Gouernour, Consuls, Assistants and whole company assembled this day in open court, committeth and authorizeth Richard Gray and George Killingworth, iointly and seuerally to be Agents, Factors, and Atturneis generall and speciall, for the whole body of this company, to buy, sel, trucke, change and permute al, and every kind and kindes of wares, marchandises and goods to the said company appertaining, now laden and shipped in the good ship called the Edward Bonauenture, appointed for Russia, the same to vtter and sell to the best commoditie, profit and aduantage of the said corporation, be it for ready money, wares and merchandises, or truck, presently, or for time, as occasion and benefit of the company shal require: and all such wares as they or either of them shal buy, trucke, or prouide, or cause to be bought for the company to lade them homeward in good order and condition, as by prudent course of marchandises, shall, and ought to appertaine, which article extendeth also to Iohn Brooke for the Wardhouse, as in the 17. and 18. articles of this commission appeareth.

2. Item, it is also committed, as aboue, to the said Agents, to binde and charge the said company by debt for wares vpon credit, as good opportunitie and occasion shal serue, with power to charge and bind the said company, and their successors, for the paiments of such things as shalbe taken vp for credite, and the said Agents to be relieued ab opere satis dandi.

3. Item full authoritie and power is committed to the said first named factors, together with Richard Chancelor grand Pilot of this fleete, to repaire to the Emperors court, there to present the king and Queenes Maiesties letters, written in Greeke, Polish, and Italian, and to giue and exhibite the marchants presents at such time and place as shalbe thought most expedient, they, or one of them to demand, and humbly desire of the Emperour such further grants and priuiledges to be made to this companie, as may be beneficiall for the same, to continue in traffike with his subiects, according to such instructions as bee in this behalfe deuised and deliuered to the Agents whereunto relation is to be had, and some one of these

persons to attend vpon the court for the obtaining of the same, as to their discretions shalbe thought good.

4. Item, that all the saide Agents doe well consider, ponder and weigh such articles as bee deliuered to them to know the natures, dispositions, lawes, customes, maners and behauiours of the people of the countries where they shal traffike, as well of the Nobilitie as of the Lawyers, Marchants, Mariners and common people, and to note diligently the subtilties of their bargaining, buying and selling, making as fewe debtes as possiblie may bee, and to bee circumspect, that no lawe neither of religion nor positiue bee broken or transgressed by them or any minister vnder them, ne yet by any mariner or other person of our nation, and to foresee that all tolles, customes, and such other rites be so duely paid, that no forfeiture or confiscation may ensue to our goods either outward or inward, and that al things passe with quiet, without breach of the publike peace or common tranquilitie of any of the places where they shall arriue or traffique.

5. Item, that prouision bee made in Mosco or elsewhere, in one or mo good townes, where good trade shall be found for a house or houses for the Agents, and companie to inhabite and dwell at your accustomed diets, with warehouses, sellers, and other houses of offices requisite, and that none of the inferiour ministers of what place or vocation soeuer he be, doe lie out of the house of the Agents without licence to be giuen, and that euery inferiour officer shalbe obedient to the orders, rules and gouernments of the said Agents, and in case any disobedient person shall be found among any of them, then such person to be punished for his misbehauiour, at the discretion of the said Agents, or of one of them in the absence of the other.

6. Item, if any person of the said ministers shall be of such pride or obstinacie, that after one or two honest admonitions, hee will not bee reformed nor reconciled from his faultes, then the saide Agents to displace euery such person from the place or roume to him heere committed, and some other discreete person to occupie the same, as to the saide Agents by their discretions shal seeme meete.

7. Item, if any person shall be found so arrogant, that he will not be ordered nor reformed by the said Agents or by one of them in the absence of the other, then the sayde person to bee deliuered to the Iustice of the countrey, to receiue such punishment, as the lawes of the countrey doe require.

8. Item, that the Agents and factours shall daily one houre in the morning conferre and consult together what shall bee most conuenient and beneficial for the companie, and such orders as they shall determine, to bee written by the Secretarie of the companie in a booke to bee prouided for that purpose, and no inferiour person to infringe and breake any such order

or deuise, but to obserue the same exactly, vpon such reasonable paine as the Agents shall put him to by discretion.

9. Item, that the said Agents shall in the ende of euerie weeke, or oftener as occasion shall require, peruse, see, and trie, not onely the Casshers, bookes, reckonings and accounts, firming the same with their handes, but also shall receiue and take weekly the account of euery other officer, as well of the Vendes, as of the empteous, and also of the state of the houshold expenses, making thereof a perfect declaration as shall appertaine, the same accounts also to bee firmed by the saide Agents hands.

10. Item, that no inferior minister shall take vpon him to make any bargains or sale of any wares, marchandises or goods, but by the Commission and Warrantise of the sayde Agents vnder their handes, and hee not to transgresse his Commission by any way, pretense or colour.

11. Item, that euery inferiour minister, that is to vnderstand, all Clerks and yong merchants, being at the order of the saide Agents, shall ride, goe, saile and trauaile to all such place, and places, as they or hee shall be appointed vnto by the saide Agents, and effectually to follow and do all that which to him or them shall be committed, well and truely to the most benefite of the company, according to the charge to him or them committed, euen as by their othes, dueties and bondes of their masters they be bounden and charged to doe.

12. Item, that at euery moneths end, all accounts and reckonings shalbe brought into perfect order, into the Lidger or memoriall, and the decrees, orders, and rules of the Agents together with the priuileges, and copies of letters, may and shall be well and truely written by the secretarie, in such forme as shalbe appointed for it, and that copies of all their doings may be sent home with the said ship at her returne.

13. Item, that all the Agents doe diligently learne and obserue all kinde of wares, as wel naturals as forrein, that be beneficiall for this Realme, to be sold for the benefit of the company, and what kinde of our commodities and other things of these West partes bee most vendible in those Realmes with profite, giuing a perfect aduise of all such things requisite.

14. Item, if the Emperour will enter into bargain with you for the whole masse of your stock, and will haue the trade of it to vtter to his owne subiects, then debating the matter prudently among your selues, set such high prises of your commodities, as you may assure your selues to be gainers in your owne wares, and yet to buy theirs at such base prises, as you may here also make a commoditie and gaine at home, hauing in your mindes the notable charges that the companie haue diffrayed in aduancing this voyage: and the great charges that they sustaine dayly in wages, victuals

and other things: all which must bee requited by the wise handling of this voyage, which being the first president shalbe a perpetual president for euer: and therefore all circumspection is to be vsed, and foreseene in this first enterprise, which God blesse and prosper vnder you, to his glorie, and the publike wealth of this Realme, whereof the Queenes Maiestie, and the Lords of the Councell haue conceiued great hope, whose expectations are not to be frustrated.

15. Item, it is to be had in minde, that you vse all wayes and meanes possible to learne howe men may passe from Russia, either by land or by sea to Cathaia, and what may be heard of our other ships, and to what knowledge you may come, by conferring with the learned or well trauailed persons, either naturall or forrein, such as haue trauailed from the North to the South.

16. Item, it is committed to the said Agents, that if they shall be certified credibly, that any of our said first ships be arriued in any place whereunto passage is to be had by water or by land, that then certaine of the company at the discretion of the Agents shall bee appointed to be sent to them, to learne their estate and condition, to visite, refresh, relieue, and furnish them with all necessaries and requisites, at the common charges of the companie, and to imbrace, accept, and intreat them as our deare and wel-beloued brethren of this our societie, to their reioycing and comfort, aduertising Syr Hugh Willoughbie and others of our carefulnes of them and their long absence, with our desire to heare of them, with all other things done in their absence for their commoditie, no lesse then if they had bene present.

17. Item, it is decreed, that when the ships shal arriue at this going foorth at the Wardhouse, that their Agents, with master Chancelor grand pilot, Iohn Brooke, merchant, deputed for the Wardhouse, with Iohn Buckland master of the Edward, Iohn Howlet master, and Iohn Robins pilot of the Philip and Marie, shall conferre and consult together, what is most profitable to be done therfore for the benefit of the company, and to consider whether they may bargaine with the captaine of the castle, and the inhabitants in that place, or alongst the coast for a large quantitie of fish, drie or wet, killed by the naturals, or to be taken by our men at a price reasonable for trucke of cloth, meale, salt, or beere, and what traine oyle, or other commodity is to be had there at this time, or any other season of the yeere, and whether there will be had or found sufficient lading for both the sayd shippes, to be bought there, and how they may conferre with the naturals for a continuance in hanting the place, if profit wil so arise to the company, and to consider whether the Edward in her returne may receiue at the Wardhouse any kind of lading homeward, and what it may amount vnto, and whether it shall be expedient for the Philip to abide at the Wardhouse the returne of the Edward out of Russia, or getting that she may returne

with the first good wind to England, without abiding for the Edward, and so to conclude and accord certainely among themselues vpon their arriuall, that the certaintie may (vpon good deliberation) be so ordered and determined betweene both ships, that the one may be assured of the other, and their determinations to be put in writing duplicate to remaine with ech ship, according to such order as shall be taken betweene them.

18. Item, that Iohn Brooke our marchant for the Wardhouse take good aduise of the rest of our Agents, how to vse himselfe in al affaires, whiles the ship shalbe at the Wardhouse, he to see good order to be kept, make bargains aduisedly, not crediting the people vntill their natures, dispositions and fidelities shal be well tried, make no debts, but to take ware for ware in hand, and rather be trusted then to trust. Note diligently what be the best wares for those parts, and howe the fishe falleth on the coast, and by what meane it is to bee bought at the most aduantage, what kindes and diuersities of sortes in fishes be, and whether it will keepe better in bulke piled, or in caske.

19. Item, he to haue a diligent eye and circumspection to the beere, salt, and other liquid wares, and not to suffer any waste to be made by the companie, and he in all contracts to require aduise, counsel, and consent of the master and pilot, the marchant to be our houswife, as our special trust is in him, he to tender that no lawes nor customes of the countrey be broken by any of the company, and to render to the prince, and other officers, all that which to them doth appertaine, the company to be quiet, voide of all quarrelling, fighting, or vexation, absteine from all excesse of drinking as much as may bee, and in all to vse and behaue themselues as to quiet marchants doeth, and ought to apperteine.

20. Item, it is decreed by the companie, that the Edward shall returne home this yeere with as much wares as may be conueniently, and profitably prouided, bought, and laden in Russia, and the rest to be taken in at the Wardhouse, as by the Agents shall be accorded. But by all meanes it is to be foreseene and noted, that the Edward returne home, and not to winter in any forrein place, but to come home and bring with her all the whole aduertisements of the marchants, with such further aduise for the next yeeres prouision, as they shall giue.

21. Item, it is further decreed and ordeined, inuiolably to be obserued, that when the good ships, or either of them (by Gods grace) shall returne home to the coastes of England, that neither of them shall stay or touch in any Hauen or Port of England, other wise then wind and weather shall serue, but shall directly saile and come to the Port of the citie of London, the place of their right discharge, and that no bulke be broken, hatches opened, chest, fardell, trusse, barrel, fat, or whatsoeuer thing it shall be, be brought

out of the shippe, vntill the companie shall giue order for the same, and appoint such persons of the companie as shall be thought meet for that purpose, to take viewe, and consider the shippe and her lading and shall giue order for the breaking vp of the saide bulke, or giue licence by discretion, for things to be brought to land. And that euery officer shall shewe the inuoise of his charge to him first committed, and to examine the wastes and losses, and to deliuer the remainder to the vse and benefit of the company, according to such order as shall be appointed in that behalfe.

22. Item, the company exhorteth, willeth, and requireth, not onely all the said Agents, pilots, masters, marchants, clerkes, boatswaines, stewards, skafemasters, and all other officers and ministers of this present voyage, being put in charge and trust daily to peruse, reade, and studie such instructions as be made, giuen, and deliuered to them for perfect knowledge of the people of Russia, Moscouia, Wardhouse and other places, their dispositions, maners, customes, vses, tolles, cariages, coines, weights, numbers, measures, wares, merchandises, commodities, and incommodities, the one to be accepted and imbraced, the other to be reiected and vtterly abandoned, to the intent that euery man taking charge, may be so well taught, perfited, and readily instructed in all the premisses, that by ignorance, no losse or preiudice may grow or chance to the company: assuring themselues, that for asmuch as the company hath trauelled and laboured so in these their instructions to them giuen, that euery man may bee perfect, and fully learned to eschew all losses, hurts and damages that may insue by pretence or colour of none knowledge, the company entendeth not to allow, or accept ignorance for any lawfull or iust cause of excuse, in that which shall be misordered by negligence, the burden whereof shall light vpon the negligent offending person, especially vpon such as of their owne heads, or temeritie, will take vpon him or them to doe or to attempt any thing, whereby preiudice may arise, without the commission of the Agents as aboue is mentioned, whereunto relation must be had.

23. Forasmuch as it is not possible to write and indite such prescribed orders, rules and commissions to the Agents and factours, but that occasion, time and place, and the pleasures of the princes, together with the operation or successe of fortune shall change or shift the same, although not in the whole, yet in part, therefore the said company doe commit to you their deare and intire beloued Agents and factors to doe in this behalfe for the commodity and wealth of this company, as by your directions, vpon good aduised deliberations shalbe thought good and beneficiall. Prouided alwayes, that the honour, good name, fame, credite, and estimation of the same companie be conserued and preserued: which to confirme we beseech

the liuing Lord to his glory, the publike benefite of this realme, our common profits, and your praises.

Finally for the seruice, and due accomplishment of all the premisses, euery Agent and minister of and for this voyage, hath not onely giuen a corporall othe vpon the Euangelists, to obserue, and cause to be obserued, this commission, and euery part, clause and sentence of the same, as much as in him lyeth, as well for his owne part as for any other person, but also haue bounde themselues and their friendes to the companie in seuerall summes of money, expressed in the actes and records of this societie, for the trueth and fidelities of them, for the better, and also manifester testification of the trueth, and of their othes, promises, and bands aforesaid, they haue to this commission subscribed particularly their seuerall hands, and the company also in confirmation of the same, haue set their seale. Yeuen the day, moneth, and yeeres first aboue mentioned.

The othe ministred to the seruants of the fellowship.

Ye sweare by the holy contents of that booke, that ye shal wel, faithfully and truely, and vprightly, and with all your indeuour, serue this right worshipfull company in that order, which by this fellowships Agent or Agents in the dominions of the Emperours of Russia, &c. shall bee vnto you committed, by commission, commandement, or other his direction. And that you shall bee obedient and faithfull to the same our Agent or Agents, and that well, and truely and vprightly according to the commission, charge, commandement, or other direction of the said Agent or Agents to you from time to time giuen and to be giuen, you shall prosecute and doe all that which in you lieth, for the good renowme, commoditie, benefite and profite of the said fellowship: and you shall not directly or indirectly, openly or couertly doe, exercise or vse any trade or feate of marchandises for your owne priuate account, commodity, gaine or profite, or for the account of or for any other person or persons, without consent or licence of this said fellowship, first obtained in writing. And if you shall know or vnderstand any other person or persons to vse, exercise or doe any trade, traffike or feat of marchandise, to or for his or their own account or accounts, at any time or times hereafter, that then ye shall truely and plainly disclose, open, vtter and reueale, and shew the same vnto this said fellowship, without fraude, colour, couin or delay: So helpe you God, &c.

* * * * *

The letter of M. George Killingworth the companies first Agent in Moscouie, touching their interteinement in their second voyage. Anno 1555. the 27. of Nouember in Mosco.

Right worshipful, my duetie, considered, &c. It may please your worship to vnderstand, that at the making hereof we all be in good health, thanks be to God, saue onely William our cooke as we came from Colmogro fell into the river out of the boate, and was drowned. And the 11. day of September wee came to Vologda, and there we laide all our wares vp, and sold very little: but one marchant would haue giuen vs 12. robles for a broad cloth, and he said he would haue had them all, and 4. altines for a pound of sugar, but we did refuse it because he was the first, and the marchants were not come thither, nor would not come before Winter, trusting to haue more: But I feare it will not be much better. Yet notwithstanding we did for the best. And the house that our wares lie in costs from that day vntil Easter ten robles. And the 28. day of September we did determine with our selues that it was good for M. Gray, Arthur Edwards, Thomas Hautory, Christopher Hudson, Iohn Segewicke, Richard Ionson, and Richard Iudde, to tarie at Vologda, and M. Chancelor, Henry Lane, Edward Prise, Robert Best and I should goe to Mosco. And we did lade the Emperours suger, with part of all sorts of wares to haue had to the Mosco with vs, but the way was so deepe, that we were faine to turne back, and leaue is stil at Vologda till the frost. And we went forth with poste horse, and the charge of euery horse being stil ten in number, comes to 10 s. 7 d. halfe penie, besides the guides. And we came to the Mosco the 4. day of October, and were lodged that night in a simple house: but the next day we were sent for to the Emperour his secretarie, and he bade vs welcome with a cheerefull countenance and cheerefull wordes, and wee shewed him that we had a letter from our Queenes grace to the Emperour his grace, and then he desired to see them all, and that they might remain with him, to haue them perfect, that the true meaning might be declared to the Emperour, and so we did: and then we were appointed to a better house: and the seuenth day the secretary sent for vs againe, and then he shewed vs that we should haue a better house: for it was the Emperour his will, that we should haue all things that we did lacke, and did send vs meade of two sorts, and two hens, our house free, and euery two dayes to receiue eight hens, seven altines, and two pence in money, and meade a certaine, and a poore fellow to make cleane our house, and to doe that wherunto we would set him. And wee had giuen many rewards before, which you shal perceiue by other, and so we gaue the messengers a reward with thanks: and the ninth day we were sent to make vs readie to speak, with the Emperour on the morow. And the letters were sent vs, that wee might deliuer them our selues, and we came before him the tenth day: and before we came to his presence we went thorow a great chamber, where stood many small tunnes, pailes, bowles and pots of siluer, I meane, like washing bowles, all parsel gilt: and within that another chamber, wherein sate (I thinke) neere a hundred in cloth of gold, and then into the chamber where his grace sate, and there I thinke were more then in the other chamber also in cloth of gold, and we did our duety, and shewed his grace our Queenes graces letters, with a note of your present which was left in Vologda: and then his grace did aske how our Queenes grace did, calling her cousin, saying that hee was glad that wee were come in health into his Realme, and we went one by one vnto him, and tooke him by the hand, and then his grace did bid vs goe in health, and come to dinner againe, and we dined in his presence, and were set with our faces towards his grace, and none in the chamber sate with their backes towards him, being I thinke neere a hundred at dinner then, and all serued with golde, as platters, chargers, pottes, cuppes, and all not slender but very massy, and yet a great number of platters of golde, standing still on the cupboord, not moued: and diuers times in the dinner time his grace sent vs meat and drinke from his owne table, and when we had dined we went vp to his grace, and receiued a cuppe with drinke at his owne hand, and the same night his grace sent certaine gentlemen to us with diuers sortes of wine and mede, to whome wee gaue a rewarde. And afterwarde we were by diuers Italians counselled to take heed whom we did trust to make the copie of the priuiledges that we would desire to haue, for feare it should not be written in the Russie tongue, as we did meane. So first a Russian did write for us a breuiat to the Emperor, the tenour wherof was, that we did desire a stronger priuilege: and when the Secretary saw it, he did deliuer it to his grace, and when we came againe, his grace willed vs to write our minds, and hee would see it, and so we did. And his grace is so troubled with preparations to warres, that as yet wee haue no answere: but we haue byn required of his Secretary, and of the vnder Chancelor, to know what wares we had brought into the Realme, and what wares we doe intend to haue, that are, or may bee had in this Realme: and we shewed them, and they shewed the Emperor therof. And then they said his graces pleasure was, that his best marchants of the Mosco should be spoken to, to meet and talk with vs. And so a day was appointed, and wee mette in the Secretarie his office, and there was the vnder Chancelor, who was not past two yeeres since the Emperors marchant, and not his Chancelour: and then the conclusion of our talke was, that the Chancelour willed vs to bethinke vs, where we would desire to haue a house or houses, that wee might come to them as to our owne house, and for marchandize to be made preparation for vs, and they would know our prises of our wares and frise: and we answered, that for our prices they must see the wares before we coulde make any price thereof, for the like in goodnesse hath not bene brought into the Realme, and we did looke for an example of all sorts of our wares to come from Vologda, with the first sledway, and then they should see them, and then we would shew them the prices of them: and likewise we could not tell them what we would giue them iustly, till we did knowe as well their iust weights as their measures: for in all places where we did come, al weights and measures did vary. Then the Secretary (who had made promise vnto vs before) saide, that we should haue all the iust measures vnder seale, and he that was found faulty in the contrary, to buy or sel with any other measure then that, the law was, that he should be punished: he said moreouer, that if it so happen that any of our marchants do promise by couenant at any time to deliuer you any certain sum of wares in such a place, and of such like goodnesse, at such a day, for such a certaine price, and then because of variance, we should cause it to be written, according as the bargain is, before a iustice or the next ruler to the place: if he did not keepe couenant and promise in all points, according to his couenant, that then looke what losse or hinderance we could iustly proue that we haue therby, he should make it good if he be worth so much: and in like case we must do to them: and to that we did agree, saue onely if it were to come ouer the sea, then if any such fortune should bee (as God forbid) that the ship should mischance or be robbed, and the proofe to be made that such kind of wares were laden, the English marchants to beare no losse to the other marchant. Then the Chancelor said, me thinks you shall do best to haue your house at Colmogro, which is but 100. miles from the right discharge of the ships, and yet I trust the ships shall come neerer hereafter, because the ships may not tary long for their lading, which is 1000. miles from Vologda by water, and all our marchants shall bring all our marchandize to Colmogro to you, and so shall our marchants neither go empty nor come empty: for if they lacke lading homeward, there is salt, which is good ware here, that they may come loden againe. So we were very glad to heare that, and did agree to his saying: for we shal neuerthelesse, if we lust, haue a house at Vologda, and at the Mosco, yea, and at Nouogrode, or where we wil in Rusland: but the three and twentieth of this present we were with the Secretary, and then among other talke, we moued, that if we should tary at Colmogro with our wares, and should not come to Vologda, or further to seeke our market, but tary still at Colmogro, and then the merchants of the Mosco and others should not come and bring their wares, and so the ships should come, and not haue their lading ready, that then it were a great losse and hinderance for vs: then saide hee againe to vs, that the marchants had beene againe together with him, and had put the like doubt, that if they should come and bring their wares to Colmogro, and that they should not find wares there sufficient to serue them, that then they should be at great losse and hinderance, they leauing their other trades to fal to that: and to that we did answere, that after the time that we do appoint with them to bring their wares to Colmogro, God willing, they should neuer come thither, but at the beginning of the yere, they should find that our marchants would haue at the least for a thousand robles, although the ships were not come: so that he saide, that then wee must talke further with the marchants: so that as yet I know not, but that we shall haue neede of one house at Colmogro, and another at Vologda, and that if they bring not their wares to Colmogro, then wee shalbe sure to buy some at Vologda, and to be out of bondage.

And thus may we continue three or foure yeeres, and in this space we shall know the countrey and the marchants, and which way to saue our selues best, and where to plant our houses, and where to seeke for wares: for the Mosco is not best for any kind of wares for vs to buy, saue onely waxe, which we cannot haue vnder seuen pence the Russe pound, and it lackes two ounces of our pound, neither will it be much better cheape, for I haue bidden 6. pence for a pound. And I haue bought more, fiue hundred weight of yarne, which stands mee in eight pence farthing the Russe pound one with another. And if we had receiued any store of money, and were dispatched heere of that we tarry for, as I doubt not but we shalbe shortly (you know what I meane) then as soone as we haue made sale, I doe intend to goe to Nouogrode and to Plesco, whence all the great number of the best tow flaxe, cometh, and such wares as are there I trust to buy part. And feare you not but we will do that may be done, if God send vs health, desiring you to prepare fully for one ship to be ready in the beginning of April to depart off the coast of England.

Concerning all those things which we haue done in the wares, you shal receiue a perfect note by the next bearer (God willing) for he that carieth these from vs is a marchant of Terwill and he was caused to cary these by the commandement of the Emperour his secretarie, whose name is Iuan Mecallawich Weskawate, whom we take to be our very friend. And if it please you to send any letters to Dantiske to Robert Elson, or to William Watson's seruant Dunstan Walton to be conueyed to vs, it may please you to inclose ours in a letter sent from you to him, written in Polish, Dutch, Latine, or Italian: so inclosed, comming to the Mosco to his hands, he wil conuey our letters to vs wheresoeuer we be. And I haue written to Dantiske already to them for the conueyance of letters from thence.

And to certifie you of the weather here, men say that these hundred yeeres was neuer so warme weather in this countrey at this time of the yeere. But as yesternight wee receiued a letter from Christopher Hudson [Footnote: Mr. John M. Read, in his "Historical Enquiry respecting Henry Hudson," printed by the Clarendon Historical Society, is of opinion that both Christopher Hudson and the Henry Hudson named in Queeu Mary's Charter as one of the founders of the Muscovy Company, were related to the discoverer of Delaware Bay. (Clarendon Hist. Soc. Reprints, Series I. p. 149.)] from a citie called Yeraslaue, who is comming hither with certaine of our wares, but the winter did decieue him, so that he was faine to tarie by the way: and he wrote that the Emperours present was deliuered to a gentleman at Vologda, and the sled did ouerthrow, and the butte of Hollocke was lost, which made vs all very sory.

I pray you be not offended with these my rude letters for lacke of time: but assoone as sales be made, I will finde the meanes to conuey you a letter with speed: for the way is made so doubtful, that the right messenger is so much in doubt, that he would not haue any letters of any effect sent by any man, if he might, for he knowes not of these: and to say the truth, the way is not for him to trauell in. But I will make another shift beside, which I trust shall serue the turne till he come, if sales be made before he be readie, which is and shall be as pleaseth God: who euer preserue your worship, and send us good sales. Written in haste.

By yours to commaund

GEORGE KILLINGWORTH
Draper.

* * * * *

(George Killingworth was furnished with a copy of the following notice of the coines, weights and measures vsed in Russia, written by Iohn Hasse, in the yeere, 1554:—)

Forasrauch as it is most necessary for al marchants which seeks to haue traffique in any strange regions, first to acquaint themselues with the coines of those lands with which they do intend to ioyne in traffique, and how they are called from the valuation of the highest piece to the lowest, and in what sort they make their paiments, as also what their common weights and measures be: for these causes I haue thought good to write something thereof according to mine owne knowledge and experience, to the end that, the marchants of that new aduenture, may the better vnderstand how the wealth of that new frequented trade will arise.

First, it is to be noted that the Emperour of Russia hath no other coines then siluer in all his land, which goeth for paiment amongst merchants, yet notwithstanding there is a coine of copper, which serueth for the reliefe of the poore in Mosco, and no where els, and that is but only for quasse, water and fruit, as nuts, apples, and such other like. The name of which money is called Pole or Poles of which Poles there goe to the least of the siluer coines, 18. But I will not stand vpon this, because it is no currant money among marchants.

Of siluer coines there be three sortes of pieces: the least is a Poledenga, the second a Denga, the third, Nowgrote, which is as much to say in English as halfepenie, penie and twopence, and for other valued money then this, there is none: there are oftentimes there coines of gold, but they come out of forrein countreys, whereof there is no ordinarie valuation, but they passe according to the agreement of marchants.

Their order in summing of money is this: as we say in England, halfpenie, penie, shilling, and pound, so say they Poledenga, Denga, Altine and Rubble: there goeth two Poledengas to a Denga, six Dengaes to an Altine, and 23 Altines, and two Dengaes to a Rubble.

Concerning the weights of Russia they are these: There are two sortes of pounds in vse amongst them, the one great, the other small: the great pound is iust two small pounds: they call the great weight by the name of Beasemar, and the smal they call the Skalla weight: with this smal weight they weigh their siluer coines, of the which the Emperor hath commanded to put to euery small pound three Rubbles of siluer, and with the same weight they weigh all Grocerie wares, and almost al other wares which come into the land, except those which they weigh by the Pode, as hops, salt, iron, lead, tinne and batrie with diuers others, notwithstanding they vse to weigh batrie more often by the small weight then by the great.

Whensoever you find the prices of your wares rated by the Pode, consider that to the great weight, and the pound to be the small. Also they divide the small pound into 48 parts, and they call the eight and fortieth part a Slotnike, by the which Slotnike the retailers sell their wares out of their shops, as Goldsmiths, Grocers, Silkesellers, and such other like as we doe vse to retaile by the ounce: and as for their great weight which they cal the Beasemar, they sel by pode or shippond. The pode doth containe of the great weight, 40 pounds, and of the small 80; there goe 10. podes to a shippond.

Yet you must consider that their great weight is not full with ours: for I take not their great pound to be full 13 ounces, but aboue 12 I thinke it be. But for your iust proofe, weigh 6 Rubbles of Russia money with our pound weight, and then shal you see what it lacketh: for 6 Rubbles of Russia is by the Emperors standerd, the great pound: so that I thinke it the next way to know the iust weight, as well of the great pound as of the small.

There is another weight needfull to be knowen, which is the weight of Wardhouse, for so much as they weigh all their drie fish by weight, which weight is the Baesemar, as they of Russia doe vse, notwithstanding there is another sorte in it: the names of those weights are these: the marke pound, the great pound, the weie, and the shippond. The marke pound is to be vnderstood as our pound, and their great pound is 24 of their marke pound: the weie is 3 great pound, and 8 weie is a shippound.

Now concerning their measures. As they haue two sortes of weights, so they haue also two sortes of measures: wherewith they measure cloth both linnen and wollen: they cal the one an Areshine, and the other a Locut: the Areshine I take to bee as much as the Flanders ell, and their Locut halfe an English yard: with their Areshine they may mete all such sorts of clothes as come into the land, and with the Locut all such cloth both linnen and wollen, as they make themselues. And whereas we vse to giue yard and inch, or yard and handfull, they do giue nothing but bare measure.

They haue also measure wherewith they doe mete their corne, which they cal a Setforth, and the halfe of that an Osmine: this Setforth I take to bee three bushels of London measure. And as for their drinke measure, they call it a Spanne, which is much like a bucket, and of that I neuer saw any true rate, but that some was greater then other some. And as for the measures of Wardhouse wherewith they mete their cloth, there is no difference between that and the measure of Danske, which is halfe an English ell.

Concerning the tolles and customs of Russia, it was reported to me in Moscouia, that the Turkes and Armenians pay the tenth penie custome of all the wares they bring into the Emperors land, and aboue that they pay for all such goods as they weigh at the Emperours beame, two pence of the Rubble, which the buyer or seller must make report to the Master of the beame: they also pay a certaine horse toll, which is in diuers places of his Realme four pence of a horse.

The Dutch nation are free of this: notwithstanding for certaine offences, they had lost their priuiledges which they haue recouered this Summer to their great charge. It was reported to me by a Iustice of that countrey, that they paied for it thirtie thousand Rubbles, and also that Rye, Dorpte and Reuel haue yeelded themselues vnder the gouernment of the Emperor of Russia: whether this was a bragge of the Russes or not, I know not, but thus he sayd, and in deed whiles we were there, there came a great Ambassadour out of Liefland, for the assurance of their priuiledges.

To speake somewhat of the commodities of this countrey, it is to be vnderstood, that there is a certaine place foure score miles from the Sea called Colmogro: to which place there resorte all the sortes of Wares that are in the North parts, as Oyles, Salt, Stockefish, Salmon, Fethers and Furres: their Salt they make of saltwater by the sea side: their Oyles they make of Seales, whereof they haue great store which is brought out of the Bay where our shippes came in: they make it in the Spring of the yeere, and bring it to Colmogro to sell, and the marchants there carie it to Nouogrode, and so sell it to the Dutch nation. Their Stockefish and Salmon commeth from a place called Mallums, not farre from Warehouse: their Salmon and their Salt they carrie to Mosco, and their drie fish they carrie to Nouogrode, and sell it there to the Lieflanders.

The Furres and Fethers which come to Colmogro, as Sables, Beauers, Minkes, Armine, Lettis, Graies, Wooluerings, and white Foxes, with Deere skinnes, they are brought thither, by the men of Penninge, Lampas, and Powstezer, which fetch them from the Sarnoedes that are counted sauage people: and the merchants that bring these Furres doe vse to trucke with the marchants of Colmogro for Cloth, Tinne, Batrie, and such other like, and the merchants of Colmogro carie them to Nouogrode, Vologda, or Mosco, and sell them there. The Fethers which come fom Penning they doe little esteeme.

If our marchants do desire to know the meetest place of Russia for the standing house, in mine opinion I take it to be Vologda, which is a great towne standing in the heart of Russia, with many great and good towns about it. There is great plenty of corne, victuals, and of all such wares as are raised in Rusland, but specially, flaxe, hempe, tallow and bacon: there is also great store of waxe, but it commeth from the Mosko.

The towne of Vologda is meetest for our marchants, because it lieth amongst all the best towns of Russia, and there is no towne in Russia but trades with it: also the water is a great commoditie to it. If they plant themselues in Mosco or Nouogrode their charge will be great and wonderfull, but not so in Vologda: for all things will there be had better cheape by the one half. And for their vent, I know no place so meet. It is likely that some will think the Mosko to be the meetest by the reason of the court, but by that reason I take it to be woorse: for the charge there would be so great by crauers and expenses, that the moitie of the profite would bee wholly consumed, which in the other place will be saued. And yet notwithstanding our marchants may bee there in the Winter to serue the Emperour and his court. The Emperour is a great marchant himselfe of waxe and sables, which with good foresight may bee procured to their hands: as for other commodities there are little or none in Moscouia, besides those aboue rehearsed: if there bee other, it is brought thither by the Turkes, who will be daintie to buy our clothes considering the charges of cariage ouer land.

Our marchants may doe well to prouide for the Russes such wares as the Dutch nation doeth serue them of, as Flanders and Holland clothes, which I beleeue, they shal serue better and with lesse charge than they of Rye or Dorpt, or Reuel: for it is no smal aduenture to bring their clothes out of Flanders to either of these places, and their charge not litle to cary them ouer lande to Nouogrode, which is from Rye nine hundred Russian miles.

This Nouogrode is a place wel furnished with flaxe, Waxe, Hides, tallow and many other things: the best flaxe in Russia is brought thither, and there, sold by the hundred bundles, which is done also at Vologda, and they that bring the flaxe to Nouogrode, dwell as neere Vologda, as Nouogrode, and when they heare of the vtterance which they may haue with our nation, they will as willingly come to them as goe to other.

They haue in Russia two sortes of flaxe, the one is called great flaxe, and the other small: that which they call great flaxe is better by foure rubbles in 100. bundels than the small: It is much longer than the other, and cleaner without wood: and whereas of the small flaxe there goe 27. or 28. bundles to a shippound, there goeth not of the greater sort aboue 22. or 24. at the most. There are many other trifles in Russia, as sope, mats, &c. but I thinke there will bee no great account made of them.

* * * * *

A copie of the first Priuileges graunted by the Emperour of Russia to the English Marchants in the yeere 1555.

Iohn Vasiliuich, by the grace of God Emperor of Russia, great duke of Nouogrode, Moscouia, &c. To all people that shall see, reade, heare or vnderstand these presents, greeting. Forasmuch as God hath planted al realmes and dominions in the whole world with sundry commodities, so as the one hath neede of the amity and commodities of the other, and by means thereof traffike is vsed from one to another, and amity therby increased: and for that as amongst men nothing is more to be desired than amity, without the which no creature being of a naturall good disposition can liue in quietnes, so that it is as troublesome to be vtterly wanting, as it is perceiued to be grieuous to the body to lacke aire, fire, or any other necessaries most requisite for the conseruation and maintenance thereof in health: considering also how needfull marchandize is, which furnisheth men of all that which is conuenient for their liuing and nouriture, for their clothing, trimming, the satisfying of their delights, and all other things conuenient and profitable for them, and that marchandize bringeth the same commodities from diuers quarters in so great abundance, as by meanes thereof, nothing is lacking in any part, and that all things be in euery place (where entercourse of marchandizes is receiued and imbraced) generally in such sort, as amity thereby is entred into, and planted to continue, and the inioyers thereof be as men liuing in a golden world: Vpon these respects and other weighty and good considerations, vs hereunto mouing, and chiefly vpon the contemplation of the gracious letters, directed from the right high, right excellent, and right mighty Queene Mary, by the grace of God Queene of England, France, &c. in the fauour of her subiects, merchants, the gouernour, consuls, assistants, and communaltie of merchants aduenturers for discouery of lands, &c.

Know ye therefore, that we of our grace speciall, meere motion, and certaine knowledge, have giuen and graunted, and by these presents for vs, our heires and successours, do giue and graunt as much as in vs is and lieth, vnto Sebastian Cabota Gouernour, Sir George Barnes knight, &c. Consuls: Sir Iohn Gresham, &c. Assistants, and to the communaltie of the aforenamed fellowship, and to their successours for euer, and to the successours of euerie of them, these articles, graunts, immunities, franchises, liberties and priuileges, and euery of them hereafter following, expressed and declared. Videlicet:

1. First, we for vs, our heires and successors, do by these presents giue and graunt free licence, facultie, authority and power vnto the said Gouernour, Consuls, Assistants, and communalty of the said fellowship, and to their successors for euer, that all and singular the marchants of the same company, their Agents, factours, doers of their businesse, atturneys, seruants, and ministers, and euery of them may at all times hereafter for euer more surely, freely and safely, with their shippes, merchandizes, goods and things whatsoeuer saile, come and enter into all and singular our lands, countreis, dominions, cities, townes, villages, castles, portes, iurisdictions, and destraicts by sea, land or fresh waters, and there tary, abide and soiourne, and buy, sell, barter and change all kind of merchandizes with al maner of marchants and people, of whatsoeuer nation, rite, condition, state or degrees they be, and with the same or other ships, wares, marchandizes, goods and things whatsoeuer they be, vnto other empires, kingdomes, dukedomes, parts, and to any other place or places at their pleasure and liberty by sea, land or fresh waters may depart, and exercise all kinde of merchandizes in our empire and dominions, and euery part thereof freely and quietly without any restraint, impeachment, price, exaction, prest, straight custome, toll, imposition, or subsidie to be demanded, taxed or paid, or at any time hereafter to be demanded, taxed, set, leuied or inferred vpon them or any of them, or vpon their goods, ships, wares, marchandizes, and things, of, for or vpon any part or parcell thereof, or vpon the goods, ships, wares, merchandizes, and things of any of them, so that they shall not need any other safe conduct or licence generall, ne speciall of vs, our heires or successours, neither shall be bound to aske any safe conduct or licence in any of the aforesaid places subiect vnto vs.

2. Item, we giue and graunt, to the said marchants this power and liberty, that they, ne any of them, ne their goods, wares, marchandizes or things, ne any part thereof, shal be by any meanes within our dominions, landes, countreyes, castles, townes, villages, or other place or places of our iurisdiction, at any time heereafter attached, staied, arrested ne disturbed for anie debt, duetie or other thing, for the which they be not principall debters or sureties, ne also, for any offence or trespasse committed, or that shall be committed, but onely for such as they or any of them shall actually commit,

and the same offences (if any such happen,) shall bee by vs onely heard, and determined.

3. Item, we giue and graunt, that the said Marchants shal and may haue free libertie, power and authoritie to name, choose and assigne brokers, shippers, packers, weighers, measurers, wagoners, and all other meet and necessary laborers for to serue them in their feat of marchandises, and minister and giue vnto them and euery of them a corporall othe, to serue them well and truely in their offices, and finding them or any of them doing contrary to his or their othe, may punish and dismisse them, and from time to time choose, sweare, and admit other in their place or places, without contradiction, let, vexation or disturbance, either of vs, our heires or successors, or of any other our Iustices, officers, ministers or subiects whatsoeuer.

4. Item, we giue and graunt vnto the saide Marchants and their successours, that such person as is, or shalbe commended vnto vs, our heires or successours by the Gouernour, Consuls and assistants of the said fellowship residant within the citie of London within the realme of England, to be their chiefe Factor within this our empire and dominions, may and shal haue ful power and authoritie to gouerne and rule all Englishmen that haue had, or shall haue accesse, or repaire in or to this said Empire and iurisdictions, or any part thereof, and shal and may minister vnto them, and euery of them good iustice in all their causes, plaints, quarrels, and disorders between them moued, and to be moued, and assemble, deliberate, consult, conclude, define, determine, and make such actes, and ordinances, as he so commended with his Assistants shall thinke good and meete for the good order, gouernment and rule of the said Marchants, and all other Englishmen repairing to this our saide empire or dominions, or any part thereof, and to set and leuie vpon all, and euery Englishman, offender or offenders, of such their acts and ordinances made, and to be made, penalties and mulcts by fine and imprisonment.

5. Item, if it happen that any of the saide Marchants, or other Englishmen, as one or more doe rebell against such chiefe Factor or Factors, or his or their deputies, and will not dispose him or themselues to obey them and euery of them as shall appertaine if the saide Rebels or disobedients doe come, and bee founde in our our saide Empire and iurisdictions, or any part and place thereof, then wee promise and graunt, that all and euery our officers, ministers, and subiects shall effectually ayde and assist the saide chiefe Factour or Factours, and their deputies, and for their power shall really woorke, to bring such rebell or disobedient rebels, or disobedients to due obedience: and to that intent shall tende vnto the same Factour or Factours, and their deputies vpon request therefore, to be made, prisons, and instruments for punishments from time to time.

6. Item, we promise vnto the saide Marchants, and their sucessours, vpon their request to exhibite and doe vnto them good, exact and fauourable iustice, with expedition in all their causes, and that when they or any of them shall haue accesse, or come to or before any of our Iustices, for any their plaints mooued, and to bee mooued betweene any our subiects or other stranger, and them, or any of them, that then they shalbe first and forthwith heard, as soon as the party which they shal find before our Iustices shalbe depeached, which party being heard forthwith, and assoone as may be, the said English marchants shall be ridde and dispatched: And if any action shall be mooued by or against any of the said Marchants being absent out of our saide empire and dominions, then such Marchants may substitute an Atturney in all and singular his causes to be followed as need shall require, and as shall seeme to him expedient.

7. Item, wee graunt and promise to the saide Marchants, and to their successours, that if the same Marchants or any of them shall bee wounded, or (which God forbid) slaine in any part or place of our Empire or dominions, then good information thereof giuen, Wee and our Iustices and other officers shall execute due correction and punishment without delay, according to the exigence of the case: so that it shall bee an example to all other not to commit the like. And if it shall chaunce the factors, seruants, or ministers of the saide Marchants or any of them to trespasse or offende, whereby they or any of them shall incurre the danger of death or punishment, the goods, wares, marchandizes, and things of their Masters shall not therefoore bee forfaited, confiscated, spoiled ne seised by any meanes by vs, our heires or successours, or by any our officers, ministers or subiects, but shall remaine to their vse, franke, free, and discharged from all punishment and losse.

8. Item, we graunt that if any of the English nation be arrested for any debt, he shal not be laid in prison, so farre as he can put in sufficient suretie and pawne: neither shall any sergeant, or officer leade them or any of them to prison, before he shall have knowen whether the chiefe Factor or factors, or their deputies shalbe sureties, or bring in pawne for such arrested: then the officers shal release the partie, and shall set him or them at libertie.

9. Moreouer, we giue, graunt and promise to the saide Marchants, that if any of their ships or other vessels shall bee spoyled, robbed, or damnified in sayling, anckoring or returning to or from our saide Empires and Dominions, or any part thereof, by any Pirats, Marchants, or other person, whatsoeuer hee or they bee, that then and in such case, wee will doe all that in vs is to cause restitution, reparation, and satisfaction to bee duely made to the said English marchants by our letters and otherwise, as shall stand with our honour, and be consonant to equitie and iustice.

10. Item, for vs, our heires and successours, wee doe promise and graunt to performe, mainteine, corroborate, autenticate and obserue all and singular the aforesaide liberties, franchises, and priuiledges, like as presently we firmely doe intend, and will corroborate, autentike and performe the same by all meane and way that we can, as much as may be to the commoditie and profite of the said English Marchants, and their successours for euer.

And to the intent that all and singuler the saide giftes, graunts and promises, may bee inuiolably obserued and performed, we the said Iohn Vasiliuich by the grace of God Emperor of Russia, great Duke of Nouogrode, Mosco, &c. for vs, our heires and successors, by our Imperiall and lordly word in stead of an othe, haue and doe promise by these presents, inuiolably to mainteyne and obserue, and cause to be inuiolably obserued and mainteined all and singuler the aforesayde giftes, graunts and promises from time to time, and at all and euery time and times heereafter. And for the more corroboration hereof haue caused our Signet hereunto to be put: Dated in our Castle of Mosco the 20. day of * * * in the yeere * * *.

* * * * *

The Charter of the Marchants of Russia, graunted vpon the discouerie of the saide Countrey by King Philip and Queene Marie.

Philip and Marie, by the grace of God King and Queene, &c. To all manner of officers, true Iurie men, ministers and subiects, and to all other people as well within this our Realme or elsewhere vnder our obeysance, iurisdiction, and rule, or otherwise vnto whome these our letters shall bee shewed, seene, or read, greeting.

Whereas wee be credibly informed that our right trusttie, right faithfull, and welbeloued Counsailors, William Marques of Winchester Lord high Treasurer of this our Realme of England, Henrie Earle of Arundel Lord Steward of our housholde, Iohn Earle of Bedford Lord keeper of our priuie Seale, William Earle of Pembroke, William Lorde Howard of Effingham Lorde high Admirall of our saide Realme of England, &c. Haue at their own aduenture, costs and charges, prouided, rigged, and tackled certaine ships, pinnesses, and other meete vessels, and the same furnished with all things necessary haue aduanced and set forward, for to discouer, descrie, and finde Isles, landes, territories, Dominions, and Seigniories vnknowen, and by our subiects before this not commonly by sea frequented, which by the sufferance and grace of Almightie God, it shall chaunce them sailing Northwards, Northeastwards, and Northwestwards, or any partes thereof, in that race or course which other Christian Monarches (being with vs in league and amitie) haue not heeretofore by Seas traffiqued, haunted, or frequented, to finde and attaine by their said aduenture, as well for the glorie of God, as for the illustrating of our honour and dignitie royall, in the increase of the reuenues of our Crowne, and generall wealth of this and other our Realmes and Dominions, and of our subiects of the same: And to this intent our subiects aboue specified and named, haue most humbly beseeched vs, that our abundant grace, fauour and clemencie may be gratiously extended vnto them in this behalfe: whereupon wee inclined to the petition of the foresaide our Counsailours, subiects and marchants, and willing to animate, aduance, further and nourish them in their said godlie, honest, and good purpose, and, as we hope, profitable aduenture, and that they may the more willingly, and readily atchieue the same. Of our especiall grace, certaine knowledge and meere motion, haue graunted, and by these presents doe graunt, for vs, our heires and successours, vnto our said right trustie, and right faithfull, and right wel beloued Counsailours, and the other before named persons, that they by the name of marchants aduenturers of England, for the discouery of lands, territories, Iles, Dominions, and Seigniories vnknowen, and not before that late aduenture or enterprise by sea or Nauigation, commonly frequented as aforesaid, shalbe from henceforth one bodie and perpetuall fellowship and communaltie of themselues, both in deede and in name, and them, by the names of Marchants aduenturers for the discouerie of lands, territories, Iles and seigniories vnknowen, and not by the seas, and Nauigations, before their saide late aduenture or enterprise by sea or Nauigation commonly frequented, We doe imcorporate, name, and declare by these presents, and that the same fellowship or communalty from henceforth shalbe, and may haue one Gouernour of the saide fellowship, and communaltie of Marchants aduenturers.

And in consideration that one Sebastian Cabota hath bin the chiefest setter forth of this iourney or voyage, therefore we make, ordeine, and constitute him the said Sebastian to be the first and present gouernour of the same fellowship and communaltie, by these presents. To haue and enioy the said office of Gouernour, to him the said Sebastian Cabota during his naturall life, without amouing or dismissing from the same roome.

And furthermore, we graunt vnto the same fellowship and communaltie and their successors, that they the saide fellowship and communaltie, and their successors after the decease of the saide Sebastian Cabota, shall, and may freely and lawfully in places conuenient and honest, assemble themselues together, or so many of them as will or can assemble together, as well within our citie of London, or elsewhere, as it shall please them, in such sort and maner, as other worshipfull corporations of our saide citie haue vsed to assemble, and there yeerely name, elect and choose one Gouernour or two of themselues, and their liberties, and also as well yeerely during the natural life of the said Sebastian Cabota now Gouernour, as also at the election of such saide Gouernour or gouernours before his decease, to choose, name, and appoint eight and twentie of the most sad, discreete, and honest persons of the saide fellowship, and communaltie of Marchant aduenturers, as is aboue specified, and 4. of the most expert and skilfull persons of the same 28. to be named and called Consuls, and 24. of the residue, to be named and called Assistants to the saide Gouernour or gouernours, and Consuls for the time being, which shal remaine and stand in their authorities for one whole yeere then next following. And if it shall fortune the saide Gouernour, Consuls, and assistants, or any of them so to be elected, and chosen as is aforesaid, to die within the yeere after his or their election, that then and so often, it shall and may be lawfull to and for the said fellowship, and communalty, to elect and choose of themselues other Gouernour or gouernours, Consuls and assistants, in the place and steade of such as so shall happen to die, to serue out the same yeere.

And further we do make, ordeine, and constitute George Barnes knight and Alderman of our Citie of London, William Garret Alderman of our saide Citie, Anthonie Husie, and Iohn Suthcot, to be the first and present 4. Consuls of the said fellowship and communalty by these presents, to haue and enioy the said offices of Consuls to them the said George Barnes, William Garret, Anthony Husie, and Iohn Suthcot, for terme of one whole yere next after the date of these our letters patents: And we doe likewise make, ordeine and constitute Sir Iohn Gresham knight, Sir Andrew Iudde knight, Sir Thomas White knight, Sir Iohn Yorke knight, Thomas Offley the elder, Thomas Lodge, Henry Herdson, Iohn Hopkins, William Watson, Will. Clifton, Richard Pointer, Richard Chamberlaine, William Mallorie, Thomas Pallie the elder, William Allen, Henry Becher, Geffrey Walkenden, Richard Fowles, Rowland Heyward, George Eaton, Iohn Ellot, Iohn Sparke, Blase Sanders, and Miles Mording, to be the first and present 24. Assistants to the saide Gouernour or governours, and Consuls, and to the said fellowship and communaltie by these presents, to haue and enioy the said offices of assistants to them for terme of one whole yere, next after the date of these our letters-patents. And further, we for vs, our heires and successors, as much as in vs is, wil and graunt by these presents vnto the saide Gouernour, Consuls, assistants, fellowship and company of Marchants aduenturers aforesaid, and to their successors, that the said gouernour or gouernours, 4. Consuls, and 24. assistants, that now by these patents are nominated and appointed, or that hereafter by the saide fellowship and communaltie of marchants aduenturers, or the more part of them, which shalbe then present, so from time to time to be chosen, so that there be 15. at the least wholy agreed therof, the said Gouernour or gouernours, or one of them, and 2. of the said Consuls shalbe there, and 12. of the residue of the said number of 15. shall be of the saide assistants, and in the absence of such Gouernour, that then 3. of the said Consuls, and 12. of the saide assistants at the least for the time being shal and may haue, vse and exercise ful power and authority to rule and gouerne all and singuler the Marchants of the said fellowship and communaltie, and to execute and doe full and speedie iustice to them, and euery of them, in all their causes, differences, variances, controuersies, quarrels, and complaints, within any our realmes, dominions and iurisdictions onely moued, and to be moued touching their merchandise, traffikes, and occupiers aforesaid, or the good order or rule of them or any of them.

Also wee for vs, our heires and successours, so much as in vs is, doe likewise by these presents graunt, that the said Gouernour, Consuls, assistants, fellowship and communaltie, and their successors shall and may haue perpetuall succession, and a common Seale which shall perpetually serue for the affaires and businesse of the saide fellowship and communaltie. And that they and their successours, shall and may bee for euer able persons, and capax in the lawe, for to purchase and possesse in fee and perpetuitie, and for term of life or liues, or for terme of yeeres or otherwise, lands, tenements, rents, reuersions, and other possessions, and hereditaments whatsoeuer they bee, by the name of the Gouernour, Consuls, assistants, fellowship and communaltie of the Marchants aduenturers by Seas and Nauigations for the discouerie of landes, territories, Iles, Dominions, and Seigniories vnknowen, and before the saide last aduenture or enterprise by seas not frequented, as before is specified, and by the same names shall and may lawfully alien, graunt, let and set the same or any part thereof to any person or persons able in the lawe to take and receiue the same. So that they doe not graunt nor alien the same, or any part thereof into mortmaine, without speciall licence of vs, our heires or successours, first had and obtained.

Also wee for vs, our heires and successours haue graunted, and by these presents doe graunt vnto the saide Gouernours, Consuls, assistants, fellowship and communaltie of the saide Marchants and to their successours, that they and their successours, shall and may lawfully purchase vnto them and their successors for euer, landes, tenements and hereditaments whatsoeuer, of the cleare yeerely value of threescore sixe pounds, thirteen shillings and foure pence of lawful money of England and not aboue, as well of such lands, tenements and hereditaments, as be holden or shall be holden of vs, our heires or successours, as of any other person or persons, the statutes prouided against alienations into mortmaine, or any of them, or any article or clause in them or any of them contained, or any other lawe, custome, statute or prouision to the contrary in any wise notwithstanding. And that they by the name of the Gouernour, Consuls, assistants, fellowship and communaltie of Marchants aduenturers, for the discouerie of lands, territories, Isles, dominions and Seigniories vnknowen by the Seas and Nauigations, and not before the said late aduenture or enterprise by seas frequented as aforesaid, shall and may be able in the law to implead, and be impleaded, to answere, and to be answered, to defende, and to be defended before whatsoeuer Iudge or Iustice, temporall or spirituall, or other persons whatsoeuer, in whatsoeuer court, or courts, and in all actions personall, reall, and mixt, and in euery of them, and in all plaints of nouel disseison, and also in all plaints, suites, quarels, affaires, businesses and demaunds whatsoeuer they bee, touching and concerning the saide fellowship and communaltie, and the affaires and businesse of the same onely, in as ample manner and forme, as any other corporation of this our Realme may doe.

Moreouer, wee for vs, our heires and successours, haue giuen and graunted, and by these presents doe giue and graunt vnto the said Gouernour, Consuls, assistants, fellowshippe, and communaltie of Marchants aduenturers aforesaide, and to their successours, that the saide Gouernour, or Gouernours, Consuls and assistants, and their successors, in maner, forme, and number afore rehearsed, shall haue full power and authoritie from time to time hereafter, to make, ordein, establish and erect all such statutes, actes and ordinaunces, for the gouernement, good condition, and laudable rule of the saide fellowship and communaltie of Marchants aduenturers aforesaid, as to them shall bee thought good, meete, conuenient and necessarie, and also to admit vnto the saide Corporation and fellowship to be free of the same, such and as many persons, as to them shal bee thought good, meete, conuenient and necessarie. And that euery such person or persons, as shall fortune heereafter to bee admitted into the saide fellowshippe, communaltie and corporation, shal from the time of his or their admittance, be free of the same. And also wee will, and by these presents, graunt for vs, our heires and successours, vnto the saide Gouernours, Consuls, assistants, fellowship, communaltie of Marchants aduenturers aforesaid, and to their successours, that the Gouernour, or gouernors, Consuls and assistants of the same, in maner, forme, and number afore rehearsed, and their successours for the time being, shall, and may haue full power and authoritie by these presents from time to time, as to them shal seeme good, to limite, set, ordeine and make, mulcts, and penalties by fines, forfeitures, and imprisonments, or any of them vpon any offender of the saide fellowship and communaltie, for any offence touching the same fellowhip and communaltie, and also that all acts and ordinances by them or their successours to bee made, which time shall thinke not necessarie or preiudiciall to the saide fellowship or communaltie, at al times to reuoke, breake, frustrate, annihilate, repeale and dissolue at their pleasure and liberty. And further, wee will, that if any of the saide fellowship and communaltie shalbe found contrarious, rebellious, or disobedient to the saide Gouernour or gouernours, Consuls, and the said assistants for the time being, or to any statutes, acts or ordinances by them made or to be made, that then the saide Gouernour or gouernours, Consuls, and the saide assistants, in maner, forme, and number aboue specified, for the time being, shall and may by vertue of these presents, mulct, and punish euery such offender or offenders, as the quality of the offence requireth, according to their good discretions.

And further, we will that none of the saide offender or offenders shall decline from the power of the saide Gouernour, or gouernours, Consuls and assistants, in maner, forme, and number abouesaide for the time being: so always, that the saide actes, statutes and ordinances, doe onely touch and concerne the saide Gouernour or gouernours, Consuls, assistants, and the saide fellowship and communaltie of our before named Marchants aduenturers, or the men of the same fellowship and communaltie, and none other; And so always, that such their acts, statutes and ordinances bee not against our prerogatiue, lawes, statutes, and customes of our realmes and Dominions, nor contrary to the seuerall duetie of any our subiects towards vs, our heires and successours, nor contrarie to any compacts, treaties, or leagues, by vs or any our progenitours heretofore had or made, or hereafter by vs, our heires and successours to bee made, to or with any forreine Prince or potentate, nor also to the preiudice of the corporation of the Maior, communalties and Citizens of our Citie of London, nor to the preiudice of any person or persons, bodie politique, or corporate or incorporate, iustly pretending, clayming, or hauing any liberties, franchises, priuiledges, rightes or preheminences, by vertue or pretext of anie graunt, gift, or Letters patents, by vs, or anie our Progenitours, heeretofore giuen, graunted, or made.

Moreouer, we for vs, our heires, and successours, will, and by these presents, doe graunt vnto the said Gouernors, Consuls, assistants, fellowship and communaltie of our Marchants aforesaid, that their said Gouernour or gouernours, Consuls and assistants, and their successors for the time being, in maner, forme and number aboue rehearsed, shal haue full power and authoritie to assigne, constitute and ordaine one officer, or diuers officers as well within our aforesaide Citie of London, as also in any other place or places of this our Realme of England, or else where within our dominions, which officer or officers, wee will to be named and called by the name of Sergeant or Serjeants to the fellowship or communalty of the said marchants, and that the said sergeant or sergeants, shall and may haue full power and authoritie by these presents, to take, leuie and gather all maner fines, forfeitures, penalties and mulcts of euery person and persons, of the saide fellowship and communaltie conuict, and that shalbe conuicted, vpon or for breaking of any statutes, acts, ordinances, to bee made by the saide Gouernour or gouernours, Consuls and assistants for the time being.

And further, we will and also graunt for vs, our heires, and successours, that the saide officer or officers shall haue further power and authoritie for the default of payment, or for disobedience in this behalfe (if neede be) to set hands and arrest aswell the bodie and bodies, as the goods and chattels of such offender, and offenders, and transgressers, in euery place and places not franchised. And if it shall fortune any such offender or offenders, their goods and chattels or any part thereof, to be in any citie, borough, towne incorporate, or other place franchised or priuiledged, where the said officer or officers may not lawfully intromit or intermeddle, that then the Maior, shirifes, baylifes, and other head officers, or ministers, within euery such citie, borough, towne incorparate or place or places franchised, vpon a precept to them, or any of them, to be directed from the gouernour or gouernours, Consuls and assistants of the said fellowship, in number and forme aforesaid, vnder the common seale of the sayd fellowship and communaltie for the time being, shall and may attach and arrest the body or bodies of such offender or offenders, as also take, and seise the goods and chattels of all and euery such offender or offenders, being within any such place or places franchised, and the same body and bodies, goods and chattels of all and euery such offender and offenders, being within any such place or places franchised, and every part therof so attached and seazed, shall according to the tenor and purport of the sayd precept, returne, and deliuer vnto the sayd officer or officers of the aforesaid fellowship, and communaltie.

And further, we will and grant for vs, our heires and successours by these presents, that all, and euery such Maior, shirife, baylife, or other head officers or ministers of any citie, borough, towne incorporate, or other places franchised, shall not be impeached, molested, vexed or sued in any our court or courts, for executing or putting in execution of any of the said precept or precepts.

[Sidenote: K. Philip and Queene Mary hereby do disannul Pope Alexanders diuision. [Footnote: Alexander VI, the father of Lucretia and Cæsar Borgia, had divided the Indies between Spain and Portugal.]]. And furthermore, we of our ample and abundant grace, meere motion, and certaine knowledge, for vs, our heires, and successors, as much as in vs is, haue giuen and granted, and by these presents doe giue and grant vnto the sayd gouernour, Consuls, assistants, fellowship, and conimunaltie of Marchants aduenturers, and to their successors, and to the Factor and Factors, assigne and assignes of euery of them, ful and free authoritie, libertie, facultie and licence, and power to saile to all portes, regions, dominions, territories, landes, Isles, Islands, and coastes of the sea, wheresoeuer before their late aduenture or enterprise vnknowen, or by our Marchants and subiects by the seas not heretofore commonly frequented, vnder our banner, standerd, flags and ensignes, with their shippe, ships, barke, pinnesses, and all other vessels of whatsoeuer portage, bulke, quantitie, or qualitie they may be, and with any Mariners, and men as they will leade with them in such shippe or shippes, or other vessels at their owne and proper costs and expences, for to traffique, descrie, discouer and finde, whatsoeuer Isle, Islands, countreis, regions, prouinces, creekes, armes of the sea, riuers and streames, as wel of Gentiles, as of any other Emperor, king, prince, gouernor or Lord whatsoeuer he or they shalbe, and in whatsoeuer part of the world they be situated, being before the sayd late aduenture or enterprise vnknowen, and by our Marchants and subiects not commonly frequented, and to enter and land in the same, without any maner of denying, paine, penaltie or forfeiture to be had or taken by anie our lawes, customes or statutes to our vse, or to the vse of our heires or successors for the same.

And we haue also granted, and by these presents, for vs, our heires and successors, doe graunt vnto the sayd Gouernours, Consuls, assistants, fellowship and communalty, and to their successours, and to their Factors and assignes, and to euery of them, licence for to reare, plant, erect, and fasten our banners, standards, flags, and Ensignes, in whatsoeuer citie, towne, village, castle, Isle, or maine lande, which shall be by them newly found, without any the penalties, forfeitures, or dangers aforesayde, and that the sayd fellowship and communalty, and their successors, Factors and assignes and euery of them shall and may subdue, possesse, and occupie, all maner cities, townes, Isles, and maine lands of infidelitie, which is or shal be by them, or any of them newly founde or descried, as our vassals and subiects, and for to acquire and get the Dominion, title, and iurisdiction of the same Cities, Townes, Castles, Villages, Isles, and maine landes, which shall bee by them, or any of them newly discouered or found vnto vs, our heires and successours for euer.

And furthermore, whereas by the voyage of our subiects in this last yeere [Footnote: Anno 1554.] attempted by Nauigation, towards the discouerie and disclosure of vnknowen places, Realmes, Islandes, and Dominions by the seas not frequented, it hath pleased Almighty God to cause one of the three shippes by them set foorth for the voyage, and purpose aboue mentioned, named the Edward Bonaventure, to arriue, abide, and winter within the Empire and dominions of the high and mightie Prince our cousin and brother, Lord Iohn Basiliuich Emperour of all Russia, Volodomer, great duke of Moscouie, &c. Who, of his clemencie, for our loue and zeale, did not onely admitte the Captaine, and marchants our subiects into his protection, and Princely presence, but also receiued and interteined them very graciously, and honourably, granting vnto them by his letters addressed vnto vs, franke accesse into all his Seigniories and dominions, with license freely to traffique in and out with all his Subiects in all kinde of Marchandise, with diuers other gracious priuiledges, liberties and immunities specified in his sayde letters vnder his Signet: Know yee therefore that wee of our further royall fauour and munificence, of our meere motion, certaine knowledge, and speciall grace, for vs our heires and successours, haue giuen and graunted, and by these presents doe giue and graunt vnto the same Gouernours, Consuls, assistants, fellowship, and comunalty aboue named, and to their successours, as much as in vs is, that all the mayne landes, Isles, Portes, hauens, creekes, and riuers of the said mighty Emperour of all Russia, and great Duke of Mosco, &c. [Sidenote: The largenes of the priuiledge of the Moscouite companie.] And all and singuler other lands, dominions territories, Isles, Portes, hauens, creekes, riuers, armes of the sea, of al and euery other Emperor, king, prince, ruler, and gouernour, whatsoeuer he or they before the said late aduenture or enterprise not knowen, or by our foresayd marchants and subiects by the seas not commonly frequented, nor by any part nor parcell thereof lying Northwards, Northeastwards, or Northwestwards, as is aforesayd, by sea shall not be visited, frequented nor hanted by any our subiects, other then of the sayd company and felowship, and their successours without expresse licence, agreement and consent of the Gouernour, Consuls, and Assistants of the said felowship and communaltie aboue named, or the more part of them, in manner and number aforesayd, for the time being, vpon paine of forfeiture and losse, as well of the shippe and shippes, with the appurtenances, as also of all the goods, marchandises, and things whatsoeuer they be, of those our subiects, not being of the sayd felowship and communalty, which shall attempt and presume to saile to any of those places, which bee, or hereafter shall happen to bee found, and traffiked vnto: the one hafe of the same forfeiture to be to the vse of vs, our heires and successors, and the other halfe to be to the vse of the sayd fellowship and communaltie. And if it shall fortune, anie stranger or strangers, for to attempt to hurt, hinder, or endamage the same marchants, their factors, deputies, or assignes, or any of them in sailing, going or returning at any time in the sayd aduenture, or for to saile or trade to or from any those places, landes or coastes, which by the sayd marchants, their factors, deputies and assignes haue bene, or shall bee descried, discouered and found, or frequented, aswell within the coastes and limites of gentility, as within the dominions and Seigniories of the sayd mighty Emperour and Duke, and of all and euery other Emperour, King, Prince, Ruler and gouernour whatsoeuer he or they be, before the sayd late aduenture or enterprise not knowen by any our said marchants and subiects, by the seas not commonly frequented, and lying Northwards, Northwestwards or Northeastwards as aforesaid, then wee will and grant, and by these presents doe licence, and authorise for vs, our heires and successors, the said marchants, their factors, deputies, and assignes, and euery of them to doe their best in their defence, to resist the same their enterprises and attempts. Willing therefore, and straightly commanding and charging al and singular our Officers, Maiors, Sherifes, Escheators, Constables, Bailifes, and all and singuler other our ministers and liege men, and subiects whatsoeuer, to bee aiding, fauouring, helping and assisting vnto the sayd gouernour or gouernours, Consuls, assistants, fellowship and communalty, and to their successors and deputies, factors, seruants, and assignes, and to the deputies, factors and assignes of euery of them, in executing and enioying the premisses, as well on land as in the sea, from time to time, and at all times when you or any of you shall be thereunto required. In witnesse whereof, &c.

Apud Westmonasterium, 6 die Feb. Annis Regnorum nostrorum, primo et secundo. [Footnote: Anno 1555.]

* * * * *

Certaine instructions deliuered in the third voyage, Anno 1556. for Russia, to euery Purser and the rest of the seruants, taken for the voyage, which may serue as good and necessary directions, to all other like aduenturers.

1. First you before the ship doth begin to lade, goe aboord, and shall there take, and write one inuentorie, by the aduise of the Master, or of some other principall officer there aboord, of all the tackle, apparell, cables, ankers, ordinance, chambers, shot, powder, artillerie, and of all other necessaries whatsoever doth belong to the sayd ship: and the same iustly taken, you shall write in a booke, making the sayd Master, or such officer priuie of that which you haue so written, so that the same may not be denied, when they shall call accompt thereof: that done, you shall write a copie of the same with your owne hand, which you shall deliuer before the shippe shall depart, for the voyage to the companies booke keeper here to be kept to their behalfe, to the ende that they may be iustly answered the same, when time shall require: and this order to be seene and kept euery voyage orderly, by the Pursers of the companies owne ship, in any wise.

2. Also when the shippe beginneth to lade, you shall be ready a boord with your booke, to enter such goods as shall be brought aboord, to be laden for the company, packed, or vnpacked, taking the markes and numbers of euery packe, fardell, trusse, or packet, corouoya, chest, fatte, butte, pipe, puncheon, whole barrell, halfe barrell, firken, or other caske, maunde, or basket, or any other thing, which may, or shall be packed by any other manner of waies or deuise. And first, all such packes, or trusses, &c. as shal be brought aboord to be laden, not marked by the companies marke, you shall doe the best to let that the same be not laden, and to enquire diligently to know the owners thereof, if you can, and what commoditie the same is, that is so brought aboord to be laden: if you can not know the owners of

such goods, learne what you can thereof, as well making a note in your booke, as also to send or bring word thereof to the Agent, and to some one of the foure Marchants with him adioined so speedily as you can, if it be here laden or to be laden in this riuer, being not marked with the companies marke, as is aforesaid: and when the sayd shippe hath receiued in all that the companies Agent will have laden, you shall make a iust copie of that which is laden, reciting the parcels, the markes and numbers of euery thing plainely, which you shall likewise deliuer to the sayd bookekeeper to the vse aforesayd.

3. Also when the ship is ready to depart, you shall come for your cockets and letters to the Agent, and shall shew him all such letters as you haue receiued of any person or persons priuately or openly, to be deliuered to any person or persons in Russia or elsewhere, and also to declare if you know any other that shall passe in the ship either master or mariner that hath receiued any letters to be priuily deliuered to any there, directed from any persons or persons, other then from the Agent here to the Agent there: which letters so by you receiued, you shall not carie with you, without you be licensed so to doe by the Agent here, and some of the foure merchants, as is aforesaid: and such others as doe passe, hauing receiued any priuie letters to be deliuered, you shal all that in you lieth, let the deliuerie of them at your arriuing in Russia: and also if you haue or do receiue, or shal know any other that doth or hath receiued any goods or ready money to be imployed in Russia, or to bee deliuered there to any person or persons from any person or persons, other then such as bee the companies goods, and that vnder their marke, you shall before the ship doeth depart, declare the same truely to the sayd Agent, and to some of the other merchants to him adioyned, as it is before declared.

4. Also when the shippe is ready to depart, and hath the master and the whole company aboord, you shall diligently foresee and take heede, that there passe not any priuie person, or persons, other then such as be authorized to passe in the said ship, without the licence and warrant of one of the Gouernours and of the assistants, for the same his passage, to be first shewed. And if there be any such person or persons that is to passe and will passe without shewing the same warrant, you shall let the passage of any such to the vttermost of your power: And for that there may no such priuie person passe vnder the cloke and colour of some mariner, you shall vpon the weying of your ships anker, call the master and the manners within boord by their names and that by your bookes, to the ende that you may see that you haue neither more nor lesse, but iust the number for the voyage.

5. Also you must have in remembrance, that if it shall chance the shippe to bee put into anie harbour in this coast by contrary windes or otherwise in

making the voyage, to send word thereof from time to time as the case shall require, by your letters in this maner. To Master I. B. Agent for the company of the New trades in S. in London: If you doe hier any to bring your letters, write that which he must haue for the portage. And for your better knowledge and learning, you shall doe very well to keepe a dayly note of the voyage both outwards and homewards.

6. And principally see that you forget not dayly in all the voiage both morning and euening, to call the company within boord to prayer, in which doing you shall please God, and the voiage will haue the better successe thereby, and the company prosper the better.

7. Also in calme weather and at other times when you shall fortune to come to anker in the seas during the voyage, you shall for the companies profite, and for the good husbanding of the victuals aboord, call vpon the Boateswaine and other of the company to vse such hookes and other engines as they haue aboord to take fish with, that such fish so taken may bee eaten for the cause aforesayd: and if there bee no such engines aboord, then to prouide some before you goe from hence.

8. And when God shall send you in safetie into the Bay of S. Nicholas at an anker, you shall goe a shore with the first boate that shall depart from the ship, taking with you such letters as you haue to deliuer to the Agent there: and if he be not there at your comming a land, then send the companies letters to Colmogro to him by some sure mariner or otherwise, as the master and you shall thinke best, but goe not your selfe at any hand, nor yet from aboord the ship, vnlesse it be a shore to treate with the Agent for the lading of the ship that you be appointed in, which you shall applie diligently to haue done so speedily as may be. And for the discharging of the goods therein in the Bay, to be carried from thence, see that you doe looke well to the vnlading thereof, that there be none other goods sent a shore then the companies, and according to the notes entred in your booke as is aforesaid: if there be, inquire diligently for whom they bee, and what goods they be, noting who is the receiuer of the sayd goods, in such sort that the company may haue the true knowledge thereof at your comming home.

9. Also there a shore, and likewise aboord, you shall spie and search as secretly as you may, to learne and know what bargaining, buying and selling there is with the master and the mariners of the shippe and the Russes, or with the companies seruants there: and that which you shall perceiue and learne, you shall keepe a note thereof in your booke secretly to your selfe, which you shall open and disclose at your comming home to the gouernours and assistants, in such sort as the trueth of their secret trades and occupyings may be reuealed and knowen. You shall need alwayes to haue Argos eyes, to spie their secret packing and conueyance, aswell on

land as aboord the shippe, of and for such furres and other commodities, as yeerely they doe vse to buy, packe and conuey hither. If you will bee vigilant and secrete in this article, you cannot misse to spie their priuie packing one with another, either on shore or aboord the shippe: worke herein wisely, and you shall deserue great thanks of the whole company.

10. Also at the lading againe of the shippe, you shall continue and abide abord, to the ende that you may note and write in your booke all such goods and marchandises as shall be brought and laden, which you shall orderly note in all sortes as heretofore, as in the second article partly it is touched: and in any wise put the Master and the company in remembrance, to looke and foresee substantially to the roomaging of the shippe, by faire meanes or threats, as you shall see and thinke will serue for the best.

11. Thus when the shippe is full laden againe, and all things aboord in good order, and that you doe fortune to goe a shore to the Agent for your letters, and dispatch away: you shall demand whether all the goods be laden that were brought thither, and to know the trueth therof, you shal repaire to the companies storehouse there at S. Nicholas, to see if there be any goods left in the sayd storehouse: if there be, you shal demand why they be not laden, and note what kinde of goods they be that be so left: and seeing any of the shippes there not fully laden, you shall put the Agent in remembrance to lady those goods so left, if any such be to be laden, as is aforesayd. And thus God sending you a faire wind, to make speede and away.

12. Finally, when God shall send you to arriue againe vpon this coast in safetie, either at Harewich, or elsewhere, goe not you aland, if you may possiblie, to the ende that when you be gone a shore, there may no goods be sent priuily ashore to be solde, or else to be solde aboord the ship in your absence, but keepe you still aboord, if you can by any meanes, for the causes aforesaid, and write the company a letter from the shippe of your good arriuall, which you may conuey to them by land by some boy or mariner of the shippe, or otherwise as you shall thinke best: and likewise when God shall send you and the shippe into the riuer here, doe not in any wise depart out of the shippe that you be in, vntil the company doe send some other aboord the shippe, in your steede and place, to keepe the shippe in your absence.

* * * * *

The Nauigation and discouerie toward the riuer of Ob, made by Master Steuen
  Burrough, Master of the Pinnesse called the Serchthrift, with diuers
  things worth the noting, passed in the yere 1556.

We departed from Ratcliffe to Blackewall the 23 of April. Satturday being S. Markes day, we departed from Blackewall to Grays.

The 27 being Munday the right worshipfull Sebastian Cabota came aboard our Pinnesse at Grauesende, accompanied with diuers Gentlemen, and Gentlewomen, who after that they had viewed our Pinnesse, and tasted of such cheere as we could make them aboord, they went on shore, giuing to our mariners right liberall rewards: and the good olde Gentleman Master Cabota [Footnote: Sebastian Cabot was then 79 years old.] gaue to the poore most liberall almes, wishing them to pray for the good fortune, and prosperous successe of the Serchthrift our Pinnesse. And then at the signe of the Christopher, hee and his friends banketted, and made me, and them that were in the company great cheere: and for very ioy that he had to see the towardnes of our intended discouery, he entred into the dance himselfe, amongst the rest of the young and lusty company: which being ended, hee and his friends departed most gently, commending vs to the gouernance of almighty God.

Tuesday (28) we rode still at Grauesend, making prouision for such things as we wanted.

Wednesday (29) in the morning we departed from Grauesende, the winde being at Southwest, that night we came to an anker thwart our Lady of Hollands.

Thursday (30) at three of the clocke in the morning we weyed, and by eight of the clocke, we were at an anker in Orwell wannes, and then incontinent I went aboord the Edward Bonauenture, [Footnote: The ship that had successfully carried Chancellor in the expedition of 1553-4.] where the worshipfull company of marchants appointed me to be, vntill the sayd good ship arriued at Wardhouse. Then I returned againe into the pinnesse.

Friday the 15 of May we were within 7 leagues of the shore, on the coast of Norway: the latitude at a South sunne, 58 degrees and a halfe, where we saw three sailes, beside our owne company: and thus we followed the shoare or land, which lieth Northnorthwest, North and by West, and Northwest and by North, as it doth appeare by the plat.

Saturday (16) at an East sunne we came to S. Dunstan's Island, [Footnote: Bommeloe Island.] which Island I so named. It was off vs East two leagues and a halfe, the wind being at Southeast: the latitude this day at a South sunne 59 degrees, 42 minutes. Also the high round mountains bare East of vs, at a south sunne: and when this hill is East of you, and being bound to the Northward, the land lyeth North and halfe a point Westerly, from this sayd South sunne, vnto a North sunne twenty leagues Northwest alongst the shoare.

Vpon Sunday (17) at sixe of the clocke in the morning, the farthest land that we could see that lay Northnorthwest, was East of vs three leagues, and then it trended to the Northwards, and to the Eastwards of the North, which headland I iudged to be Scoutsnesse. At seuen of the clocke we changed our course and went North, the wind being at Southsoutheast, and it waxed very thicke and mistie, and when it cleered, we went Northnortheast. At a South sunne we lost sight of the Serchthrift, because of the mist, making our way North. And when we lost sight of the shoare and pinnesse, we were within two leagues and a halfe of the shoare: the last land that we saw when this mist came vpon vs, which is to the Northwards of Scoutsnesse, lay Northnortheast, and Southsouthwest, and we made our way North vntill a west sunne fiue leagues.

From that vntill Munday (18) three a clocke in the morning ten leagues Northnortheast: and then we went North and by East, because the winde came at the Westsouthwest with thicke miste: the latitude this day at a South sunne sixtie three degrees and a halfe truely taken: at this season we had sight of our Pinnesse againe.

From that vntill Tuesday (19) a South sunne Northnortheast fortie foure leagues, and then Northeast From a South sunne vntill eight of the clocke, fifteene leagues Northeast.

From that vntill Wednesday (20) a South sunne Northnortheast, except the first watch Northeast: then had we the latitude in sixtie seuen degrees, thirtie nine minutes. From that vnto a Northwest sunne eighteen leagues Northeast, and then we were within two leagues off the shore, and saw the high land to the Southwards of Lowfoot [Footnote: The Lofoden Islands lie between 67 deg. 30 min. N. Latitude and 12 deg. and 16 deg. E. longitude. They consist of ten large and many small islands, all rocky and mountainous. The largest Islands are: Hindoen, E. and W. Waagen, Langoen, Andoe, Rost &c.] breake out through the mist, and then we went North and by east.

From the sayd Northwest sunne vntill foure of the clocke in the morning (21) North and by East ten leagues and a halfe: and then Northnortheast vntill a South sunne, the latitude being sixtie nine degrees, and a halfe. From that vntill halfe an houre past seuen of the clocke, Northnortheast eleuen leagues and a halfe, and then we went Northeast ten leagues. From that 3 leagues and a halfe Eastnortheast, and then we sawe the land through the cloudes and hazie thwart on the broadside of vs the winde being then at Southsouthwest.

From that vntill Saturday (22), at eight of the clocke in the morning Eastnortheast, and to the Northwards fortie eight leagues, and then the wind came vp at North, wee being aboord the shore, and thwart of the

Chappell, which I suppose is called Kedilwike [Footnote: Probably Hammerfest, the most northern town in Europe]: then we cast the shippes head to the seawards, because thee winde was verie scant: and then I caused the Pinnesse to beare in with the shore, to see whether she might find an harborough for the ships or not, and that she found and saw two roaders ride in the sound: and also they sawe houses. But notwithstanding, God be praysed, the winde enlarged vpon vs, that we had not occasion to goe into the harborough: and then the Pinnesse bare her Myssen mast ouer boord with flagge and all, and lost the flagge: with the mast there fell two men ouer boord, but God be praised, they were saued: the flagge was a token, whereby we might, understand whether there were a good harbour there or not.

[Sidenote: The North Cape so named by Steuen Burrowe.] At the North sunne the North Cape (which I so named the first voyage) was thwart of vs, which is nine leagues to the Eastwards of the foresayd Chappell from the Eastermost point of it. [Footnote: This is a slight error, if by the "Chappell" is meant the present site of Hammerfest, as North Cape, which is in 71 deg. 10 min. N. latitude, and 25 deg. 46 min. E. longitude, is only distant 14-1/2 miles N.E. from that town. Von Herbertstein states that Istoma and other Russians had sailed round the North of Norway, in 1496. North Cape, or rather Nordkyn, was called then Murmunski Nos (the Norman Cape). When Hulsius, in his Collection of Travels, gives Von Herbertstein's account of Istoma's voyage, he considers Swjatoi Nos, on the Kola peninsula, to be North Cape. (Hamel, *Tradescant*, St. Petersburg, 1847, p. 40, quoted by Nordenskiöld; *Voyage of the Vega*. Vol. I., p. 218.)]

Iune.

The Sunday (7) we weied in Corpus Christi Bay, at a Northeast and by East sunne: the Bay is almost halfe a league deepe: the headland which is Corpus Christi point, lyeth Southeast and by East, one league from the head of the Bay, where we had a great tyde, like a race ouer the flood: the Bay is at the least two leagues ouer: so doe I imagine from the fayre foreland to Corpus Christi poynt ten leagues Southeast and by East: It floweth in this Bay, at a South and by West moone full sea. From that we went vntill seuen a clocke at after noone twentie leagues Southeast and by South: and then we tooke in all our sailes, because it was then very mistie, and also we met with much ice that ran out of the Bay, and then wee went Southsoutheast with our foresayle: at eight of the clocke, we heard a piece of ordinance, which was out of the Edward, which bade vs farewell, and then we shot off another piece, and bade her farewell: wee could not one see the other, because of the thicke miste: at a Northwest sunne it began somewhat to cleere, and then we sawe a head lande, and the shoare trended to the Southwestward, which I iudged to be about Crosse Island: it was off vs at a Northnorthwest sunne, Westsouthwest.

From this Northnorthwest sunne, vntill Munday (8), we went Southeast, and this morning we came at anker among the shoales that lie off of point Looke out, at a Northeast and by East sunne, the wind being at Eastsoutheast. At this poynt Looke out, a south Moone maketh a full sea. Cape good fortune lyeth from the Isle of Crosses Southeast, and betweene them is tenne leagues: point Looke out lyeth from Cape Good fortune Eastsoutheast, and betweene them are sixe leagues. S. Edmonds point lieth from point Looke out Eastsoutheast, and halfe a point to the Southwards, and betweene them are sixe leagues. There is betweene these two points, a Bay that is halfe a league deepe, and is full of shoales and dangers. At a Southeast sunne we weyed, and turned to the windwards, the winde being at Eastsoutheast: and at a Southeast sunne, we came to an anker, being then a full sea, in fiue fadoms and a halfe water. It hieth at this place where we roade, and also at point Looke out, foure fadome water. At a Westnorthwest sunne we weyed, and driued to the windewards, vntill Tuesday (9), a Northnortheast sunne, and then being a high water, we came to an anker open of the riuer Cola, in eight fadome water. Cape S. Bernard lyeth from S. Edmondes point, Southeast and by South, and betwixt them are sixe leagues, and also betwixt them is the Riuer Cola, into which Riuer we went this euening.

Wednesday (10) we roade still in the sayd riuer, the winde being at the north: we sent our skiffe aland to be dressed: the latitude of the mouth of the riuer Cola is sixtie fiue degrees, fortie and eight minutes. [Footnote: This is another error, the latitude being 68 deg. 51 min.]

Thursday (11) at 6 of the clocke in the morning, there came aboord of vs one of the Russe Lodiaes, rowing with twentie oares, and there were foure and twenty men in her. The master of the boate presented me with a great loafe of bread, and six ringes of bread, which they call Colaches, and foure dryed pikes, and a pecke of fine otemeale, and I gaue vnto the Master of the boate, a combe, and a small glasse: and he declared vnto me, that he was bound to Pechora, and after that, I made them to drinke, the tide being somewhat broken, they gently departed. The Masters name was Pheodor.

Whereas the tenth day I sent our Pinnesse on shoare to be mended, because she was leake, and weake, with the Carpenter and three men more to helpe him, the weather chanced so, that it was Sunday before they could get aboord our shippe. All that time they were without prouision of victuals, but onely a little bread, which they spent by Thursday at night, thinking to haue come aboord when they had listed, but winde and weather denied them: insomuch that they were faine to eate grasse, and such weedes as they could find then aboue grounde, but fresh water they had plentie, but the meate with some of them could scant frame by reason of their queazie stomackes.

From Thursday at afternoone, vntill Sunday (14) in the morning, our barke did ride such a roadsted that it was to be marueiled, without the helpe of God, how she was able to abide it.

[Illustration: Russian "LODJA." After G. de Veer.]

In the bight of the Southeast shoare of the riuer Cola, there is a good roade in fiue fadome, or foure fadome and a halfe, at a lowe water: but you shall haue no land Northnortheast of you then, I proued with our pinnesse, that the depth goeth on the Southeast shoare.

Thursday (18) we weyed our ankers in the riuer Cola, and went into the Sea seuen or eight leagues, where we met with the winde farre Northerly, that of force it constrained vs to goe againe backe into the sayd riuer, where came aboord of vs sundry of their Boates, which declared vnto me that they were also bound to the northwards, a fishing for Morse, and Salmon, and gaue me liberally of their white and wheaten bread.

As we roade in this riuer, wee sawe dayly comming downe the riuer many of their Lodias, and they that had least, had foure and twenty men in them, and at the last they grew to thirtie saile of them: and amongst the rest, there was one of them whose name was Gabriel, who showed me very much friendshippe, and he declared vnto mee, they all were bound to Pechora, a fishing for Salmons, and Morses: insomuch that hee shewed mee by demonstrations, that with a faire winde wee had seuen or eight dayes sailing to the Riuer Pechora, so that I was glad of their company. This Gabriel, promised to giue mee warning of shoales, as hee did indeede.

Sunday (21) being the one and twentieth day, Gabriel gaue me a barrell of Meade, and one of his speciall friends gaue me a barrell of beere, which was caryed vpon mens backs at least 2 miles.

Munday (22) we departed from the riuer Cola, with all the rest of the said Lodias, but sailing before the wind, they were all too good for vs [Footnote: It is curious to find that the Russian Lodias (of which an engraving is annexed) were better sailors than the ships of the more civilised Englishmen]: but according to promise, this Gabriel and his friend did often strike their sayles, and taried for vs forsaking their owne company.

Tuesday (23) at an Eastnortheast sunne we were thwart of Cape S. Iohn. [Footnote: Cape Krasnoj.] It is to be vnderstood, that from the Cape S. Iohn vnto the riuer or bay that goeth to Mezen, it is all sunke land, and full of shoales and dangers, you shall haue scant two fadome water, and see no land. And this present day wee came to an anker thwart of a creeke, which is 4 or 5 leagues to the Northwards of the sayd Cape, into which creeke Gabriel and his fellow rowed, but we could not get in: and before night there were aboue 20 saile that went into the sayd creeke, the wind being at the Northeast. We had indifferent good landfang.

This aftenoone Gabriel came aboord with his skiffe, and then I rewarded him for the good company that he kept with vs ouer the shoales with two small iuory combes, and a steele glasse, with two or three trifles more, for which he was not vngratefull. But notwithstanding, his first company had gotten further to the Northwards.

Wednesday (24) being Midsummer day, we sent our skiffe aland to sound the creeke, where they found it almost drie at a low water. And all the Lodias within were on ground.

Although the harborough were euil, yet the stormie similitude of the Northerly winds tempted vs to set our sayles, and we let slip a cable and an anker, and bare with the harborough, for it was then neere a high water: and as alwaies in such iournies varieties do chance, when we came vpon the barre in the entrance of the creeke, the wind did shrink so suddenly vpon vs, that we were not able to lead it in, and before we could haue slatted the shippe before the winde, we should haue bene on ground on the lee shore, so that we were constrained to let fall an anker vnder our sailes, and rode in a very breach, thinking to haue warpt in. Gabriel came out with his skiffe, and so did sundry others also, shewing their good will to helpe vs, but all to no purpose, for they were likely to haue bene drowned for their labour, in so much that I desired Gabriel to lend me his anker, because our owne ankers were too big for our skiffe to lay out, who sent me his owne, and borrowed another also and sent it vs. Then we layd out one of those ankers, with a hawser which he had of 140 fadom long, thinking to haue warpt in, but it would not be: for as we shorted vpon the said warpe the anker came home, so that we were faine to beare the end of the warpe, that we rushed in vpon the other small anker that Gabriel sent aboord, and layd that anker to seawards: and then betweene these two ankers we trauersed the ships head to seawards, and set our foresaile and maine sayle, and when the barke had way, we cut the hawser, and so gate the sea to our friend, and tryed out al that day with our maine corse.

The Thursday (25) we went roome with Cape S. Iohn, where we found indifferent good rode for a Northnortheast wind, and for a neede, for a North and by West winde.

Friday (26) at afternoone we weyed, and departed from thence, the wether being meetly faire, and the winde at Eastsoutheast, and plied for the place where we left our cable and anker, and pur hawser: and as soone as we were at an anker, the foresaid Gabriel came aboord of vs, with 3 or foure more of their small boats, and brought with them of their Aquauitæ and Meade, professing vnto me very much friendship, and reioiced to see vs againe, declaring that they earnestly thought that we had bene lost. This Gabriel declared vnto me, that they had saued both the ankers and our hauser, and after we had thus communed, I caused 4 or 5 of them to goe into my cabbin, where I gaue them figs, and made them such cheere as I could. While I was thus banketing of them, there came another of their skiffes aboord with one who was a Keril, [Footnote: Karelian.] whose name afterwards I learned, and that he dwelt in Colmogro, and Gabriel dwelled in the towne of Cola, which is not far from the riuers mouth. This foresaid Keril said vnto me that one of the ankers which I borowed was his, I gaue him thanks for the lone of it, thinking it had bene sufficient. And as I continued in one accustomed maner, that if the present which they brought were worth entertienment they had it accordingly, he brought nothing with him, and therefore I regarded him but litle. And thus we ended, and they took their leaue and went ashore. At their comming ashore, Gabriel and Keril were at vnconuenient words, and by the eares, as I vnderstand: the cause was because the one had better entertienment then the other: but you shal vnderstand that Gabriel was not able to make his party good, because there were 17 lodias of the Kerils company who tooke his part, and but 2 of Gabriels company.

The next high water Gabriel and his company departed from thence, and rowed to their former company and neighbours, which were in number 28 at the least, and all of them belonging to the riuer Cola.

And as I vnderstood Keril made reckoning that the hawser which was fast in his anker should haue bene his owne, and at first would not deliuer it to our boat, insomuch that I sent him worde that I would complaine vpon him, whereupon he deliuered the hawser to my company.

The next day being Saturday, (27) I sent our boat on shore to fetch fresh water and wood, and at their comming on shore this Keril welcomed our men most gently, and also banketed them: and in the meane time caused some of his men to fill our baricoes with water, and to help our men to beare wood into their boat: and then he put on his best silke coate, and his coller of pearles, and came aboord againe, and brought his present with him: and thus hauing more respect vnto his present then to his person, because I perceiued him to be vainglorious, I bade him welcome, and gaue him a dish of figs: and then he declared vnto me that his father was a gentleman, and that he was able to shew me pleasure, and not Gabriel, who was but a priests sonne.

After their departure from vs we weied, and plied all the ebbe to the windewards, the winde being Northerly, and towards night it waxed very stormy, so that of force we were constrained to go roome with Cape S. Iohn againe, in which storme wee lost our skiffe at our sterne, that wee bought at Wardhouse, and there we rode vntil the fourth of Iuly. The latitude of Cape S. Iohn is 66 degrees 50 minutes. And it is to be noted, that the land of Cape S. Iohn is of height from the full sea marke, as I iudge, 10 fadomes, being cleane without any trees growing, and also without stones or rockes, and consists onely of blacke earth, which is so rotten, that if any of it fall into the sea, it will swimme as though it were a piece of wood. In which place, about three leagues from the shore you shall not haue aboue 9 fadom water, and clay ground.

Iulie.

Saturday (4) at a Northnorthwest sunne the wind came at Eastnortheast, and then we weied, and plied to the Northwards, and as we were two leagues shot past the Cape, we saw a house standing in a valley, which is dainty to be seene in those parts, and by and by I saw three men on the top of the hil. Then I iudged them, as it afterwards proued, that they were men which came from some other place to set traps to take vermin [Footnote: Probably mountain foxes. Remains of fox-traps are still frequently met with along the coast of the Polar Sea, where the Russians have carried on hunting.] for their furres, which trappes we did perceiue very thicke, alongst the shore as we went.

Sunday (5) at an East sunne we were thwart off the creeke where the Russes lay, and there came to an anker, and perceiuing the most part of the Lodias to be gone we thought it not good to tary any longer there, but weyed and spent all the ebbe, plying to the windewards.

Munday (6) at a South sunne it was high water. All alongst the coast it floweth little, onely a South moone makes a full sea: and as we were a weying we espied the Russe Lodias, which we first lost. They came out of a creeke amongst the sandy hilles, [Footnote: Kija Bay.] which hilles beginne 15 leagues Northnortheast from Cape S. Iohn.

Plying this ebbe to an end, we came (7) to an anker 6 leagues Northnortheast from the place where we saw the Russes come out: and there the Russes harboured themselues within a soonke banke, but there was not water enough for vs.

At a North sunne we weyed and plied to the Northwards, the land lying Northnortheast, and Southsouthwest, vntill a South sunne, and then we were in the latitude of 68 degrees and a halfe: and in this latitude ende those sandy hilles, and the land beginneth to lie North and by West, South and by

East, and Northnorthwest, and to the Westwards, and there the water beginneth to waxe deepe.

At a Northwest sunne we came to an anker within halfe a league of the shore, where wee had good plenty of fish, both Haddocks and Cods, riding in 10 fadom water.

Wednesday (8) we weyed, and plyed neerer the headland, which is called Caninoz, [Footnote: Canin Nos, latitude 68 deg. 30 min. N.] the wind being at East and by North.

Thursday (9) the wind being soant we turned to windwards the ebbe, to get about Caninoz: the latitude this day at noone was 68 degrees 40 minutes.

Friday (10) we turned to the windward of the ebbe, but to no purpose: and as we rode at an anker, we saw the similitude of a storme rising at Northnorthwest, and could not tell where to get rode nor succor for that winde, and harborough we knew none: and that land which we rode vnder with that winde was a lee shore. And as I was musing what was best to be done, I saw a saile come out of a creeke vnder the foresayd Caninoz, which was my friend Gabriel, who forsooke his harborough and company, and came as neere vs as he might, and pointed vs to the Eastwards, and then we weyed and followed him, and went East and by South, the wind being at Westnorthwest, and very mistie.

Saturday (11) we went Eastsoutheast and followed Gabriel, and he brought vs into an harborough called Morgiouets, which is 30 leagues from Caninoz, and we had vpon the barre going in two fadome and a fourth part: and after we were past in ouer the barre, it waxed deeper, for we had 5 fadoms, 4 and a half, and 3 fadom &c. Our barke being mored, I sent some of our men to shoare to prouide wood, where they had plenty of drift wood, but none growing: and in this place we found plenty of young foule, as Gulles, Seapies [Footnote: Probably the little Auk (*Mergulus Alle*, L.)], and others, whereof the Russes would eate none, whereof we were nothing sory, for there came the more to our part.

Sunday (12) our men cut wood on shoare, and brought it aboord, and wee balasted our shippe with stones.

This morning Gabriel saw a smoke on the way, who rowed vnto it with his skiffe, which smoke was two leagues from the place where we road: and at a Northwest sunne he came aboord again, and brought with him a Samoed, [Footnote: This was the first meeting between West Europeans and Samoyeds.] which was but a young man: his apparell was then strange vnto vs, and he presented me with three young wild geese, and one young barnacle [Footnote: *Anser bernicla*, L.].

Munday (13) I sent a man to the maine in Gabriels boat and he brought vs aboord 8 barricoes of fresh water: the latitude of the said Morgiouets is sixtie eight degrees and a terce. It floweth there at a Southsouthwest moone full sea, and hyeth two fadome and a halfe water.

At a Westnorthwest sunne we departed from this place, (14) and went East 25 leagues, and then saw an Island by North and by West of vs eight leagues, which Island is called Dolgoieue: [Footnote: Dolgoi Island.] and from the Eastermost part of this Island, there lyeth a sand East and by South 7 leagues long.

Wednesday (15) at a North and by East sunne Swetinoz [Footnote: Swjatoi Nus.] was South of vs 5 leagues. This day at aftemoone we went in ouer the dangerous barre of Pechora, and had vpon the barre but one fadome water [Footnote: The capes at the Mouth of the Petchora, Cape Ruski Savorot, and
Cape Medinski Savorot are very nearly in lat. 69 deg.].

Thursday (16) we road still.

Friday (17) I went on shoare and obserued the variation of the Compasse, which was three degrees and a halfe from the North to the West: the latitude this day was, sixtie nine degrees ten minutes.

From two or three leagues to the Eastward of Swetinoz, vntill the entering of the riuer Pechora, it is all sandie hilles, and towards Pechora the sandie hilles are very low.

It higheth on the barre of Pechora foure foote water, and it floweth there at a Southwest moone a full sea.

Munday (20) at a North and by East sunne, we weyed, and came out ouer the sayd dangerous barre, where we had but fiue foote water, insomuch that wee found a foote lesse water comming out then wee did going in. I thinke the reason was, because when we went in the winde was off the sea, which caused the sands to breake on either side of vs, and we kept in the smoothest betweene the breaches, which we durst not haue done, except we had seene the Russes to haue gone in before vs: and at our comming out the winde was off the shoare, and fayre weather, and then the sands did not appeare with breaches as at our going in: we thanke God that our ship did draw so little water.

When we were a seaboord the barre the wind scanted vpon vs, and was at Eastsoutheast, insomuch that we stopped the ebbes, and plyed all the floods to the windewards, and made our way Eastnortheast.

Tuesday (21) at a Northwest sunne we thought that we had seen land at East, or East and by North of vs: which afterwards prooued to be a monstrous heape of ice.

Within a little more than halfe an houre after we first saw this ice, we were inclosed within it before we were aware of it, which was a fearefull sight to see: for, for the space of sixe houres, it was as much as we could doe to keepe our shippe aloofe from one heape of ice, and beare roomer from another, with as much wind as we might beare a coarse. And when we had past from the danger of this ice, we lay to the Eastwards close by the wind.

The next day (22) we were againe troubled with the ice.

Thursday (23) being calme, we plyed to the windwards, the winde being Northerly. We had the latitude this day at noone in 70 degrees 11 minutes.

We had not runne past two houres Northwest, the wind being at Northnortheast and Northeast and by North a good gale, but we met againe with another heape of ice: we wethered the head of it, and lay a time to the seawards, and made way West 6 leagues.

Friday (24) at a Southeast sunne we cast about to the Eastwards, the wind being at Northnortheast: the latitude this day at noone was 70 degrees 15 minutes.

On S. Iames his day (25) bolting to the windewardes, we had the latitude at noone in seuenty degrees twentie minutes. The same day at a Southwest sunne, there was a monstrous Whale aboord of us, so neere to our side that we might haue thrust a sworde or any other weapon in him, which we durst not doe for feare hee should haue ouerthrowen our shippe: and then I called my company together, and all of vs shouted, and with the crie that we made he departed from vs: there was as much aboue water of his backe as the bredth of our pinnesse, and at his falling downe, he made such a terrible noyse in the water that a man would greatly haue maruelled, except hee had knowen the cause of it: but God be thanked, we were quietly deliuered of him. [Footnote: Of the various species of Whales, the Narwhal occurs very rarely off Novaya Zemlya. It is more common at Hope Island, and Witsen states that large herds have been seen between Spitzbergen and Novaya Zemlya. The White Whale (*Delphinapterus leucas*, Pallas), on the other hand, occurs in large shoals on the coasts of Spitzbergen and Novaya Zemlya. In 1871, 2167 White Whales were taken by the Tromsoe fleet alone, an estimated value of £6500. In 1880, one vessel had 300 whales at one cast of the net, in Magdalena Bay. In former times they appear to have been caught at the mouth of the Yenisej, which river they ascend several hundred miles. Nordenskiold also saw large shoals off the Taimur peninsula. Other species occur seldom off Novaya Zemlya. It is rather amusing to find the meeting with a whale mentioned as very remarkable and dangerous. When Nearchus sailed with the fleet of Alexander the Great from the Indus to the Red Sea, a whale also caused so great a panic that it was only with difficulty that the commander could restore order among the frightened seamen, and get the rowers to row to the place where the Whale spouted water and caused a commotion in the sea like that of a whirlwind. All the men shouted, struck the water with their oars, and sounded their trumpets, so that the large, and, in the judgment of the Macedonian Heroes, terrible animal, was frightened. *(See the "Indica" of Nearchus, preserved to us by Arrian, an excellent translation of which, by J. W. McCrindle, appeared in 1879.)* Quite otherwise was the Whale regarded on Spitsbergen some few years after Burrough's voyage. At the sight of a Whale all men were beside themselves with joy, and rushed down into the boats in order to attack and kill the valuable, animal. The fishery was carried on with such success, that the right Whale *(Balaena mysticetus L.)*, whose pursuit then gave full employment to ships by hundreds, and to men by tens of thousands, is now practically extirpated. As this Whale still occurs in no limited numbers in other parts of the Polar Sea, this state of things shows how easily an animal is driven away from a region where it is so much hunted. Captain Svend Foeyn, from 1864 to 1881, exclusively hunted another species *(Balænoptera Sibbaldii* Gray), on the coast of Finmark; and other species still follow shoals of fish on the Norwegian coast, where they sometimes strand and are killed in considerable numbers. (Nordenskiöld's *Voyage of the Vega*, vol. I., p. 165).] And a little after we spied certaine Islands, with which we bare, and found good harbor in 15 or 18 fadome, and blacke oze: we came to an anker at a Northeast sunne, and named the Island S. Iames his Island, [Footnote: Evidently one of the Islands at the south of Novaya Zemlya.] where we found fresh water.

Sunday, (26) much wind blowing we rode still.

Munday (27) I went on shoare and tooke the latitude, which was 70 degrees 42 minutes: the variation of the compasse was 7 degrees and a halfe from the North to the West.

Tuesday (28) we plyed to the Westwards alongst the shoare, the wind being at Northwest, and as I was about to come to anker, we saw a sayle comming about the point, whereunder we thought to haue ankered. [Sidenote: The relation of Loshak.] Then I sent a skiffe aboord of him, and at their coming aboord they tooke acquaintance of them and the chiefe man said hee had bene in our company in the riuer Cola, and also declared unto them that we were past the way which should bring vs to the Ob. This land, sayd he, is called Noua Zembla, that is to say, the New land: and then he came aboord himselfe with his skiffe, and at his comming aboord he told me the like, and sayd further, that in this Noua Zembla is the highest mountaine in the worlde, as he thought, [Footnote: The highest mountains in Novaya Zemlya hardly exceed 3500 feet.] and that Camen Boldshay, which is on the maine of Pechora, is not to be compared to this mountaine, but I saw it not: he made me also certaine demonstrations of the way to the Ob, and seemed to make haste on his owne way, being very lothe to tarie, because the yeere was farre past, and his neighbour had fet Pechora, and not he: so I gaue him a steele glasse, two pewter spoones, and a paire of veluet sheathed knives: and then he seemed somewhat the more willing to tary, and shewed me as much as he knew for our purpose: he also gaue me 17 wilde geese, and shewed me that foure of their lodias were driuen perforce from Caninoze to this Noua Zembla. This mans name was Loshak.

Wednesday, (29) as we plied to the Eastwards, we espied another saile, which was one of this Loshaks company, and we bare roome, and spake with him, who in like sort tolde vs of the Ob, as the other had done.

Thursday, (30) we plied to the Eastwards, the winde being at Eastnortheast.

Friday, (31) the gale of winde began to increase, and came Westerly withall, so that by a Northwest sunne we were at an anker among the Islands of Vaigats, where we saw two small lodias, the one of them came aboard of vs, and presented me with a great loafe of bread: and they told me that they were all of Colmogro, except one man that dwelt at Pechora, who seemed to be the chiefest among them in killing of the Morse.

There were some of their company on shoare, which did chase a white beare ouer the high clifs into the water, which beare the lodia that was aboard of vs killed in our sight.

This day there was a great gale of wind at North, and we saw so much ice driuing a seaboord, that it was then no going to sea.

August.

Saturday (1) I went ashore, and there I saw three morses that they had killed: they held one tooth of a Morse, which was not great, at a roble, and one white beare skin at three robles and two robles: they further tolde me, that there were people called Samoeds on the great Island, and that they would not abide them nor vs, who haue no houses, but only couerings made of Deere skins, set ouer them with stakes: they are men expert in shooting, [Footnote: That the Samoyeds were archers is shewn by old drawings, one of which I reproduce from Linschoten. Now the bow has completely gone out of use, for Nordenskiöld did not see a single archer. Wretched old flint firelocks are, however, common.] and have great plenty of Deere.

This night there fell a cruell storme, the wind being at West.

Sunday (2) we had very much winde, with plenty of snow, and we rode with two ankers a head.

[Illustration: Samoiedarum, trahis a rangiferis protractis insidentium. Nec non Idolorum ab ijsdem cultorum effigies. SAMOYED SLEIGH AND IDOLS. After an old Dutch engraving.]

Munday (3) we weyed and went roome with another Island, which was fiue leagues Eastnortheast from vs, and there I met againe with Loshak, and went on shore with him, and hee brought me to a heap of the Samoeds idols, which were in number aboue 300, the worst and the most vnartificiall worke that euer I saw: the eyes and mouthes of sundrie of them were bloodie, they had the shape of men, women and children, very grosly wrought, and that which they had made for other parts, was also sprinckled with blood. Some of their idols were an old sticke with two or three notches, mode with a knife in it. [Footnote: The accompanying *fac-simile* of a quaint old engraving of a Samoyed sleigh and idols gives an excellent idea of both.] I saw much of the footing of the sayd Samoeds, and of the sleds that they ride in. There was one of their sleds broken, and lay by the heape of idols, and there I saw a deers skinne which the foules had spoyled: and before certaine of their idols blocks were made as high as their mouthes, being all bloody, I thought that to be the table whereon they offered their sacrifice: I saw also the instruments, whereupon they had roasted flesh, and as farre as I could perceiue, they make their fire directly under the spit.

Loshak being there present tolde me that these Samoeds were not so hurtful as they of Ob are, and that they haue no houses, as indeede I saw none, but onely tents made of Deers skins, which they vnderproppe with stakes and poles: their boates are made of Deers skins, and when they come on shoare they cary their boates with them upon their backes: for their cariages they haue no other beastes to serue them, but Deere onely. As for bread and corne they haue none, except the Russes bring it to them: their knowledge is very base, for they know no letter. [Footnote: This is one of the oldest accounts of the Samoyeds we possess. Giles Fletcher, who in 1588 was Queen Elizabeth's Ambassador to the Czar, writes, in his accounts of Russia, of the Samoyeds in the following way:—

"The *Samoyt* hath his name (as the *Russe* saith) of eating himselfe: as if in times past they lived as the *Cannibals*, eating one another. Which they make more probable, because at this time they eate all kind of raw flesh, whatsoeuer it bee, euen the very carrion that lyeth in the ditch. But as the *Samoits* themselves will say, they were called *Samoit*, that is, *of themselves*, as though they were *Indigenæ*, or people bred upon that very soyle that never changed their seate from one place to another, as most Nations have done.

They are clad in Seale-skinnes, with the hayrie side outwards downe as low as the knees, with their Breeches and Netherstocks of the same, both men and women. They are all Blacke hayred, naturally beardless. And therefore the Men are hardly discerned from the Women by their lookes: saue that the Women wear a locke of hayre down along both their eares." (*Treatise of Russia and the adjoining Regions*, written by Doctor Giles Fletcher, Lord Ambassador from the late Queen, Everglorious Elizabeth, to Theodore, then Emperor of Russia, A.D. 1588. *Purchas*, iii. p. 413.)

In nearly the same way the Samoyeds are described by G. De Veer, in his account of Barents's Second Voyage in 1595.

Serebrenikoff, according to Nordensköld, maintains that *Samodin* should be written instead of *Samoyed*. For *Samoyed* means "self eater," while *Samodin* denotes an "individual," "one who cannot be mistaken for another," and, as the Samoyeds were never cannibals, Serebrenikoff gives a preference to the latter name, which is used by the Russians at Chabarova, and appears to be a literal translation of the name which the Samoyeds give themselves. Nordenskiöld, however, considers it probable that the old tradition of man-eaters (*androphagi*), living in the north, which originated with Herodotus, and was afterwards universally adopted in the geographical literature of the Middle Ages, reappears in Russianised form in the name *Samoyed*. With all due respect for Nordenskiöld, I am inclined to agree with Serebrenikoff. In the account of the journey which the Italian minorite, Joannes de Piano Carpini, undertook in High Asia in 1245-47, an extraordinary account of the Samoyeds and neighbouring tribes is given. (See Vol. II. of these Collections, pp. 28 and 95).—I give a very curious engraving of Samoyeds from Schleissing.—Nordenskiöld inserts, in his *Voyage of the Vega*, the following interesting communication from Professor Ahlquist, of Helsingfors:—.

"The Samoyeds are reckoned, along with the Tungoose, the Mongolian, the Turkish and the Finnish-Ugrian races, to belong to the so-called Altaic or Ural-Altaic stem. What is mainly characteristic of this stem, is that all the languages occurring within it belong to the so-called agglutinating type. For in these languages the relations of ideas are expressed exclusively by terminations or suffixes—inflections, prefixes and prepositions, as expressive of relations, being completely unknown to them. Other peculiarities characteristic of the Altaic languages are the vocal harmony occurring in many of them, the inability to have more than one consonant in the beginning of a word, and the expression of the plural by a peculiar affix, the case terminations being the same in the plural as in the singular. The affinity between the different branches of the Altaic stem is thus founded mainly on analogy or resemblance in the construction of the languages, while the different tongues in the material of language (both in the words themselves and in the expression of relations) show a very limited affinity or none at all. The circumstance that the Samoyeds for the present have as their nearest neighbours several Finnish-Ugrian races (Lapps, Syrjaeni, Ostjaks, and Voguls), and that these to a great extent carry on the same modes of life as themselves, has led some authors to assume a close affinity between the Samoyeds and the Fins and the Finnish races in general. The speech of the two neighbouring tribes, however, affords no ground for such a supposition. Even the language of the Ostjak, which is the most closely related to that of the Samoyeds, is separated heaven-wide from it and has nothing in common with it, except a small number of borrowed words (chiefly names of articles from the Polar nomad's life), which the Ostjak has taken from the language of his northern neighbour. With respect to their language, however, the Samoyeds are said to stand at a like distance from the other branches of the stem in question. To what extent craniology or modern anthropology can more accurately determine the affinity-relationship of the Samoyed to other tribes, is still a question of the future."

At the present day, the Samoyeds dwell in skin tents. They dress principally in reindeer-skins, and the women's holiday-dress is particularly showy. Their boots, also of reindeer-skin, are beautifully and tastefully embroidered. In summer, the men go bare-headed: the women divide their hair into tresses, and use artificial plaits, ornamented with pearls, buttons, &c. Like the man, the woman is small, with coarse black hair, face of a yellow colour, small and sunken eyes, a flat nose, broad cheek-bones, slender legs, and small feet and hands. She competes with the man in dirt. Nordenskiöld places the Samoyeds in the lowest rank of all the Polar races. The women have perfectly equal rights with the men.]

Tuesday (4) we turned for the harborough where Loshaks barke lay, whereas before we road vnder an Island. And there he came aboord of vs and said vnto me: if God sende winde and weather to serue, I will goe to the Ob with you, because the Morses were scant at these Islands of Vaigats, but if he could not get to the riuer of Ob, then he sayd hee would goe to the riuer of Naramzay, where the people were not altogether so sauage as the Samoyds of the Ob are: hee shewed me that they will shoot at all men to the vttermost of their power, that cannot speake their speech.

Wednesday (5) we saw a terrible heape of ice approach neere vnto vs, and therefore wee thought good with al speed possible to depart from thence, and so I returned to the Westwards againe, to the Island where we were the 31. of Iuly.

[Illustration: SAMOYED ARCHERS. After Unschoten.]

[Illustration: SAMOYEDS. From Schleissing's Nou-entdecktes Sieweria, worinnen die Zobeln gefangen werden. Zittan 1693.]

Thursday (6) I went a shoare, and tooke the latitude, which was 70 degrees 25 minutes: and the variation of the compasse was 8 degrees from the North to the West.

Loshak and the two small Lodias of Pechora departed from this Island, while I was on shoare taking the latitude, and went to the Southwards: I maruailed why he departed so suddenly, and went ouer the shoales amongst the Islands where it was impossible for vs to follow them. But after I perceiued them to be weatherwise.

Friday (7) we road still, the winde being at Northnortheast, with a cruel storme. The ice came in so abundantly about vs at both ends of the Island that, we rode vnder, that it was a fearefull sight to behold: the storme continued with snow, raine, and hayle plenty.

Saturday (8) we rode still also, the storme being somewhat abated, but it was altogether misty, that we were not able to see a cables length about vs, the winde being at Northeast and by East.

Sunday (9) at foure of the clocke in the morning we departed from this Island, the winde being at Southeast, and as we were cleere a sea boord the small Islandes and shoales, it came so thick with mistes that we could not see a base shotte from vs. Then we took in all our sailes to make little way.

At a Southeast sunne it waxed cleere, and then we set our sayles, and lay close by the wind to the Southwards alongst the Islands of Vaigats. At a west sunne we tooke in our sayle againe because of the great mist and raine. Wee sounded at this place, and had fiue and twenty fadomes water, and soft black oze, being three leagues from the shoare, the winde being at South and by East, but still misty.

Munday (10) at an East sunne we sounded, and had 40 fadomes, and oze, still misty: at noone wee sounded againe, and had 36 fadome, still misty.

Tuesday (11) at an Eastnortheast sunne we let fall our anker in three and twenty fadome, the mist still continuing.

Wednesday (12) at three of the clocke in the morning the mist brake vp, the wind being at Northeast and by East, and then we saw part of the Islands of Vaigats, which we bare withall, and went Eastsoutheast close by the winde: at a West sunne we were at an anker vnder the Southwest part of the said Vaigats, and then I sent our skiffe to shoare with three men in her, to see if they might speake with any of the Samoeds, but could not: all that day was rainie, but not windie.

Thursday (13) the wind came Westerly, so that we were faine to seeke vs another place to ride in, because the wind came a seaboord land, and although it were misty, yet wee followed the shoare by our lead: and as we brought land in the wind of vs, we let fall our anker. At a West sunne the mist brake up, so that we might see about vs, and then we might perceiue that we were entred into a sound.

This afternoone we tooke in two or three skiffes lading of stones to ballast our shippe withall. It hyeth here four foot water, and floweth by fits, vncertaine to be iudged.

Friday (14) we rode still in the sound, the wind at Southwest, with very much raine, and at the end of the raine it waxed againe mistie.

Saturday (15) there was much wind at West, and much raine, and then againe mistie.

Sunday (16) was very mistie and much winde.

Munday (17) very mistie, the winde at Westnorthwest.

Tuesday (18) was also mistie, except at noone: then the sunne brake out through the mist, so that we had the latitude in 70 degrees 10 minutes: the afternoone was misty againe, the wind being at Westnorthwest.

Wednesday (19) at three of the clocke afternoone the mist brake vp, and the wind came at Eastnortheast, and then we weyed, and went South and by East, vntil seuen of the clocke, eight leagues, thinking to haue had sight of the sandie hilles that are to the Eastwards of the riuer Pechora. At a Northwest sunne we took in our maine saile, because the wind increased, and went with a foresaile Westnorthwest, the wind being at Eastnortheast: at night there grewe so terrible a storme, that we saw not the like, although we had indured many stormes since we came out of England. It was wonderfull that our barke was able to brooke such monstrous and terrible seas, without the great helpe of God, who neuer fayleth them at neede, that put their sure trust in him.

Thursday (20) at a Southsouthwest sunne, thanks be to God, the storme was at the highest, and then the winde began to slake, and came Northerly withall, and then I reckoned the Westermost point of the riuer Pechora to be South of vs 15 leagues. At a Westsouthwest sunne we set our maine sayle, and lay close by the winde, the winde being at Northwest and by North, making but little way, because the billow went so high: at midnight wee cast about, and the shippe caped Northnortheast, making little way.

Friday (21) at noone we had the latitude in 70 degrees 8 minutes, and we sounded, and had 29 fadomes sand, and in maner, stremy ground. At West sunne we cast about to the Westwards, and a little after the wind came vp at West.

Saturday (22) was calme: the latitude this day at noone was 70 degrees and a terce, we sounded heere, and had nine and forty fadomes and oze, which oze signified that we drew towards Noua Zembla.

And thus we being out of al hope to discouer any more to the Eastward this yeere, wee thought it best to returne, and that for three causes.

The first, the continuall Northeast and Northerly winds, which haue more power after a man is past to the eastwards of Caninoze, then in any place that I doe know in these Northerly regions.

Second, because of great and terrible abundance of ice which we saw with our eies, and we doubt greater store abideth in those parts: I aduentured already somewhat too farre in it, but I thanke God for my safe deliuerance from it.

Third, because the nights waxed darke, and the winter began to draw on with his stormes: and therefore I resolued to take the first best wind that God should send, and plie towards the bay of S. Nicholas, and to see if wee might do any good there, if God would permitt it.

This present Saturday we saw very much ice, and were within two or three leagues of it: it shewed vnto vs as though it had beene a firme land as farre as we might see from Northwest off vs to the Eastwards: and this afternoone the Lord sent vs a little gale of wind at South, so that we bare cleere of the Westermost part of it, thanks be to God. And then against night it waxed calme againe, and the winde was at Southwest: we made our way vntill Sunday (23) noone Northwest and by West, and then we had the latitude in 70 degrees and a halfe, the winde at Southwest: there was a billow, so that we could not discerne to take the latitude exactly, but by a reasonable gesse.

Munday (24) there was a pretie gale of wind at South, so that wee went West and by South, the latitude this day at noone was 70 degrees 10 minutes: wee had little winde all day: at a Westnorthwest sunne we sounded, and had 29 fadoms blacke sandie oze, and then we were Northeast 5 leagues from the Northeast part of the Island Colgoieue.

Tuesday (25) the wind all Westerly we plyed to the windwards.

Wednesday (26) the wind was all Westerly, and calme: wee had the latitude this day in 70 degrees 10 minutes, we being within three leagues of the North part of the Island Colgoieue.

Thursday, (27) we went roome about the Westermost part of the Island, seeking where we might finde a place to ride in for a Northwest wind, and could not find none, and then we cast about againe to the seawards, and the winde came at Westsouthwest, and this morning we had plenty of snow.

Friday, (28) the winde being at Southwest and by West, we plied to the windewards.

Saturday (29) the winde being at South we plyed to the Westwards, and at afternoone the mist brake vp, and then we might see the land seuen or eight leagues to the Eastwards of Caninoz: we sounded a little before and had 35 fadoms and oze. And a while after wee sounded againe, and had 19. fadome and sand: then we were within three leagues and a halfe of the shore, and towards night there came downe so much winde, that we were faine to bring our ship a trie, and laide her head to the Westwards.

Sunday, (30) the winde became more calme, and when it waxed verie mystie: At noone wee cast about to the Eastwards, the winde beeing at South, and ranne eight houres on that boorde, and then we cast about and caped West southwest: we sounded and had 32 fathomes, and found oaze like clay.

Munday, (31) we doubled about Caninoze, and came at an anker there, to the intent that we might kill some fish if God permit it, and there we gate a great Nuse, which Nuses were there so plentie, that they would scarcely suffer any other fish to come neere the hookes: the said Nuses caried away sundrie of our hookes and leads.

A little after at a West Sunne, the winde began to blow stormie at West southwest, so that we were faine to wey and forsake our fishing ground, and went close by the winde Southwest, and Southwest and by West, making our way South southwest.

September.

Tuesday (1) at a West Sunne we sounded and had 20. fathoms, and broken Wilkeshels: I reckoned Caninoze to be 24 leagues Northnortheast from vs.

The eleuenth day we arriued at Colmogro, and there we wintered, expecting the approch of the next Summer to proceede farther in our intended discouerie for the Ob: which (by reason of our imploiments to Wardhouse the next spring for the search of some English ships) [Footnote: The fate of the three vessels that were employed on the first English Expedition to the North-East (see p. 29) was equally unfortunate. The *Edward Bonaventure*, commanded, as we have seen, by Chancellor, sailed in 1553 from England to the White Sea, returned to England in 1554, and was on the way plundered by the Dutch (Purchas, iii., p. 250); started again with Chancellor for the Dwina in 1555, and returned the same year to England under John Buckland; accompanied Burrough in 1556 to the Kola Peninsula: went thence to the Dwina to convey to England Chancellor and a Russian Embassy, the vessel, besides, carrying £20,000 worth of goods. It was wrecked in Aberdour Bay, near Aberdeen, on the 20th (10th) November, and Chancellor, his wife, and seven Russians were drowned.—The *Bona Esperanza*, commanded by Willoughby in 1553, carried him and his crew to perish at the mouth of the Varzina. The vessel was recovered, and was to have been used in 1556 to carry to England the Embassy already mentioned. It reached a harbour near Trondhjeim, but after leaving there, was never heard of again.—The *Bona Confidenzia* was also saved after the fatal wintering at the Varzina, and was employed in escorting the Embassy in 1556, but stranded on the Norwegian coast, every soul on board perishing. (See the account of the Russian Embassy to England, pp. 142-3.)—The vessels alluded to by Burrough are the *Edward Bonaventure* and *Bona Confidenzia*.] was not accordingly performed.

* * * * *

Certaine notes vnperfectly written by Richard Iohnson seruant to Master
  Richard Chancelour, which was in the discouerie of Vaigatz and Noua
  Zembla, with Steuen Burrowe in the Serchthrift 1556. and afterwarde
among
  the Samoedes, whose deuilish rites hee describeth.

First, after we departed out of England we fell with Norway, and on that coste lieth Northbern or Northbergen, and this people are vnder the King of Denmarke: But they differ in their speech from the Danes, for they speake Norsh. And North of Northbern lie the Isles of Roste and Lofoot, and these Islands pertaine vnto Finmarke, and they keepe the laws and speake the language of the Islanders. And at the Eastermost part of that land is a castle which is called the Wardhouse, and the King of Denmarke doeth fortifie it with men of warre: and the Russes may not goe to the Westward of that castle. And East Southeast from that castle is a lande called Lappia: in which lande be two maner of people, that is to say, the Lappians and the Scrickfinnes, which Scrickfinnes are a wilde people which neither know God, nor yet good order: and these people liue in tents made of Deares skinnes: and they haue no certaine habitations, but continue in heards and companies by one hundred and two hundreds. And they are a people of small stature, and are clothed in Deares skinnes and drinke nothing but water, and eate no bread but flesh all raw. And the Lappians bee a people adioyning to them and be much like to them in al conditions: but the Emperour of Russia hath of late ouercome manie of them, and they are in subiection to him. And this people will say that they beleeue in the Russes God. And they liue in tents as the other doe. And Southeast and by

South from Lappia lyeth a prouince called Corelia, and these people are called Kerilli. And South southeast from Corelia lyeth a countrey called Nouogardia. And these three nations are vnder the Emperour of Russia, and the Russes keepe the Lawe of the Greekes in their Churches, and write somewhat like as the Greekes write, and they speake their owne language, and they abhorre the Latine tongue, neither haue they to doe with the Pope of Rome, and they holde it not good to worshippe any carued Image, yet they will worshippe paynted Images on tables or boords. And in Russia their Churches, steeples, and houses are all of wood: and their shippes that they haue are sowed with withes and haue no nayles. The Kerilles, Russians or Moscouians bee much alike in all conditions. And South from the Moscouians lye the Tartarians, which bee Mahumetans, and liue in tentes and wagons, and keepe in heardes and companies: and they holde it not good to abide long in one place, for they will say, when they will curse any of their children, I woulde thou mightest tary so long in a place that thou mightest smell thine owne dung, as the Christians doe: and this is the greatest curse that they haue. And East Northeast of Russia lieth Lampas, which is a place where the Russes, Tartars, and Samoeds meete twise a yeere, and make the faire to barter wares for wares. And Northeast from Lampas lieth the countrey of the Samoeds, which be about the riuer of Pechere, and these Samoeds bee in subiection to the Emperour of Russia, and they lie in tentes made of Deere skinnes, and they vse much witchcraft, and shoot well in bowes. And Northeast from the river Pechere [Footnote: Or, Pechora.] lieth Vaygatz, and there are the wilde Samoeds which will not suffer the Russes to land out of the Sea, but they will kill them and eate them, as wee are tolde by the Russes: and they liue in heards, and haue all their carriages with deere, for they haue no horses. Beyond Vaygatz lyeth a lande called Noua Zembla, which is a great lande, but wee sawe no people, and there we had Foule inough, and there wee sawe white Foxes and white Beares And the sayde Samoeds which are about the bankes of Pechere, which are in subiection to the Emperour of Russia, when they will remoue from one place to another, then they will make sacrifices in manner following. Euerie kinred doeth sacrifice in their owne tent, and hee that is most auncient is their Priest. And first the Priest doth beginne to play vpon a thing like to a great sieue, with a skinne on the one ende like a drumme: and the sticke that he playeth with is about a spannne long, and one ende is round like a ball, couered with the skinne of an Harte. Also the Priest hath vpon his head a thing of white like a garlande, and his face is couered with a piece of a shirt of maile, with manie small ribbes, and teeth of fishes, and wilde beastes hanging on the same maile. Then he singeth as wee vse heere in Englande to hallow, whope, or showte at houndes, and the rest of the company answere him with this Owtis, Igha, Igha, Igha, and then the Priest replieth againe, with his voyces. And they answere him with the selfsame wordes so manie times, that in the ende he becommeth as it were madde, and falling downe as hee were dead, hauing nothing on him but a shirt, lying vpon his backe I might perceiue him to breathe. I asked them why hee lay so, and they answered mee, Now doeth our God tell him what wee shall doe, and whither we shall goe. And when he had lyen still a little while, they cried thus three times together, Oghao, Oghao, Oghao, and as they vse these three calles, hee riseth with his head and lieth downe againe, and then hee rose vp and sang with like voyces as hee did before: and his audience answered him, Igha, Igha, Igha. Then hee commaunded them to kill fiue Olens or great Deere, and continued singing still both hee and they as before. Then hee tooke a sworde of a cubite and a spanne long, (I did not mete it my selfe) and put it into his bellie halfeway and sometime lesse, but no wounde was to bee seene, (they continuing in their sweete song still). Then he put the sworde into the fire till it was warme, and so thrust it into the slitte of his shirte and thrust it through his bodie, as I thought, in at his nauill and out at his fundament: the poynt beeing out of his shirt behind, I layde my finger vpon it, then hee pulled out the sworde and sate downe. This beeing done, they set a kettle of water ouer the fire to heate, and when the water doeth seethe, the Priest beginneth to sing againe they answering him, for so long as the water was in heating, they sate and sang not. Then they made a thing being foure square, and in height and squarenesse of a chaire, and couered with a gown very close the forepart thereof, for the hinder part stood to the tents side. Their tents are rounde and are called Chome in their language. The water still seething on the fire, and this square seate being ready, the Priest put off his shirt, and the thing like a garland which was on his head, with those things which couered his face, and he had on yet all this while a paire of hosen of deeres skins with the haire on, which came vp to his buttocks. So he went into the square seate, and sate down like a tailour and sang with a strong voyce or hallowing. Then they tooke a small line made of deeres skinnes of four fathoms long, and with a smal knotte the Priest made it fast about his necke, and vnder his left arme, and gaue it vnto two men standing on both sides of him, which held the ends together. Then the kettle of hote water was set before him in the square seat, al this time the square seat was not couered, and then it was couered with a gown of broad cloth without lining, such as the Russes do weare. Then the 2. men which did hold the ends of the line stil standing there, began to draw, and drew til they had drawn the ends of the line stiffe and together, and then I hearde a thing fall into the kettle of water which was before him in the tent. Thereupon I asked them that sate by me what it was that fell into the water that stoode before him. And they answered me, that it was his head, his shoulder and left arme, which the line had cut off, I meane the knot which I sawe afterwarde drawen hard together. Then I rose vp and would haue looked whether it were so or not, but they laid hold on me, and said, that if they should see him with their bodily eyes, they shoulde liue no longer. And the most part of them can speake the Russe tongue to be vnderstood: and they tooke me to be a Russian. Then they beganne to hallow with these wordes. Oghaoo, Oghaoo, Oghaoo, many times together. And as they were thus singing and out calling, I sawe a thing like a finger of a man two times together thrust through the gowne from the Priest. I asked them that sate next to me what it was that I sawe, and they saide, not his finger; for he was yet dead: and that which I saw appeare through the gowne was a beast, but what beast they knew not nor would not tell. And I looked vpon the gowne, and there was no hole to bee seene; and then at the last the Priest lifted vp his head with his shoulder and arme, and all his bodie, and came forth to the fire. Thus farre of their seruice which I sawe during the space of certaine houres: but how they doe worship their Idols that I saw not: for they put vp their stuffe for to remoue from that place where they lay. And I went to him that serued the Priest, and asked him what their God saide to him when he lay as dead. Hee answered, that his owne people doeth not know: neither is it for them to know, for they must doe as he commanded. This I saw the fift day of Ianuarie in the yere of our Lord 1556, after the English account.

* * * * *

A discourse of the honourable receiuing into England of the first Ambassador from the Emperor of Russia, in the yeere of Christ 1556. and in the third yeere of the raigne of Queene Marie, seruing for the third voyage to Moscouie. Registred by Master Iohn Incent Protonotarie.

It is here recorded by writing and autenticall testimonie, partly for memorie of things done, and partly for the veritie to be knowen to posteritie in time to come, that whereas the most high and mightie Iuan Vasiliuich Emperour of all Russia, great Duke of Volodemer, Moscouia and Nouogrode, Emperor of Cassan, and of Astrachan, Lord of Pleskie, and great Duke of Smolenskie, Tuerskie, Yowgoriskie, Permskie, Viatskie, Bolgarskie and Sibierskie, Emperour and great Duke of many others, as Nouogrode in the nether countries, Chernigoskie, Rezanskie, Polodskie, Rezewskie, Bielskie, Rostoskie, Yeraslaueskie, Bealozarskie, Oudarskie, Obdorskie, Condenskie, and manie other countries, and lord ouer all those partes, in the yeere of our Lord God, folowing the account of the Latin church, 1556. sent by the sea from the port of S. Nicholas in Russia, his right honorable ambassador sirnamed Osep Napea, [Footnote: Ossip Gregorjevitsch Nepeja.] his high officer in the towne and countrey of Vologda, to the most famous and excellent princes, Philip and Mary by the grace of God king and Queene of England, Spaine, France and Ireland, defenders of the faith, Archdukes of Austria, dukes of Burgundie, Millaine, and Brabant, counties of Haspurge, Flanders and Tyroll, his ambassador and Orator with certaine letters tenderly conceiued, together with certaine presents and gifts mentioned in the foot of this memorial, as a manifest argument and token of a mutual amity and friendship to be made and continued betweene their maiesties and subiects respectiuely, for the commoditie and benefit of both the realmes and people: which Orator was the 20. day of Iuly imbarked and shipped in, and vpon a good English ship named the Edward Bonauenture, belonging to the Gouernour, Consuls and company of English marchants. Richard Chancelor being grand Pilot, and Iohn Buckland master of the said ship. In which was laden at the aduenture of the foresaid Ambassador and marchants at seueral accounts, goods and merchandizes, viz. in waxe, trane oyle, tallow, furres, felts, yarne and such like, to the summe of 20000. li. sterling, together with 16. Russies attendant vpon the person of the said Ambassador. [Sidenote: Foure ships.] Ouer and aboue ten other Russies shipped within the said Bay of S. Nicholas, in one other good ship to the said company also belonging called the Bona Speranza, with goods of the said Orators and marchants to the value of 6000. lib. sterling, as by the inuoices and letters of lading of the said seueral ships (whereunto relation is to be had) particularly appeareth. Which good ships comming in good order into the seas, and trauersing the same in their iourney towards the coast of England, were by the contrary winds and extreme tempests of weather seuered the one from the other, that is to say, the saide Bona Speranza with two other English ships also appertaining to the saide company, the one sirnamed the Philip and Mary, the other the Confidentia, were driuen on the coast of Norway, into Drenton water, where the saide Confidentia was seene to perish on a Rocke, and the other, videlicet, the Bona Speranza, with her whole company, being to the number of foure and twentie persons seemed to winter there, whereof no certaintie at this present day is knowen. The third, videlicet, the Philip and Mary arriued in the Thames nigh London the eighteenth day of April, in the yeere of our Lord one thousand fiue hundred fiftie and seuen. [Sidenote: The Edward Bonauenture arriued in Scotland, in the Bay of Pettuslego, November 7. 1556.] The Edward Bonauenture trauersing the seas foure moneths, finally the tenth day of Nouember of the aforesaide yeere of our Lorde one thousand fiue hundred fiftie and sixe, arriued within the Scottish coast in a Bay named Pettislego, where by outragious tempests, and extreme stormes, the said ship being beaten from her ground tackles, was driuen vpon the rockes on shoare, where she brake and split in pieces in such sort, as the grand Pilot vsing all carefulnesse for the safetie of the bodie of the sayde Ambassadour and his trayne, taking the boat of the said ship, trusting to attaine the shore, and so to save and preserue the bodie, [Sidenote: Richard Chancelor drowned.] and seuen of the companie or attendants of the saide Ambassadour, the same boat by rigorous waues of the seas, was by darke night ouerwhelmed and drowned, wherein perished not only the bodie of the said grand Pilot, with seuen Russes, but also diuers of the Mariners of the sayd ship: the noble personage of the saide Ambassadour with a fewe others (by Gods preseruation and speciall fauour) onely with much difficultie saued. In which shipwracke not onely the saide shippe was broken, but also the whole masse and bodie of the goods laden in her, was by the rude and rauenous people of the Countrey thereunto adioyning, rifled, spoyled and caried away, to the manifest losse and vtter destruction of all the lading of the said ship, and together with the ship apparell, ordinance and furniture belonging to the companie, in value of one thousand pounds, of all which was not restored toward the costs and charges to the summe of fiue hundred pounds sterling.

As soone as by letters addressed to the saide companie, and in London delivered the sixt of December last past, it was to them certainely knowen of the losse of their Pilote, men, goods and ship, the same merchants with all celeritie and expedition, obtained not onely the Queenes maiesties most gracious and fauourable letters to the Ladie Dowager and lordes of the Councell of Scotland for the gentle comfortment and entertainment of the saide Ambassadour, his traine and companie, with preseruation and restitution of his goods, as in such miserable cases, to Christian pitie, princely honour and meere Iustice appertaineth, but also addressed two Gentlemen of good learning, grauitie and estimation, videlicet, Master Lawrence Hussie Doctor of the Ciuill Lawe, and George Gilpin with money and other requisites into the Realme of Scotland, to comfort, ayde, assist, and relieue him and his there, and also to conduct the Ambassadour into England, sending with them by poste a Talmach or Speachman for the better furniture of the seruice of the sayde Ambassadour, trusting thereby to haue the more ample and speedie redresse of restitution: which personages vsing diligence, arriued at Edenborough (where the Queenes court was) the three and twentieth day of the saide moneth of December, who first visiting the saide Ambassadour, declaring the causes of their comming and Commission, shewing the letters addressed in his fauour, the order giuen them for his solace and furniture of all such things as hee would haue, together with their daily and readie seruice to attend vpon his person and affaires, repaired consequently vnto the Dowager Queene, deliuering the letters. Whereupon they receiued gentle answeres, with hope and comfort of speedie restitution of the goods, apparell, iewels, and letters: for the more apparance whereof, the Queene sent first certaine Commissioners with an Harold of armes to Pettislego, the place of the Shipwracke, commaunding by Proclamation and other Edictes, all such persons (no degree excepted) as had any part of such goods as were spoyled and taken out or from the ship to bring them in, and to restore the same with such further order as her grace by aduise of her Council thought expedient: by reason whereof not without great labours, paines and charges (after long time) diuers small parcels of Waxe, and other small trifling things of no value, were by the poorer sort of the Scottes brought to the Commissioners, but the Iewels, rich apparell, presents, gold, siluer, costly furres, and such like, were conueyed away, concealed and vtterly embezelled. Whereupon, the Queene at the request of the said Ambassadour, caused diuers persons to the number of 180. or moe, to be called personally before her princely presence, to answer to the said spoile, and really to exhibit and bring in all such things as were spoiled and violently taken, and caried out of the same, whereof not onely good testimonie by writing was shewed, but also the things themselues found in the hands of the Scottish subiects, who by subtile and craftie dealings, by conniuence of the commissioners, so vsed or rather abused themselues towards the same Orator & his attendants, that no effectuall restitution was made: but he fatigated with daily attendance and charges, the 14. day of February next ensuing, distrusting any reall and effectual rendring of the saide goods and marchandizes and other the premisses, vpon leaue obtained of the saide Queene, departed towards England, hauing attending vpon him the said two English Gentlemen and others (leauing neuerthelesse in Scotland three Englishmen to pursue the deliuerie of such things as were collected to haue bene sent by ship to him in England: which being in Aprill next, and not before imbarked for London, was not at this present day here arriued) came the 18. day of Februarie to Barwike within the dominion and realme of England, where he was by the Queenes maiesties letters and commandement honourably receiued, vsed and interteined by the right honourable lord Wharton, lord Warden of the East marches, with goodly conducting from place to place, as the dayly iourneys done ordinarily did lie, in such order, maner and forme, as to a personage of such estate appertaineth. He prosecuting his voyage vntil the 27. of Februarie [Footnote: 1557.] approched to the citie of London within twelue English miles, where he was receiued with fourscore merchants with chaines of gold and goodly apparell, as wel in order of men seruants in one vniforme liuerie, as also in and vpon good horses and geldings, who conducting him to a marchants house foure miles from London, receiued there a quantitie of gold, veluet and silke, with all furniture thereunto requisite, wherewith he made him a riding garment, reposing himselfe that night. The next day being Saturday and the last day of Februarie, he was by the merchants aduenturing for Russia, to the number of one hundred and fortie persons, and so many or more seruants in one liuerie, as abouesaid, conducted towards the citie of London, where by the way he had not onely the hunting of the Foxe and such like sport shewed him, but also by the Queenes maiesties commandement was receiued and embraced by the right honourable Viscount Montague, sent by her grace for his entertainment: he being accompanied with diuers lustie knights, esquiers, gentlemen and yeomen to the number of three hundred horses led him to the North partes of the Citie of London, where by foure notable merchants richly apparelled was presented to him a right faire and large gelding richly trapped, together with a footcloth of Orient crimson veluet, enriched with gold laces, all furnished in most glorious fashion, of the present, and gift of the sayde merchants: where vpon the Ambassadour at instant desire mounted, riding on the way towards Smithfield barres, the first limites of the liberties of the Citie of London. The Lord Maior accompanied with all the Aldermen in their skarlet did receiue him, and so riding through the Citie of London in the middle, betweene the Lord Maior and Viscount Montague, a great number of merchants and notable personages riding before, and a large troupe of seruants and apprentises following, was conducted through the Citie of London (with great admiration and plausibilitie of the people running plentifully on all sides, and replenishing all streets in such sort as no man without difficultie might passe) into his lodging situate in Fant church streete, where were prouided for him two chambers richly hanged and decked, ouer and aboue the gallant furniture of the whole house, together with an ample and rich cupboord of plate of all sortes, to furnish and serue him at all meales, and other seruices during his abode in London, which was, as is vnderwritten, vntil the third day of May: during which time daily diuers Aldermen and the grauest personages of the said companie did visite him, prouiding all kind of victuals for his table and his seruants, with al sorts of Officers to attend vpon him in good sort and condition, as to such an ambassadour of honour doeth and ought to appertaine.

It is also to be remembred that at his first entrance into his chamber, there was presented vnto him on the Queenes Maiesties behalfe for a gift and present, and his better furniture in apparel, one rich piece of cloth of tissue, a piece of cloth of golde, another piece of cloth of golde raised with crimosin veluet, a piece of crimosin veluet in graine, a piece of purple veluet, a piece of Damaske purpled, a piece of crimosin damaske, which he most thankfully accepted. In this beautifull lodging refreshing and preparing himselfe and his traine with things requisite he abode, expecting the kings maiesties repaire out of Flanders into England, whose highnesse arriuing the one and twentie of March, the same Ambassadour the fiue and twentieth of March being the Annunciation of our Ladie (the day tweluemoneth he took his leaue from the Emperour his master) was most honourably brought to the King and Queenes maiesties court at Westminster, where accompanied first with the said Viscount and other notable personages, and the merchants, hee arriuing at Westminster bridge, was there receiued with six lords, conducted into a stately chamber, where by the lords, Chancellor, Treasurer, Priuie seale, Admirall, bishop of Elie, and other Counsellers, hee was visited and saluted: and consequently was brought vnto the Kings and Queenes maiesties presence, sitting vnder a stately cloth of honour, the chamber most richly decked and furnished, and most honourably presented. Where, after that hee had deliuered his letters, made his Oration, giuen two timber of Sables, and the report of the same made both in English and Spanish, in most louing maner embraced, was with much honour and high entertainment, in sight of a great confluence of people, Lordes and Ladies eftsoones remitted by water to his former lodging, to the which, within two dayes after by the assignement of the King and Queenes maiesties, repaired and conferred with him secretly two graue Counsellers, that is, the lord Bishop of Elie, and Sir William Peter Knight, chiefe Secretary to their Highnesse, who after diuers secret talkes and conferences, reported to their highnesse their proceedings, the grauitie, wisedome, and stately behauior of the sayd Ambassadour, in such sort as was much to their maiesties contentations.

Finally concluding vpon such treaties and articles of amitie, as the letters of the Kings and Queenes maiesties most graciously vnder the greate seale of England to him by the sayd counsellers deliuered, doth appeare.

The three and twentieth of April, being the feast of S. George, wherein was celebrated the solemnitie of the Noble order of the Garter at Westminster, the same lord ambassadour was eftsoones required to haue audience: and therefore conducted from the sayd lodging to the court by the right Noble the lords Talbot and Lumley to their maiesties presence: where, after his Oration made, and thanks both giuen and receiued, hee most honourably tooke his leaue with commendations to the Emperour. Which being done, he was with special honour led into the chappell, where before the Kings and Queens maiesties, in the sight of the whole Order of the Garter, was prepared for him a stately seate, wherein he accompanied with the Duke of Norfolke, the lords last aboue mentioned, and many other honourable personages, was present at the whole seruice, in ceremonies which were to him most acceptable: the diuine seruice ended, he eftsoones was remitted and reduced to his barge, and so repaired to his lodging, in like order and gratulation of the people vniuersally as before.

The time of the yeere hasting the profection and departure of the Ambassador, the merchants hauing prepared foure goodly and well trimmed shippes laden with all kinds of merchandises apt for Russia, the same Ambassadour making prouision for such things as him pleased, the same ships in good order valed downe the Riuer of Thames, from London to Grauesend, where the same Ambassadour with his traine and furniture was imbarked towards his voyage homeward, which God prosper in all felicitie.

It is also to be remembred, that during the whole abode of the sayd Ambassadour in England, the Agents of the sayde marchants did not onely prosecute and pursue the matter of restitution in Scotland, and caused such things to be laden in an English shippe hired purposely to conuey the Ambassadours goods to London, there to be deliuered to him, but also during his abode in London, did both inuite him to the Maior, and diuers worshipfull mens houses, feasting and banquetting him right friendly, shewing vnto him the most notable and commendable sights of London, as the kings palace and house, the Churches of Westminster and Powles, the Tower and Guild hall of London, and such like memorable spectacles. And also the said 29. day of April, the said merchants assembling themselues together in the house of the Drapers hal of London, exhibited and gaue vnto the said Ambassador, a notable supper garnished with musicke, Enterludes and bankets: in the which a cup of wine being drunke to him in the name and lieu of the whole companie, it was signified to him that the whole company with most liberall and friendly hearts, did frankly giue to him and his all maner of costs and charges in victuals riding from Scotland to London during his abode there, and vntill setting of saile aboord the ship, and requesting him to accept the same in good part as a testimonie and witnes of their good hearts, zeale and tendernesse towards him and his countrey.

It is to be considered that of the Bona Speranza no word nor knowledge was had at this present day, nor yet of the arriual of the ships or goods from Scotland.

The third day of May the Ambassadour departed from London to Grauesend, accompanied by diuers Aldermen and merchants, who in good gard set him aboord the noble shippe, the Primrose Admirall to the Fleete, where leaue was taken on both sides and parts, after many imbracements and diuers farewels not without expressing of teares.

[Sidenote: The King and Queens second letters to the Emperour of Russia.] Memorandum, that the first day of May the Councillers, videlicet, the Bishop of Elye, and Sir William Peter on the behalfe of the Kings and Queens Maiesties repairing to the lorde Ambassadour did not onely deliuer vnto him their highness letters of recommendations vnder the great seale of England to the Emperour, very tenderly and friendly written, but also on their Maiesties behalf gaue and deliuered certaine notable presents to the Emperours person, and also gifts for the lord Ambassadours proper vse and behoof, as by the particulars vnder written appeareth, with such further good wordes and commendations, as the more friendly haue not bin heard, whereby it appeareth how well affected their honours be to haue and continue amitie and traffique betweene their honours and their subiects: which thing as the kings and Queenes maiesties haue shewed of their princely munificences and liberalities, so haue likewise the merchants and fellowship of the Aduenturers, for and to Russia, manifested to the world their good willes, mindes and zeales borne to this new commensed voyage, as by the discourse aboue mentioned, and other the notable actes ouer long to be recited in this present memoriall, doeth and may most clearely appeare, the like whereof is not in any president or historie to bee shewed.

Forasmuch as it may bee doubted how the ship named the Edward Bonauenture suffered shipwracke, what became of the goods, howe much they were spoiled and deteined, how little restored, what charges and expenses ensued, what personages were drowned, how the rest of the ships either arriued or perished, or howe the disposition of almightie God hath wrought his pleasure in them, how the same ambassadour hath bene after the miserable case of shipwracke in Scotland vnreuerently abused, and consequently into England receiued and conducted, there intertained, vsed, honoured, and finally in good safetie towards his returne, and repaire furnished, and with much liberalitie and franke handling friendly dismissed, to the intent that the trueth of the premisses may be to the most mightie Emperour of Russia sincerely signified in eschewment of all events and misfortunes that may chance in this voyage (which God defend) to the Ambassadours person, traine, and goods, this present memoriall is written, and autentikely made, and by the sayde Ambassadour his seruants, whose names be vnderwritten, and traine in presence of the Notarie, and witnesses vndernamed, recognized, and acknowledged. Giuen the day, moneth, and yeere vnderwritten, of which instrument into euery of the sayde Shippes one testimoniall is deliuered, and the first remaineth with the sayde Companie in London.

Giftes sent the King and Queenes Maiesties of England by the Emperour of
  Russia, by the report of the Ambassadour, and spoyled by the Scots after
  the Shipwracke.

1 First, sixe timber of Sables rich in colour and haire.
2 Item, twentie entire Sables exceeding beautifull with teeth, eares and
    clawes.
3 Item, foure living Sables with chaines and collars.
4 Item, thirtie Lusarnes large and beautifull.
5 Item, sixe large and great skinnes very rich and rare, worne onely by
    the Emperour for worthinesse.
6 Item, a large and faire white Ierfawcon [Footnote: Gerfalcon] for the
    wild Swanne, Crane, Goose, and other great Fowles, together with a
    drumme of siluer, the hoopes gilt, vsed for a lure to call the sayd
    Hawke.

Giftes sent to the Emperour of Russia by the King and Queenes Maiesties of
England.

1 First, two rich pieces of cloth of Tissue. 2 Item, one fine piece of Scarlet 3 Item, one fine Violet in graine. 4 Item, one fine Azur cloth. 5 Item, a notable paire of Brigandines with a Murrian couered with crimson veluet and gilt nailes. 6 Item, a male and Female Lions.

Giftes giuen to the Ambassadour at his departure, ouer and aboue such as were deliuered vnto him at his first arriual.

1 First, a chaine of golde of one hundred pound. 2 Item, a large Bason and Euer, siluer and gilt. 3 item, a paire of pottle pots gilt. 4 Item, a paire of flaggons gilt.

The names of all such Russies as, were attendant vpon the Ambassadour, at and before his departure out of England.

Isaak Fwesscheneke.
Demetre.
Gorbolones.
Symonde.
Yeroffia.
Stephen.
Lowca.
Andria.
Foma.

Memorandum, the day and yeere of our Lord aboue mentioned, in the house of the worshipfull Iohn Dimmocke Citizen and Draper of London, situate within the famous Citie of London in the Realme of England, the abouenamed honourable Osep Gregorywich Napea, Ambassadour and Orator aboue mentioned, personally constituted and present, hauing declared vnto him by the mouth of the right worshipfull master Anthony Hussie Esquire, the effect of the causes and contents, of, and in this booke, at the interpretation of Robert Best his interpreter sworne, recognized, and knowledged in presence of me the Notarie and personages vnderwritten, the contents of this booke to be true, as well for his owne person as for his seruants aboue named, which did not subscribe their names as is aboue mentioned, but onely recognized the same. In witness whereof, I Iohn Incent, Notary Publike, at the request of the said master Anthonie Hussie, and other of the Marchants haue to these presents vnderwritten set my accustomed signe, with the Subscription of my name, the day and yeere aboue written, being present the right Worshipfull,

Andrew Iudde, Knight.
George Barne, " and Alderman of London.
William Chester " "
Rafe Greeneaway, "
Iohn Mersh Esquier.
Iohn Dimmock.
Blase Sanders.
Hubert Hussie, and
Robert Best aboue mentioned.

* * * * *

The voyage of the foresaid M. Stephen Burrough, An. 1557. from Colmogro to Wardhouse, which was sent to seeke the Bona Esperanza, the Bona Confidentia, and the Philip and Mary, which were not heard of the yeere before. [Footnote: This voyage of Burrough's, undertaken at his own instance, to the coast of Russian Lapland, has attracted little notice: we learn from it, however, that the Dutch, even at this time, carried on an extensive trade with Russian Lapland.]

May.

Vpon Sunday the 23 of May, I departed with the Searchthrift from Colmogro, the latitude whereof is 64. degrees, 25. minutes, and the variation of the compasse, 5 degrees, 10. minutes from the North to the East.

Wednesday (26) we came to the Island called Pozanka, which Island is within foure leagues of the barre Berozoua. It floweth here at an East and by South moone full sea.

Saturday (29) in the morning we departed from Pozanka, and plied to the barre of Berozoua Gooba, whereupon wee came to anker at a lowe water, and sounded the said Barre with our two Skiffes, and found in the best upon the shoaldest of the barre 13. foote water by the rule. It higheth vpon this barre, in spring streames 3. foote water: and an East Moone maketh a full sea vpon this barre.

Sunday (30) in the morning wee departed from the barre of Berozoua, and plied along by the shoalds in fiue fadome, vntill I had sight of S. Nicholas roade, and then wee cast about to the Northwards, and went with a hommocke, which is halfe a mile to Eastwards of Coya Reca, which hommocke and S. Nicholas abbey lye Southsouthwest, and Northnortheast, and betweene them are 11. leagues. Coia Reca is halfe a mile to the Eastwards of Coscaynos. Coscaynos and the middles of the Island called Mondeustoua ostroue, which is thwart of the barre of Berozoua lieth South and by East, North and by West, and betweene them are 4. leagues, or as you may say from the Seaboord part of the barre to Coscaynos are 3. leagues and a halfe.

Munday (31) at a Northeast and by East sunne we were thwart of Coscaynos.

Dogs nose lieth from Coscaynos Northnorthwest, and betweene them are eight leagues: and Dogs nose sheweth like a Gurnerds head, if you be inwardly on both sides of it: on the lowe point of Dogs nose there standeth a crosse alone.

Iune.

1. From Dogs nose to Foxnose are three leagues, North, and by West.

The 2 day of Iune I went on shoare 2. miles to the Northwards of Dogs nose, and had the latitude of that place in 65. degrees, 47. minutes. It floweth a shoare at this place, at an East moone full sea, and the ship lay thwart to wende a flood, in the off, at a Southsoutheast moone. So that it is to be vnderstoode, that when it is a full sea on the shoare, it is two points to ebbe, before it be a lowe water in the off. The variation of the Compasse at this place is 4. degrees from the North to the East.

This day (3) the Northnorthwest winde put vs backe againe with Dogs nose, where a ship may ride thwart of a salt house, in 4. fadome, or 4. fadome and a halfe of water, and haue Landfange for a North and by West winde: which Salt house is halfe a mile to the Southwards of Dogs nose.

Friday (4) at a Southsouthwest Sunne, wee departed from this Salt house. It is to be noted that foure miles to the Norhwards of Dogs nose there growe no trees on the banke by the water side and the bankes consist of fullers earth. Ouer the cliffes there growe some trees: so that Dogs nose is the better to be knowen because it is fullers earth, and the like I haue not seene in all that Countrey.

A head of Foxe nose a league from the shoare there are 15. fadome: betwixt Foxe nose and Zolatitsa there are 6. leagues, I meane the Southerly part of Foxe nose.

Sunday (6) I sounded the barre of Zolatitsa, which the Russes told me was a good harborow, but in the best of it I found but 4. foote water.

Munday (7) I had the latitude in 66. degrees, and then was point Pentecost six leagues south of vs.

Wednesday (9) I went on land at Crosse Island, and tooke the latitude, which was 66. degrees, 24. minutes.

We being one league Northeast of Crosse Island, I sawe the land on the Eastside, which I iudged to be Cape good fortune, and it was then Eastsoutheast of vs 9 leagues.

Cape grace is 7. leagues and a halfe Northeast from Crosse Island.

There are 2. Islands 5. leagues Northnortheast from Cape grace, the Southermost of them is a little long Island almost a mile long, and the Northermost a little round island, and they are both hard aboord the shore.

Cape Race is from the Southermost Island North and by West, betweene them are two leagues, and from that and halfe a league Northnorthwest, there is another poynt. Betweene which poynt and Cape Race, the Russes haue a Stanauish or harborow for their Lodias: and to the Westwards of the sayd poynt, there is a shoale bay.

Three leagues and a halfe to Northwards of Cape Race, we had the latitude on the 10. day of this moneth in 67. degrees 10. minutes. Riding within half a league of the shoare in this latitude I found it to be a full sea at a North and by East moone. I had where we roade, two and twentie fadoome, and the tallow which is taken vp is full of great broken shels, and some stones withal like vnto small sand congealed together.

From a South sunne that wee weyed, the winde being at North and by East, wee driued to the windwards halfe the ebbe, with the ships head to the Eastwards. [Sidenote: Frost in Iune] And then when we cast her head to the Westwards, we sounded, and had 22. fadome broken shels, and gray sand; this present day was very mistie, with frost on the shrowds as the mist fell.

Friday (11) in the morning at an East sunne, the mist brake up a little, the winde being at North and by West a stiffe gale, our shrowdes and roapes ouer head being couered with frost, and likely to be a storme: I thought it good to seeke an harborow, and so plied roome with the Islands which are two leagues to the Southwards of Cape Race, and within these Islands (thankes bee to God) we found harborow for vs. It higheth at these Islands two fadome water: it floweth in the harborow at this place at a Southsoutheast moone ful sea: and a sea boord it floweth at a Southsouthwest moone a full sea. The Russes call this Island Tri Ostroue.

You may come in betweene the little Island and the great Island, and keepe you in the mids of the Sound, and if you borrowe on any side, let it bee on the greatest Island, and you shall haue at a low water, foure fadome, and three fadome and a halfe, and three fadome, vntill that you be shot so farre in as the narrowest, which is between the Northermost point of the greatest Island, and the Southerne point of the maine which is right against it, and then hale to the Northwards with the crosse which standeth in the maine, and you shall haue at a lowe water 10. foote water, and faire sand. And if you be disposed to goe through the Sound to the Southwards, keepe the Northwest shoare aboorde, for on the Island side after you be shotte so far in as the crosse, it is a shoale of rockes halfe the sound ouer: which rockes do last vnto the Southerly part of the great Island, and rather to the Southwards. And if you be constrained to seeke a harbor for Northerly windes, when you come out of the sea hale in with the Southerly part of the great Island, gluing the Island a faire birth, and as you shoote towards the maine, you shall finde roade for all Northerly windes, in foure fadome, fiue, sixe, and seuen fadome, at a lowe water.

Also within this great Island (if neede bee) you may haue a good place to ground a ship in: the great Island is almost a mile long and a quarter of a mile ouer.

This storm of Northerly winde lasted vntill the 16. of this moneth and then the winde came Southerly, but we could not get out for ice. I went on shore at the crosse, and tooke the latitude, which is 66. degrees, 58. minutes, 30. seconds: the variation of the Compasse 3. degrees and a halfe from the North to the East.

Thursday (17) being faire weather, and the winde at North we plied to the winde-wards with sailes and oares: wee stopped the flood this day three leagues to the Northwards of Cape Race, two miles from the shore, and had twentie fadome water, faire gray and blacke sand, and broken shels. And when the slake came wee wayed and made aboord to the shoare-wards, and had within two cables length of the shoare, eighteene fadomes faire gray and blacke sand: a man may finde roade there for a North winde, and so to the Westwards.

Two leagues to the Southward of Corpus Christi poynt, you may haue Landfang for a North and by East-winde, and from that to the Westwards in 23. fadome almost a mile from shoare, and faire sand, and amongst the sand little yong small limpets, or such like as growe vpon muscles: and within two cables length and lesse of the shoare are eighteene fadomes, and the sounding aforesayd, but the yong limpets more plentifull. It was a full sea where we roade, almost a mile from shoare, at a South and by West moone: two leagues to the Southwards of Corpus Christi point is the vttermost land, which land and Cape Race lyeth South and halfe a point to Westwards, and North and halfe a point to the Eastwards, and between them are sixe leagues. Riding this day (19) sixe leagues to the Northwards of Cape Race, the winde at Northnorthwest, with mist and frost, at noone the sunne appeared through the mist, so that I had the latitude in 67. degrees, 29. minutes.

Munday (21) we were thwart of Corpus Christi point, two leagues and a halfe from shoare, or rather more, where we sounded, and had 36. fadoms, and broken cocle shels, with brannie sand, but the broken shels very thicke.

Tuesday (22) in the morning we were shotte a head of Cape gallant, which the Russes call Sotinoz. And as were shot almost halfe a league betwixt it, and Cape comfort, the wind came vp at the Northwest, and after to the Northwards, so that we were faine to beare roome to seeke a harbour, where we found good harbour for all windes, and the least 7. fadome water betweene S. Iohns Islands and the maine.

After that we came to an ancre, we tooke the latitude, which was 68. degrees, 1 minute, after noone, the winde at North with plentie of snowe.

At a West Sunne there came aboord us certaine Lappians in a boate, to the number of sixteene persons, and amongst them there were two wenches, and some of them could speake the Russe tongue: I asked them where their abiding was, and they tolde mee that there was a companie or heard of them, to the number of 100. men, besides women and children, but a little from vs in the riuer Iekonga.

They tolde me that they had bene to seeke meate among the rockes, saying, If wee get no meate, wee eate none. I sawe them eate rocke weedes as hungerly, as a cowe doeth grasse when shee is hungrie. I sawe them also eate foules egges rawe, and the yong birdes also that were in the egges.

I obserued certaine wordes of their language, which I thought good to set downe for their vse, that hereafter shall haue occasion to continue this voyage.

COWGHTIE COTEAT, what call you this.
PODDYTHECKE, come hither.
AUANCHYTHOCKE, get the hence.
ANNA, farewell.
TEYRUE, good morrowe.
IOMME LEMAUFES, I thanke you.
PASSEUELLIE, a friend.
OLMUELKE, a man.
CAPTELLA, a woman.
ALKE, a sonne.
NEIT, a daughter, or yong wench.
OVUIE, a head.
CYELME, an eye.
NENNA, a nose.
NEALMA, a mouth.
PANNEA, teeth.

NEUGHTEMA, a tongue.
SEAMAN, a beard.
PEALLEE, an eare.
TEAPPAT, the necke.
VOAPT, the haire.
KEAT, a hand.
SOARME, fingers.
IOWLKIE, a legge.
PEELKIE, the thombe, or great toe.
SARKE, wollen cloth.
LEIN, linnen cloth.
PAYTE, a shirt.
TOL, fire.
KEATSE, water.
MURR, wood.
VANNACE, a boate.
ARICA, an oare.
NURR, a roape.
PEYUE, a day.
HYR, a night.
PEVUEZEA, the Sunne.
MANNA, the Moone.
LASTE, starres.
COSAM VOLKA, whither goe you.
OTTAPP, sleepe.
TALLYE, that.
KEIEDDE PIEUE, a weeke.
ISCKIE, a yeere.
KESSE, Sommer.
TALUE, Winter.
IOWKSAM, colde.
PAROX, warme.
ABRYE, raine.
YOUGHANG, yce.
KEATYKYE, a stone.
SELLOWPE, siluer.
SOLDA, golde.
TENNAE, tinne.
VESKUE, copper.
ROWADT, yron.
NEYBX, a knife.
AXSHE, a hatchet.
LEABEE, bread.

IEAUEGOAT, meale.
PENCKA, the winde.
IOWTE, A platter.
KEMNIE, a kettle.
KEESTES, gloues.
SAPEGE, shoes.
CONDE, a wilde Deare.
POATSA, the labouring Deare.

Their wordes of number are these as followeth.

OFTE, One.
NOUMPTE, Two.
COLME, Three.
NELLYE, Four.
VITTE, Five.
COWTE, Six.
KEYDEEM, Seven.
KAFFTS, Eight
OWGHCHTE, Nine.
LOCKE, Ten.
OSTRETUMBELOCKE, Eleven.
COWGHTNUMBELOCKE, Twelve.
COLMENONBELOCKE, Thirteen.
NELLYNOMBELOCKE, Fourteen.
VITTIENOMBELOCKE, Fifteen.
COWTENOMBELOCKE, Sixteen.
KEYDEMNOMBELOCKE Seventeen.
KAFTSNOMBELOCKE, Eighteen.
OWGHTNOMBELOCKE, Nineteen.
COFFTEYLOCKE, Twenty.
COLMELOCKE, Thirty.
NELLY LOCKE. Forty.
VITTELOCKE, Fifty.
COWTELOCKE, Sixty.
KEYDEMLOCKE, Seventy.
KAFFTSELOCKE, Eighty.
OUGHCHETELOKE, Ninety.
TEWET, One hundred.

Friday (25) in the morning we departed from Saint Iohns Island: to the Westwards thereof, a mile from the shoare, we sounded, and had 36. fadoms, and oazie sand.

Iuana Creos is from Cape gallant Westnorthwest, and halfe a point to the Northwards, and betweene them is 7. leagues. The point of the Island, which is Cape comfort, lyeth from Iuana Creos, Northwest and by North, and almost the 3. part of a point to the Westwards, and betweene them are 3. leagues.

The Eastermost of S. Georges Islands, or the 7. Islands, lyeth from Iuana Creos Northwest, and halfe a point to the Northwards, and betweene them are 14. leagues and a halfe. The vttermost of the 7. Islands, and Cape Comfort, lieth Northwest, and by North, Southeast, and by South.

Vnder the Southermost Island you shall finde good roade for all Northerly windes from the Northwest to the Northeast. From the Southeast part of the 7. Islands, vnto the Northwest part of them, are 3. leagues and a halfe.

From the Northwest part of the Islands aforesaid, vnto S. Peters Islands, are 11. leagues Northwest.

(26). S. Peters Islands rise an indifferent low point, not seeming to be an Island, and as if it had a castle vpon it.

S. Pauls Islands lie from S. Peters Islands Northwest and to the Westwards, and betweene them are 6. leagues. Within these Islands there is a faire sandy bay, and there may be found a good roade for Northerly windes.

Cape Sower beere lyeth from S. Pauls Islands Northwest and by West, and betweene them are 5. leagues.

Cape comfort, which is the Island of Kildina, lieth from Cape Sower beere, 6. leagues West Northwest, and it is altogether a bay betweene them seeming many Islands in it.

From Cape Bonauenture, to Chebe Nauoloche are 10. leagues Northwest, and a litle to the Westwards. Chebe Nauoloche is a faire point, whereon standeth a certaine blacke, like an emptie butte standing a head.

From Chebe Nauoloch to Kegor, is 9. leagues and a halfe Northwest, and halfe a poynt to the Westwards. Kegor riseth as you come from the Eastwards like 2. round homocks standing together, and a faire saddle betweene them.

It floweth where we road this Sunday (27) to the Eastwards of Kegor, at a Southeast and by East moone, a full sea: we roade in 15. fadome water within halfe a mile of the shoare: at a Northwest Sunne the mist came downe so thicke, that we were faine to come to an ancre within lesse then a mile of the point that turneth to Doms haff, where we had 33. fadome, and the sounding like to the skurfe of a skalde head.

Munday (28) at afternoone, wee came into the Sound of Wardhouse, although it were very mistie. Then I sent a man a shoare to know some newes, and to see whether they would heare any thing of our ships [Marginal note: Which were the Bona Esperanza, the Bona confidentia and the Philip and Marie. Whereof the two first were lost].

Tuesday (29) I went on shoare, and dined with the Captaines deputie, who made mee great cheere: the Captaine himselfe was not as yet come from Bergen: they looked for him euery houre, and they said that he would bring newes with him.

At a Northwest and by North sunne we departed from Wardhouse, toward Colmogro.

Wednesday (30) we came to Kegor, where we met with the winde at East Southeast, so that we were faine to go in to a bay to the Westwards of the point Kegor, where a man may moare 2. or 3. small ships, that shall not draw past 11. or 12. foote water, for all windes, an East Northeast winde is the worst. It is a ledge of rocks that defendeth the Northerly winds from the place where they moare. When we came into the bay we saw there a barke which was of Dronton [Marginal note: Or, Trondon], and three or foure Norway yeaghes, belonging to Northberne: so when I came a shoare, I met first with the Dutchmen, amongst whom was the Borrowmasters sonne of Dronton, who tolde me that the Philip and Mary wintered at Dronton, and departed from thence for England in March: and withall he shewed me that the Confidence was lost, and that he had bought her sailes for his ship. Then the Dutchmen caried me to their Boothe, and made me good cheere, where I sawe the Lappians chepen of the said Dutchmen, both siluer platters and dishes, spoones, gilt rings, ornaments for girdles of siluer and gilt, and certaine things made to hang about the necke, with siluer chaines belonging to them.

The Dutchmen bring hither mightie strong beere, I am certain that our English double beere would not be liked of the Kerile and Llappians, as long as that would last.

Here I sawe the Dutchmen also haue course cloth, both blew, greene, and redde, and sad horseflesh colour. And hither they bring also Ottars cases and foxe cases, both blacke and redde: our English foxe cases are but counterfaits vnto them.

They would not let me vnderstand any of their prises, but as I otherwise vnderstood they bartered 2. load of siluer for 100 of stockfish, and 2. loade is a doller. And the Dutchmen told me, and they had made a notable good yeere this present yeere 1557. They tolde me that they should be faine to goe to Wardhouse with one lading, and lay it on land there, and so come againe and fetch another. The Borrowmasters sonne told me, that he would go to Amsterdam with his lading of stockfish, who gaue me a barrell of strong beere, and brought it in aboord our ship himseelf.

After this I went among the Russes and Kerils, who offered me fish to sell, and likewise the Lappians desired me to look vpon their fish. I made them answere, that I had nowe no wares nor money to barter with them, and said that I came only to see if I might meete with our English ships. Then they desired me that I would come thither the next yeere: I said to them, If I should come the next yeere, I think here would not be fish ynough to serue the Dutch and vs also. They answered me, that if more ships did resort thither, there would more people labour to kill and make fish: and further they said, that some of them came thither a fishing 8 weekes iourney with Deere, which Deere will trauaile more speedily then horses will.

As I was thus in talke with the Kerils and Lappians, the Emperour of Russia his deputie (who was there to gather the tribute of the Lappians) sent for me to come to his tent, who after familiar salutations, made me good cheere. He demanded of me why none of our ships came thither. I answered him, because we knew not the place before now, neither yet heard of any faire that was kept there. Then said he, If you will come hither, here would more people resort to kill fish, I think it good (said he) that you make a beginning. I tolde him, that by the grace of God the next yeere, one English ship should come thither.

Because I sawe the seruants of the King of Denmarke there also gathering the tribute, I asked Vasilie Pheodoruich the Russie deputie, whether the Denmarks would not be a let to vs, if we should come to this Kegor. And he said no, they should not: for this land is my kings, and therefore be bolde to come hither.

The Kerils and the Lappians solde no fish, vntil the said deputie had looked upon it, and giuen them leaue to sell. I asked him what wares were best for vs to bring thither, and he said, siluer, pearles, cloth, blewe, red, and greene, meale, strong beere, wine, pewter, foxe cases, and gold.

The Lappians pay tribute to the Emperour of Russia, to the king of Denmarke, and to the king of Sweden. He told me that the Riuer Cola is little more then 20. leagues to the Southwards of Kegor, where we should haue great plentie of salmon, if corne were any thing cheape in Russia: for then poore men would resort thither to kill salmon.

The Dutchmen tolde me that they had made a good yeere of this, but the Kerils complained of it because they could not sell all their fish, and that which they sold was as pleased the Dutchmen, and at their own price. I asked the Kerils at what price they sold their fish to the Russes, and they said good cheape: wee sell 24. fishes for 4. altines. I thinke they solde little aboue 20. pence, the 25. fishes this yeere.

The Dutchmen tolde me that the best stockfish is made at Kegor. I sawe at Vasiltes tent 7. or 8. iauelins, and halfe a dozen of bowes bent, with their budgets of arrowes, and likewise swords with other weapons: Otherwise
I sawe no weapons there.

I was also conueyed to their lodgings, which gathered tribute for the king of Denmarke, where I sawe a pair of bilbowes: and I asked whether they were for the Lappians (if neede were,) and they said no, but onely for their owne company if they should chance to be vnruly.

The Kerils and the Lappians are not to be trusted, for they will steale as well as the Russes, if they may conueniently come by any thing.

Concerning my voyage, because the winde was scant to goe backe againe to Colmogro, I tarried to the Eastwards of the poynt Kegor, and sent to land, and baked two batches of bread in the ouens that the Kerils haue for their prouision.

* * * * *

Instructions giuen to the Masters and Mariners to be obserued in and about this Fleete, passing this yeere 1577. toward the Bay of S. Nicolas in Russia, for this present Race to be made and returne of the same by Gods grace to the port of London, the place of their right discharge, as in the Articles ensuing is deduced.

First, it is accorded and agreed betweene the seuerall proprietaries and owners, masters and companies of the foure ships, surnamed the Primrose, the Iohn Euangelist, the Anne and the Trinitie, and the Lieutenant, Consuls, assistants and companie of the Marchant aduenturers, that the aboue named foure ships shall in good order and conduct, saile, passe, and trauaile together in one flote, ging, and conserue of societie, to be kept indissolubly and not to be seuered, but vnited within continuall sight, so farre foorth as (by winde and weather) by possibilitie shall or may be without any separation or departure of one from the other.

2 Item, it is agreed that the good ship named the Primerose, shalbe Admirall of this flote, and that Anthonie Ienkinson Gentleman, shalbe captaine thereof: and that all the other 3. ships shall ensue and follow her in all courses, and that no course or waying (in harborough especially) shall be made without aduice, consent and agreement of the sayd Captaine, the Master, his mate, and two other officers of the said ship, or of three of them at the least.

3 Item, that the said Anthonie is and shalbe reputed and taken for Captaine general of the said flote together with all such orders, preeminences, priuiledges and preferments as by the order of seas is due and accustomed to a Captaine during his abode and exercise of the same.

4 If is also ordeined, that if any one or moe of the said 3. ships shalbe out of sight either before or behinde the Admirall, that then the rest of the ships shall tacke or take off their sailes in such sort as they may meete and come together, in as good order as may be, to the intent to keepe the consortment exactly in all poynts.

5 It is constituted, that if any ships shalbe seuered by mist or darke weather, in such sort as the one cannot haue sight of the other, then and in such case the Admiral shall make sound and noise by drumme, trumpet, horne, gunne or otherwise or meanes, that the ships may come as nigh together, as by safetie and good order they may.

6 It is also to be obserued, that euery day once the other three shippes shall send and come aboord the Admirall, and there consult and determine of such matter and things as shall be for the assurance of their Nauigation, and most expedition of the same.

7 Item, that notes and entries be daily made of their Nauigations put in writing and memory, and that the yong Mariners and apprentices may be taught and caused to learne and obserue the same.

8 It is accorded that the said Captaine shall haue the principall rule and gouernement of the apprentices: And that not onely they, but also all the other sailers, shalbe attendant and obedient to him, as of duetie and reason appertaineth.

9 Also that no beere nor broth, or other liquor be spilt vpon the balast, or other place of the ship, whereby any anoyance, stinke, or other vnsauorinesse shall growe in the shippe to the infection or hurt of the persons in the same.

10 Item, that the Captaine by discretion shall from time to time disship any artificer or English seruingman or apprentice out of the Primrose into any other of the three ships, and in lieu of him or them, take any such apprentice as he shall thinke conuenient and most meete to serue the benefite of the companie.

11 Item, that great respect be had to the Gunners and Cookes roomes, that all danger and perill of powder and fire may be eschewed and auoyded.

12 Item, that singular care and respect be had to the ports of the ship, aswell in Nauigation as in harborow, and especially in lading and vnlading of the shippes, that nothing be lacking or surcharged: and that the bookes

may oftentimes be conferred and made to agree in eschuement of such losses, as may ensue.

13 Special foresight is to be had, that at the Wardhouse no trecherie, inuasion, or ether peril of molestation be done or procured to be attempted to our ships by any kings, princes, or companies, that do mislike this new found trade by seas to Russia, or would let and hinder the same, where of no small boast hath bene made; which giueth occasion of more circumspection and diligence.

14 If the winde and weather will serue, it is thought good rather to goe by the Wardhouse then to come in and ancre there, lest any male engine, or danger may be the rather attempted against vs, our goods and ships as aboue.

15 It is thought good that Richard Iohnson, late seruant to M. Chanceler, shall be sent home in this next returne to instruct the company of the state of the Countrey, and of such questions as may be demanded of him, for our better aduertisements and resolutions, in such doubts as shall arise here: and that he shall haue the roome of the Captaine in such sort as Master Ienkinson is in this present cocket assigned vnto. And if Iohnson can not, may not, nor will not returne and occupie the said place, then any other person to be preferred thereunto, as by the discretion of our said Captaine, with consent of our Agents, shall be thought meete and apt to supply the same.

16 Prouided alway, that the ships returning be not disfurnished of one such able man, as shall occupie the Captainship in like order, as is, and hath bene in such case appoynted, as reason and good order requireth.

17 Item that all other former orders, rules, and deuises, made and prouided for the good order of our ships, wares, and goods, being not repugnant, contrary or diuerse to these articles, and the contents of the same, shall be, and stand in full force and effect to be in all respects obserued and kept of all and euery person and persons, whom the same doth or shall touch or concerne.

In witnesse of the premisses faithfully to be obserued and kept, the owners and Masters of the said foure ships, together with the said Captaine, to these seuenteene articles, contained in two sheetes of paper, haue subscribed their hands. Given in London the third of May, in the yeere of our Lord God 1557.

Owners, of the Primerose
  Andrewe Iudde,
  William Chester,

Anthony Hickman,
Edward Casteline.

Owners of the Iohn Euangelist
Andrew Iudde,
William Chester.

Owner of the Anne
Iohn Dimocke.

Owner of the Trinitie
R. T.

* * * * *

A letter of the Company of the Marchants aduenturers to Russia vnto
George Killingworth, Richard Gray, and Henry Lane their Agents there, to
be deliuered in Colmogro or els where: sent in the Iohn Euangclist.

After our heartie commendations vnto you and to either of you: your
generall letter and other particular letters with two bookes of the sale and
remainders of our goods, and the buying of wares there with you, we
receiued about the ende of Nouember out of the Edward, with heauie
newes of the losse of the sayde good shippe and goods at Petslego in
Scotland, with the death of Richard Chancelor and his Boy, with certaine of
the Embassadours seruants, and he himselfe with nine of his seruants
escaped very hardly onely by the power of God: but all his goods and ours
in maner were lost and pilfred away by the Scots, and that that is saued is
not yet come to our hands, but we looke for it daily, and it will skant pay
the charges for the recouering of it. No remedy but patience: and to pray to
God to send vs better fortune hereafter. As touching the receiuing and
entertaining of the Embssadour and his retinewe since his comming to
England at the king and Queenes Maiesties hands, with the Counsell and
Lords of this Realme, and the Marchants that be free in Russia with feasting
and beneuolence giuen him, wee referre it to his report and others. The like
we thinke haue not bene seene nor shewed here of a long time to any
Ambassadour. The Philip and Marie arriued here tenne dayes past: she
wintered in Norway. The Confidence is lost there. And as for the Bona
Esperanza, as yet we haue no newes of her. We feare it is wrong with her.
By your billes of lading receiued in your generall letters we perceiue what
wares are laden in them both. Your letters haue no date nor mention where
they were made, which were written by Henry Lane, and firmed by you
George Killingworth, and Richard Gray: both it and the other letters and
Bookes came so sore spoyled and broken with water that we cannot make
our reckoning by them. You shall vnderstand we haue fraighted for the
parts of Russia foure good shippes to be laden by you and your order: That

is to say, The Primerose of the burthen of 240. Tunnes, Master vnder God Iohn Buckland: The Iohn Euangelist of 170. Tunnes, Master vnder God Laurence Roundal: The Anne of London of the burthen of 160. tunnes. Master vnder God Dauid Philly, and the Trinitie of London of the burthen of 140. Tunnes Master vnder God Iohn Robins, as by their Charter parties may appeare: which you may require to see for diuerse causes. You shall receiue, God willing, out of the said good ships, God sending them in safety for the vse of the Company, these kinds of wares following, all marked with the general marke of the Company as followeth. 25. fardels containing 207. sorting clothes, one fine violet in graine, and one skarlet, and 40. cottons for wrappers, beginning with number 1. and ending with number 52. The sorting clothes may cost the first peny 5. li. 9. s. the cloth, one with the other. The fine violet 18. li. 6. s. 6. d. The skarlet 17. li 13. s 6. d., the cottons at 9. li. 10. s. the packe, accompting 7. cottons for a packe, more 500. pieces of Hampshire kersies, that is 400. watchets, 43. blewes, 53. reds, 15. greenes, 5. ginger colours, and 2. yelowes which cost the first penny 4. li. 6. s. the packe, and 3. packes containing 21. cottons at 9. li. 10. s. the packe, and part of the clothes is measured by Arshines. More 9. barrels of Pewter of Thomas Hasels making, &c. Also the wares bee packed and laden as is aforesayde, as by an Inuoyce in euery Shippe more plainly may appear. So that when it shall please God to send the said good ships to you in safetie, you are to receiue our said goods, and to procure the sales to our most aduantage either by ready money, time or barter: hauing consideration that you doe make good debts, and giue such time, if you give any, as you may employ and returne the same against the next voyage; and also foreseeing that you barter to a profit, and for such wares as be here most vendible, as waxe, tallowe, traine oyle, hempe and flax. Of furres we desire no great plentie, becuase they be dead wares. And as for Felts we will in no wise you send any. And whereas you have provided tarre, and as we suppose, some hempe ready bought, our aduise is, that in no wise you send any of them hither vnwrought, because our fraight is 4. li a tunne or little lesse which is so deare as it would not beare the charges: and therefore we haue sent you 7. ropemakers, as by the copies of their covenants here inclosed shall appeare. Whom we wil you set to work with al expedition in making of cables and ropes of al sorts, from the smallest rope to xii. inches: And that such tarre and hempe as is already brought to the water side, they may there make it out, and after that you settle their worke in Vologhda or Colmogro as you shall thinke good, where their stuffe may be neerest to them: at which place and places you doe assigne them a principall overseer aswell to see the deliuerie of the stuffe vnwrought, as also to take charge of the stuffe wrought, and to foresee that neither the yarne be burnt in tarring, nor the hempe rotted in the watering: and also to furnish them so with labourers, workemen and stuffe, as hereafter when these workmen shall come away, we be not destitute of good workmen, and that these may dispatch as much as possibly they may, doing it substancially: for we esteme it a principal commoditie, and that the Counsel of England doth well allowe. Let all diligence be vsed, that at the returne of these shippes we may see samples of all ropes and cables if it be possible, and so after to continue in worke, that we may haue good store against the next yeere. [Sidenote: Danske the old chiefe place for Cables.] Therefore they haue neede to haue a place to worke in, in the winter: and at any hand let them haue helpe enough to spinne their stuffe: for seeing you haue great plentie of hempe there, and at a reasonable price, we trust we shallbe able to bring as good stuffe from thence, and better cheape then out of Danske: if it be diligently vsed; and haue a good ouerseer. Let the chiefest lading of these foure shippes be principally in wexe, flaxe, tallowe, and traine oyle. And if there be any more wares than these ships be able to take in, then leaue that which is least in valew and grossest in stouage vntill the next shipping: for wee doe purpose to ground our selues chiefly vpon these commodities, as wexe, cables and ropes, traine oyle, flaxe and some linen yarne. [Sidenote: Commodities not bearing the charges of long fraight.] As for Masts, Tarre, Hempe, Feathers, or any such other like, they would not beare the charges to haue any, considering our deere fraight. We haue sent you a Skinner to be there at our charges for meate, drinke, and lodging, to viewe and see such furres as you shall cheape or buye, not minding neuerthelesse, that you shall charge your selues with many, except those which bee most vendible, as good marterns, miniuers, otherwise called Lettis and Mynkes. Of these you may send vs plentie, finding them good and at a reasonable price. As for Sables and other rich Furres, they bee not euery mans money: therefore you may send the fewer, vsing partly the discretion of the skinner in that behalfe.

Wee heare that there is great plentie of steele in Russia and Tartarie, whereof wee would you sent vs part for an example, and to write your mindes in it what store is to be had: for we heare say there is great plentie, and that the Tartars steele is better then that in Russia. And likewise we be informed that there is great plentie of Copper in the Emperours Dominions: we would he certified of it what plentie there is, and whether it be in plates or in round flat cakes, and send vs some for an example. Also we would haue you to certifie vs what kinde of wollen cloth the men of Rie and Reuel, and the Holes and Lettoes doe bring to Russia, and send the skantlings of them with part of the lists and a full aduise of the lengths and breadths, colours and prices, and whether they be strained or not: and what number of them may be vttered in a yeere, to the intent we may make prouision for them for the like sortes, and all other Flemish wares which they bring thither and be most vendible there. And to certifie vs whether our set clothes be vendible there or not: and whether they be rowed and shorne: because ofttimes they goe vndrest. Moreouer, we will you send vs of euery commoditie in that Countrey part, but no great quantitie other then such as is before declared. And likewise euery kinde of Lether, whereof wee bee informed there is great store bought yeerely by the Esterlings and Duches for hie Almaigne and Germaine.

More, that you doe send vs for proofe a quantity of such earth, hearbes, or what thing soeuer it be, that the Russes do die and colour any kinde of cloth linen or wollen, Lether or any other thing withall: and also part of that which the Tartars and Turkes doe bring thither, and how it must be vsed in dying and colouring. Moreouer, that you haue a speciall foresight in the chusing of your Tallowe, and that it may be well purified and tried, or els it will in one yeere putrifie and consume.

Also that you certifie vs the trueth of the waights and measures, and howe they doe answere with ours, and to send vs 3. robles in money, that we may trie the iust value of them.

Also we doe send you in these ships ten young men that be bound Prentises to the Companie, whom we will you to appoynt euery of them as you shall there finde most apt and meete, some to keepe accompts, some to buy and sell by your order and Commission, and some to send abroad into the notable Cities of the Countrey for vnderstanding and knowledge. And we will you send vs aduertisement from time to time as well as of the demeanours of our Prentises which we doe send now as also of such other as bee already there with you. And if you finde any of them remisse, negligent, or otherwise misuse themselues and will not be ruled, and then you doe send him home, and the cause why.

And because we doe perceiue the Countrey to be large, and that you haue three housholds, we doe appoynt Henry Lane to be one of our Agents, and to ioin with you in all your doings, and to haue like authoritie and power as you George Killingworth and Rich and Gray haue: not doubting but you three will so conferre together, as both our Prentises and others may be appoynted and diuided euery of them to his office, and to that he can best skill of: and you also so diuide your selues euery of you to an house, as by aduertisement one from another, our businesse and trafficke may take good successe. And for diuers considerations, to auoyde many troubles and businesse that might happen, wee haue appoynted that hee which shall abide at Colmogro (which we doe think to bee most meetest Henry Lane) shall haue with him there such of our young men, as can best skill in keeping of accompts after the maner of Marchants, that is, by Debitor and Creditor: And that there shall be the place, where our bookes shalbe kept: because it is nearer the sea side, where our goods shalbe discharged and our ships laden. And the said Henry Lane to be charged with all such goods as we shall discharge there out of our ships, according to our Inuoyces. Which goods are to be sent from Colmogro to Vologhda or to Mosco, or to any other place where you three or two of you do appoynt them to be sold, so that Henry Lane be one. And so from time to time immediately as any thing is sold, doe you certifie the same to Henry Lane, that he may enter it into the Bookes as apperteineth: otherwise he should be too farre behinde in his Bookes at the comming of our ships, when he should send vs the accompt of the whole yeere passed. And we will also that you George Killingworth and Richard Gray doe in the fine of April next send either of you vnto Henry Lane a whole, perfit, and iust accompt firmed with your owne hands of all the goods you haue solde and bought vntill that time, and what remaineth vnsolde: and also the accompt of all maner costs of wares, and charges of you and the yong men vnder you particularly in such sort as the said accompt may bee with him in Colmogro at the fine of May at the furthest: to the intent that hee may make all our accompts perfite against the comming of our ships: and in any wise to keepe accompt of euery voyage by it selfe, and not minde one voyage with another at no hand. And as we will haue you to keepe accompt of euery voyage by it selfe, euen so wee would haue all the whole costes and charges of euery yeere put into the voyage of that yeere. As the charges of all the last yeere must be put to the accompt of the third voyage: and the charges of this yeere present, must in the fine of April next, be put to the fourth voyage. Not doubting but your wisedome is such that you will not take it in euill part, that wee doe appoynt Henry Lane to take the accompt of the rest. For we doe it for none other cause, but to keepe a good order in our bookes, that his bookes and ours may by this meanes agree: and hee being the yonger man, may best take paines: and that you doe keepe accompt of euery kinde of wares by it selfe, to the intent wee may perceiue wherein is our most gaine. And also in the making of your returne, in any wise name in your billes of lading, letters, and accompts, what wares doe appertaine to the first, second, and third voyage: and that wee may knowe the same by the numbers or otherwise as you shall thinke good by your wisedomes, putting the charges of the said wares vnto them, as nigh as you can. And all such money as shall bee made of your goods in any place, wee referre that to your discretion, where it shall remaine vntill it bee employed, either at Vologhda, Mosco, or els where. And likewise wee will that Henry Lane doe make in a readinesse about the beginning of Iune euery yeere our whole accompt of the voyage in that yeere passed: in such sort that wee may receiue the same by our shippes: and that wee may plainely perceiue what sales are made, and what remaineth of the first, second, third, and fourth voyage, and what charges haue been layde out for the sayd voyages, and what wares bee bought, and laden, and what they cost, and for what voyage euery parcell thereof is: and to send vs a copie of the same accompt in euery shippe. And also forasmuch as at this time we haue sent you but small store of wares in comparison of that we haue hope will bee vttered in short space, and yet neuerthelesse much more then you wrote for, whereby there shall not be sufficient to make any ample returne: and vnderstandinig that there is great quantitie of goods stayed for our trade there by the Emperour, wee haue mooued the Embassador that you may haue credite for such quantitie as shall seeme good to you to prouide for our benefite. Which credite if you may by his means obtaine, or otherwise haue, we would you bought as much Wexe principally as you may get. For if there be in that countrey so great quantitie, as we be informed there is, it will be the best commoditie we may haue: for hauing that wholly in our hands, we may serue our owne countrey and others. Therefore seeing the Emperour doth minde, that such commodities as bee in his dominions shall not passe to Rie and Reuel and Poland as they haue done, but bee reserued for vs: therefore we must so lay for it, that it may not ly upon their hands that haue it to sell, always hauing consideration in the price and time as our next dispatch may correspond. Whereof you may send a certaine aduise, as well what you shall receiue of credit, and to what quantite, as also what wares are remaining in your hands: which together well considered, you may aduertise vs as well for how many hundreth tonnes we must prouide fraight against the next yeere, as also what sortes, quantities and qualities of wares we shall send you, as well to pay your credite, as also to furnish the next aduenture after. Of this we would be answered largely. For we trust by this time you are able to giue full instructions of the state of the countrey: according to the articles of your first Commissions, and what commodities doe principally abound there with their prices: and likewise what of our commodities haue most vtterance there, and what prices will be given for them there: and all other things requisite and necessary to be knowen.

Also we doe vnderstand that in the Countrey of Permia or about the river of Pechora, is great quantitie of Yewe, and likewise in the Countrey of Vgory, which we be desirous to haue knowledge of because it is a special commoditie for our Realme. [Sidenote: Leonard Brian sent to search out Yewe in the North parts of Russia.] Thereon wee haue sent you a yong man, whose name is Leonard Brian, that hath some knowledge in the wood, to show you in what sorte it must be cut and clouen. So our minde is if there be any store, and that it bee found to be good, that there you doe prouide a good quantitie against the next yeere for the comming of our shippes and if there can bee found none that will serue for our purpose then you may set the sayd Leonard Brian to any other businesse that you shall finde most fittest for him, vntill the returne of our ships the next yeere. For he is hired by the yeere onely for that purpose. We doubt not but that hee shall doe you good seruice there. For hee hath good knowledge of wares of that Countrey for his bringing vp hath bene most in Danske, and hath good vnderstanding in making of Ropes and Cables. Also we doe send you two Coopers to remaine there with you at our finding hogmeat and drinke and lodging to make in a readinesse all such caske as shalbe needfull for traine oyle, tallowe, or any thing else One of them may goe with Leoonard Brian to cut and cleue such Yewe as he shall like there. And because we be not sure what timber they shall finde there to make Caske, we haue laden in these ships 140. tunnes emptie Caske, that is 94. tunnes shaken Caske and 46. tunnes whole, and ten thousand hoopes, and 480. wrethes of twigs: they may be doing with that till they can prouide other timber, which we would be glad to heare of. They haue an example with them of the bigness of the Caske they shall make. Neuerthelesse, all such Buttes and Hoggesheads as may be found to serue we will shalbe filled with Traine Oyle.

Also we charge you that you suffer no goods nor marchandise of any persons being not free of the Company, and of the accompt of the Company to be laden in any wise in our ships either now or at any time hereafter: except the Emperour or Ambassadour minde to send any thing to the King and Queenes Maiesties, or to any noble man, or to the Marchants of the Companie: Nor likewise that you suffer any goods that goe in these ships to be brought on land there, except the Ambassadours goods, and the Physitions and Apothecaries, and others that he hath with him, who carie no Marchandise. And because our ships be freighted by the great, it shalbe very needful that you do appoynt certaine to see the romaging of the ships, and to giue the master or Boatswaine, or him that will take vpon him to romage, a good reward for his labour to see the goods well romaged. If it be iii d. or iiii d. the tunne, it shall not be amisse. For if it be not substantially well looked into, it may bee a great deale of money [illegible] of our wayes.

Also because we reckon that from the Mosco will bee always better conueyance of letters to vs by land: our minde is that from time to time as occasion shall serue, our Agents shall write to him that shall lie at Mosco of all things that shall passe, that hee may giue vs large instructions, as well what is solde and bought as also what lading we shall take, and what quantitie and kinde of goodes we shall send. For hitherto we haue had but a slender aduise, more like a bill to serue a Chapman, then for quantitie of wares to serue a kingdom. For we must procure to vtter good quantities of wares, especially the commodities of our Realme, although we affoord a good penyworth, to the intent to make other that haue traded thither, wearie, and so to bring our selues and our commodities in estimation, and likewise to procure to haue the chiefe commodities of that countrey in our hand, as waxe and such others, that other nations may be serued by vs and at our hands. For wee doe vnderstand that the greatest quantitie of waxe that commeth to Danske, Lubeck, and Hambourgh, commeth out of Russia. Therefore if wee should buy part, and they also buy, it would raise the price there, and would bee little woorth here. And all such letters of importance and secrecie as you doe send by land for any wares or otherwise, you must write them in Cyphers, after the order of a booke sent you in the shippes: always taking good heede in placing of your letters and cyphers, that wee may vnderstand them by the same booke heere, and to send them in such sort that we may haue them here by Christmas or Candlemas, if it be possible. And because you cannot so certainly aduertise vs by letters of your doings, but some doubt may arise, whereof we would most gladly be certified: our mind is therefore that with these ships you send vs home one such yong man as is most expert in knowledge of that countrey, and can best certifie vs in such questions as may be demanded, whome we will remit vnto you again in the next ships. We thinke Arthur Edwards wilbe fittest for that purpose: neuerthelesse vse your discretion in that matter.

As touching our goods that were robbed and pilfred out of our ships at Colmogro and Vologda we trust by this time they are restored againe, and the malefactors so punished that other may take example for doing the like, otherwise it will be an euil president. Moreouer, we doe perceiue that Richard Gray doeth buy mastes to send into England; they will not quit the costes, except we had a ship of purpose for them. And likewise that Steuen Burrow is returned from his discouere with the Serchthrift and wintereth at Colmogro, and is minded to set forth in the beginning of Iune next to seeke the riuer of Ob. We pray God to speede him well, and trust to haue him here in England this yeere to bring vs good newes.

We doe perceiue there is a riuer found about the mouth of S. Nicholas Bay that hath thirteen foot vpon the barre at a lowe water, and is as neere Colmogro as S. Nicholas: which will be a great pleasure vnto vs. We will that Steuen Burrowe doe proceed on his voiage to discouer. [Sidenote: M. Anthonie Ienkinson his first trauaile intended for Cathay by the Caspian sea and Beghar.] Also we haue sent you one Anthonie Ienkinson Gentleman, a man well trauelled, whom we mind to vse in further travelling, according to a Commission deliuered him, subscribed by master Antonie Huse and others. Wherefore we will you deliuer him one or more of such painfull young men as he shal thinke meetest for his purpose: and likewise such money and wares as he shal think best to take with him. He must haue fourty pounds a yeere for foure yeeres, to be paid him by the halfe yeere, or as he wil demaund it of you, so let him haue it from Easter last. Also the prices of wares here at this present are, bale flaxe twenty pound the packe and better, towe flaxe twentie eight pound the hundred, traine oyle at nine pound the tunne, waxe at foure pound the hundred, tallow at sixteen shillings the hundred, cables and ropes very deare: as yet there are no shippes come out of Danske.

Kept vntill the tenth day of this present. As this day came the goods, out of Scotland that were recouered out of the Edward Bonauenture: and nowe we doe preceiue that the caske that the trayne oyle came in, is verie good, and much better then ours. Therefore our minde is, that you shall lade it all in such barrels of the biggest sort as you laded in the Edward, and no long barrels nor small. And that caske that wee haue sent may serue for the Tallowe or anie other ware that is not leakage. Neuerthelesse this voyage you must take such as you can get.

Also if the Emperour bee minded to deliuer you any summe of money, or good Waxe, at as reasonable a price as you may buye for readie money, wee will that you shall take it and lade it for our accomptes, and to come at our aduenture, and hee to bee payed at the return of the Shippes in Veluets, Sattens, or any other kinde of silk, or cloth of golde, cloth of tissue, or according as his Commission shall bee that hee shall sende vs in the shippes and according to such paternes as hee shall send. Wee doe not finde the Ambassadour nowe at the last so conformable to reason as wee had thought wee shoulde. Hee is very mistrustfull, and thinketh euery man will beguile him. Therefore you had neede to take heede howe you haue to doe with him or with any such, and to make your bargaines plaine, and to set them downe in writing. For they bee subtill people, and doe not alwaies speake the trueth, and thinke other men to bee like themselues. Therefore we would haue none of them to send any goods in our shippes at any time, nor none to come for passengers, vnless the Emperour doe make bargaine with you, as is aforesaid, for his owne person.

Also we charge you not to suffer any of our nation to send any wares to their wiues or friends in any of our ships; but to take their money there to be paid heere by the companie and not otherwise: and to haue consideration how you doe take the roble. For although we doe rate it after sixteene shillings eight pence of our money, yet it is not worth past 12 or 13 shillings sterling. Moreouer, you had neede to sende newe accomptes, for them that came in the Edward bee marred and torne, so that we can make no reckoning by them: and likewise to write vs a perfect note of all the goodes which you receiued the last voyage out of the Edward, and heerein not to faile.

Andrew Iudde.
George Barne.
Anthonie Huse.
William Garrand.
William Chester.

* * * * *

A Letter of Master Thomas Hawtrey to the worshipfull Master Henrie Lane
 Agent at Colmogro, written in Vologda the 31. of Ianuarie 1557.

Worshipfull Sir, heartie commendations premised. These may bee to
aduertise you, that yesterday the thirtieth, of this present came hither
Robert Best, and brought with him two hundred robles, that is, one
hundred for this place, and one hundred for you at Colmogro. As for
hempe which is here at two robles and a halfe the bercouite, Master Gray
hath written to buy no more at that price: for Iohn Sedgewicke hath bought
for sixe or seuen hundred robles worth at Nouogrode for one roble and a
halfe the bercouite, and better cheape: and white Nouogrode flaxe is there
at three robles the bercouite. I trust hee will doe much good by his going
thither. As I doe vnderstand, Richard Iohnson is gone to Nouogrode with
money to him, I doubt not but Master Gray hath aduertised you of all their
doings, both at the Mosco and the Nouogrod. And touching our doings
heere, you shall perceiue that wee haue solde wares of this fourth voyage
for one hundred and fourtie robles, besides fiftie robles of the second and
third voyage since the giuing vp of my last account, and for wares of the
Countrey, you shall vnderstand that I haue bought tried and vntried for 77.
robles foure hundred podes of tried tallowe, beside foure hundred podes
that I haue giuen out money for, whereof God graunt good receipt when
the time commeth, which is in lent. And in browne flaxe and hempe I haue
bought seuenteene bercouites, sixe podes and sixteene pound, which cost
28. robles, eleuen altines two pence. And as for other kindes of wares I
haue bought none as yet And for mastes to bee prouided, you shall
vnderstand that I wrote a letter to Totma the 28. of this present for fiftie
mastes to wit, for 25. of fifteene fathoms, and 25. of foureteene fathoms, to
be an arshine and a halfe at the small ende. [Sidenote: An Arshine is 3.
quarters of a yard or more.] And more, I haue written for 30. great trees to
be two arshines and a halfe at the small ende, and for the other that were
prouided the last yeere, I trust they will be sent downe in the spring of the
yeere. [Sidenote: A rope house erected by Colmogro.]And as concerning
the Ropemakers, you shall vnderstand that their abiding place shall bee with
you at Colmogro, as I doe thinke Master Gray has aduertised you. For, as
Roger Bontigne Master of the woorkes doeth say, there is no place more
meete for their purpose then with you: and there it will be made with lesser
cost, considering that the pale is the one halfe of it: which is to set one pale
more to that, and so for to couer it ouer, which as they say, will be but little
cost. They doe pray that it may bee made sixteene foote broade, and one
hundred and eightie fathoms long: and that in the midde way twentie foote
from the pale towarde the water side there may be a house made to tarre in,
standing alone by it selfe for danger of fire. The Tarre house that they

woulde haue made, is to bee fifteene fathoms long, and ten fathoms broade, and they would that house should be made first: for I thinke they will not tarre before they come there. And farther they desire that you will prouide for as much tarre as you may, for heere wee haue small store, but when the time commeth that it shoulde be made, I will prouide as much as I can here, that it may bee sent downe when the Nasade commeth. The stuffe that they haue readie spunne is about fiue thousand waight, and they say that they trust to haue by that time they come downe yarne ynough to make 20. cables. As concerning a copie of the Alphabet in ciphers Master Gray hath written hither that Robert Austen had one, which he willed that he shoulde deliuer to you. Thus I surcease, beseeching God to preserue you in health, and to send you your hearts desire.

By yours to command to his power,

Thomas Hawtrey.

* * * * *

A letter of master Richard Gray one of the first Agents of the Moscouie companie to Master Henrie Lane at Mosco, written in Colmogro the 19. of Februarie 1558.

[Sidenote: Lampas a great mart for the Samoeds in the North.] Worshipfull Sir, after heartie commendations &e. You shall vnderstand that this Lent commeth to Lampas such a number of men of diuers nations with wares, as hath not bene seene these ten yeeres. Thither came many out of Vgori: therefore I would haue bene there my selfe, and also haue receiued such money as is owning vs in wares by Kerill his brother and Osep Boscouo. For as you well know, thence they will go with their wares to the Mosco, and make vs payment with delayes, as they haue done these other yeeres past. Colobone and his partner be departed towards Lampas with seuen sleddes laden with victuals. Others also are gone to that Mart. As touching the bringing of money with you, it will bee good, for I assure you since our comming to this countrey haue not so many persons gone to the Sea, as will doe this yeere. Trusting that God will send good store of traine oyle, I will cause as much caske to bee in a readinesse as I can, if you shall think it meete to send some money before. All our old hempe is spunne and wrought in tenne cables from fifteene ynches to ten the least, and thirteene Hausers from six ynches to three ynches: and all may weigh white eight and twenty thousand pound weight and vpwarde. There is in hempe ockam fiue thousand pound two hundred weight in twelue sackes at the least: the flaxe that came downe in the Nassadaes with those seuen podes that came last is all spunne with a good part of that hempe that came last. God send more shortly, for all that is here and that is comming in the three other sleddes will bee dispatched by the fourth weeke in Lent. Within these few dayes I bought thirteen podes, seuen pound of hempe that cost two robles, twenty eight altines, foure pence, which together with that that was bought before, shall bee laide in dipping and sounding lines, for it is very good. There are spent aboue fiftie barrels of tarre alreadie: you shall vnderstand that these eight workemen will spinne and lay aboue fourescore and tenne thousand pound of hempe, so it bee dressed readie to their hands, hauing two to turne the wheeles, and two to winde vp. Therefore I haue agreed with these two boyes to serue the worshipfull companie foure yeeres a piece. One of them windeth vp and is very apt to spinne: therefore I will haue two other young men Russes to spinne, if they can finde good sureties for their trueth. I haue bene in hand with these two yong men that came put of the Trinitie, and they with me, but vnder seuen pound a year they will not serue, nor Thomas Bunting that was Roger Bunting his seruant. Therefore I would haue three Russes at the least to spinne, fiue of them will be as good as these three, and will not be so chargeable all, as one of these would be. I thinke it were good that our Nassada were somewhat strengthened in her floore on both sides with plankes of fiue or sixe ynches thicke, from the stemme to the sterne, as I haue written to Thomas Hawtrey at Vologda. Also if you shall so thinke meet, your waxe and tallowe shall be laden in two Dosnickes, for they bee meete to goe aboord the shippes: I doe intend to set vp an house at Boroseua ouer against the place whereat the shippes shall ride, your aduise therein I expect it shall not cost aboue three robles, and yet if we will, there shall be two warme roomes in it. As for other matter at this present I haue not to trouble you withall, and if it would please yow I would be glad to heare some good newes of Master Ienkinson. Thus Iesus be with you and be his guide.

Postscriptum.

[Sidenote: White hawks and white beares prohibited without licence.] As for these our Hawkes they bee not white, but white and mayled, but indeede be Iarfawkons. These dayes past our Olen died. So this yeere our Masters of the companie are like to haue none, nor any white beares. Neither may any passe out of the realme without a special licence from the Emperour.

I intend God willing to goe to Lampas, if I doe I will take foure or fiue kerseys with me, but as for money there is small store here to carie.

Yours, Richard Gray.

* * * * *

A letter of Thomas Alcocke to the worshipfull Richard Gray, and Henrie Lane

Agents in Moscouia from Tirwill in Polonia, written in Tirwill the 26. of Aprill 1558.

My duety premised vnto your worships, with commendations &c. It may please you to be aduertised, that my last I sent from Smolensco, which I trust you haue receiued with other letters to diuers of our Englishmen, wherein I certified you of my long retayning there, as also of my departure from thence, and howe that I had hired a Totar to bring mee to Danske. We came to a certaine village on Satterday the sixe and twentieth of Februarie, and there remained that night and Sunday to refresh our horses, intending to haue gone away on Munday earely. But on Saterday at night one of his neighbours departed to Tirwill, and there declared to the Captaine howe that at such a place there was a Dutch man that was come from the Mosco, and woulde ride to Danske, saying, for the one, I cannot tell what he is. The Captaine incontinent ridde to the King to shewe him thereof, so that without any delay there was sent out for mee one of the Gentlemen of the Kings house, and one of the Mesnickes of the Towne with sixe Officers to take mee. They came thither in the night about midnight, and there apprehended mee and tooke all that I had from me: they left me nothing but my clothes to put on my backe, and so brought mee to Tirwill to the Captaines house, where before I dyned, I had a payre of fetters clapped on my legges, wherewithall I sate vntill it was Munday in the Easter-weeke. On which day, after long and earnest calling to the Captaine as he ridde by the windowe, he commaunded the Marshall that mine yrons shoulde be taken off, but no worde I could heare when I should be deliuered out of captiuitie till it was Saint George his day: on which day I was had before the Marshall, who declared vnto me that the Kings Maiestie had shewed his mercie and goodnesse towardes mee: for his pleasure was that I should be deliuered out of prison to depart into England, but no way else. So after I had giuen thankes for the Kings Maiesties goodnesse shewed vnto me, I desired him that he woulde be a meane that I might haue the remaynder of such thinges as were taken from me restored vnto me againe. Hee made me answere, that I might thanke God that I escaped with my head, and that if euer there came any more of vs through the land, they should not so doe. The weeke before Easter they deliuered mee my Corobia againe with all thinges that were therein. They tooke from mee in money nine Hungers gylderns in golde, fiue shillings foure pence in Lettoes money, fourtie Altines in Russe money, whereof twentie and more were for tokens, halfe an angell and a quarter of Master Doctour Standishes, with his golde ring.[Sidenote: Doctor Standish the Emperours Phisition.] Your two pieces of money (Master Gray) that you sent to your wife and daughter, with my two pieces of Boghary money. Of all this I had eight Hungers gilderns deliuered mee the thirde weeke of mine imprisonment to paye for my charges, which stoode mee in a Doller a weeke. So that at the day of my deliuerie I had but three gyldernes left me. For the rest I made a supplication to the Captaine and had the like answere giuen mee as the Marshall gaue me. So that all the rest of the thinges before written are lost, and no recouerie to bee had, which grieueth me more for the tokens sake then doeth mine eight weeks imprisonment. They haue also my sword, my bootes, my bowe and arrowes that I bought at Smolensco, which cost me foure marks, my sled, my felt, the comhold, a booke of the Flowres of godly prayers, and my booke wherein my charges were written. Of all these I can get nothing againe, not so much as my two bookes.

After I had remayned there fiue and thirtie dayes, I was had before the Captaine vp into a great chamber to bee examined for letters and of the cause of my comming through the Countrey. In the Captaines companie was one of the Lordes of Danske. They demaunded of mee where my letters were, I declared vnto them that I had none: your Officers (sayd I) tooke me when I was in my bedde, they searched mee and tooke all that I had from mee, if there be any they shall finde them among my stuffe which they haue. They asked mee then, for what cause I went home ouer lande? I declared vnto them, that the Winter beeing a warme season, and hauing intelligence that the frozen Sea was not much frozen, and supposing this Sommer it would be nauigable, I was onely sent to prouide a Shippe to be sent to passe the sayde Seas to discouer Cataia: which if God graunted wee might doe, it woulde not onely bee a commoditie to the Realme of Englande, but vnto all Christian landes, by the riches that might be brought from thence, if the histories bee true that are written thereof. Much other communication I had with them concerning the same voyage. Then he demaunded of mee what wares wee brought into Russia, and what we carried from thence. I declared the same vnto them. Then they burdened mee, that wee brought thither thousandes of ordinance, as also of harneis, swordes, with other munitions of warre, artificers, copper, with many other things; I made them answere, that wee had brought thither about one hundred shirtes of mayle, such olde thinges newe scowred as no man in Englande woulde weare. Other talke they had with mee concerning the trade of Moscouia too long to commit to writing.

[Sidenote: An attempt to hinder our trade to Mosvouia by the Hans townes and Easterlings.] At my comming hither heere were Ambassadours from the townes of Danske, Lubeck, and Hamburgh, as also out of Liefland to desire this King to bee their Captaine and head their intended voyage, which was to stoppe all such shippes as shoulde goe out of England for Mocouia. Whereunto the King graunted, and immediately they departed to prepare their shippes. So that I am afraide that either these our enemies, or the great warres that we haue with France and Scotland will be an occasion that you shall haue no shippes at Colmogro this yeere.

To conclude, although I haue no tokens to deliuer them, that the tokens taken from me were sent vnto, yet I will declare vnto them that I had tokens for them, with the mischance. And thus I commit you to Almightie God with the rest of the companie who keepe you in health to his holy will and pleasure.

By yours to commaund

THOMAS ALCOCKE.

* * * * *

A Letter of Master Anthonie Ienkinson vpon his returne from Boghar to the worshipful Master Henrie Lane Agent for the Moscouie compante resident in Vologda, written in the Mosco the 18. of September, 1559.

Worshipfull Sir, after my heartie commendations premised with most desire to God of your welfare and prosperous successe in all your affaires. It may please you to bee aduertised that the fourth of this present I arriued with Richard Iohnson and Robert Iohnson all in health, thankes bee to God. Wee haue bene as farre as Boghar, [Footnote: Bokhara.] and had proceeded farther on our voyage toward the lande of Cathay, had it not bene for the vncessant any continuall warres, which are in all these brutall and wilde countrey, that it is at this present impossible to passe, neither went there any Carauan of people from Boghar that way these three yeere. And although our iourney hath bene so miserable, dangerous, and chargeable with losses, charges and expenses, as my penne is not able to expresse the same: yet shall wee bee able to satisfie the woorshipfull Companies mindes, as touching the discouerie of The Caspian Sea, with the trade of merchandise to bee had in such landes and countreyes as bee thereabout adiacent, and, haue brought of the wares and commodities of those Countries able to answere the principall with profite: wishing that there were vtterance for as great a quantitie of kersies and other wares as there is profile to bee had in the sales of a small quantitie, (all such euill fortunes beeing escaped as to vs haue chaunced this present voyage,) for then it woulde be a trade woorthie to bee followed. Sir, for that I trust you will be here shortly (which I much desire) I will deferre the discourse with you at large vntill your comming, as well touching my trauel, as of other things. Sir, Iohn Lucke departed from hence toward England the seuenth of this present, and intendeth to passe by the way of Sweden, by whom I sent a letter to the worshipfull Companie, and haue written that I intend to come downe vnto Colmogoro to be readie there at the next shipping to imbarke my selfe for England, declaring that my seruice shal not be needful here, for that you are a man able to serne their worships in greater affaires then they haue heere to doe, so farre as I perceiue. As touching the Companies affaires heere, I referre you to Christopher Hudsons letters, for that I am but newly arriued. Hauing heere but litle businesse to doe, I send you Richard Iohnson to helpe you there in your affaires. Thus giuing you most heartie thanks for my wench Aura Soltana, I commend you to the tuition of

God, who send you health with hearts desire. [Sidenote: This was a yong Tartar girle which he gaue to the Queene afterwards.]

Your assured to command,

Anthonie Ienkinson.

* * * * *

A Letter of the Moscouie companie to their Agents in Russia, Master Henrie Lane, Christopher Hudson, and Thomas Glouer sent in their seuenth voyage to Saint Nicholas with three ships, the Swallowe, the Philip and Marie, and the Iesus the fifth of May, 1560.

After our heartie commendations to you. The twelfth day of the last moneth here arriued in safety, thanks be to God, our two ships, and by them we receiued your letters and inuoices very well perceiuing what you haue laden in them. The tallowe came euill conditioned and broken, by reason it came in Corrobias, wee lose and spoyle more then the Caske will cost, and much of this tallowe is verie euill, blacke, soft and putrified. Touching the Waxe, as yet wee knowe not howe the weight will rise, by reason that some of it was lost in the barkes. The weight of the last yeeres waxe did not rise so well as the other yeeres before it did. There had neede good heede bee taken in the weighing. Also much of this Waxe had a great foote, and is not so faire waxe as in times past wee baue had. You must cause the foote to bee taken off before you doe weigh it, or else you must seeke to haue a good allowance for it. The traine Oyles which you laded this yeere came well conditioned, and the caske was good and of a good sise. But if they were made a little bigger, it were the better, for they be not hogsheads. You haue written to vs to send you caske which is not heere to be had, neither doe wee thinke it so best if it were heere, considering it must goe either shaken and bounde vp, or else emptie, which will bee pesterable, and likewise will shrinke and drie, and not be fitte to lade oyles in. Therefore our minde is, you shall cause so much caske to bee made there of the sise of hogsheads as will serue both for; your oyles and tallowe, and let them be well trimmed with pitch on the heads and seames, and stand full of water three or foure dayes before you put Oyles in them; Your Cowper may bee ouerseer to them that make them, that they be well hooped and cleere tymber without knottes, the woorst caske you may put the tallowe in. Hee that seeth the filling of the oyles had neede to looke well to it, for there was much water in this that, came nowe. Wee perceiue you haue bought and haue in a readinesse one hundred and fourtie tunnes of oyles, and that if neede bee you may haue more store. Wherefore we doe minde to send, you shipping for three hundred tunnes and vpwards, because we would haue this next Summer as great a returne as you can of the commodities of that Countrey, as also such of our wares as you haue that are not vendible, or will not be solde or bartered, because we would haue a ful knowledge and state of our accounts. The Sables which you sent this yeere be very base, among them all we could not make one principall timber: wee haue alwayes written vnto you to send them that bee good or else none. The Woluerings were indifferent, and some of the wolues, the rest verie base, the Lusernes but meane, the Lettes not so large skinnes as we hane had: the best is, they were of a new death. As for the Ermines, they cost more there with you, then we can sell them for here. Therefore buy no more of them, nor of Squirels, for wee lost the one halfe in the other. The wares that we would haue you prouide against the comming of the shippes are, Waxe, Tallowe, trayne Oyles, Flaxe, Cables and Ropes, and Furres, such as we haue written to you for in our last letters by the shippes: and from hencefoorth not to make any great prouision of any rich Furres except principall Sables and Lettes: for now there is a Proclamation made that no furres shall be worne here, but such as the like is growing here within this our Realme. Also we perceiue that there might be a great deale of tallowe more prouided in a yeere than you send. Therefore our minde is, you should enlarge somewhat more in the price, and to send vs if you can three thousand podes a yeere: for we doe most good in it. And likewise the Russes, if you would giue them a reasonable price for their wares, woulde be the willinger to buy and sell with you, and not to carie so much to Nouogrode as they doe, but woulde rather bring it to Vologda to you, both Waxe, Tallowe, Flaxe, Hempe, and all kinde of other wares fitte for our Countrey. Our minde is you should prouide for the next ships fiue hundred Losh hides, of them that be large and faire, and thickest in hand, and to be circumspect in the choosing, that you buy them that bee killed in season and well dryed and whole. If they be good we may sell them here for sixteene shillings and better the piece, wee would haue the whole skinnes that is, the necke and legges withal, for these that you sent now lacke their neckes and legges. Neuerthelesse for this time you must sende them as you may get them: if you coulde finde the meanes that the haire might bee clipped off them, they woulde not take so much roome in the shippes as they doe. We perceiue by your letters that the prices of Waxe doe rise there with you, by reason that the Poles and Lifelanders doe trade into Russia by licence: which, if there shoulde bee peace betweene them, would be an occasion that all other commodities in Russia woulde rise to a bigger price, and not be sufficient to serue them and vs too, and likewise woulde bring downe there the price of our commodities. Therefore we thinke it good you shoulde make a supplication to the Emperour in the name of The Companie to returne the trade from Rye and Reuel to vs, especially for such wares as wee doe buy: promising that wee will bee bounde to take them at a reasonable price, as wee haue bought them in times past: and likewise that wee will bring to them such wares of ours, as are thought fitte for the Countrey, and so sell them at such reasonable prices as wee haue done. If this shoulde not come to passe, wee might be out of hope of doing any good by the trade there: but that we haue a further hope of some good trade to be found out by Master Antonie Ienkinson: by reason we doe perceiue by your letters, that raw silke is as plentifull in Persia, as flaxe is in Russia: beside other commodities that may come from thence. Wee vnderstand by your letters that you be at a point with the Russe for the Waxe, Tallow, and traine oyles that he shipped the last yere for 311 robles 20 altines, which is well: although much be not gotten by it, but because they should not vnderstand our reckonings. We much maruel what you mean to buy Seale skins and tanne them. All that you haue sent in times past lie here vnsold, and will yeelde no money. If you send 100 of them tawed with the haire on, they will bee solde, or else not. In our shippe we will send you such things as you write to haue for the ropers: and wee would they should make more store of small cables and ropes, as cables of 7, 8, 9, 10, 11, 12. inches. For these great cables be not for euery man; and the greatest cables bee not best laded: and likewise small ropes for shroudes, sholes, and other small tackeling: and that you looke better to the spinning of their yarne that it be euen and well tarred. The sables that you doe mind to send vs let them be principall and fayre, and not past foure or fine timbars. For they will not be so commonly worne here as they haue bin with noble men: and likewise of Luserns send fewe and principal good. We mind to send you in our shippes 100 tunnes of salte. And because we perceiue that balast is hardly to be had at our lading place there with you, we would you shoulde haue in a readinesse 100 tunnes of the white stones whereof you sent vs home an example two yeres past. And likewise to haue in a readinesse mastes of all sortes for our shippes: for we know not what neede wee shall haue of them. The bringer hereof is Thomas Alcock, he could not be suffered the last yeare to passe through Poland. And as we, wrote vnto you in our shippes, hee is our seruant for yeares: And for that we know him to be honest, true and painefull, our mind is he shalbe placed where he may do best seruice. He doth know the commodities and discommodities of all kinde of wares which you doe send vs. Therefore we would you should credite his sayings both in quantitie of wares and goodnes, as also wherin is most our profit. We see by your letters that your opinion is that the rope-makers should remaine there two yeres more; and that you haue prouided great plentie of hempe, which we are content withall. But as yet we haue solde none of our cables or halsers, neither is the proofe of them knowen; because the first you sent vs were made of flaxe, which are worth no money: for after they be once wet they will rotte and moulder away like mosse. And those which you sent vs now last, by misfortune there with you at the lading were wette and fretted in many places, and haue lost their colour: by meanes whereof they be not so vendible as if they had come well conditioned. Of an hard beginning we trust God will send vs a good ending. We hope in your next letters to heare good newes of the proceedings of Master Antonie Ienkinson. We perceiue by his letters that Astracan is not so good a Mart towne as the fame hath gone of it: and maruell much that round pewter should be so good, and good chepe there, and from whence it should come. And whereas you write that you wil come for England in our next shippes, we would gladly haue you to remaine there vntill the next yere following, for the better instruction of our seruants there; who have not had so long time of continuance for the language and knowledge of the people, countrey, and wares as you haue had. [Sidenote: Christopher Hodson and Thomas Glouer appointed Agents 1560.] Neuerthelesse if you will needs come away, we haue no doubt, but that you will leaue good order with our seruants there, namely with Christopher Hodson and Thomas Glouer, whom we appoint to remaine there as Agents in your roome, till further order bee taken: not doubting but that they will vse themselues so discreetely and wisely in all their doings, as shall be to the worship and benefite of this company. And as we haue a good hope in them that they will be carefull, diligent and true in all their doings: so haue we no lesse hope, in all the rest of our seruants there, that they will bee not onely obedient to them (considering what roome they be in) but also will be carefull, diligent and true euery one in his roome and place for the benefite and profite of the company: That hereafter in the absence of others they may be called and placed in the like roome there or elsewhere. And if you find any to be disobedient and stobborne, and will not be ruled; wee will you shall send him home in our shippes: who shall find such small fauour and friendship during the time that he hath to serue, as by his disobedience and euill seruice hee hath deserued. And whereas Christopher Hodson hath written to come home, as partly he hath good cause, considering the death of his father and mother: yet in regard that Sir George Barne and the Ladie his wife were his special friends in his absence, we doubt not but that he wil remain in the roome, which we haue appointed him, if you doe not tarie and remaine there, till farther order be taken: and for his seruice and paines hee shall be considered, as reason is, as friendly as if his friends were liuing. Thus we trust you will take such order the one to remaine at the Mosco, and the other at Colmogro, or elsewhere, as most neede is. Thomas Alcocke is desirous to be in the Mosco: neuerthelesse you shall find him reasonable to serue where he may doe most good. The 62 robles which you receiued of Iohn Boucher we haue payed him here, and also the 8 robles, which you receiued the yere before of Christopher Rose, and the money which you receiued more of George Burton, for the which we haue you our debtors. Thus we rest, referring that which is here omitted to the report of the bringer: and so God haue you in his keeping. Also we would that you should send vs in our shippes 200 horse-clothes more. The things before written wee would that you should let our seruants see and reade, to the intent they may perceiue our mindes.

Another letter to the foresaid parties. 1560.

This letter before written is the copie of one sent you by Thomas Alcock, trusting that hee was with you long since. [Sidenote: Stockholme.] The 26 day of the last moneth we receiued a letter from him, dated in Stockholme in Sweden the 14 day of Ianuary, and we perceiue by his letter that hee had talked with a Dutch man that came lately from the Mosco, who informed him that our friend Master Antony Ienkinson was returned to the Mosco in September last past, but how farre he had beene, or what he had done, he could not tell. [Sidenote: Iohn Luck taken prisoner in Lieflande.] Also he wrote that one Iohn Lucke a Ioyner was taken by the Liefelanders, and put in prison. As yet wee haue not heard from the sayd Iohn Lucke, nor know not whether he be released out of prison or not. We suppose that by him you wrote some letter which as yet is not come to our hands: so that we thinke hee is yet in prison, or otherwise dispatched out of the way. The fifteenth day of December wee receiued a letter from Christopher Hodson, dated in the Mosco the 29 of Iuly, by the way of Danske: which is in effect a copie of such another receiued from him in our shippes. [Sidenote: The Swallow.] You shal vnderstand that we haue laden in three good shippes of ours these kind of wares following: to wit, in the Swallowe of London, Master vnder God Steuen Burrow, 34 fardels N'o 136 broad short clothes, and foure fardels N'o 58 Hampshire Kersies: and 23 pipes of bastards and seckes, and 263 pieces of raisins and 4 hogsheds N'o 154 pieces of round pewter, and ten hogsheds and poncheons of prunes, and one dryfatte with Almonds. [Sidenote: The Philip and Marie.] And in the Philip and Marie, Master vnder God Thomas Wade, 25 fardels N'o 100 broad clothes, and three fardels N'o 42 Hampshire Kersies and thirtie pipes of seckes and bastards, and 100 pieces of raisins. [Sidenote: The Iesus.] And in the Iesus of London, Master vnder God Arthur Pette, 10 fardels N'o 40 broade shorte clothes, and twenty seuen pipes of bastards and seckes, as by the Inuoices herewith inclosed may appeare: Also you shall receiue such necessaries as you did write to bee sent for the rope makers: trusting that you shall haue better successe with them which you shall send vs in these ships, then with the rest which you haue sent vs yet: for we as yet haue sold none of them. And whereas we wrote vnto you in our former letter, that we would send you a hundred tunnes of salte, by reason it is so deare here we doe send you but nine tunnes and a halfe, for it cost here tenpence the bushell the first penie: namely in the Swallow 6 tunnes and a halfe, in the Philip and Marie one tunne and a halfe, and in the Iesus one tunne and a halfe: The 4 hogsheads of round pewter goe in the Swallow and in the Philip and Marie N'o 154 pieces, as is aforesaid. We send you three ships, trusting that you haue prouided according to our former writing good store of lading for them. If yee haue more wares then will lade the ships, let it be Traine oyles that you leaue behinde: the price is not here so good as it was; it is worth here 9 pound the tunne. We thinke it good you should let the smaller ship bring as much of the traine as she can cary: And that the masters of the ships do looke wel to the romaging, for they might bring away a great deale more than they doe, if they would take paine in the romaging: and bestowe the traine by it selfe, and the waxe and tallowe by it selfe: for the leakage of the traine doth fowle the other wares much. As for Allard the skinner, if you thinke good he may come home in these shippes. We haue no doubt but that you Henrie Lane, if you minde to come home now in these ships as you requested, will leaue such good order there with our seruants as shall bee for our most profite and their preferment, if they doe their dueties diligently and truely. If our friend Master Antonie Ienkinson bee returned, and meane to come away in these ships to declare his mind and opinion of his trauaile, if need require and he be so minded he may returne thither by land and be there by the fine of Ianuarie or before. But as we be vncertaine whether he be returned or not: so we know not what he hath done, nor what benefite may arise hereafter of his trauaile. Therefore in this wee remit it to his and your good discretions. Wee send you Thomas Hawtrey which is our seruant for yeeres: our minde is he should be placed, where he may doe best seruice.

Also we send you Nicholas Chancelour to remaine there, who is our apprentice for yeeres: our minde is hee should be set about such businesse as he is most fit for: he hath been kept at writing schoole along: he hath his Algorisme, and hath vnderstanding of keeping of bookes of reckonings. We send you now but 100 Kersies: but against the next yeere, if occasion serue, wee will send you a greater quantitie, according as you shall aduise vs: One of the pipes of seckes that is in the Swallow, which hath 2 round compasses upon the bung, is to be presented to the Emperour: for it is special good. The nete waight of the 10 puncheons of prunes is 4300. 2 thirds 1 pound. It is written particularly vpon the head of euery puncheon: and the nete weight of the fatte of almonds is 500 li. two quarters. The raisins, prunes, and almonds you were best to dispatch away at a reasonable price, and principally the raisins, for in keeping of them will be great losse in the waight, and the fruit will decay. We thinke it good that you prouide against the next yeere for the comming of our shippes 20 or 30 bullockes killed and salted, for beefe is very deare here. Therefore you were best to saue some of this salt that we doe send you in these ships for the purpose. [Sidenote: The salt of Russia is not so good as Baye salt.] The salte of that countrey is not so good. In this you may take the opinion of the masters of the shippes. [Sidenote: Foxe skinnes white, blacke and russet vendible in England.] Foxe skins, white, blacke, and russet will be vendible here. The last yere you sent none: but there were mariners that bought many. If any of the mariners doe buy any trifling furres or other commodities, we will they shall be registred in our pursers bookes, to the intent we may know what they be. We desire to know how the Emperour tooke the letter which we sent in our ships, as an answere to the letter that came in his name and vnder his seale for the sixe thousand dallers. [Sidenote: May 5. 1560.] Thus wee rest, committing you to God, from London the fift day of May 1560.

For lacke of time the gouernours haue not firmed this letter: which is the copie of the other two letters firmed by them.

Yours, William Mericke.
Yours, Blase Sanders.

* * * * *

The maner of Iustice by lots in Russia, written by Master Henrie Lane, and executed in a controuersie betweene him and one Sheray Costromitskey in Mosco. 1560.

After the comming home into Russia of Ioseph Napea the first ambassadour to Queene Marie, I remaining the Agent there, sundrie Russian marchants by Iosephs procurement obtained letters from the Emperour to freight goods and passe in our ships for England: which thing vpon good consideration I answered and refused. They were then driuen to credite vs and compound in value vntill the next returne. At which time, notwithstanding good accompt in the value of 600 robles, there grewe question by their double demand. [Sidenote: Triall by combat or lot.] So in April Anno 1560. before my comming from Moscouia, they obtained trial by combat or letter to haue their summe double, or as I proffered 600 robles. For combatte I was prouided of a strong willing Englishman, Robert Best, one of the companies seruants: whome the Russes with their Champion refused. So that we had the words of our priuiledge put in effect, which were to draw lots. The day and maner of triall appointed by the Emperour at his castle in his palace and high Court of Moscouia was thus. The Emperours two Treasurers, being also Chancelours and chiefe Iudges, sate in court. They appointed officers to bring me, mine interpreter, and the other, through the great presse within the rayle or barre, and permitted me to sit downe some distance from them: the aduerse parties being without at the barre. Both parties were first perswaded with great curtesie, to wit, I to enlarge mine offer, and the Russes to mitigate their challenge. Notwithstanding that I protested my conscience to be cleere, and their gaine by accompt to bee sufficient, yet of gentlenes at the magistrates request, I made proffer of 100 robles more: which was openly commended, but of the plaintifes not accepted. Then sentence passed with our names in two equall balles of waxe made and holden vp by the Iudges, their sleeues stripped vp. Then with standing vp and wishing well to the trueth attributed to him that should be first drawen, by both consents among the multitude they called a tall gentleman, saying: Thou with such a coate or cap, come vp: where roome with speede was made. He was commanded to holde his cappe, wherein they put the balles, by the crowne vpright in sight, his arme not abasing. With like circumspection, they called at aduenture another tall gentleman, commanding him to strip vp his right sleene, and willed him with his bare arme to reach vp, and in Gods name seuerally to take out the two balles: which he did, deliuering to either Iudge one. Then with great admiration the lotte in ball first taken out was mine: which was by open sentence so pronounced before all the people, and to be the right and true parte. The chiefe plaintifes name was Sheray Costromitsky. I was willed forthwith to pay the plaintifes the summe by me appointed. Out of which for their wrong or sinne, as it was termed, they payd tenne in the hundred to the Emperor. Many dayes after, as their maner is, the people took our nation to be true and vpright dealers, and talked of this iudgement to our great credite.

The former letters dated 1558, 1559, and 1560, should all followe M. Ienkinsons voyage to Boghar.

* * * * *

The first voyage made by Master Anthonie Ienkinson, from the Citie of London toward the land of Russia, begun the twelfth of May, in the yeere 1557.

First by the grace of God, the day and yeere aboue mentioned, I departed from the sayd Citie, and the same day at Grauesend embarked my selfe in a good shippe, named the Primerose, being appointed, although vnworthy, chiefe captaine of the same, and also of the other 3 good ships, to say, the Iohn Euangelist, the Anne, and the Trinitie, hauing also the conduct of the Emperour of Russia his ambassadour named Osep Nepea Gregoriwich, who passed with his company in the sayde Primerose. And thus our foure tall shippes being well appointed, aswell for men as victuals as other necessarie furniture, the saide twelfth day of the moneth of May, we weyed our ankers, and departed from the saide Grauesend, in the after noone, and plying down the Thames, the wind being Easterly, and fayre weather, the 13 day we came a ground with the Primerose, upon a sand called the blacke taile, where we sate fast vntill the 14 day in the morning, and then God be praysed, she came off: and that day we plyed downe as ferre as our Ladie of Holland, and there came to an anker, the wind being Easterly, and there remayned vntill the 20 day: then we weyed and went out at Goldmore gate, and from thence in at Balsey slade, and so into Orwel wands, where we came to an anker: but as we came out at the sayd Goldemore gate, the

Trinitie came on ground on certaine rockes, that lye to the Northward of the said gate, and was like to be bilged and lost. But by the aide of God, at the last she came off againe, being very leake: and the 21 day the Primerose remaining at an anker in the wands, the other three shippes bare into Orwel hauen where I caused the sayd Trinitie to be grounded, searched, and repaired. So we remayned in the said hauen, vntill the 28. day: and then the winde being Westerly, the three shippes that were in the hauen, weyed and came forth, and in comming forth the Iohn Euangelist came on ground vpon a sand, called the Andros, where she remained one tide, and the next full sea she came off againe without any great hurt, God be praised.

The 29 day in the morning all foure ships weied in the Wands, and that tide went as farre as Orfordnesse, where we came an anker, because the wind was Northerly: And about sixe of the clocke at night, the wind vered to the Southwest and we weyed anker, and bare cleere of the nesse, and then set our course Northeast and by North vntill midnight, being then cleare of Yarmouth sands. [Sidenote: Iune.] Then we winded North and by West, and Northnorthwest, vntill the first of Iune at noone, then it waxed calme and continued so vntill the second day at noone: then the winde came at Northwest, with a tempest, and much raine, and we lay close by, and caped Northnortheast, and Northeast and by North, as the winde shifted, and so continued vntill the third day at noone: then the wind vered Westerly againe, and we went North our right course, and so continued our way vntill the fourth day, at three of the clocke in the afternoone, at which time the wind vered to the Northwest againe and blew a fresh gale, and so continued vntill the seuenth day in the morning, we lying with all our shippes close by, and caping to the Northwards: and then the wind vering more Northerly, we were forced to put roomer with the coast of England againe, and fell ouerthwart Newcastle, but went not into the hauen, and so plied vpon the coast the eighth day and the ninth.

The tenth day the winde came to the Northnorthwest, and we were forced to beare roomer with Flamborow head, where we came to an anker, and there remained vntil the seuenteenth day. Then the winde came faire, and we weyed, and set our course North and by East, and so continued the same with a mery winde vntill the 21 at noone, at which time we tooke the sunne, and had the latitude in sixty degrees. Then we shifted our course, and went Northnortheast, and Northeast and by North, vntill the 25. day. [Sidenote: Heilick Islands in 66 degrees 40 minutes.] Then we discouered certaine Islands, called Heilick Islands, lying from vs Northeast, being in the latitude of sixtie sixe degrees, 40 minutes. [Sidenote: Rost Islands.] Then we went north and by West, because we would not come too nigh the land, and running that course foure houres, we discouered, and had sight of Rost Islands, ioining to the main land of Finmarke. Thus continuing our course along the coast of Norway and Finmark, the 27 day we tooke the Sunne, being as farre shot as Lofoot, and had the latitude in 69 degrees. And the same day in the afternoone appeared ouer our heads a rainebow, like a semicircle, with both ends vpwarde. [Sidenote: Malestrand a strange whirle poole.] Note that there is between the said Rost Islands and Lofoot, a whirle poole called Malestrand, [Footnote: Maelström.] which from halfe ebbe vntill halfe flood, maketh such a terrible noise, that it shaketh the ringes in the doores of the inhabitants houses of the sayd Islands tenne miles off. Also if there commeth any Whale within the current of the same, they make a pitifull crie. Moreouer, if great trees be caried into it by force of streams, and after with the ebbe be cast out againe, the ends and boughs of them haue bene so beaten, that they are like the stalkes of hempe that is bruised. Note, that all the coaste of Finmarke is high mountaines and hils, being couered all the yere with snow. And hard aboord the shoare of this coast, there is 100 or 150 fadomes of water in depth. [Sidenote: Zenam Island.] Thus proceeding and sailing forward, we fell with an Island called Zenam, being in the latitude of 70 degrees. About this Island we saw many Whales, very monstrous, about our ships, some, by estimation of 60 foot long: and being the ingendring time they roared and cried terriblie. [Sidenote: Kettelwike Island.] From thence we fell with an Island, called Kettelwicke.

This coast from Rost vnto Lofoot lieth North and south, and from Lofoot to Zenam Northeast and southwest, and from Zenam to Kettelwike Eastnortheast and Westsouthwest. [Sidenote: Inger sound.] From the said Kettelwike we sailed East and by North 10 leagues, and fell with a land called Inger sound, where we fished, being becalmed, and tooke great plenty of Cods. [Sidenote: The North Cape.] Thus plying along the coast, we fell with a Cape, called the North Cape, which is the Northermost land that wee passe in our voyage to S. Nicholas, and is in the latitude of 71 degrees and ten minutes, and is from Inger sound East, and to the Northwards 15 leagues. And being at this North Cape the second day of Iuly, we had the sunne at North 4 degrees aboue the Horizon. The third day wee came to Wardhouse, hauing such mists that we could not see the land. [Sidenote: Wardhouse] This Wardhouse is a Castle standing in an Island 2 miles from the maine of Finland, subiect to the king of Denmarke, and the Easternmost land that he hath. There are two other Islands neere adioining vnto that, whereon the Castle of Wardhouse standeth. The inhabitants of those three Islands liue onely by fishing, and make much, stockefish which they dry with frost: their most feeding is fish; bread and drinke they haue none, but such as is brought them from other places. [Sidenote: Cattell fed with fish.] They haue small store of cattell, which are also fed with fish. From Wardhouse we sailed Southsoutheast ten leagues, and fell with a Cape of land called Kegor, [Footnote: Cape Njemetsky.] the

Northermost part of the land of Lappia. [Sidenote: The Monastery of Pechinchow.] And betweene Wardhouse, and the said Cape is a great Bay, called Dommeshaff, [Footnote: Varanger fjord.] in the South part whereof is a Monasterie of Monkes of the Russes religion, called Pechinchow. Thus proceeding forward and sayling along the coast of the said land of Lappia, winding Southeast, the fourth day through great mists and darkenes we lost the company of the other three ships, and met not with them againe, vntill the seuenth day, when we fell with a Cape or head land called Swetinoz, [Footnote: Cape Swjatojnos.] which is the entring into the Bay of S. Nicholas. At this Cape lieth a great stone, to the which the barkes that passed thereby, were wont to make offrings of butter, meale, and other victuals, thinking that vnlesse they did so, their barkes or vessels should there perish, as it hath bene oftentimes seene: and there it is very darke and mistie. [Sidenote: Arzina reca the riuer where Hugh Willoughbie was frozen.] Note that the sixt day we passed by the place where Sir Hugh Willoughbie, with all his company perished, which is called Arzina reca, that to say, the riuer Arzina. [Footnote: Varzina.]

The land of Lappia is an high land, hauing snow lying on it commonly all the yere. The people of the Countrey are halfe Gentiles: they liue in the summer time neere the sea side, and vse to take fish, of the which they make bread, and in the winter they remoue vp into the countrey into the woods, where they vse hunting, and kill Deere, Beares, Woolues, Foxes, and other beasts, with whose flesh they be nourished, [Sidenote: The Lappians couered all sauing their eies.] and with their skinnes apparelled in such strange fashion, that there is nothing seene of them bare but their eies. They haue none other habitation, but onely in tents, remouing from place to place according to the season of the yeere. They know no arte nor facultie, but onely shooting, which they exercise dayly, as well men as women, and kill such beasts as serue them for their foode. Thus proceeding along the coast from Swetinoz aforesaid, the ninth day of Iuly wee came to Cape Grace, [Footnote: Cape Krasnoj.] being in the latitude of 66 degrees and 45 minutes, and is at the entring in of the Bay of S. Nicholas. Aboord this land there is 20 or 30 fadoms water, and sundry grounds good to anker in. [Sidenote: The current at Cape Grace.] The current at this Cape runneth Southwest and Northeast. From this Cape wee proceeded along vntill we came to Crosse Island, which is seuen leagues from the sayd Cape Southwest: and from this Island, wee set ouer to the other side of the Bay, and went Southwest, and fell with an head land called Foxenose, which is from the sayd Island 25 leagues. [Sidenote: The entering of the Bay of S. Nicholas is seuen leagues broad at the least.] The entring of this Bay from Crosse Island to the neerest land on the other side is seuen leagues ouer. From Foxenose proceeding forward the twelfth day of the sayd moneth of Iuly, all our foure ships arriued in safetie at the road of Saint Nicholas in the land of Russia, where we ankered, and had sailed from London vnto the said roade seuen hundred and fifty leagues. The Russian ambassadour and his company with great ioy got to shore, and our ships here forthwith discharged themselues: and being laden againe, and hauing a faire winde, departed toward England the first of August. [Sidenote: August.] The third of the sayd moneth I with other of my company came vnto the citie of Colmogro, being an hundred verstes from the Bay of Saint Nicholas, and in the latitude of 64 degrees 25 minutes. I taried at the said Colmogro vntill the fifteenth day: and then I departed in a little boate vp the great riuer of Dwina, which runneth very swiftly, [Sidenote: Pinego River.] and the selfe same day passed by the mouth of a riuer called Pinego, leauing it on our lefte hand fifteen verstes from Colmogro. On both sides of the mouth of this riuer Pinego is high land, great rockes of Alablaster, great woods, and Pineapple trees lying along within the ground, which by report haue lien there since Noes flood. [Sidenote: The towne of Yemps.] And thus proceeding forward the nineteenth day in the morning, I came into a town called Yemps, an hundred verstes from Colmogro. All this way along they make much tarre, pitch and ashes of Aspen trees. [Sidenote: Vstiug.] From thence I came to a place called Vstiug, an ancient citie the last day of August. At this citie meete two riuers: the one called Iug, and the other Sucana, both which fall into the aforesaid riuer of Dwina. The riuer Iug hath his spring in the land of the Tartars called Cheremizzi, ioining to the countrey of Permia: and Succana hath his head from a lake not farre from the citie of Vologda. Thus departing from Vstiug, and passing by the riuer Succana, we came to a towne called Totma. About this place the water is verie shallow, and stonie, and troublesome for Barkes and boats of that countrey, which they call Nassades, and Dosneckes, to passe that way: wherein marchandise are transported from the aforesayd Colmogro to the citie of Vologhda. [Sidenote: The description of their Nassades.] These vessels called Nassades, are very long builded, broade made, and close aboue, flatte bottomed, and draw not aboue foure foote water; and will came two hundred tunnes: they haue none iron appertaining to them but all of timber, and when the winde serueth, they are made to sayle. Otherwise they haue many men, some to hale and drawe by the neckes with long small ropes made fast to the sayd boats, and some set with long poles. There are many of these barks vpon the riuer of Dwina: And the most part of them belongeth vnto the citie of Vologhda: for there dwell many marchants, and they occupie the said boates with carying of salte from the sea side vnto the sayd Vologhda. The twentieth of September I came vnto Vologhda, which is a great citie, and the riuer passeth through the midst of the same. The houses are builded with wood of Firre trees, ioyned one with another, and round without: the houses are foure square without any iron or stone worke, couered with birch barkes, and wood ouer the same: Their Churches are all of wood, two for euery parish, one to be heated for Winter, and the other for Summer.

On the toppes of their houses they laye much earth, for feare of burning: for they are sore plagued with fire. This Vologhda is in 59 degrees, eleuen minutes, and is from Colmogro, 1000 verstes.

All the way I neuer came in house, but lodged in the wildernesse, by the riuers side, and caried prouision for the way. [Sidenote: Good counsell for trauellers.] And he that will trauell those wayes, must carie with him an hatchet, a tinder boxe, and a kettle, to make fire and seethe meate, when he hath it: for there is small succour in those parts, vnlesse it be in townes.

[Sidenote: December.] The first day of December, I departed from Vologhda in poste in a sled, as the maner is in Winter. And the way to Moscua is as followeth. From Vologda to Commelski, 27 verstes, so to Olmor 25 verstes, so to Teloytske 20 verstes, so to Vre 30 verstes, so to Voshansko 30 versus, then to Yeraslaue 30 verstes, which standeth vpon the great riuer Volga, so to Rostoue, 50 verstes, then to Rogarin 30 verstes, so to Peraslaue 10 verstes, which is a great town, standing hard by a faire lake. From thence to Dowbnay 30 verstes, so to Godoroke 30 verstes, so to Owchay 30 verstes, and last to the Mosco 25 verstes, where I arriued the sixt day of December.

There are 14 postes called Yannes betweene Vologhda and Mosco, which are accompted 500 verstes asunder.

The 10 day of December I was sent for to the Emperors Castle by the sayd Emperour, and deliuered my letters vnto the Secretary, who talked with me of diuers matters, by the commandement of the Emperour. And after that my letters were translated, I was answered that I was welcome, and that the Emperour would giue me that I desired.

The 25 day, being the day of the natiuitie, I came into the Emperours presence, and kissed his hand, who sate aloft in a goodly chaire of estate, hauing on his heade a crowne most richly decked, and a staffe of gold in his hand, all apparelled with golde, and garnished with precious stones.

There sate distant from him about two yardes his brother, and next vnto him a boy of twelue yeares of age, who was inheritor to the Emperor of Casan, conquered by this Emperor 8 yeares past. Then sate his nobilitie round about him, richly apparelled with gold and stone. And after I had done obeisance to the Emperour, he with his own mouth calling me by my name, bade me to dinner, and so I departed to my lodging till dinner time, which was at six of the clocke, by candle light.

The Emperour dined in a fayre great hall, in the midst whereof was a pillar foure square, very artificially made, about which were diuers tables set, and at the vppermost part of the hall, sate the Emperour himselfe, and at his table sate his brother, his Vncles sonne, the Metropolitane, the young Emperour of Casan, and diuers of his noble men, all of one side. There were diuers Ambassadors, and other strangers, as well Christians as heathens, diuersly apparelled, to the number of 600 men, which dined in the sayd hall, besides 2000 Tartars, men of warre, which were newly come to render themselues to the Emperour, and were appointed to serue him in his wars against the Lieflanders, but they dined in other hals. I was set at a litle table, hauing no stranger with me, directly before the Emperors face. Being thus set and placed, the Emperour sent me diuers bowles of wine, and meade, and many dishes of meat from his own hand, which were brought me by a Duke, and my table serued all in gold and siluer, and so likewise on other tables, there were set bowles of gold, set with stone, worth by estimation 400 pounds sterling one cup, besides the plate which serued the tables.

There was also a cupbord of plate, most sumptuous and rich, which was not vsed: among the which, was a piece of golde of two yardes long, wrought in the toppe with towers, and dragons heads, also diuers barrels of gold and siluer, with Castles on the bungs, richly and artificially made. The Emperour and all the hall throughout was serued with Dukes: and when dinner was ended, the Emperour called me by name, and gaue me drinke with his own hand, and so I departed to my lodging.

Note, that when the Emperour drinketh, all the company stand vp, and at euery time he drinketh or tasteth of a dish of meate he blesseth himselfe. Many other things I sawe that day, not here noted.

The 4 of Ianuary, which was Twelftide with them, the Emperour, with his brother and all his nobles, all most richly appareled with gold, pearles, precious stones, and costly furres, with a crowne vpon his head, of the Tartarian fashion, went to the Church in procession, with the Metropolitan, and diuers bishops and priests. That day I was before the Emperour again in Russe apparell, and the Emperour asked if that were not I, and his Chancelor answered yea. Then he bad me to dinner: then came he out of the church, and went with the procession vpon the riuer, being all frozen, and there standing bare headed, with all his Nobles, there was a hole made in the ice, and the Metropolitan hallowed the water with great solemnitie and seruice, and did cast of the sayd water vpon the Emperors sonne and the Nobility. That done, the people with great thronging filled pots of the said water to carie home to their houses, and diuers children were throwen in, and sicke people, and plucked out quickly againe, and diuers Tartars christened: all which the Emperour beheld. Also there were brought the

Emperours best horses, to drink at the sayd hallowed water. All this being ended, he returned to his palace againe, and went to dinner by candle light, and sate in a woodden house, very fairely gilt. There dined in the place, about 300 strangers, and I sate alone as I did before, directly before the Emperour, and had my meat, bread and drinke sent me from the Emperour.

The citie of Mosco is great, the houses for the most part of wood, and some of stone, with windowes of yron, which serue for summer time. There are many faire Churches of stone, but more of wood, which are made hot in the winter time. The Emperors lodging is in a faire and large castle, walled foure square of bricke, high, and thicke, situated vpon a hill, 2 miles about, and the riuer on the Southwest side of it, and it hath 16 gates in the walles, and as many bulwarks. [Footnote: The Kremlin Palace.] His palace is separated from the rest of the Castle, by a long wall going north and south, to the riuer side. In his palace are Churches, some of stone and some of wood, with round towers fairely gilded. In the Church doores and within the Churches are images of golde: the chiefe markets for all things, are within the sayd Castle, and for sundry things sundry markets, and euery science by it selfe. And in the winter there is a great market without the castle, vpon the riuer being frozen, and there is sold corne, earthen pots, tubs, sleds, &c. The castle is in circuit 2900 pases.

The coontrey is ful of marish ground, and plaine, in woods and riuers abundant, but it bringeth forth good plenty of corne. This Emperour is of great power: for he hath conquered much, as wel of the Lieflanders, Poles, Lettoes, and Swethens, as also of the Tartars, and Gentiles, called Samoeds, hauing thereby much inlarged his dominions. He keepeth his people in great subiection: all matters passe his iudgement, be they neuer so small. The law is sharpe for all offenders.

The Metropolitan dealeth in matters of religion, as himselfe listeth, whome the Emperour greatly honoreth. They vse the ceremonies, and orders of the Greeke Church. They worship many images painted on tables, and specially the image of S. Nicholas. Their Priests be maried, but their wiues being dead, they may not marie the second time, and so become Monkes, whereof there are a great number in the land.

They haue foure Lents in the yeere, and the weeke before Shrofetide, they call the Butter weeke, &c.

They haue many sortes of meats and drinkes, when they banket and delight in eating of grosse meates, and stinking fishe. Before they drinke they vse to blowe in the cup: their greatest friendship is in drinking: they are great talkers and lyers, without any faith or trust in their words, flatterers and dissemblers. The women be there very obedient to their husbands, and are kept straightly from going abroad, but at some seasons.

At my being there, I heard of men and women that drunke away their children, and all their goods at the Emperors tauerne, and not being able to pay, hauing impauned himselfe, the Tauerner bringeth him out to the highway, and beates him vpon the legges: then they that passe by, knowing the cause, and hauing peraduenture compassion vpon him, giue the money, and so he is ransomed.

In euery good towne there is a drunken Tauerne called a Cursemay, which the Emperour sometime letteth out to farme, and sometimes bestoweth for a yeare or two on some duke or gentleman, in recompense of his seruice: and for that time he is Lord of all the towne, robbing and spoiling, and doing what pleaseth him: and then he be growen rich, is taken by the Emperor, and sent to the warres againe, where he shall spend all that which he hath gotten by ill meanes: so that the Emperour in his warres is little charged, but all the burden lieth vpon the poore people.

They vse sadles made of wood and sinewes, with the tree gilded with damaske worke, and the seat couered with cloth sometimes of golde, and the rest Saphian leather, well stitched. They vse little drummes at their sadle bowes, by the sound whereof their horses vse to runne more swiftly.

The Russe is appareled in this manner: his vpper garment is of golde, silke, or cloth, long, downe to the foot, and buttoned with great buttons of siluer, or els laces of silke, set on with brooches, the sleeues thereof very long, which he weareth on his arme, ruffed vp. Vnder that he hath another long garment, buttoned with silke buttons, with a high coller standing vp of some colour and that garment is made straight. Then his shirt is very fine, and wrought with red silk, or some gold, with a coller of pearle. Vnder his shirt he hath linnen breeches, vpon his legs, a paire of hose without feete, and his bootes of red or yellow leather. On his head hee weareth a white Colepecke, with buttons of siluer, gold, pearle, or stone, and vnder it a black Foxe cap, turned vp very broad.

When he rideth on horsebacke to the warres, or any iourney, he hath a sword of the Turkish fashion, and his bowe and arrowes of the same maner. In the towne he weareth no weapon, but onely two or three paire of kniues, hauing the hafts of the tooth of a fish, called the Morse.

In the Winter time, the people trauell with sleds, in towne and countrey, the way being hard, and smooth with snow; the waters and riuers are all frozen, and one horse with a sled, will draw a man vpon it 400 miles, in three daies: but in the Summer time, the way is deepe with mire, and trauelling is very ill.

The Russe, if he be a man of any abilitie, neuer goeth out of his house in the winter, but vpon his sled, and in Summer vpon his horse: and in his sled he sits vpon a carpet, or a white Beares skinne: the sled is drawen with a horse well decked, with many Foxes and Wooulues tailes at his necke, and is conducted by a little boy vpon his backe: his seruants stand vpon the taile of the sled &c.

* * * * *

The voyage, wherein Osep Napea the Moscouite Ambassadour returned home into his countrey, with his entertainement at his arriuall, at Colmogro: and a large description of the maners of the Countrey.

The twelfth of Maye, in the yeare of our Lorde 1557 there departed from Grauesend, foure good shippes well appointed for Marchants, which were presently bound into the Baye of S. Nicholas in Russia, with which shippes was transported, or caried home, one Osep Gregoriwich Napea, who was sent Messenger from the Emperour and great Duke of Moscouia. The foure ships were these, whose names follow, viz.

The Primerose Admirall.
The Iohn Euangelist Viceadmirall.
The Anne and the Trinitie Attendants.

The 13 of Iuly, the foresayd foure shippes came to an anker in the Baye of S. Nicholas, befor an Abbey, called the Abbey of S. Nicholas, whereas the sayde Messenger, Osep Gregoriwich Napea went a shoare, and as many English men as came to serue the Emperour remained with him at the Abbey for the space of sixe daies, vntill he had gotten all his things a shoare, and laden the same in the barkes, to goe vp the riuer Dwina, vnto Vologhda, which is by water 1000 verstes, and euery verste is about three quarters of an English mile.

[Sidenote: Presents vsed in Russia are all for the most part of victuals.] The 20 of Iuly, we departed from S. Nicholas, and the 24 of the same, we came to Colmogro, where we remained eight daies and the sayd Messenger was there of all his acquaintance welcommed home, and had presents innumerable sent vnto him, but it was nothing but meate, and drinke. Some sent white bread, some rie bread, and some buttered bread and pancakes, beefe, mutton, bacon, egges, butter, fishes, swannes, geese, duckes, hennes, and all maner of victuals, both fish and flesh, in the best maner, that the rude people could deuise: for among them, these presents are highly esteemed.

The 29 of Iuly, we departed from Colmogro, and the 14 of August we came to
Vstiug, where we remained one day, and changed our barkes or boates.

The 27 of August, we came to Vologhda, where we remained 4 dayes vnlading the barkes, and lading our chestes and things in small waggons, with one horse in a piece, which in their tongue are called Telegos, and with these Telegoes they caried our stuffe from Vologhda vnto the Mosco, which is 500 verstes: and we were vpon the same way 14 daies: for we went no faster then the Telegoes.

[Sidenote: The citie of Boghar.] There are three great townes betweene the Mosco and Vologhda, that is to say, Yeraslaue, Rostaue, and Pereslaue. Vpon one side of Yeraslaue runneth a famous riuer which is called Volga. It runneth into the Caspian sea, and it diuideth it selfe before it come into the Mare Caspium, in 50 parts or more, and neere vnto the same sea there stands a great Citie, called Boghar, the inhabitants of which are called by the same name.

The people of the said Citie doe traffique vnto the Citie of Mosco: their commodities are spices, muske, ambergreese, rubarbe, with other drugs. They bring also many furres, which they buy in Siberia coming towards the Mosco: the sayd people are of the sect of Mahomet.

[Sidenote: They arrived at Mosco.] The 12 of September we came vnto the citie of Mosco, where we were brought by Napea, and two of the Emperours gentlemen vnto a large house, where euery one of vs had his chamber appointed.

The 14 of September we were commanded to come vnto the Emperour, and immediately after our coming we were brought into his presence, vnto whom each of vs did his duetie accordingly, and kissed his right hand, his maiestie sitting in his chaire of estate, with his crowne on his bead, and a staffe of goldsmiths worke in his left hand well garnished with rich and costly stones: and when we had all kissed his hand and done our dueties, his maiestie did declare by his interpreter that we were all welcome vnto him, and into his countrey, and thereupon willed vs to dine with him: that day we gaue thanks vnto his maiestie, and so departed vntil the dinner was readie.

When dinner time approached, we were brought againe into the Emperour's dining chamber, where we were set on one side of a table that stoode ouer against the Emperours table, to the end that he might wel behold vs al: and when we came into the foresayd chamber, we found there readie set these tables following.

First at the vpper end of one table were set the Emperour his maiestie, his brother, and the Emperour of Cazan, which is prisoner. About two yardes lower sate the Emperour of Cazan his sonne, being a child of fiue yeeres of age, and beneath him sate the most part of the Emperors noble men.

And at another table neere vnto the Emperours table, there was set a Monke all alone, which was in all points as well serued as the Emperour. At another table sate another kinde of people called Chirkasses, [Footnote: Kirghis.] which the Emperour entertaineth for men of warre to serue against his enemies. Of which people and of their countrey, I will hereafter make mention.

All the tables aforesayde were couered onely with salt and bread, and after that we had sitten awhile, the Emperour sent vnto euery one of vs a piece of bread, which were given and deliuered vnto euery man seuerally by these words: The Emperour and great Duke giueth the bread this day, and in like manner three or foure times before dinner was ended, he sent vnto euery man drinke, which was giuen by these words, The Emperour and great Duke giueth thee to drinke. All the tables aforesayd were serued in vessels of pure and fine golde, as well basons and ewers, platters, dishes and sawcers, as also of great pots, with an innumerable sorte of small drinking pottes of diuers fashions, whereof a great number were set with stone. As for costly meates I haue many times seene better: but for change of wines, and diuers sorts of meads, it was wonderfull: for there was not left at any time so much void roome on the table, that one cuppe more might haue bin set, and as far as I could perceiue, all the rest were in the like maner serued.

In the dinner time, there came in six singers which stood in the midst of the chamber, and their faces towards the Emperour, who sang there before dinner was ended three seuerall times, whose songs or voyces delighted our eares little or nothing.

The Emperour neuer putteth morsell of meate in his mouth, but he first blesseth it himselfe, and in like maner as often as he drinketh: for after his maner he is very religious, and he esteemeth his religious men aboue his noble men.

This dinner continued about the space of fiue houres, which being ended, and the tables taken vp, we came into the midst of the chamber, where we did reuerence vnto the Emperors maiestie, and then he deliuered vnto euery one of vs with his own hands a cup of mead, which when euery man had receiued and drunke a quantity thereof, we were licensed to depart, and so ended that dinner. And because the Emperour would haue vs to be mery he sent to our lodging the same Euening three barrels of meade of sundry sortes, of the quantitie in all of one hogshed.

The 16 day of September the Emperour sent home vnto our lodging for euery of vs a Tartarie horse to ride from place to place as we had occasion, for that the streetes of Mosco are very fowle and mirie in the Summer.

[Sidenote: M. Standish doctor of Phisicke.] The 18 of September there were giuen vnto master Standish doctor in Physick, and the rest of our men of our occupations, certaine furred gownes of branched veluet and gold, and some of red damaske, of which master Doctors gowne was furred with Sables, and the rest were furred some with white Ermine, and some with gray Squirel, and all faced and edged round about with blacke beauer.

The 1 of October in the morning we were commanded to come vnto the Emperors court, and when we came thither, we were brought vnto the Emperor vnto whom we did our duties accordingly: whereupon he willed vs to dine with him that day, and so with thanks vnto his maiestie, we departed vntill dinner time, at which time we came, and found the tables couered with bread and salt as at the first: and after that we were all set vpon one side of the table, the Emperors maiestie according to his accustomed maner sent vnto euery man a piece of bread by some of the Dukes which attended on his highnesse.

And whereas the 14 of September we were serued in vessels of gold, we were now serued in vessels of siluer, and yet not so abundantly as was the first of gold: they brought drinke vnto the table in siluer boles which conteined at the least sixe gallons a piece, and euerie man had a smal siluer cuppe to drinke in, and another to dip or to take his drinke out of the great boll withall: the dinner being ended, the Emperour gaue vnto euery one of vs a cup with meade, which when we had receiued, we gaue thanks and departed.

Moreouer, whensoeuer the Emperors pleasure is that any stranger shall dine with him, he doth send for them in the morning, and when they come before him, he with his owne mouth biddeth them to dinner, and this order he alwaies obserueth.

The 10 of October the Emperour gaue vnto M. Standish 70 rubles in money, and to the rest of our men of occupations 30 rubles apiece.

The 3 of Nouember we dined againe with the Emperour, where we were serued as before.

[Sidenote: Long Dinners.] The 6 of December being S. Nicholas day, we dined againe at the Emperours, for that is one of the principall feasts which the Moscouites hold: we were serued in siluer vessels and ordered in all points as before, and it was past 7 of the clocke at night before dinner was ended.

The Emperours maiestie vseth euery yeare in the moneth of December, to haue all his ordinance that is in the citie of Mosco caried into the field which is without the Suburbs of the citie, and there to haue it planted and bent vpon two houses of Wood filled within with earth: against which two houses there were two faire white markes set vp, at which markes they discharge all their ordinance, to the ende the Emperour may see what his Gunners can doe. [Sidenote: Ordinance in Russia.] They haue faire ordinance of brasse of all sortes, bases, faulcons, minions, sakers, culuerings, cannons double and royall, basiliskes long and large, they haue sixe great pieces whose shot is a yard of height, which shot a man may easily discerne as they flee: they haue also a great many of morter pieces or potguns, out of which pieces they shoote wild fire. [Footnote: The cannon in use in the 16th century were all cast, and in England font metal or bronze was mostly employed. The falcon seems to have been of 2-1/2 inches bore; the minion 3-1/2 inches; the saker about the same; the culverin 5-1/2 inches—the weight of the shot not being proportionate to the bore. The falconet, minion, falcon, saker, and demi-culverin were known respectively as 2, 3, 4, 6, and 9-pounders; while the heavier pieces, or culverins, ranged from 15-pounders up to the "cannon-royall," or 63-pounders. Mortars were first introduced in the reign of Henry VIII. According to Stowe, those made for this monarch in 1543 were "at the mouth from 11 to 19 inches wide," and were employed to throw hollow shot of cast iron, filled like modern bombs with combustibles, and furnished with a fuse. Some of these 16th century guns may still be seen at the Tower of London.]

[Sidenote: A yerely triumph.] The 12 of December the Emperours Maiestie and all his nobility came into the field on horsebacke, in most goodly order, hauing very fine Iennets and Turkie horses garnished with gold and siluer abundantly. The Emperors maiestie hauing on him a gowne of rich tissue, and a cap of skarlet on his head, set not only with pearles, but also with a great number of rich and costly stones: his noble men were all in gownes of cloth of gold, which did ride before him in good order by 3. and 3. and before them there went 5000 harquebusiers, which went by 5 and 5 in a rank in very good order, euery of them carying his gun vpon his left shoulder, and his match in his right hand, and in this order they marched into the field whereas the foresayd ordinance was planted.

And before the Emperors maiestie came into the field, there was a certaine stage made of small poles which was a quarter of a mile long, and about threescore yardes off from the stage of poles were certaine pieces of ice of two foot thicke, and six foote high set vp, which ranke of ice was as long as the stage of poles, and as soone as the Emperors maiestie came into the field, the harquebusiers went vpon the stage of poles where they settled themselues in order. And when the Emperors maiestie was setled where he would be, and where he might see all the ordinance discharged and shot off, the harquebusiers began to shoot off at the banke of ice, as though it had bin in any skirmish or battel, who ceased not shooting vntill they had beaten all the ice flat on the ground.

After the handguns, they shot off their wild fire vp into the aire, which was a goodly sight to behold. And after this, they began to discharge the smal pieces of brasse, beginning with the smallest and so orderly bigger and bigger, vntill the last and biggest. When they had shot them all off, they began to charge them againe, and so shot them al off 3 times after the first order, beginning with the smallest and ending with the greatest. And note that before they had ended their shooting, the 2 houses that they shot vnto were beaten in pieces, and yet they were strongly made of Wood and filled with earth, being at the least 30 foote thicke. This triumph being ended, the Emperour departed and rode home in the same order that he came foorth into the field. The ordinance is discharged euery yeare in the moneth of December, according to the order before mentioned.

On Christmas day we were all willed to dine with the Emperors Maiestie, where for bread, meat and drinke, we were serued as at other times before: but for goodly and rich plate, we neuer saw the like or so much before. There dined that day in the Emperors presence aboue 500 strangers, and two hundred Russes, and all they were serued in vessels of gold, and that as much as could stand one by another vpon the tables. Besides this there were foure cupbords garnished with goodly plate both of gold and siluer. Among the which there were 12 barrels of siluer, conteining aboue 12 gallons a piece, and at each end of euery barrell were 6 hoopes of fine gold: this dinner continued about sixe houres.

[Sidenote: The hallowing of the riuer of Mosco.] Euery yeare vpon the 12 day they vse to blesse or sanctifie the riuer Moscua, which runneth through the citie of Mosco, after this maner.

First they make a square hole in the ice about 3 fadoms large euery way, which is trimmed about the sides and edges with white boords. Then about 9 of the clocke they come out of the church with procession towards the riuer in this wise.

First and foremost there goe certaine young men with waxe tapers burning, and one carying a great lanterne: then follow certaine banners, then the crosse, then the images of our Lady, of S. Nicholas, and of other Saints, which images men carie vpon their shoulders: after the images follow certaine priests to the number of 100 or more: after them the Metropolitan who is led betweene two priests, and after the Metropolitan came the Emperour with his crowne vpon his head, and after his maiestie all his noble men orderly. Thus they followed the procession vnto the water, and when they came vnto the hole that was made, the priests set themselues in order round about it. And at one side of the same poole there was a scaffold of boords made, vpon which stood a faire chaire in which the Metropolitan was set, but the Emperours maiestie stood vpon the ice.

After this the priests began to sing, to blesse and to sense, and did their seruice, and so by that time that they had done, the water was holy, which being sanctified, the Metropolitan tooke a litle thereof in his hands, and cast it on the Emperour, likewise vpon certaine of the Dukes, and then they returned againe to the church with the priests that sate about the water: but that pressse that there was about the water when the Emperor was gone, was wonderful to behold, for there came aboue 5000 pots to be filled of that water: for that Moscouite which hath no part of that water, thinks himselfe vnhappy.

And very many went naked into the water, both men and women and children: after the presse was a litle gone, the Emperours Iennets and horses were brought to drinke of the same water, and likewise many other men brought their horses thither to drinke, and by that means they make their horses as holy as themselues.

All these ceremonies being ended, we went to the Emperour to dinner, where we were serued in vessels of siluer, and in all other points as we had bene beforetime.

[Sidenote: The Russes Lent.] The Russes begin their Lent alwaies 8 weekes before Easter: the first weeke they eate egs, milke, cheese and butter, and make great cheare with pancakes and such other things, one friend visiting another, and from the same Sunday vntil our Shrofesunday there are but few Russes sober, but they are drunke day by day, and it is accompted for no reproch or shame among them.

The next weeke being our first weeke of Lent, or our clensing weeke, beginning our Shrofesunday, they make and keepe a great fast. It is reported, and the people do verily beleeue that the Metropolitan neither eateth nor drinketh any maner of thing for the space of seuen dayes, and they say that there are many religious men which doe the like.

The Emperors Maiestie eateth but one morsel of bread, and drinketh but one draught of drinke once in the day during that weeke, and all men that are of any reputation come not out of their houses during that time, so that the streetes are almost void of company, sauing a few poore folkes which wander to and fro. The other sixe weeks they keepe as we do ours, but not one of them will eate either butter, cheese, egs or milke.

On Palme Sunday they haue a very solemne procession in this maner following.

First, they haue a tree of a good bignesse which is made fast vpon two sleds, as though it were growing there, and it is hanged with apples, raisins, figs and dates, and with many other fruits abundantly. In the midst of the same tree stand 5 boyes in white vestures, which sing in the tree before the procession: after this there followed certaine yong men with waxe tapers in their hands burning, and a great lanterne that al the light should not go out: after them followed two with long banners, and sixe with round plates set vpon long staues: the plates were of copper very ful of holes and thin: then followed 6 carying painted images vpon their shoulders, after the images followed certaine priests to the number of 100 or more, with goodly vestures, whereof 10 or 12 are of white damaske set and imbrodered round about with faire and orient pearles, as great as pease, and among them certaine Sapphires and other stones. After them followed the one halfe of the Emperours noble men: then cometh the Emperors maiestie and the Metropolitane, after this maner.

First, there is a horse, couered with white linen cloth down to the ground, his eares being made long with the same cloth like to an asses ears. Vpon this horse the Metropolitane sitteth sidelong, like a woman: in his lappe lieth a faire booke, with a crucifix of Goldsmiths worke vpon the couer which he holdeth fast with his left hand, and in his right hand he hath a crosse of gold, with which crosse he ceaseth not to blesse the people as he rideth.

There are to the number of 30 men which spread abroad their garments before the horse, and as soone as the horse is past ouer any of them, they take them vp againe and run before, and spread them againe, so that the horse doth alway go on some of them. They which spread the garments are all priests sonnes, and for their labours the Emperour giueth vnto them new garments.

[Sidenote: The Emperor leadeth the Metropolitans horse in procession.] One of the Emperors noble men leadeth the horse by the head, but the Emperour himselfe going on foote leadeth the horse by the ende of the reine of his bridle with one of his hands, and in the other of his hands he had a branch of a Palme tree: after this followed the rest of the Emperors Noble men and Gentlemen, with a great number of other people. In this order they went from one church to another within the castle, about the distance of two flights shot: and so returned againe to the Emperours Church, where they made an end of their seruice. Which being done, the Emperours maiestie and certaine of his noble men went to the Metropolitane his house to dinner, where of delicate fishes and good drinks there was no lacke.

The rest of this weeke vntil Easter day they kept very solemnely, continuing in their houses for the most part, and vpon Munday or Thursday the Emperour doth alwayes vse to receiue the Sacrament, and so doe most of his nobles.

Vpon good Friday they continue all the day in contemplation and prayers, and they vse euery yere on good Friday to let loose a prisoner in the stead of Barrabas. The night following they go to the Church where they sleepe vntil the next morning, and at Easter they haue the resurrection, and after euery of the Lents they eat flesh the next weeke following, Friday, Saturday and all.

They haue an order at Easter which they alwaies obserue, and that is this: euery yere against Easter to die or colour red with Brazell a great number of egs, of which euery man and woman giueth one vnto the priest of their Parish vpon Easter day in the morning. And moreouer the common people vse to carie in their hands one of their red egs, not onely vpon Easter day, but also three or foure dayes after, and gentlemen and gentlewomen haue egs gilded which they cary in like maner. They vse it as they say for a great loue, and in token of the resurrection, whereof they reioyce. [Sidenote: Kissing vsed in the Greek church.] For when two friends meete during the Easter holy dayes, they come and take one another by the hand: the one of them sayth, the Lord or Christ is risen, the other answereth, it is so of a truth, and then they kisse and exchange their egs both men and women, continuing in kissing 4 dayes together.

The 12 of Aprill being Tuesday in the Easter weeke, Master Ienkinson and Master Graie, and certayne other of vs English men dined with the Emperor, where we were serued as we had bin before time. And after diner the Emperours maiestie gave vnto master Ienkinson and vnto M. Gray, and so orderly vnto euery one of vs a cup of Mead, according to his accustomed maner which when euery man had received and giuen thanks, M. Ienkinson stepped into the midst of the chamber before the Emperours maiestie, and gaue thankes to his highnesse for his goodnesse vnto him extended, desiring his grace to licence him to depart, and in like maner did M. Gray. His maiestie did not only licence them to depart, but also graunted vnto Master Ienkinson his letters vnder his great seale, vnto all princes through whose dominions master Ienkinson should haue occasion to passe, that he might the sooner and quietlier passe by meanes thereof. [Sidenote: With these letters M. Ienkinson tooke his voyage the same April to Boghar.] Which being granted, master Ienkinson and Gray lowly submitted themselues, thanking his maiestie. So the Emperour gaue vnto either of them a cuppe of mead to drinke, and willed them to depart at their pleasure in Gods peace.

The 14. of Aprill in the morning, when M. Gray and I were ready to depart towards England, the Chancellors sent vnto vs and willed vs to come to their office in the Chancerie, where at our comming they shewed vs a great number of the Emperors iewels, and rich robes, willing vs to marke and beholde them well, to the end that at our arriuall into England, we might make report what we had seene there.

[Sidenote: The Emperors wardrobe.] The chiefest was his maiesties crowne, being close vnder the top very faire wrought: in mine opinion, the workmanship of so much gold few men can amend. It was adorned and decked with rich and precious stones abundantly, among the which one was a rubie, which stood a handfull higher then the top of the crown vpon a small wier, it was as big as a good beane: the same crown was lined with a faire blacke Sable, worth by report 40. robles.

Wee sawe all his maiesties robes which were very richly set with stones, they shewed vs manie other great stones of diuers kindes, but the most part of them were vneuen, in maner as they came out of the worke, for they doe more esteeme the greatnesse of stones, then the proportion of them.

We saw two goodlie gownes which were as heauie as a man could easily carrie, all set with pearles ouer and ouer: the gards or borders round about them were garnished with saphires and other good stones abundantly. One of the same gownes was very rich, for the pearles were very large, round and orient: as for the rest of his gownes and garments, they were of rich tissue and cloth of gold and all furred with very blacke Sables.

When we had sufficiently perused all these things, they willed master Gray at his arriuall in England, to prouide if he could, such iewels and rich clothes as he had seene there, and better if he could, declaring that the Emperour would gladly bestow his money vpon such things.

So we tooke our leaue the same time, and departed towards Vologda immediatly.

The maners, vsages, and ceremonies of the Russes.

Of the Emperour.

The Emperours name in their tongue is Iuan Vasiliuich, that is as much to say, as Iohn the sonne of Vasilie [Marginal note: Or, Basilius.] and by his princely state hee is called Otesara [Footnote: Czar.] as his predecessors haue bene before, which to interprete, is a king, that giueth not tribute to any man. And this word Otesara his maiesties interpreters haue of late dayes interpreted to be Emperour, so that now hee is called Emperour and great Duke of all Russia, &c. Before his father they were neither called Emperours nor kings but onely Ruese Velike, that is to say, great Duke.

And as this Emperor which now is Iuan Vasiliuich, doeth exceede his predecessors in name, that is, from a Duke to an Emperour, euen so much by report he doeth exceede them in stoutnesse of courage and valiantnesse, and a great deale more: for he is no more afraid of his enemies which are not few, then the Hobbie of the larks.

His enemies with whom he hath warres for the most part are these: Litto, Poland, Sweden, Denmarke, Lifland, the Crimmes, Nagaians, and the whole nation of the Tartarians, which are a stoute and a hardie people as any vnder the Sunne.

This Emperour vseth great familiaritie, as wel vnto all his nobles and subiects, as also vnto strangers which serue him either in his warres, or in occupations: for his pleasure is that they shall dine oftentimes in the yeere in his presence, and besides that he is oftentimes abroad, either at one Church or another, and walking with his noble men abroad. And by this meanes he is not onely beloued of his nobles and commons, but also had in great dread and feare through all his dominions, so that I thinke no prince in Christendome is more feared of his owne then he is, nor yet better beloued. For if he bid any of his Dukes goe, they will runne, if he giue any euil or angrie worde to any of them, the partie will not come into his maiesties presence againe of a long time if he be not sent for, but will faine him to be very sicke, and will let the haire of his head grow very long, without either cutting or shauing, which is an euident token that hee is in the Emperors displeasure: for when they be in their prosperity, they account it a shame to weare long haire, in consideration whereof, they vse to haue their heads shauen.

[Sidenote: Note.] His maiesty heareth all complaints himselfe, and with his owne mouth giueth sentence, and iudgement of all matters, and that with expedition: but religious matters he medleth not withall, but referreth them wholly vnto the Metropolitane.

His maiestie retaineth and well rewardeth all strangers that come to serue him, and especially men of warre.

Hee delighteth not greatly in hawking, hunting, or any other pastime, nor in hearing instruments or musicke, but setteth all his whole delight vpon two things: First, to serue God, as vndoubtedly he is very deuoute in his religion, and the second, howe to subdue and conquere his enemies.

He hath abundance of gold and siluer in his owne handes or treasurie: but the most part of his subiects know not a crowne from a counter, nor gold from copper, they are so much cumbred therewithall, and he that is worth 2. 3. or 4. grotes, is a rich man.

Of their religious men.

The Metropolitane is next vnto God, our Lady and S. Nicholas excepted: for the Emperors maiestie iudgeth and affirmeth him to be of higher dignitie then himselfe; for that, saith he, he is Gods spiritual officer, and I the Emperour am his temporall officer, and therefore his maiestie submitteth himselfe vnto him in many things concerning religious matters, as in leading the Metropolitans horse vpon Palme Sunday, and giuing him leaue to sitte on a chaire vpon the 12. day, when the riuer Mosco was in blessing, his maiestie standing on the yce.

All matters of religion are reformed by the Metropolitane, he heareth the causes and giueth sentence as himselfe listeth, and is authorized so to doe, whether it be to whip, hang or burne, his will must needs be fulfilled.

They haue both monks, friers and nunnes, with a great number of great and rich monasteries: they keepe great hospitalitie, and doe relieue much poore people day by day. I haue bene in one of the monasteries called Troietes, [Footnote: There was a monastery answering this description, but its name was Trajetski.] which is walled about with bricke very strongly like a castle, and much ordinance of brasse vpon the walles of the same. They told me themselues that there are seuen hundred brethren of them which belong vnto that house. The most part of the lands, towns, and villages which are within 40. miles of it, belong vnto the same. They shewed me the church, wherein were as many images as could hang about, or vpon the wals of the Church round about, and euen the roofe of the church was painted ful of images. The chiefe image was of our Ladie, which was garnished with gold, rubies, saphirs and other rich stones abundantly. In the midst of the church stood 12. waxe tapers of two yards long, and a fathom about in bignesse, and there stands a kettle full of waxe with about 100. weight, wherein there is alwayes the wicke of a candle burning, as it were a lampe which goeth not out day nor night.

They shewed me a coffin couered with cloth of gold which stoode vpon one side within their church, in which they told me lay a holy man, who neuer eate or dranke, and yet that he liueth. And they told me (supposing that I had beleeued them) that he healeth many diseases, and giueth the blind their sight, with many other miracles, but I was hard of belief because I saw him worke no miracle whilest I was there.

After this they brought me into their sellers, and made me taste of diuers kinds of drinks, both wine and beere, mead and quassie, of sundry colours and kinds. Such abundance of drink as they haue in their sellers, I doe suppose few princes haue more, or so much at once.

Their barrels or vessels are of an vnmeasurable bignes and sise: some of them are 3. yards long and more, and 2. yards and more broad in their heads: they conteine 6. or 7. tunnes a piece: they haue none in their sellers of their owne making that are lesse then a tunne. They haue 9. or 10. great vautes which are full of those barrels which are seldome remooued: for they haue trunks which come downe through the roofe of the vautes in sundry places, through which they powre drinke downe, hauing the caske right vnder it to receiue the same, for it should be a great trouble to bring it all downe the stayres.

[Sidenote: The hospitalitie of their monasteries.] They giue bread, meat and drinke vnto all men that come to them, not onely while they are at their abbey, but also when they depart, to serue them by the way.

There are a great number of such monasteries in the Realm, and the Emperors maiesty rideth oftentimes from one to another of them, and lieth at them 3. or 4. daies together.

The same monkes are as great merchants as any in the land of Russia, and doe occupy buying and selling as much as any other men, and haue boats which passe too and fro in the riuers with merchandize from place to place where any of their countrey do traffike.

They eate no flesh during their liues as it is reported: but vpon Sunday, Munday, Tuesday, Thursday and Saturday it is lawfull for them to eate egges, butter, cheese, and milke, and at all times to eate fish, and after this sort they lead their liues.

They weare all blacke garments, and so doe none other in all the lande, but at that abbey onely.

[Sidenote: Want of preachers cause of great ignorance and idolatry.] They haue no preachers no not one in al the land to instruct the People, so that there are many, and the most part of the poore in the countrey, who if one aske them how many gods there be, they wil say a great many, meaning that euery image which they haue is a god: for all the countrey and the Emperours maiesty himselfe wil blesse and bowe, and knocke their heads before their images, in so much that they will crie earnestly vnto their images to helpe them to the things which they need. Al men are bound by their law to haue those images in their houses, and ouer euery gate in all their townes and cities are images set vp, vnto which the people bow and bend, and knocke their heads against the ground before them: as often as they come by any church or crosse they do in like maner. And when they come to any house, they blesse themselues 3. or 4. times before they will salute any man in the house.

They reckon and hold it for great sinne to touch or handle any of their images within the circle of the boord where the painting is, but they keep them very daintily, and rich men deck them ouer and about with gold, siluer and stones, and hang them ouer and about with cloth of gold.

The priestes are married as other men are, and weare all their garments as other men doe, except their nightcaps, which is cloth of some sad colour, being round, and reacheth vnto the eares: their crownes are shauen, but the rest of their haire they let grow as long as nature will permit, so that it hangeth beneath their eares vpon their shoulders: their beards they neuer shaue: if his wife happen to die, it is not lawfull for him to mary againe during his life.

They minister the Communion with bread and wine after our order, but he breaketh the bread and putteth it into the cup vnto the wine, and commonly some are partakers with them: and they take the bread out againe with a spoon together with part of the wine, and so take it themselues, and giue it to others that receiue with them after the same maner.

Their ceremonies are al as they say, according to the Greeke Church vsed at this present day, and they allow no other religion but the Greeks, and their owne: and will not permit any nation but the Greeks to be buried in their sacred burials, or churchyards.

All their churches are full of images, vnto the which the people when they assemble, doe bowe and knocke their heads, as I haue before said, that some will haue knobbes vpon their foreheads with knocking, as great as egges.

[Sidenote: Al their seruice is in their mother tongue.] All their seruice is in the Russe tongue, and they and the common people haue no other praiers but this, *Ghospodi Iesus Christos esine voze ponuloi nashe.* That is to say, O Lorde Iesus Christ, sonne of God haue mercy upon vs: and this is their prayer, so that the most part of the vnlearned know neither Pater noster, nor the Beliefe, nor Ten commandements, nor scarcely vnderstand the one halfe of their seruice which is read in their Churches.

Of their Baptisme.

When any child is borne, it is not baptised vntil the next Sunday, and if it chance that it be not baptized then, it must tary vntil the next Sunday after the birth, and it is lawfull for them to take as manie Godfathers and Godmothers as they will, the more the better.

When they go to the Church, the midwife goeth foremost, carrying the childe, and the Godfathers and Godmothers follow into the midst of the Church, where there is a small table ready set, and on it an earthen pot ful of warme water, about the which the Godfathers and Godmothers, with the childe, settle themselues: then the clerke giueth vnto euery of them a smal waxe candle burning, then commeth the priest, and beginneth to say certaine words, which the Godfathers and Godmothers must answere word for word, among which one is, that the childe shal forsake the deuill, and as that name is pronounced, they must all spit at the word as often as it is repeated. Then he blesseth the water which is in the pot, and doth breathe ouer it: then he taketh al the candles which the gosseps haue, and holding them all in one hand letteth part of them drop into the water, and then giueth euery one his candle againe, and when the water is sanctified, he taketh the childe and holdeth it in a small tubbe, and one of the Godfathers taketh the pot with warme water, and powreth it all vpon the childs head.

After this he hath many more ceremonies, as anoynting eares and eyes with spittle, and making certaine crosses with oyle vpon the backe, head, and brest of the childe: then taking the childe in his armes, carieth it to the images of S. Nicholas, and our Ladie, &c. and speaketh vnto the images, desiring them to take charge of the childe, that he may liue, and beleeue as a Christian man or woman ought to doe, with many other words. Then comming backe from the images, he taketh a paire of sheares and clippeth the yong and tender haires of the childes head in three or foure places, and then deliuereth the childe, whereunto euery of the Godfathers and Godmothers lay a hand: then the priest chargeth them, that the childe be brought vp in the faith and feare of God or Christ, and that it be instructed to clinege and bow to the images, end so they make an end: then one of the Godfathers must hang a crosse about the necke of the childe, which he must alwayes weare, for that Russe which hath not a crosse about his necke they esteeme as no Christian man, and thereupon they say that we are no Christians, because we do not weare crosses as they do.

Of their Matrimonie.

Their matrimonie is nothing solemnized, but rather in most points abominable, and as neere as I can learne, in this wise following.

First, when there is loue betweene the parties, the man sendeth vnto the woman a small chest or boxe, wherein is a whip, needles, threed, silke, linnen cloth, sheares, and such necessaries as shee shall occupie when she is a wife, and perhaps sendeth therewithall raisins, figs or some such things, giuing her to vnderstand, that if she doe offend she must be beaten with the whip, and by the needles, threed, cloth, &c. that she should apply her selfe diligently to sowe, and do such things as shee could best doe, and by the raisins or fruites he meaneth if she doe well, no good thing shalbe withdrawn from her, nor be too deare for her: and she sendeth vnto him a shirt, handkerchers, and some such things of her owne making. And now to the effect.

When they are agreed, and the day of marriage appointed when they shall goe towardes the Church, the bride will in no wise consent to go out of the house, but resisteth and striueth with them that would haue her out, and faineth her selfe to weepe, yet in the end, two women get her out, and lead her towards the church, her face being couered close, because of her dissimulation, that it should not be openly perceiued: for she maketh a great noise, as though she were sobbing and weeping, vntil she come at the Church, and then her face is vncouered. The man commeth after among other of his friends, and they cary with them to the church a great pot of wine or mead: then the priest coupleth them together much after our order, one promising to loue and seme the other during their liues together, &c. which being done, they begin to drinke, and first the woman drinketh to the man, and when he hath drunke he letteth the cuppe fell to the ground, hasting immediately to tread vpon it, and so doth she, and whether of them tread first vpon it must haue the victorie and be master at all times after, which commonly happeneth to the man, for he is readiest to set his foot on it, because he letteth it fall himselfe, then they goe home againe, the womans face beeing vncouered. The boyes in the streetes crie out and make a noyse in the meanetime, with very dishonest wordes.

When they come home, the wife is set at the vpper end of the table, and the husband next vnto her: they fall then to drinking till they bee all drunke, they perchance haue a minstrell or two, and two naked men, which led her from the Church daunce naked a long time before all the companie. When they are wearie of drinking, the bride and the bridegrome get them to bed, for it is in the euening alwayes when any of them are married: and when they are going to bedde, the bridegrome putteth certain money both golde and siluer, if he haue it, into one of his boots, and then sitteth down in the chamber, crossing his legges, and then the bride must plucke off one of his boots, which she will, and if she happen on the boote wherein the money is, she hath not onely the money for her labor, but is also at such choyse, as she need not euer from that day forth to pul off his boots, but if she misse the boot wherin the money is, she doth not onely loose the money, but is also bound from that day forwards to pull off his boots continually.

Then they continue in drinking and making good cheere three daies following, being accompanied with certaine of their friends, and during the same three daies he is called a Duke, and shee a dutches, although they be very poore persons, and this is as much as I haue learned of their matrimony: but one common rule is amongst them, if the woman be not beaten with the whip once a weeke, she will not be good, and therefore they looke for it orderly, and the women say, that if their husbands did not beate them, they should not loue them.

They vse to marry there very yong, their sonnes at 16. and 18. yeeres old, and the daughters at 12. or 13. yeeres or yonger: they vse to keepe their wiues very closely, I meane those that be of any reputation, so that a man shall not see one of them but at a chance, when she goeth to church at Christmas or at Easter, or els going to visite some of her friends.

The most part of the women vse to ride a stride in saddles with styropes, as men do, and some of them on sleds, which in summer is not commendable.

[Sidenote: The women of Russia paint their faces.] The husband is bound to finde the wife colours to paint her withall, for they vse ordinarily to paynt themselues: it is such a common practise among them, that it is counted for no shame: they grease their faces with such colours, that a man may discerne them hanging on their faces almost a flight shoote off: I cannot so well liken them as to a millers wife, for they looke as though they were beaten about the face with a bagge of meale, but their eye browes they colour as blacke as ieat.

The best propertie that the women haue, is that they can sowe well, and imbroder with silke and golde excellently.

Of their buriall.

When any man or woman dieth, they stretch him out, and put a new paire of shooes on his feete, because he hath a great iourney to goe: then doe they winde him in a sheet, as we doe, but they forget not to put a testimonie in his right hand, which the priest giueth him, to testifie vnto S. Nicholas that he died a Christian man or woman. And they put the coarse alwayes in a coffin of wood, although the partie be very poore: and when they goe towards the Church, the friends and kinsemen of the partie departed carrie in their hands small waxe candles, and they weepe and howle, and make much lamentation.

They that be hanged or beheaded, or such like, haue no testimonie with them: how they are receiued into heauen, it is a wonder, without their passport.

There are a great number of poore people among them which die daily for lacke of sustenance, which is a pitifull case to beholde: for there hath beene buried in a small time, within these two yeeres, aboue 80. persons young and old, which haue died onely for lacke of sustenance: for if they had had straw and water enough, they would make shift to liue: [Sidenote: Bread made of straw.] for a great many are forced in the winter to drie straw and stampe it, and to make bread thereof, or at the least they eate it in stead of bread. In the summer they make good shift with grasse, herbes and rootes: barks of trees are good meat with them at all times. [Sidenote: The vnmercifulnesse of the Russes toward the poor.] There is no people in the world, as I suppose, that liue so miserably as do the pouerty in those parts, and the most part of them that haue sufficient for themselues, and also to relieue others that need, are so vmnerciful that they care not how many they see die of famine or hunger in the streets.

[Sidenote: Stooues or baths vsuall with the Muscovites.] It is a countrey full of diseases, diuers, and euill, and the best remedy is for anie of them, as they holde opinion, to goe often vnto the hote houses, as in a maner euery man hath one of his owne, which hee heateth commonly twise euery weeke, and all the bouseholde sweate, and wash themselues therein.

The names of certaine sortes of drinkes vsed in Russia, and commonly drunke in the Emperours Court.

[Sidenote: Reported by Thomas Bulley.] The first and principall meade is made of the iuice or liccour taken from a berrie called in Russia, Malieno, which is of a marueilous sweete taste, and of a carmosant colour, which berry I haue seene in Paris.

The second meade is called Visnoua, because it is made of a berry so called, and is like a black gooseberrie: but it is like in colour and taste to the red wine of France.

The third meade is called Amarodina or Smorodina, short, of a small berry much like to the small rezin, and groweth in great plentie in Russia.

The fourth meade is called Chereunikyna, which is made of the wilde blacke cherry.

The fift meade is made of hony and water, with other mixtures.

There is also a delicate drinke drawn from the root of the birch tree, called in the Russe tongue Berozeuites, which drinke the noble men and others vse in Aprill, May, and Iune, which are the three moneths of the spring time: for after those moneths, the sappe of the tree dryeth, and then they cannot haue it.

* * * * *

The voyage of Master Anthony Ienkinson, made from the citie of Mosco in Russia, to the citie of Boghar in Bactria, in the yeere 1558: written by himselfe to the Merchants of London of the Moscouie company.

The 23. day of April, in the yeere 1558. (hauing obtained the Emperor of Russia his letters, directed vnto sundry kings and princes, by whose dominions I should passe) I departed from Mosco by water, hauing with mee two of your seruants, namely, Richard Iohnson, and Robert Iohnson, and a Tartar Tolmach, with diuers parcels of wares, as by the inuentory appeareth: and the 28. day we came to a town called Collom, distant from the Mosco 20. leagues, and passing one league beyond the saide Collom, we came vnto a riuer called Occa, into the which the riuer Mosco falleth, and looseth his name: and passing downe the said riuer Occa 8. leagues, we came vnto a castle called Terreuettisko, which we left vpon our right hand, and proceeding forward, the second day of May, we came vnto another castle called Peroslaue, distant 8. leagues, leauing it also on our right hand. The third day we came vnto the place where olde Rezan was situate, beeing now most of it ruined and ouergrowen, and distant from the said Peroslaue, 6. leagues: the 4. day we passed by a castle called Terrecouia, from Rezan 12. leagues, and the 6. day we came to another castle called Cassim, vnder the gouernment of a Tartar prince named Vtzar Zegoline, sometime Emperour of the worthy citie of Cazan, and now subiect vnto the Emperour of Russia. But leauing Cassim on our left hand, the 8. day we came vnto a faire town called Morom, from Cassim 20. leagues, where we took the sonne, and found the lattitude 56 degrees: and proceeding forward the 11. day, we came vnto another faire town and castle called Nyse Nouogrode, situated at the falling of the foresaid riuer Occa into the worthie riuer of Volga, distant from the saide Moron [Transcriber's note: sic.] 25. leagues, in the latitude of 56. degrees 18. minutes. From Rezan to this Nyse Nouogrod, on both sides the said riuer of Occa, is raised the greatest store of waxe and hony in all the land of Russia. We tarried at the foresaid Nyse Nouogrode vntil the 19. day, for the comming of a captain which was sent by the Emperour to rule at Astracan, who beeing arriued, and hauing the number of 500. great boates vnder his conduct, some laden with victuals, souldiers, and munition: and other some with merchandise, departed altogether the said 19. day from the said Nyse Nouogrode, and the 22. we came vnto a castle called Vasiliagorod, distant 25. leagues, which we left vpon our right hand. This towne or castle had his name of this Emperors father, who was called Vasilius, and gorod in the Russe tongue is as much as to say as a castle, so that Vasiliagorod is to say, Vasilius castle: and it was the furthest place that the said Emperour conquered from the Tartars. But this present Emperour his sonne, called Iuan Vasiliwich, hath had great good successe in his warres, both against the Christians and also the Mahometists and Gentiles, but especially against the Tartars, inlarging his Empire euen to the Caspian sea, hauing conquered the famous riuer of Volga, with all the countries there about adiacent. Thus proceeding on our iourney the 25. day of May aforesaide, wee came to another castle called Sabowshare, which wee left on our right hand, distant from Vasiliagorod 16. leagues. The countrey heereabout is called Mordouits, and the habitants did professe the law of the Gentiles: but nowe beeing conquered by this Emperour of Russia, most of them are christened, but lie in the woods and wildernesse, without towne or habitation.

[Sidenote: Cazan.] The 27. day we passed by another castle called Swyasko, distant from Shabowshare aforesaid 25. leagues: we left it on our, right hand, and the 29. came vnto an Island one league from the citie of Cazan, from which falleth downe a riuer called Cazanka reca, and entreth into the foresaide Volga. Cazan is a faire town after the Russe or Tartar fashion, with a strong castle, situated vpon a high hill, and was walled round about with timber and earth, but now the Emperour of Russia hath giuen order to plucke downe the old walles and to builde them againe of free stone. It hath bene a citie of great wealth and riches, and being in the hands of the Tartars it was a kingdome of it selfe, and did more vexe the Russes in their warres, then any other nation: but 9 yeres past, this Emperour of Russia conquered it, and tooke the king captiue, who being but young is nowe baptised, and brought vp in his court with two other princes, which were also kings of the said Cazan, and being ech of them in time of their raignes in danger of their subiects through ciuil discord, came and rendred themselues at seueral times vnto the said Emperor, so that at this present there are three princes in the court of Russia, which had bene Emperours of the said Cazan, whom the Emperour vseth with great honour.

[Sidenote: The Island of marchants.] We remained at Cazan till the 13. day of Iune, and then departed from thence: and the same day passed by an Island called the Island of merchants, because it was woont be a place where all merchants, as well Russes and Cazanites, as Nagayans and Crimmes, and diuers other nations did resort to keepe mart for buying and selling, but nowe it is forsaken, and standeth without any such resort thither, or at Cazan, or at any place about it, from Mosco vnto Mare Caspium. [Sidenote: The riuer of Cama.] Thus proceeding forward the 14. day, we passed by a goodly riuer called Cama, which we left on our left hand. The riuer falleth out of the countrey of Permia into the riuer of Volga, and is from Cazan 15. leagues: and the countrey lying betwixt the said Cazan and the said riuer Cama on the left hand of Volga is called Vachen, and the inhabitants be Gentiles, and liue in the wildernesse without house or habitation: and the countrey on the other side of Volga ouer against the said riuer Cama is called the land of Cheremizes, halfe Gentiles, halfe Tartars, and all the land on the left hand of the said Volga from the said riuer vnto Astracan, and so following the North and Northeast side of the Caspian sea, [Sidenote: Nagay Tartars.] to a land of the Tartars called Turkemen, is called the countrey of Magnat or Nagay, whose inhabitants are of the law of Mahomet, and were all destroyed in the yeere 1558, at my being at Astracan, through ciuill warres among them, accompanied with famine, pestilence, and such plagues, in such sort that in the said yeere there were consumed of the people, in one sort and another, aboue one hundred thousand: the like plague was neuer seen in those parts, so that the said countrey of Nagay being a countrey of great pasture, remaineth now vn-replenished to the great contentation of the Russes, who haue had cruel warres a long time together.

The Nagayans when they flurished, liued in this maner: they were diuided into diuers companies called Hords, and euery hord had a ruler, whom they obeyed as their king, and was called a Murse. [Sidenote: Hords.] Towne or house they had none, but liued in the open fields, every Murse or King hauing his Hords or people about him, with their wives, children and cattell, who hauing consumed the pasture in one place, remooued vnto another; and when they remooue they haue houses like tents set vpon wagons or carts, which are drawen from place to place with camels, and therin their wiues, children, and all their riches, which is very litle, is caried about, and euery man hath at the least foure or fiue wives besides concubines. Vse of money they haue none, but doe barter their cattell for apparell and other necessaries. They delight in no arte nor science, except the warres, wherein they are expert, but for the most part they be pasturing people, and haue great store of cattell, which is all their riches. They eate much flesh, and especially the horse, and they drinke mares milk, wherewith they be oftentimes drunke: they are seditious and inclined to theft and murther. Corne they sowe not, neither do eate any bread, mocking the Christians for the same, and disabling our strengths, saying we liue by eating the top of a weede, and drinke a drinke made out of the same, allowing their great deuouring of flesh, and drinking of milke to be the increase of their strength. But now to proceed forward to my iourney.

[Sidenote: The Crimme Tarters.] All the countrey vpon our right hand the riuer Volga, from ouer against the riuer Cama, vnto the towne of Astracan, is the land of Crimme, whose inhabitants be also of the lawe of Mahomet, and liue for the most part according to the fashions of the Nagayes, having continuall wars with the Emperour of Russia, and are valiant in the fielde, hauing countenance, and support from the great Turke.

[Sidenote: The River of Samar.] The 16. day of Iune we passed by certaine fishermens houses called Petowse twenty leagues from the riuer Cama, where is great fishing for sturgeon, so continuing our way untill the 22. day, and passing by another great riuer called Samar, which falleth out of the aforesaide countrey, and runneth through Negay, and entreth into the saide riuer of Volga. The 28. day wee came vnto a great hill, where was in times past a castle made by the Crimmes, but now it is ruined, being the iust midway betweene the said Cazan and Astrachan, which is 200. leagues or thereabout, in the latitude of 51. degrees 47. minutes. [Sidenote: Licoris in great plentie.] Vpon all this shore groweth great abundance of Licoris, whose root runneth within the ground like a vine.

Thus going forward the sixt day of Iuly we came to a place called Perouolog, so named because in times past the Tartars caried theit bortes from Volga vnto the riuer Tanais, otherwise called Don, by land, when they would robbe such as passed downe the said Volga to Astracan, and also such as passed downe by the riuer Tanais, to Asou, Caffa, or any other towne situated vpon Mare Euxinum, into which sea Tanais falleth, who hath his springs in the countrey of Rezan, out of a plaine ground. It is at this straight of Perouolog from the one riuer to the other two leagues by land, and is a dangerous place for theeues and robbers, but now it is not so euill as it hath bene, by reason of the Emperour of Russia his conquests.

Departing from Perouolog, hauing the wildernesse on both sides, wee sawe a great heard of Nagayans, pasturing, as is abouesaid, by estimation aboue a thousand camels drawing of cartes with houses vpon them like tents, of a strange fashion, seeming to bee a farre off a towne: that Hord was belonging to a great Murse called Smille, the greatest prince in all Nagay, who had slaine and driuen away all the rest, not sparing his owne brethren and children, and hauing peace with this Emperour of Russia he hath what he needeth, and ruleth alone: so that now the Russes liue in peace with the Nagayans, who were wont to haue mortall warres together.

The 14. day of Iuly passing by an old castle, which was Old Astracan, and leauing it vpon our right hand, we arriued at New Astracan, which this Emperour of Russia conquered six yeeres past, in the yeere 1552. It is from the Mosco vnto Astracan six hundred leagues, or thereabout. [Sidenote: Astracan.] The towne of Astracan is situated in an Island vpon a hill side, hauing a castle within the same, wailed about with earth and timber, neither faire nor strong: The towne is also walled about with earth; the buildings and houses (except it be the captaines lodging, and certaine other gentlemens) most base and simple. [Sidenote: Store of Sturgions.] The Island is most destitute and barren of wood and pasture, and the ground will beare no corne: the aire is there most infected, by reason (as I suppose) of much fish, and specially Sturgion, by which onely the inhabitants liue, hauing great scarsitie of flesh and bread. They hang vp their fish in their streets and houses to dry for their prouision, which causeth such abundance of flies to increase there, as the like was neuer seene in any land, to their great plague. And at my being at the sayd Astracan, there was a great famine and plague among the people, and specially among the Tartars called Nagayans, who the same time came thither in great numbers to render themselues to the Russes their enemies, and to seeke succour at their hands, their countrey being destroyed, as I said before: but they were but ill entertained or relieued, for there died a great number of them for hunger, which lay all the Island through in heapes dead and like to beasts vnburied, very pitifull to behold: many of them were also sold by the Russes, and the rest were banished from the Island. At that time it had bene an easie thing to haue conuerted that wicked Nation to the Christian faith, if the Russes themselues had bene good Christians: but how should they shew compassion vnto other Nations, when they are not mercifull vnto their owne? At my being there I could haue bought many goodly Tartars children, if I would haue had a thousand, of their owne fathers and mothers, to say a boy or a wench for a loafe of bread woorth sixe pence in England, but we had more need of victuals at that time then of any such merchandise. This Astracan is the furthest hold that that this Emperour of Russia has conquered of the Tartars towards the Caspian sea, which he keepeth very strong, sending thither euery yere prouision of men and victuals, and timber to build the castle.

There is a certaine trade of merchandise there vsed, but as yet so small and beggerly, that it is not woorth the making mention, and yet there come merchants thither from diuers places. The chiefest commodities that the Russes bring thither are redde hides, redde sheepes skinnes, woodden vessels, bridles, and saddles, kniues, and other trifles, with corne, bacon, and other victuals. The Tartars bring thither diuers kindes of wares made of cotten wooll, with diuers kindes of wrought silkes: and they that come out of Persia, namely from Shamacki doe bring sowing silke, which is the coursest that they vse in Russeland, Crasco, diuers kinds of pide silkes for girdles, shirts of male, bowes, swords, and such like things: and some yeeres corne, and wallnuts, but all such things in such small quantitie, the merchants being so beggerly and poore that bring the same, that it is not worth the writing, neither is there any hope of trade in all those parts woorth the folowing.

[Sidenote: The length of the Island of Astracan] This foresaid Island of Astracan is in length twelue leagues, and in bredth three, and lieth East and West in the latitude of fortie seuen degrees, nine minutes: we taried there vntil the sixt day of August, and hauing bought and prouided a boate in company with certaine Tartars and Persians, we laded our goods and imbarked our selues; and the same day departed I, with the said two Iohnsons hauing the whole charge of the Nauigation downe the sayd riuer Volga, being very crooked, and full of flats towards the mouth thereof. [Sidenote: They enter into the Caspian sea.] We entred into the Caspian sea the tenth day of August at the Easterly side of the sayd riuer, being twentie leagues from Astracan aforesayd, in the latitude of fortie six degrees, twentie seuen minutes.

Volga hath seuentie mouthes or fals into the sea: and we hauing a large wind, kept the Northeast shore, and the eleuenth day we sailed seuen leagues Eastnortheast, and came vnto an Island hauing an high hill therein, called Accurgar, a good marke in the sea. From thence East tenne leagues, we fell with another Island called Bawhiata, much higher then the other. Within these two Islands to the Northwards, is a great Baie called the Blew sea. [Sidenote: The Blew sea.] From thence wee sailed East and by North ten leagues, and hauing a contrary wind, we came to an anker in a fadome water, and so rid vntill the fifteenth day, hauing a great storme at Southeast, being a most contrary wind, which we rid out. Then the wind came to the North, and we weyed, and set our course Southeast, and that day sailed eight leagues.

[Sidenote: Baughleata being 74 leagues from Volga.] Thus proceeding forwards, the 17. day wee lost sight of land, and the same day sailed thirtie leagues, and the 18. day twentie leagues winding East, and fell with a land called Baughleata, being 74. leagues fromm the mouth of the said Volga, in the latitude of 46. degrees 54. minutes, the coast lying neerest East and by South, and West and by North. At the point of this land lieth buried a holy Prophet, as the Tartars call him, of their law, where great deuotion is vsed of all such Mahometists as doe passe that way.

[Sidenote: Iaic riuer.] The nineteenth day the winde being West, and we winding Eastsoutheast, we sailed tenne leagues, and passed by a great riuer called Iaic, which hath his spring in the lande of Siberia, nigh vnto the foresaid riuer Cama, and runneth through the lande of Nagay, billing into this Mare Caspium. [Sidenote: Serachick] And vp this riuer one dayes tourney is a Towne called Serachick, subiect to the aforesaid Tartar prince called Murse Smille, which is nowe in friendship with the Emperour of Russia. Here is no trade of merchandize vsed, for that the people haue no vse of money, and are all men of warre, and pasturers of cattel, and giuen much to theft and murther. Thus being at an anker against this riuer Iaic, and all our men being on land, sauing I, who lay sore sicke, and fiue Tartars whereof one was reputed a holy man, because he came from Mecka, there came vnto vs a boate with thirtie men well armed and appointed, who boorded vs, and began to enter into our barke, and our holy Tartar called Azy, perceiuing that, asked them what they would haue, and withall made a prayer: with that these rouers staied, declaring that they were Gentlemen, banished from their countrey, and out of liuing, and came to see if there were any Russes or other Christians (which they call Caphars) in our barke: To whom this Azi most stoutly answered, that there were none, auowing the same by great othes of their lawe, (which lightly they will not breake) whom the rouers beleeued, and vpon his words departed. And so through the fidelitie of that Tartar, I with all my company and goods were saued, and our men being come on boord, and the wind faire, we departed from that place, and winding East and Southeast, that day being the 20. of August sailed 16. leagues.

[Sidenote: The Countrie of Colmack] The 21. day we passed ouer a Bay of 6. leagues broad, and fell with a Cape of land, hauing two Islands at the Southeast part thereof, being a good marke in the sea: and doubling that Cape the land trended Northeast, and maketh another Bay, into which felleth the great riuer Yem, springing out of the land of Colmack.

The 22. 23. and 24. dayes, we were at an anker.

The 25. the winde came faire, and wee sailed that day 20. leagues, and passed by an Island of lowe land, and thereabout are many flats and sands: and to the Northward Of this Island there goeth in a great Bay, but we set off from this Island, and winded South to come into deepe water, being much troubled with shoalds and flats, and ran that course 10. leagues, then East Southeast 20. leagues, and fel with the maine land, being full of copped hils, and passing along the coast 20. leagues, the further we sailed, the higher was the land.

The 27. day we crossed ouer a Bay, the South shore being the higher land, and fel with a high point of land: and being ouerthwart the Cape, there rose such a storme at the East, that we thought verily we should haue perished: this storme continued 3. dayes. [Sidenote: The port of Manguslaue.] From this Cape we passed to a port called Magnuslaue. The place where we should haue arriued at the Southernmost part of the Caspian sea, is 12. leagues within a Bay: but we being sore tormented and tossed with this foresaid storme, were driuen vnto another land on the other side the Bay, ouerthwart the sayd Manguslaue being very lowe land, and a place as well for the ill commoditie of the hauen, as of those brute field people, where neuer barke nor boate had before arriued, not liked of vs.

But yet here we sent certaine of our men to land to talke with the gouernour and people, as well for our good vsage at their handes, as also for prouision of camels to carry our goods from the sayd sea side to a place called Sellyzure, being from the place of our landing fiue and twentie dayes iourney. Our messengers returned with comfortable wordes and faire promises of all things. [Sidenote: They goe on land.] Wherefore the 3. day of September 1558. we discharged our barke, and I with my companie were gently entertained of the Prince and of his people. But before our departure from thence, we found them to be very bad and brutish people, for they ceased not daily to molest vs, either by fighting, stealing or begging, raising the prise of horse and camels, and victuals, dooble that it was woont there to be, and forced vs to buy the water that we did drinke: which caused vs to hasten away, and to conclude with them as well for the hire of camels, as for the prise of such as wee bought, with other prouision, according to their owne demaund: So that for euery camels lading, being but 400. waight of ours, we agreed to giue three hides of Russia, and foure woodden dishes, and to the Prince or gouernour of the sayd people, one ninth, and two seuenths: Namely, nine seuerall things, and twise seuen seuerall things: for money they vse none.

[Sidenote: The countrey of Manguslaue.] And thus being ready, the foureteenth of September we departed from that place, being a Carauan of a thousand Camels. And hauing trauailed fiue dayes iourney, we came to another Princes Dominion, and vpon the way there came vnto vs certaine Tartars on horseback, being well armed, and seruants vnto the saide Prince called Timor Soltan, gouernour of the said countrey of Manguslaue, where wee meant to haue arriued and discharged our barke, if the great storm aforesayd had not disappointed. These aforesaid Tartars stayd our Carauan in the name of their Prince, and opened our wares, and tooke such things as they thought best for their saide prince without money, but for such things as they tooke from me, which was a ninth (after much dissension) I ridde vnto the same Prince, and presented my selfe before him, requesting his fauour, and pasport to trauaile through his countrey, and not to be robbed nor spoiled of his people: which request he graunted me, and intertained me very gently, commaunding me to be well feasted with flesh and mares milke: for bread they vse none, nor other drinke except water: but money he had none to giue mee for such thinges as he tooke of mee, which might be of value in Russe money, fifteene rubbles, but he gaue me his letter, and a horse woorth seuen rubbles. And so I departed from him being glad that I was gone: for he was reported to be a very tyrant, and if I had not gone vnto him, I vnderstoode his commaundement was that I should haue beene robbed and destroyed.

This Soltan liued in the fields without Castle or towne, and sate, at my being with him, in a little rounde house made of reedes couered without with felt, and within with Carpets. There was with him the great Metropolitan of that wilde Country, esteemed of the people, as the Bishop of Rome is in most parts of Europe, with diuers other of his chiefe men. The Soltan with this Metropolitan demanded of me many questions, as wel touching our kingdoms, lawes, and Religion, as also the cause of my coming into those parts, with my further pretence. To whom I answered concerning all things, as vnto me seemed best, which they tooke in good part. [Sidenote: 20 dayes trauaile in the wildernese, with scarcite of water.] So hauing leaue I departed and ouertooke our Carauan and proceeded on our iourney, and trauailed 20 dayes in the wildernes from the sea side without seeing towne or habitation, carying prouision of victuals with vs for the same time, and were driuen by necessity to eate one of my camels and a horse for our part, as other did the like: and during the said 20 daies we found no water, but such as we drew out of old deepe welles, being very brackish and salt, and yet sometimes passed two or three dayes without the same. [Sidenote: Another gulfe of the Caspian sea.] And the 5. day of October ensuing, we came gulfe of the Caspian sea againe, where we found the vnto a water very fresh and sweete: at this gulfe the customers of the king of Turkeman met vs, who tooke custome of euery 25. one, and 7. ninthes for the saide king and his brethren, which being receiued they departed, and we remained there a day after to refresh our selues.

[Sidenote: Will. de Rubricis describeth this riuer of Ardok, cap. 4.] Note that in times past there did fal into this gulf the great river Oxus, which hath his springs in the mountains of Paraponisus in India, and now commeth not so far, but falleth into another riuer called Ardock, which runneth toward the North, and consumeth himself in the ground passing vnder ground aboue 500. miles, and then issueth out againe and falleth into the lake of Kithay. [Footnote: Oxus, the Jihun of the Arab, the Amu-darya of the Persians, and the Vak-shu of the Hindus, is a river of Central Asia, in Turkestan, draining the Great Pamir through two head streams—the Panja or southern, rising in Lake Victoria, 13,900 feet above the sea-level, and the Ak-su or Murghah, or northern, said to flow from Lake Barkal Yasin, 13,000 feet above the sea-level, and receiving the outflow of Lake Kara-kul above the junction. The united stream flows westwards towards Balkh, before reaching which it gradually trends to the northwest until, after a course of about 1300 miles, it reaches the south coast of the Aral Sea. In parts the stream has a breadth of 800 yards, with a depth of 20 feet, and a very rapid current; but the vast quantity of sedimentary matter which it brings down to the month, forming shifting sands and banks, renders it difficult to navigate. A great portion of the volume of the stream is absorbed in the irrigation of the Khivan Oasis. The tendency of the Oxus, like that of the great Siberian rivers, is to press continually on its right or east bank, and twice within historic times it has oscillated between the Caspian and Aral Seas. In the fourteenth century it is supposed to have entered the Caspian by the Uzboi channel, near Mikhailovsk. It was proposed at one time to attempt to reopen this bed, but the scheme has been abandoned in favour of the steppe river, Chagan. Herodotus seems to refer to the Oxus under the name of Araxes, but his description is confused, and many of his commentators suppose that the Araxes of Herodotus is the river of the same name in Armenia; while others suppose that it is either the Volga or the Jaxartes. Strabo says that the Oxus rose in the Indian mountains and flowed into the Caspian, which is also the opinion of Mela and Ptolemy. Pliny makes it rise in a lake called Oxus, and the truth of his statement is now confirmed.]

[Sidenote: Sellizure, or Shayzure.] We hauing refreshed our selues at the foresaide gulfe, departed thence the 4. day of October, and the seuenth day arriued at a castle called Sellizure, where the king called Azim Can, remained with 3. other of his brethren, and the 9. day I was commaunded to come before his presence, to whom I deliuered the Emporors letters of Russia: and I also gaue him a present of a ninth, who entertained me very well, and caused me to eate in his presence as his brethren did, feasting me with flesh of a wilde horse, and mares milk without bread. [Sidenote: Letters of safteconduct] And the next day he sent for me again, and asked of me diuers questions, as wel touching the affaires of the Emperour of

Russia, as of our countrey and lawes, to which I answered as I thought good: so that at my departure he gaue me his letters of safe conduct.

This Castle of Sellizure is situated vpon an high hill, where the King called the Can lyeth, whose palace is built of earth very basely, and not strong: the people are but poore, and haue litle trade of merchandise among them. The South part of this Castle is lowe lande, but very fruitfull, where grow many good fruites, among which there is one called a Dynie, of a great bignesse and full of moysture, which the people do eate after meate in steade of drinke. Also there growes another fruite called a Carbuse of the bignesse of a great cucumber, yellow and sweete as sugar: also a certaine corne called Iegur, whose stalke is much like a sugar cane, and as high, and the graine like rice, which groweth at the toppe of the cane like a cluster of grapes; the water that serueth all that countrey is drawen by ditches out of the riuer Oxus, vnto the great destruction of the said riuer, for which cause it falleth not into the Caspian sea as it hath done in times past, and in short time all that land is like to be destroied, and to become a wildernes for want of water, when the riuer of Oxus shal faile.

[Sidenote: Vrgence.] The 14. day of the moneth we departed from this Castle of Sellizure, and the 16. of the same we arriued at a citie called Vrgence, where we paid custome as wel for our own heads, as for our camels and horses. And hauing there soiourned one moneth, attending the time of our further trauaile, the king of that countrey called Aly Soltan, brother to the forenamed Azym Can, returned from a towne called Corasan, within the borders of Persia, which he lately had conquered from the Persians, with whom he and the rest of the kings of Tartaria haue continuall warres. Before this king also I was commanded to come, to whom I likewise presented the Emperors letters of Russia, and he intertained me wel, and demanded of me diuers questions, and at my departure gaue me his letters of safe conduct.

This city or towne of Vrgence standeth in a plaine ground, with walles of the earth, by estimation 4. miles about it. The buildings within it are also of earth, but ruined and out of good order: it hath one long street that is couered aboue, which is the place of their market. It hath bene wonne and lost 4. times within 7. yeeres by ciuill warres, by meanes whereof there are but few merchants in it, and they very poore, and in all that towne I could not sell about 4. kerseis. The chiefest commodities there sold are such wares as come from Boghar, and out of Persia, but in most smal quantity not worth the writing. [Sidenote: The countrey of Turkeman.] All the land from the Caspian sea to this Citie of Vrgence is called the land of Turkeman, and is subiect to the said Azim Can, and his brethren which be fiue in number, and one of them hath the name of the chiefe king called Can, but he is little obeyed sauing in his owne Dominion, and where he dwelleth: for euery one will be King of his owne portion, and one brother seeketh alwayes to destroy another, hauing no natural loue among them, by reason that they are begotten of diuers women, and commonly they are the children of slaues, either Christians or Gentiles, which the father doeth keepe as concubines, and euery Can or Sultan hath at least 4. or 5. wiues, besides young maidens and boyes, liuing most viciously: and when there are warres betwixt these brethren, (as they are seldome without) he that is ouercome if he be not slaine, flieth to the field with such companie of men as will followe him, and there liueth in the wildemesse resorting to watering places, and so robbeth and spoileth as many Carauans of Marchants and others as they be able to ouercome, continuing in this sort his wicked life, vntil such time as he may get power and aide to inuade some of his brethren againe. From the Caspian sea vnto the Castle of Sellizure aforesaid, and all the Countreis about the said Sea, the people liue without towne or habitation in the wilde fields, remouing from one place to another in great companies with their cattel, whereof they haue great store, as camels, horses, and sheepe both tame and wilde. Their sheepe are of great stature with great buttocks, weighing 60. or 80. pound in weight. There are many wild horses which the Tartars doe many times kil with their hawkes, and that in this order. The hawkes are lured to sease vpon the beasts neckes or heads, which with chafing of themselues and sore beating of the hawkes are tired: then the hunter following his game doeth slay the horse with his arrow or sword. In all this lande there groweth no grasse, but a certaine brush or heath, whereon the cattell feeding become very fat.

The Tartars neuer ride without their bow, arrowes, and sword, although it be on hawking, or at any other pleasure, and they are good archers both on horsebacke, and on foote also. These people haue not the vse of golde, siluer, or any other coyne, but when they lacke apparell or other necessaries, they barter their cattell for the same. Bread they haue none, for they neither till nor sow: they be great deuourers of flesh, which they cut in smal pieces, and eat it by handfuls most greedily, and especially the horseflesh. Their chiefest drink is mares milke sowred, as I haue said before of the Nagayans, and they wilbe drunk with the same. They haue no riuers nor places of water in this countrey, vntil you come to the foresaid gulf, distant from the place of our landing 20. dayes iourney, except it be in wels, the water whereof is saltish, and yet distant the one from the other two daies iourney and more. They eate their meate vpon the ground, sitting with their legs double vnder them, and so also when they pray. Art or science they haue none, but liue most idlely, sitting round in great companies in the fields, deuising, and talking most vainely.

[Sidenote: The riuer of Ardock falleth into the lake of Kitay.] The 26. day of Nouember, we departed from the towne of Vrgence, and hauing trauailed

- 204 -

by the riuer Oxus, 100 miles, we passed ouer another great riuer called Ardock, where we paid a certaine pety custome. This riuer Ardock is great, and very swift, falling out of the foresaid Oxus and passing about 1000. mile to the Northward, it then consumeth it selfe in the ground, and passing vnder the same about 500. mile, issueth out againe, and falleth into the lake of Kitay, as I haue before declared.

[Sidenote: The castle of Kait.] The 7. of December following, we arriued at a Castle called Kait, subiect to a Soltan called Saramet Soltan, who meant to haue robbed all the Christians in the Carauan, had it not bene for feare of his brother the king of Vrgence, as we were informed by one of his chiefest counsellers, who willed vs to make him a present, which he tooke, and deliuered: besides, we paid at the said castle for custome, of euery camel one red hide of Russia, besides pety gifts to his officers.

Thus proceeding in our iourney, the tenth day at night being at rest, and our watch set, there came vnto vs foure horsemen, which wee tooke as spies, from whom wee tooke their weapons and bound them, and hauing well examined them, they confessed that they had seene the tract of many horsemen, and no footing of camels, and gaue vs to vnderstand, that there were rouers and theeues abroade: for there trauaile few people that are true and peaceable in that Countrey, but in companie of Carauan, where there be many camels: and horsefeeting new without camels were to be doubted. Whereupon we consulted and determined amongst our selues, and sent a poste to the said Soltan of Kayte, who immediatly came himselfe with 300. men, and mette these foure suspected men which we sent vnto him, and examined them so streightly, and threatned them in such sort, that they confessed, there was a banished Prince with 40. men 3. daies iourney forward, who lay in wait to destroy vs, if he could, and that they themselues were of his companie.

The Soltan therefore vnderstanding, that the theeues were not many, appointed vs 80. men well armed with a Captaine to goe with vs, and conduct vs in our way. And the Soltan himselfe returned backe againe, taking the foure theeues with him. These souldiers trauailed with vs two dayes, consuming much of our victuals. And the 3. day in the morning very earely they set out before our Carauan, and hauing ranged the wildernes for the space of foure houres, they mette vs, comming towards vs as fast as their horse could runne, and declared that they had founde the tract of horses not farre from vs, perceiuing well that we shoulde meete with enemies, and therefore willed vs to appoint our selues for them, and asked vs what we would giue them to conduct vs further, or else they would returne. To whom we offered as we thought good, but they refused our offer, and would haue more; and so we not agreeing they departed from vs, and went back to their Soltan, who (as wee coniectured) was priuie to the conspiracie. [Sidenote: Diuination by sorcerie] But they being gone, certaine Tartars of our companie called holy men, (because they had bene at Mecha) caused the whole Carauan to stay, and would make their prayers, and deuine how wee should prosper in our iourney and whether we should meet with any ill company or no? To which, our whole Carauan did agree. And they tooke certaine sheepe and killed them, and tooke the blade bones of the same, and first sodde them and then burnt them, and tooke of the blood of the said sheepe, and mingled it with the powder of the saide bones, and wrote certaine Characters with the saide blood, vsing many other ceremonies and wordes, and by the same deuined and found, that wee shoulde meete with enemies and theeues (to our great trouble) but should ouercome them, to which sorcerie, I and my companie gaue no credit, but we found it true: for within 3. houres after that the souldiers departed from vs, which was the 15. day of December, in the morning, we escried farre off diuers horsemen which made towards vs, and we (perceiuing them to be rouers) gathered ourselues together, being 40. of vs wel appointed, and able to fight, and we made our prayers together euery one after his lawe; professing to liue and die one with another, and so prepared our selues. When the theeues were nigh vnto vs, we perceiued them to be in number 37. men well armed, and appointed with bowes, arrowes and swords, and the captaine a prince banished from his Countrey. They willed vs to yeelde our selues, or els to be slaine, but wee defied them, wherewith they shotte at vs all at once, and wee at them very hotly, and so continued our fight from morning vntil two houres within night, diuers men, horses and camels being wounded and slaine on both partes: [Sidenote: Handguns very profitable.] and had it not bene for 4. handgunnes which I and my companie had and vsed, we had bene ouercome and destroyed: for the theeues were better armed, and were also better archers than we: But after wee had slaine diuers of their men and horses with our gunnes, they durst not approch so nigh, which caused them to come to a truce with vs vntill the next morning, which we accepted, and encamped our selues vpon a hill, and made the fashion of a Castle, walling it about with packes of wares, and laide our horses and camels within the same to saue them from the shotte of arrowes: and the theeues also incamped within an arrowe shotte of vs, but they were betwixt vs and the water, which was to our great discomfort, because neither we nor our camels had drunke in 2. dayes before.

Thus keeping good watch, when halfe the night was spent, the Prince of the theeues sent a messenger halfe way vnto vs, requiring to talke with our Captaine, in their tongue, the Carauan Basha, who answered the messenger, I will not depart from my companie to goe into the halfe way to talke with thee: but if that thy Prince with all his companie will sweare by our Lawe to keepe the truce, then will I send a man to talke with thee, or els not. Which the Prince vnderstanding as well himselfe as his company, swore so loude that we might all heare. And then we sent one of our company (reputed a holy man) to talke with the same messenger. [Sidenote: Bussarmans. Caphar.] The message was pronounced aloude in this order, our Prince demaundeth of the Carauan Basha, and of all you that be Bussarmans, (that is to say circumcised) not desiring your bloods, that you deliuer into his hands as many Caphars, that is vnbeleeuers (meaning vs the Christians) as are among you with their goods, and in so doing, hee will suffer you to depart with your goods in quietnesse, and on the contrary, you shall be handled with no lesse cruelty then the Caphars, if hee ouercome you, as he doubteth not. To the which our Carauan Basha answered, that he had no Christians in his company, nor other strangers, but two Turkes which were of their Law, and although hee had, hee would rather die then deliuer them, and that we were not afraide of his threatnings, and that should he know when day appeared. And so passing in talke, the theeues (contrary to their othe) caried our holy man away to their Prince, crying with a lowde voyce in token of victory, Ollo, ollo. Wherewith we were much discomforted, fearing that that holy man would betray vs: but he being cruelly handled and much examined, would not to death confesse anything which was to vs preiudliciall, neither touching vs, nor yet what men they had slaine and wounded of ours the day before. When the night was spent, in the morning we prepared our selues to battel againe: which the theeues perceiuing, required to fall to agreement and asked much of vs: And to be briefe, the most part of our companie being loth to go to battel againe, and hauing litle to loose, and safeconduct to passe, we were compelled to agree, and to giue the theeues 20 ninths (that is to say) 20 times 9 seuerall things, and a camell to cary away the same, which being receiued, the theeues departed into the wildernes to their old habitation, and we went on our way forward. [Sidenote: The river of Oxus.] And that night came to the riuer Oxus, where we refreshed our selues, hauing bene 3. dayes without water and drinke, and tarried there all the next day, making mery with our slaine horses and camels, and then departed from that place, [Sidenote: A wildernes of sande.] and for feare of meeting with the said theeues againe or such like, we left the high way which went along, the said riuer, and passed through a wildernes of sand, and traulled 4 dayes in the same before we came to water: and then came to a wel, the water being very brackish, and we then as before were in neede of water, and of other victuals, being forced to kill our horses and camels to eate.

In this wildernes also we had almost fallen into the hands of theeues: for one night being at rest, there came certaine scouts, and caried away certaine of our men which lay a litle separated from the Carauan, wherewith there was a great shoute and crie, and we immediately laded our camels, and departed being about midnight and very darke, and droue sore till we came to the riuer Oxus againe, and then we feared nothing being walled with the said riuer: and whether it was for that we had gotten the water, or for that the same theeues were far from vs when the scouts discouered vs, we knowe not, but we escaped that danger.

[Sidenote: Boghar a citie of Bactria.] So vpon the 23 day of December we arriued at the citie of Boghar in the lande of Bactria. This Boghar is situated in the lowest part of all the land, walled about with a high wall of earth, with diuers gates into the same: it is diuided into 3 partitions, whereof two parts are the kings, and the 3 part is for Marchants and markets, and euery science hath their dwelling and market by themselues. The Citie is very great, and the houses for the most part of earth, but there are also many houses, temples and monuments of stone sumptuously builded, and gilt, and especially bathstoues so artificially built, that the like thereof is not in the world: the maner whereof is too long to rehearse. [Sidenote: A strange worme in mens legs.] There is a little riuer running through the middest of the said Citie, but the water there of is most vnholsome, for it breedeth sometimes in men that drinke thereof, and especially in them that be not there borne, a worme of an ell long, which lyeth commonly in the legge betwixt the flesh and the skinne, and is pluckt out about the ancle with great art and cunning, the Surgeons being much practised therein, and if shee breaks in plucking out, the partie dieth, and euery day she commeth out about an inch, which is rolled vp, and so worketh till she be all out. And yet it is there forbidden to drinke any other thing then water, and mares milke, and whosoeuer is found to breake that law is whipped and beaten most cruelly through the open markets, and there are officers appointed for the same, who haue authoritie to goe into any mans house, to search if he haue either Aquauitae, wine, or brage, and finding the same, doe breake the vessels, spoile the drinke, and punish the masters of the house most cruelly, yea, and many times if they perceiue but by the breath of a man that he hath drunke, without further examination he shall not escape their hands.

There is a Metropolitane in this Boghar, who causeth this to bee so streightly kept: and he is more obeyed then the king, and will depose the king, and place another at his will and pleasure, as he did by this king that raigned at our being there, and his predecessour, by the meanes of the said Metropolitan: for he betrayed him, and in the night slewe him in his chamber, who was a Prince who loued all Christians well.

This Countrey of Boghar was sometime subiect to the Persians, and do now speake the Persian tongue, but yet now it is a kingdome of it selfe, and hath most cruell warres continually with the sayd Persians about their religion, although they be all Mahometists. One occasion of their wars is, for that the Persians will not cut the haire of their vpper lips, as the

Bogharians and all other Tartars doe, which they accompt great sinne, and cal them Caphars, that is Vnbeleeuers, as they doe the Christians.

[Sidenote: The coyne of Boghar.] The king of Boghar hath no great power or riches, his reuenues are but small, and he is most meinteined by the Citie: for he taketh the tenth penie of all things that are there solde, as well by the craftsmen as by the marchants, to the great impouerishment of the people, whom he keepeth in great subiection, and when he lacketh money, he sendeth his officers to the shops of the sayd Marchants to take their wares to pay his debts, and will haue credit of force, as the like he did to pay me certaine money that he owed me for 19 pieces of Kersey. Their money is siluer and copper, for gold there is none current: they haue but one piece of siluer, and that is worth 12. pence English, and the copper money are called Pooles, and 120 of them goeth the value of the said 12. pence, and is more common paiment then the siluer, which the king causeth to rise and fall to his most aduantage euery other moneth, and sometimes twise a moneth, not caring to oppresse his people, for that he loketh not to reigne aboue 2 or 3 yeres before he be either slaine, or driuen away, to the great destruction of the countrey and merchants.

The 26 day of the moneth I was commanded to come before the said king, to whom I presented the Emperour of Russia his letters, who interteined vs most gently, and caused vs to eate in his presence, and diuers times he sent for me, and deuised with me familiarly in his secret chamber, as well of the power of the Emperour, and the great Turke as also of our countries, lawes, and religion, and caused vs to shoote in handguns before him, and did himselfe practise the vse thereof. But after all this great intertainement before my departure he shewed himselfe a very Tartar: for he went to the wars owing me money, and saw me not payd before his departure. And although indeede he gaue order for the same, yet was I verie ill satisfied, and forced to rebate part, and to take wares as payment for the rest contrary to my expectation: but of a begger better paiment I could not haue, and glad I was so to be paid and dispatched.

But yet I must needs praise and commend this barbarous king who immediately after my arriual at Boghar, hauing vnderstoode our trouble with the theeues, sent 100 men well armed, and gaue them great charge not to returne before they had either slaine or taken the sayd theeues. Who according to their commission ranged the wildernes in such sort, that they met with the said company of theeues, and slew part, and part fledde, and foure they tooke and brought vnto the king, and two of them were sore wounded in our skirmish with our gunnes: And after the king had sent for me to come to see them, he caused them all 4 to be hanged at his palace gate, because they were Gentlemen, to the example of others. And of such goods as were gotten againe, I had part restored me, and this good iustice I found at his hands.

There is yeerely great resort of Marchants to this Citie of Boghar, which trauaile in great Carauans from the countries thereabout adioining, as India, Persia, Balgh, Russia, with diuers others, and in times past from Cathay, when there was passage: but these Marchants are so beggerly and poore, and bring so little quantitie of wares, lying two or 3 yeeres to sell the same, that there is no hope of any good trade there to be had worthy the following.

The chiefe commodities that are brought thither out of these foresayd Countreys, are these following.

[Sidenote: Marchandise of India.] The Indians doe bring fine whites, which the Tartars do all roll about their heads, and al other kinds of whites, which serue for apparell made of cotton wooll and crasko, but golde, siluer, precious stones, and spices they bring none. I enquired and perceiued that all such trade passeth to the Ocean sea, and the vaines where all such things are gotten are in the subiection of the Portingals. The Indians carie them from Boghar againe wrought silkes, red hides, slaues, and horses, with such like, but of Kerseis and other cloth, they make little accompt. I offered to barter with Marchants of those Countreis, which came from the furthest parts of India, euen from the countrey of Bengala, and the riuer Ganges, to giue them Kersies for their commodities, but they would not barter for such commoditie as cloth.

[Sidenote: Marchandise of Persia.] The Persians do bring thither Craska, wollen cloth, linnen cloth, diuers kindes of wrought pide silkes, Argomacks, with such like, and doe carie from thence redde hides with other Russe warres, and slaues, which are of diuers countreies, but cloth they will by none, for that they bring themselues, and is brought vnto them as I haue inquired from Allepo in Syria, and the parts of Turkie. [Sidenote: Marchandise of Russia.] The Russes doe carie vnto Boghar, redde hides, sheepe skinnes, wollen cloth of diuers sorts, woodden vessels, bridles, saddles, with such like, and doe carie away from thence diuers kindes of wares made of cotton wooll, diuers kinds of silkes, Crasca, with other things, but there is but smal vtterance. [Sidenote: Marchandise of Cathay.] From the Countreis of Cathay are brought thither in time of peace, and when the way is open, musk, rubarbe, satten, damaske, with diuers other things. At my being at Boghar, there came Carauans out of all these foresaid Countries, except from Cathay: and the cause why there came none from thence was the great warres that had dured 3 yeeres before my comming thither, and yet dured betwixt 2 great Countries and cities of Tartars, that are directly in the way betwixt the said Boghar and the said

Cathay, and certaine barbarous field people, as well Gentiles as Mahometists bordering to the said Cities. [Sidenote: Taskent and Caskar.] The cities are called Taskent and Caskar, and the people that warre against Taskent are called Cassaks of the law of Mahomet: and they which warre with the sayd countrey of Caskar are called Kings, Gentiles and idolaters. These 2 barbarous nations are of great force liuing in the fields without house or towne, and haue almost subdued the foresaid cities, and so stopped vp the way, that it is impossible for any Carauan to passe vnspoiled: so that 3 yeeres before our being there, no Carauan had gone, or vsed trade betwixt the countries of Cathay and Boghar, and when the way is cleare, it is 9 moneths iourney.

To speake of the said countrey of Cathay, and of such newes as I haue heard thereof, I haue thought it best to reserue it to our meeting. I hauing made my solace at Boghar in the Winter time, and hauing learned by much inquisition, the trade thereof, as also of all the other countries thereto adioyning, and the time of the yeere being come, for all Carauans to depart, and also the king being gone to the warres, and newes come that he was fled, and I aduertised by the Metropolitan himselfe, that I should depart, because the towne was like to bee besieged: I thought it good and meete, to take my iourney some way, and determined to haue gone from thence into Persia, and to haue seene the trade of that countrey, although I had enformed my selfe sufficiently thereof, as well at Astracan, as at Boghar: and perceiued well the trades not to be much vnlike the trades of Tartaria: but when I should haue taken my iourney that way, it was let by diuers occasions: the one was, the great wars that did newly begin betwixt the Sophie, and the kings of Tartaria, whereby the waies were destroyed: and there was a Carauan destroied with rouers and theeues, which came out of India and Persia, by safe conduct: and about ten daies iourney from Boghar, they were robbed, and a great part slaine. [Sidenote: He returneth the eight of March 1559.] Also the Metropolitan of Boghar, who is greater then the king, tooke the Emperors letters of Russia from me, without which I should haue bene taken slaue in euery place: also all such wares as I had receiued in barter for cloth, and as I tooke perforce of the king, and other his Nobles, in paiment of money due vnto me, were not vendible in Persia: for which causes and diuers others, I was constrained to come backe againe to Mare Caspium, the same way I went: so that the eight of March 1559, we departed out of the said Citie of Boghar, being a Carauan of 600 Camels: and if we had not departed when we did, I and my company had bene in danger to haue lost life and goods. For, ten daies after our departure, the king of Samarcand came with an armie, and besieged the said Citie of Boghar, the king being absent, and gone to the wars against another prince, his kinsman, as the like chanceth in those Countries once in two or three yeres. For it is maruell, if a King reigne there aboue three or foure yeres, to the great destruction of the Countrey, and marchants.

[Sidenote: Vrgence.] The 25 of March, we came to the foresayd towne of Vrgence, and escaped the danger of 400 rouers, which lay in waite for vs backe againe, being the most of them of kindred to that company of theeues, which we met with going foorth; as we perceiued by foure spies, which were taken. [Sidenote: The king of Balke, or Balgh.] There were in my company, and committed to my charge, two ambaassadors, the one from the king of Boghar, the other from the king of Balke, and were sent vnto the Emperor of Russia. And after having taried at Vrgence, and the Castle of Sellysure, eight daies for the assembling, and making ready of our Carauan, the second of Aprill we departed from thence, hauing foure more Ambassadors in our companie, sent from the king of Vrgence, and other Soltans, his brethren, vnto the Emperor of Russia, with answere of such letters as I brought them: and the same Ambassadors were also committed vnto my charge by the sayde Kings and princes: to whome I promised most faithfully, and swore by our law, that they should be well vsed in Rusland, and suffered to depart from thence againe in safetie, according as the Emperor had written also in his letters: for they somewhat doubted, because there had none gone out of Tartaria into Russia, of long time before.

The 23 of Aprill, we arriued at the Mare Caspium againe, where we found our barke which we came in, but neither anker, cable, cocke, nor saile: neuerthelesse wee brought hempe with vs, and spunne a cable our selues, with the rest of our tackling, and made vs a saile of cloth of cotton wooll, and rigged our barke as well as we could, but boate or anker we had none. In the meane time being deuising to make an anker of wood of a cart wheele, there arriued a barke, which came from Astracan, with Tartars and Russes, which had 2 ankers, with whom I agreed for the one: and thus being in a readinesse, we set saile and departed, I, and the two Iohnsons being Master and Mariners ourselues, hauing in our barke the said sixe ambassadors, and 25 Russes which had bene slaues a long time in Tartaria, nor euer had before my comming, libertie, or meanes to get home, and these slaues serued to rowe, when neede was. Thus sailing sometimes along the coast, and sometimes out of sight of lande, the 13. day of May, hauing a contrary winde, wee came to an anker, being three leagues from the shoare, and there rose a sore storme, which continued 44. houres, and our cable being of our our owne spinning, brake, and lost our anker, and being off a lee shoare, and hauing no boate to helpe vs, we hoysed our saile, and bare roomer with the said shoare, looking for present death: but as God prouided vs, we ranne into a creeke ful of oze, and so saued our selues with our barke, and liued in great discomfort for a time. For although we should haue escaped with our liues the danger of the sea, yet if our barke had perished, we knew we should haue bene either destroyed, or taken slaues by the people of that Countrey, who liue wildly in the field, like beasts, without house or habitation. Thus when the storme was seazed, we went out of the creeke againe: and hauing set the land with our Compasse, and taken certaine markes of the same, during the time of the tempest, whilest we ridde at our anker, we went directly to the place where we ridde, with our barke againe, and found our anker which we lost: whereat the Tartars much marueiled howe we did it. While we were in the creeke, we made an anker of wood of cart wheeles, which we had in our barke, which we threw away, when wee had found our yron anker againe. Within two days after, there arose another great storme, at the Northeast, and we lay a trie, being driuen far into the sea, and had much ado to keepe our barke from sinking, the billowe was so great: but at the last, hauing faire weather, we tooke the Sunne, and knowing howe the land lay from vs we fel with the Riuer Yaik, according to our desire, wherof the Tartars were very glad, fearing that wee should haue bene driuen to the coast of Persia, whose people were vnto them great enemies.

[Sidenote: The English flag in the Caspian sea.] Note, that during the time of our Nauigation, wee set vp the redde crosse of S. George in our flagges, for honour of the Christians, which I suppose was neuer seene in the Caspian sea before. We passed in this voyage diuers fortunes: notwithstanding the 28. of May we arriued in safetie at Astracan, and there remained till the tenth of Iune following, as well to prepare vs small boates, to goe vp against the streame of Volga, with our goods, as also for the companie of the Ambassadours of Tartarie, committed vnto me, to bee brought to the presence of the Emperour of Russia.

[Sidenote: A notable description of the Caspian Sea.] This Caspian sea (to say some thing of it) is in length about two hundred leagues, and in breadth 160, without any issue to other seas: to the East part whereof, ioyneth the great desert countrey of the Tartars, called Turkemen: to the West, the countreyes of the Chyreasses, the mountaines of Caucasus, and the Mare Euxinum, which is from the said Caspian Sea a hundred leagues. To the North is the riuer Volga, and the land of Nagay, and to the South parte ioyne the countreys of Media and Persia. This sea is fresh water in many places, and in other places as salt as our great Ocean. It hath many goodly Riuers falling into it, and it auoideth not it selfe except it be vnder ground. The notable riuers that fall into it are first the great riuer of Volga, called in the Tartar tongue Edell, which springeth out of a lake in a marrish or plaine ground, not farre from the Citie of Nouogrode in Russia, and it is from the spring to the Sea, aboue two thousande English miles. It hath diuers other goodly Riuers falling into it, as out of Siberia, Yaic, and Yem: Also out of the mountaines of Caucasus, the Riuers of Cyrus and Arash, and diuers others.

As touching the trade of Shamaky in Media and Tebris, with other townes in Persia, I haue enquired, and do well vnderstand, that it is euen like to the trades of Tartaria, that is little vtterance, and small profite: and I haue bene aduertised that the chiefe trade of Persia is into Syria, and so transported into the Leuant sea. The fewe shippes vpon the Caspian Seas, the want of Mart and port Townes, the pouertie of the people, and the ice, maketh that trade naught.

At Astracan there were merchants of Shamaky, with whom I offered to barter, and to giue them kersies for their wares, but they would not, saying, they had them as good cheape in their countrey, as I offred them, which was sixe rubbles for a kersie, that I asked: and while I was at Boghar, there were brought thither out of Persia, Cloth, and diuers commodities of our countries, which were sold as good cheape, as I might sell ours.

The tenth day of Iune we departed from Astracan towards the Mosco, hauing an hundred gunners in our company at the Emperors charges, for the safe conduct at the Tartar Ambassadors and me. And the eight and twentieth day of Iuly folowing, wee arriued at the citie of Cazan, hauing bene vpon the way from Astracan thither, sixe weekes and more, without any refreshing of victuals: for in all that way there is no habitation.

[Sidenote: His arriual at Mosco the 2. of September.] The seuenth of August folowing, wee departed from Cazan, and transported our goods by water, as farre as the citie of Morum, and then by land; so that the second of September, we arriued at the citie of Mosco, and the fourth day I came before the Emperours Maiestie, kissed his hand, and presented him a white Cowes taile of Cathay, and a drumme of Tartária, which he well accepted. Also I brought before him all the Ambassadors that were committed to my charge, with all the Russe slaues: and that day I dined in his Maiesties presence, and at dinner his Grace sent me meate by a Duke, and asked me diuers questions touching the lands and countreis where I had bene. And thus I remained at the Mosco about your affaires, vntil the 17. day of February that your wares were sent downe: and then hauing a license of the Emperors Maiestie to depart, the 21. day I came to your house at Vologhda, and there remained vntil the breaking vp of the yere: and then hauing seene all your goods laden into your boates, I departed, with the same, and arriued withall in safetie at Colmogro the 9. of May 1560. And here I cease for this time, intreating you to heare with this my large discourse, which by reason of the varietie of matter, I could make no shorter, and I beseech God to prosper all your attempts.

The latitudes of certaine principall places in Russia, and other Regions.

Deg. Min.

Mosco in 55 10
Nouogrod the great 58 26
Nouogrod the lesse 56 33
Colmogro 64 10
Vologhda 59 11
Cazan 55 33
Oweke 51 40
Astracan 47 9
At the entrance into the
  Caspian sea. 46 42
Manguslaue beyond the
  Caspian sea. 45 04
Vrgence in Tartary 20.
  dayes iourney from the
  Caspian sea. 42 18
Boghar a citie in Tartary
  20. dayes iourney from
  Vrgcnce. 39 10

* * * * *

Certaine notes gathered by Richard Iohnson (which was at Boghar with M. Anthony Ienkinson) of the reports of Russes and other strangers, of the wayes of Russia to Cathaya, and of diuers and strange people.

The first note giuen by one named Sarnichoke a Tartarian subiect to the Prince of Boghar, which are also Tartars bordering vpon Kizilbash or Persia, declaring the way from Astracan, being the furthest part of Russia, to Cathaya as foloweth.

First from Astracan to Serachick by land, trauailing by leysure as Merchants vse with wares, is 10. dayes iourney.

From Serachick to a towne named [Marginal note: Or Vrgema.] Vrgenshe, 15. dayes.

From Vrgenshe to Boghar, 15. dayes.

From Boghar to Cascar, 30. dayes.

From Cascar to Cathaya, 30. dayes iourney.

* * * * *

By the same partie a note of another way more sure to traueile, as he reporteth.

From Astracan to Turkemen by the Caspian sea, 10. dayes, with barkes.

From Turkemen by lande specially with Camels, bearing the weight of 15. poodes for their common burthens, is 10. dayes to Vrgenshe.

From Vrgenshe to Boghar, 15. dayes.

Note. At this Citie of Boghar is the marte or meeting place betweene the Turkes and nations of those parts and the Cathayans.

Also the toll there is the 40. part to be payed of Merchandizes or goods.

From thence to Cascar is one moneths iourney, and from Cascar (being the frontier of the great Can, hauing many townes and fortes by the way) is also a moneths trauel for merchants by land to Cathay.

Further, as he hath heard (not hauing bene in those parts himselfe) ships may saile from the dominions of Cathaia vnto India. But of other waies, or how the seas lie by any coast hee knoweth not.

The instruction of another Tartarian merchant dwelling in the citie of Boghar, as he hath learned by other his countreymen which haue bene there.

First from Astracan by sea to Serachick is 15 dayes: affirming also that a man may trauell the other way before written by Turkemen.

From Serachick to Vrgence is 15 dayes.

From Vrgence to Boghar also 15 dayes.

Note. These last 30 daies iourney is without habitation of houses: therefore trauellers lodge in their own tents, carying with them to eate, their seuerall prouisions: and for drinesse there bee many wels of faire water at equall baiting places not farre distant dayly to be had.

From Boghar to Taskent easie travelling with goods, is 14 dayes by land.

From Taskent to Occient 7 dayes.

From Occient to Cascar 20 daies. This Cascar is the head towne or citie of another prince, lying betweene Boghar and Cathaia, called Reshit can.

From Cascar to Sowchick 30 daies iourney, which Sowchick is the first border of Kathay.

From Sowchick to Camchick 5 dayes iourney, and from Camchick to Cathay is 2 moneths iourney, all the way being inhabited, temperate, and wel replenished with innumerable fruits, and the chiefe citie in that whole land is called Cambalu, which is yet 10 dayes iourney from Cathay.

Beyond this land of Cathay, which they praise to be ciuill and vnspeakeably rich, is the countrey named in the Tartarian tongue Cara-calmack inhabited with blacke people: but in Cathay the most part thereof stretching to the sunne rising, are people white and of faire complexion. Their religion also, as the Tartars report, is christian, or after the maner of Christians, and their language peculiar, differing from the Tartarian tongue.

There are no great and furious Beares in trauelling through the waies aforesaid, but wolues white and blacke. And because that woods are not of such quantitie there, as in these parts of Russia, but in maner rather scant then plentiful, as is reported, the Beares breed not that way, but some other beasts (as namely one in Russe called Barse) are in those coasts. This Barse appeareth by a skinne of one seene here to sell, to be nere so great as a big lion, spotted very faire and therefore we here take it to be a Leopard or Tiger.

[Sidenote: Angrim] Note that 20 daies iourney from Cathay is a country named Angrim, where liueth the beast that beareth the best Muske, and the principal thereof is cut out of the knee of the male. [Sidenote: Mandeuille speaketh hereof.] The people are taunie, and for that the men are not bearded nor differ in complexion from women, they have certaine tokens of iron, that is to say: the men weare the sunne round like a bosse vpon their shoulders, and women on their priuie parts. Their feeding is raw flesh in the same land, and in another called Titay: [Marginal Note: or Kitay.] the Duke there is called Can. [Sidenote: Small people.] They worship the fire, and it is 34 dayes iourney from great Cathay, and in the way lyeth the beautifull people, eating with kniues of golde, and are called Comorom, and the land of small people is neerer the Mosko then Cathay.

* * * * *

The instructions of one of Permia, who reporteth he had bene at Cathay the way before written, and also another way neere the sea coast, as foloweth, which note was sent out of Russia from Giles Holmes.

[Sidenote: Pechora but six days iourney by land or water from Ob.] First from the prouince of Dwina is knowen the way to Pechora, and from Pechora traueiling with Olens or harts, is six dayes iourney by land, and in the Sommer as much by water to the riuer of Ob.

The Ob is a riuer full of flats, the mouth of it is 70. Russe miles ouer. And from thence three dayes iourney on the right hand is a place called Chorno-lese, to say in English, blacke woods, and from thence neere hand is a people called Pechey-cony, wearing their haire by his description after the Irish fashion.

From Pechey-cony to Ioult Calmachey three dayes iourney, and from thence to
Chorno Callachay three dayes tending to the Southeast.

These two people are of the Tartarian faith, and tributaries to the great Can.

* * * * *

Here follow certaine countreys of the Samoeds which dwell vpon the riuer Ob, and vpon the sea coasts beyond the same, taken outof the Russe tongue word by word, and trauailed by a Russe born in Colmogro, whose name was Pheodor Towtigin, who by report, was slaine in his second voyage in one of the said countreys.

Vpon the East part beyond the countrey of Vgori, the riuer Ob is the most Westernmost part thereof. Vpon the sea coast dwell Samoeds, and their countrey is called Molgomsey, whose meate is flesh of Olens, or Harts, and Fish, and doe eate one another sometimes among themselues. And if any Marchants come vnto them, then they kill one of their children for their sakes to feast them withall. And if a Marchant chance to die with them, they burie him not, but eate him, and so doe they eate them of their owne countrey likewise. [Sidenote: Travelling on dogs and harts.] They be euill of sight, and haue small noses, but they be swift and shoote very well, and they trauaile on Harts and on dogges, and their apparell is Sables and Harts skinnes. They haue no Marchandise but Sables onely.

2 Item, on the same coast or quarter beyond those people; and by the sea side also doth dwell another kinde of Samoeds in like maner, hauing another language. One moneth in the yeere they liue in the sea, and doe not come or dwell on the dry land for that moneth.

3 Item beyond these people, on the sea coast, there is another kinde of Samoeds, their meate is flesh and fish, and their merchandise are Sables, white and blacke Foxes (which the Russes call Pselts) and Harts skinnes, and Fawnes skinnes.

* * * * *

The relation of Chaggi Memet a Persian Marchant, to Baptista Ramusius, and other notable citizens of Venice; touching the way from Tauris the chiefe city of Persia, to Campion a citie of Cathay ouer land: in which voyage he himselfe had passed before with the Carauans.

From Tauris to Soltania. 6 dayes iourney
From Soltania to Casbin. 4 " "
From Casbin to Veremi. 6 " "
From Veremi to Eri. 15 " "
From Eri to Boghara. 20 " "
From Boghara to Samarchand. 5 " "
From Samarchand to Cascar. 25 " "

From Cascar to Acsu. 20 " "
From Acsu to Cuchi. 20 " "
From Cuchi to Chialis. 10 " "
From Chialis to Turfon. 10 " "
From Turfon to Camul. 13 " "
From Camul to Succuir. 15 " "
From Succuir to Gauta. 5 " "
From Gauta to Campion. 6 " "

Which Campion is a citie of the Empire of Cathay in the prouince of Tangut, from whence the greatest quantitie of Rubarbe commeth.

* * * * *

A letter of Sigismond king of Polonia, written in the 39. yeere of his reigne to Elizabeth the Queenes most excellent Maiestie of England, &c.

Sigismundus Augustus by the grace of God king of Polonia, great Duke of Lituania, Russia, Prussia, Massouia, and Samogetia, &c. Lord and heire &c. to the most Noble Princesse Ladie Elizabeth by the same grace of God Queene of England, France and Ireland, &c. our deare sister, and kinsewoman, greeting and increase of all felicitie. Whereas your Maiestie writeth to vs that you haue receiued two of our letters, wee haue looked that you should haue answered to them both. [Sidenote: The trade to Narue forbidden by the K. of Poland.] First to the one in which we intreated more at large in forbidding the voyage to Narue, which if it had bene done, we had bene vnburdened of so often writing of one matter: and might haue answered your Maiestie much better to the purpose. Now we thus answere to your Maiestie to those matters of the which you writte to vs the 3 of October from Windsore. [Sidenote: The ancient couenants of trafficke between England and Prussia.] First, forasmuch as your Maiestie at the request of our letters hath discharged the arrest of Marchants goods, and of the names of the men of Danske our subiects, which was set vpon them by the commandement of your Maiestie: and also haue restored the olde and ancient libertie of traffique, we acknowlege great pleasure done vnto vs in the same: and also think it to bee done according to common agreement made in times past. Neither were we euer at any time of any other opinion touching your Maiestie, but that wee should obtaine right and reason at your hands. Forasmuch as we likewise shall at all times be ready to grant to your Maiestie, making any request for your subiects, so farre as shall stand with iustice, yet neither will we yeeld any thing to your Maiestie in contention of loue, beneuolence, and mutuall office, but that we iudge euery good turne of yours to be recompensed by vs to the vttermost: and that shall we prooue as occasion shall serue. [Sidenote: The olde libertie of trafficke.] Therefore we shall commaund the arrests, if any be made by our subiects (as it is vnknowen to vs) of merchants goods and English names to be discharged: and shall conserue the olde libertie of trafficke, and all other things which shall seeme to apperteine to neighbourhood betweene vs and your Maiestie: so that none of the subiects of your Maiestie hereafter presume to vse the nauigation to the Narue forbidden by vs, and full of danger not onely to our parts, but also to the open destruction of all Christians and liberall nations. [Sidenote: The meanes of increase of the power of the Muscouite.] The which as we haue written afore, so now we write againe to your Maiesty that we know and feele of a surety, the Moscouite, enemy to all liberty vnder the heauens, dayly to grow mightier by the increase of such things as he brought to the Naure, while not onely wares but also weapons heretofore vnknowen to him, and artificers and arts be brought vnto him: by meane whereof he maketh himselfe strong to vanquish all others. Which things, as long as this voyage to Narue is vsed, can not be stopped. And we perfectly know your Maiesty can not be ignorant how great the cruelty is of the said enemy, of what force he is, what tyranny he vseth on his subiects, and in what seruile sort they be under him. We seemed hitherto to vanquish him onely in this, that he was rude of arts, and ignorant of policies. If so be that this nauigation to the Naure continue, what shall be vnknowen to him? Therefore we that know best, and border vpon him, do admonish other Christian princes in time, that they do not betray their dignity, liberty and life of them and their subiects to a most barbarous and cruell enemy, as we can no lesse do by the duty of a Christian prince. For now we do foresee, except other princes take this admonition, the Moscuite puffed vp in pride with those things that he brought to the Narue, and made more perfect in warlike affaires with engines of warre and shippes, will make assault this way on Christendome, to slay or make bound all that shall withstand him: which God defend. With which our admonition diuers princes already content themselues, and abstaine from the Narue. The others that will not abstaine from the sayd voyage shalbe impeached by our nauie, and incurre the danger of losse of life, liberty, wife and children. Now therefore if the subiects of your Maiesty will forbeare this voyage to Narue, there shalbe nothing denied to them of vs. Let your Maiesty well weigh and consider the reasons and occasions of our stopping of ships going to the Narue. In which stopping, our subiects of Danske be in no fault, as we haue already written to your Maiesty, neither vse we their counsell in the same. In any other matter, if there be any fault in them against your Maiesty or your subiects, we will gladly do iustice vpon them, that your Maiesty may well vnderstand that we be careful of you and your subiects. Neither thinke we it meet to take Hamburgh, or any other place to iudge the matter: for we haue our councell and iudgement seat at Rie, where your Maiesty and your subiects, or any other shal haue iustice administred vnto them, with whom we haue had ancient league and amity. And thus much we haue thought good to let your Maiesty vnderstand. Fare ye well. Dated the sixt of December the 39 of our reigne. [Footnote: A.D. 1559]

Sigismundus Augustus Rex.

* * * * *

The Queenes Maiesties Letters to the Emperour of Russia, requesting licence, and safe conduct for M. Anthony Ienkinson to passe thorow his kingdome of Russia, into Persia, to the Great Sophie, 1561.

ELIZABETHA Dei gratia, Angliae, &c. Regina, serenissimo et potentissimo principi, D. Ioanni Basiliuich, Imperatori totius Russiæ, Magno Duci, &c. Salutem, et omnium rerum prosperarum foelicissimum incrementum. Potentissime Princeps, res est nobis ad memorandum longè gratissima, illa vestræ Maiestatis erga nos et nostros amicitia. Quæ tempore foelicissimæ memoriæ Regis Edwardi sexti, fratris nostri charissimi, Dei benignitate incepta, deinceps verò vestra non solùm singulari humanitate alta atque fota, sed incredibili etiam bonitate aucta atque cumulata, nunc autem omnibus beneuolentiæ vestræ officijs sic firmata est atque constabilita, vt iam minimè dubitemus, quin ea ad laudem Dei, ad gloriam vtriusque nostrum, ad publicam nostrorum vtrobique regnorum immensam commoditatem, ad priuatam singulorum vtrinque subditorum optatam spem, certàmque foelicitatem multis sit deinceps seculis duratura. Et quanquam hæc vestra bonitas, plenissimè sese effudit in omnes nostros subditos, qui sese in ullas imperij vestri partes vnquam receperunt, (pro qua ingentes nostras, vt par est, gratias vestræ Maiestati habemus, vestrísque vicissim in omni opportunitatis loco libentissimè feremus) tamen abundantia benignitatis vestræ, in accipiendo, támque humanitèr tractando nostrum fidelem et perdilectum famulum Antonium Ienkinson, qui has perfert literas, seorsim nobis gratissima existit. Nam præterquam quòd nullis non locis vestri Imperij et magna libertate, et summa humanitate vestræ serenitatis non permissu solùm, sed iussu etiam frueretur, vestra bonitas tamen non in hac domestica benignè feciendi ratione conquieuit, sed perlibentèr et vltrò eundum nostrum hunc perdilectum famulum, varijs exteris principus, quoquouersus ipse iter suum instituerat, literis suis, suo magno Imperiali sigillo consignatis commendauit. Quod beneficium illi vbiuis gentium, et viam sine vllo periculo, propter publicam vestram fidem, et aduentum cum magno fauore, propter vestram commendationem, optatè quidem et foeliciter communiuit Itaque quemadmodum gemina hæc vestra beneuolentia, cum illa generalis exhibita in vestro regno negotiantibus subditis nostris vniuersis, tum ista seorsim præstita huic Antonio Ienkinson, perfideli nostro famulo, nobis in mente non solùm ad gratam perpetuamque memoriam, verùm etiam ad mutuam, vel opportunam compensationem, firmissimè defixa est: ita, petimus à vestra Maiestate vt vtramque beneuolentiæ vestræ rationem et communem nostris vniuersis, et priuatam huic nostro dilecto famulo, vtrisque deinceps dignetur tueri, atque conseruare. Neque nos quidem diffidemus, quin quem fauorem vestra Maiestas anteà sua sponte Antonio Ienkinson, tum quidem priuato ostendit, eundem nunc nostra rogatu eidem Antonio in nostrum iam famulatum cooptato benignè velit denuò declarere. Et propterea petimus à vestra Maiestate, vt dignetur iterum concedere eidem nostro famulo literas suas commeatus, publicæ fidei, ac saluiconductus, quarum tenore, authoritate, atque præsidio, sit illi, familiaribus suis, et seruis, tutum, liberumque, cum mercibus, sarcinis, equis, et bonis suis vniuersis, inuehendis euehendísque, per vestra regna, domicilia, atque prouincias, proficisci, ire, transire, redire, abire, et istic morari, quandiu placuerit, et inde recedere quandocunque illi aut suis libitum fuerit. Et sicut non dubitamus, quin vestra Maiestas hæc omnia humanitatis grata officia, pro immensa bonitate suæ naturæ benignè et largiter huic famulo nostro sit concessura ita valdè optamus, adeóque petimus, vt vestra Maiestas eodem nostrum famulum, vnà cum omnibus suis familiaribus, ac bonis, exteris alijs principibus literis suis dignetur commendare, presertim verò atque seorsim Magno Sophi, Persarum Imperatori, in cuius etiam imperia et ditiones idem noster famulus gratia potissimè experiundi peregrina, commercia, proficisci vnà cum suis constituit.

Confidimus igitur hæc omnia nostra postulata pro famuli spe, pro nostra expectatione, pro vestra bonitate, pro nostrorum utrinque subditorum commoditate, fausta illi, grata nobis, acccpta etiam vestræ Maiestati, et nostris vtrobíque perquam vtilia euasura. Deus vestræ Maiestatis, &c. Datum in celeberrima nostra Ciuitate Londini, anno mundi 5523. Domini ac Dei nostri Iesu Christi 1561. regnorum verò nostrorum tertio.

The same in English

Elizabeth by the grace of God, Queene of England, &c. to the right excellent, and right mightie Prince, Lord Iohn Basiliwich, Emperour of all Russia, &c. greeting, and most happie increase in all prosperitie. Right mightie Prince, the amitie of your Maiestie towards vs and our subiects is very pleasant to vs to be remembred, which being begun by the goodnesse of God in the reigne of our most deare brother of happie memorie, King Edward the sixt, and afterwards, through your not onely singular humanitie, fed, and nourished, but also through your incredible goodnesse increased, and augmented, is now firmed and established, with all maner of tokens of your beneuolence, that now we doubt not, but that from hencefoorth, during many ages, the same shall endure to the praise of God, to both our glories, to the publike great commoditie of our Realmes on either part, and to the priuate desired hope; and certeine felicitie of all our subiects. And although that this your goodnesse hath bene abundantly extended to all our subiects that have at any time repaired into any part of your Empire, for the which wee giue (as reason is) your Maiestie right heartie thanks, and will againe shew the like vnto yours, right willingly, whensoeuer opportunitie shall require: yet the abundance of your benignitie both in receiuing, and also in enterteining our faithfull and beloued seruant, Anthonie Ienkinson, the bringer of these our letters, is vnto vs for him priuately very thankefull. For besides this, that in all places of your Empire, he not onely by your Maiesties sufferance, but also by your commandement, enioyed much libertie, and great friendship, your goodnesse not ceasing in this your domesticall disposition of clemencie, did right willingly, and of your owne abundant grace, commend the same our well-beloued seruant, by your letters sealed with your Imperiall seale, to sundrie forren Princes, vnto whom he was minded to iourney: which your magnificence did purchase unto him happily, according to his desire, both passage without all perill, through your notable credit, and also atchieuing of his iourney through your commendation. Therefore like as these your duplicated beneuolences, both that one generally exhibited to all our subiects frequenting that your Realme, and also this the other extended apart to this our right faithfull seruant Anthonie Ienkinson, is right assuredly fastened in our remembrance, not onely for a perpetuall and gratefull memorial, but also for a mutuall and meet compensation: so we desire of your Maiestie, to vouchsafe from hencefoorth to conserue and continue the geminate disposition of your beneuolences, both generally to all our subiects, and also priuately to this, our beloued seruant. And we doubt not, but that at our request, you will againe graciously shew vnto the same Anthony, now admitted into our seruice, the like favor as heretofore your Maiesty of your meere motion did exhibite vnto him, being then a priuate person. And therefore we desire your Maiesty eftsones to grant to the same our seruant, your letters of licence, pasport, and safe conduct, through the tenour, authority, and helpe whereof, he, his seruants, together with their merchandises, baggages, horses, and goods whatsoeuer, that shall be brought in, or carried out, by or thorow all your empire, kingdome, dominions, and provinces, may surely and freely iourney, go, passe, repasse, depart, and there tary so long as it shall please him: and from thence returne whensoeuer it shall seeme good to him or his: and as we doubt not, but that your Maiesty in the goodnesse of your nature will graciously and abundantly grant all these good offices of humanity, so we do heartily desire that your Maiesty wil likewise vouchsafe to commend the same our seruant, together with all his goods, by your letters to other forren Princes, and especially to the great Sophy, and Emperour of Persia, into whose empire and iurisdictions the same our seruant purposeth with his for to iourney, chiefly for triall of forren merchandises.

We therefore doe trust that all these our demands shall tend, and haue effect, according to the hope of our seruant, and to our expectation, for your wealth, for the commodity of both our subiects, lucky to him, thankefull to vs, acceptable to your Maiesty, and very profitable to our subiects on either part. God grant vnto your Maiesty long and happy felicity in earth, and euerlasting in heauen. Dated in our famous city of London the 25 day of the moneth of April, in the yeere of the creation of the world 5523, and of our Lord God Iesus Christ 1561, and of our reigne the third.

* * * * *

The Queenes Maiesties Letters to the great Sophy of Persia, sent by M. Anthonie Ienkinson. 1561.

ELizabetha Dei gratia, Angliæ, Franciæ, et Hiberniæ Regina, &c. Potentissimo, et inuictissimo Principi, Magno Sophi Persarum, Medorum, Parthorum, Hircanorum, Carmanorum, Margianorum, populorum ris et vltrà Tygrim fluuium, et omnium intra Mare Caspium, et Persicum sinum nationum atque Gentium Imperatori salutem, et rerum prosperarum foelicissimum incrementum. Summi Dei benignitate factum est, vt quas gentes, non solum immensa terrarum spacia, et insuperabiles marium vastitates sed et ipsi etiam cælorum cardines longissimè disiunxerunt, ipsæ tamen literarum bono et mentis certa cogitata, et humanitatis grata officia, et intelligentiæ mutuæ multa commoda facilè inter se et opportunè possint communicare. Itaque cùm perdilectus, et fidelis noster famulus Antonius Ienkinson, qui has literas nostras perfert, cum bona venia, fauore, et gratia nostra hoc Angliæ nostræ regnum excedere, et in Persiam vsque, vestrásque alias ditiones Dei benignitate penetrare constituerit, hoc illius institutum perlaudabile quidem grato nostro fauore prosequi, et promouere studuimus: id quod eo nos libentius facimus, quoniam hoc eius propositum ex honesto studio commercij constituendi potissimum cùm vestris subditis, alijsque peregrinis hominibus, ad vestra regna confluentibus, omninò exortum sit. Propterea nobis et scribendum ad vestram Maiestatem, ab eaque petendum esse duximus, vt nostro rogatu dignetur concedere huic famulo nostro Antonio Ienkinson literas publicæ fidei et salui conductus, quarum authoritate atque præsidio, licitum, liberúmque sit illi, vnà cum suis familiaribus, seruis, sarcinis, mercibus et bonis vniuersis, per vestra regna, domicilia, ditiones, atque prouincias liberè, et sine impedimento proficisci, ire, transire, redire, abire, et istic morari, quamdiu placuerit, et inde recedere, quandocunque illi vel suis lubitum fuerit. Si hæc sancta hospitalitis iura et duleia communis humanitatis officia, inter nos, nostra regna nostrósque subditos libentèr constitui, sincerè coli, et constanter conseruari queant, speramus nos, Deum Optimum Maximum effecturum, vt ab hijs paruis initijs, grandiora rerum momenta, nobis ad magna ornamenta atque decus nostris ad summa commoda atque vsus, aliquando sint oritura: siquidem, vt non, terra, non mare, non coelum, ad nos longissimè sperandos quàm diuina ratio communis humanitatis, et mutuæ beneuolentiæ ad nos firmissimè coniungendos plus virium habuisse videatur. Deus salutem omnem, et foelicem in terris, et perpetuam in coelis, vestræ concedat Maiestati. Datum in Anglia, in celebri nostra vrbe Londino, 25 die mensis Aprilis, anno mundi 5523. Domini ac Dei nostri Iesu Christi, 1561, regnorum vero nostrorum tertio.

The same in English.

[Sidenote: This letter was also written in Hebrew and Italian.] Elizabeth by the grace of God, Queene of England, &c. To the right mightie, and right victorious Prince, the great Sophie, Emperour of the Persians, Medes, Parthians Hircans, Carmanians, Margians, of the people on this side, and beyond the river of Tygris, and of all men, and nations, betweene the Caspian sea, and the gulfe of Persia, greeting and most happie increase in all prosperitie. By the goodness of the Almightie God it is ordeined, that those people which not onely the huge distance of the lands, and the inuincible widenesse of the seas, but also the very quarters of the heavens do most farre separate, and set asunder, may neuerthelesse through good commendation by writing, both ease, and also communicate betweene them, not onely the conceiued thoughts, or deliberations, and gratefull offices of humanitie, but also many commodities of mutuall intelligence. Therefore whereas our faithfull, and right wellbeloued seruant Anthonie Ienkinson, bearer of these our letters, is determined with our licence, fauor, and grace, to passe out of this our Realme, and by Gods sufferance to trauell euen into Persia, and other your iurisdictions; we minde truely with our good favour to set forward, and aduance that his right laudable purpose: and that the more willingly, for that this his enterprise is only grounded upon an honest intent to establish trade of merchandise with your subiects, and with other strangers traffiking in your realmes. Wherfore we haue thought good, both to write to your Maiestie, and also to desire the same, to vouchsafe at our request, to grant to our sayd seruant, Anthonie Ienkinson, good passports and safe conducts, by meanes and authoritie wherof, it may be free and lawfull for him, together with his familiars, seruants, cariages, merchandise, and goods whatsoeuer, thorow your Realmes, Dominions, Iurisdictions, and Prouinces, freely, and without impeachment, to iourney, go, passe, repasse, and tarry so long as he shall please and from thence to retourne whensoeuer he or they shall thinke good. If these holy dueties of entertainment, and sweet offices of naturall humanitie may be willingly concluded, sincerely embraced, and firmly obserued between vs, and our Realmes, and subiects, then we do hope that the Almightie God will bring it to passe, that of these small beginnings, greater moments of things shall hereafter spring, both to our furniture and honours, and also to the great commodities, and vse of our peoples: so it will be knowen that neither the earth, the seas, nor the heauens, haue so much force to separate vs, as the godly disposition of naturall humanity, and mutual beneuolence haue to ioyne vs strongly together. God grant vnto your Maiestie long and happy felicity in earth, and perpetuall in heauen. Dated in England in our famous citie of London, the 25 day of the moneth of April, in the yere of the creation of the world 5523, and of our Lord and God Iesus: Christ, 1561, and of our reigne the third.

* * * * *

A remembrance giuen by vs the Gouernours, Consuls, and Assistants of the company of Merchants trading into Russia, the eight day of May 1561, to our trustie friend Anthonie Ienkinson, at his departure towards Russia, and so to Persia, in this our eight iourney.

First you shall vnderstand that we haue laden in our good ship, called the Swallow, one Chest, the keyes whereof we doe heere deliuer you, and also a bill, wherein are written particularly the contents in the sayd Chest, and what euery thing did cost: and because, as you know, the sayd Chest is of charge, we desire you to haue a speciall regard vnto it, and when God shall send you vnto Mosco, our mindes and will is, that you, with the aduise of our Agents there, doe appoint some such presents for the Emperour and his sonne, either wine, cloth of golde, scarlet, or plate, as to your good discretion shall be thought meet, and when you haue deliuercd vnto him the Queenes Maiesties letters and our sayd present in the name of the Company, we thinke it good that you make your humble sute vnto his Highnesse in our name, to get his licence or safe conduct for you and all other our seruants or Agents at all times hereafter with such wares and merchandise as you at this time, or they hereafter at all other times shall thinke good to passe out of his dominions towards Tartaria, Persia, or other places, and also to retourne vnto Mosco with such wares and merchandises as you shall bring or send from any land or countrey that is not in his dominions, and if it be thought good by you and our Agents there to make composition with the emperor or his officers for some certeine custome or tole vpon such goods as we shall passe that way, to the intent we might be the better fauored, we refer it to your discretion, foreseeing that the opening of this matter be not preiudiciall vnto our former priuileges.

And for the sale of our cloth of gold, plate, pearles, saphyres, and other iewels, we put our trust and confidence in you principally to sell them for ready money, time to good debtors, or in barter for good wares, so that you make our other Agents priuy how and for what price you sell any of the premisses, and also deliver such sums of money, billes or wares, as you shall receiue, vnto our said Agents: thinking good further, that if you perceiue that the plate or other iewels, or any part thereof will not be sold for profit before your departure from the Mosco, that then you cause them to be safe-packed, and set order they may be sent hither againe in our shippes the next yere; except you perceiue that there may be some profit in carrying some part of them into Persia, which we would not to be of any great value.

We have also laden in the sayd Swallow and the other two ships 80 fardles, conteining 400 kersies, as by youre inuoice doth appeare, which fardles be packed, and appointed to be caried into Persia: neuerthelesse, if you chance to finde good sales for them in the Mosco, we thinke it were good to sell part of them there, and to cary the lesse quantity with you, because we be vncertaine what vent or sale you shall find in Persia or other places where you shall come.

If you obtaine the Emperours licence to passe out of his dominions, and to returne, as aforesaid, and that you perceiue you may safely do the same, our minde is, that at such time as you thinke best and most conuenient for that purpose, you do apppoint so many, and such of our hired seruants or apprentices as you thinke necessary and meet for our affaires, and may best be spared, to go with you in your said voyage, whereof we would one to be such as you might make priuy of all your doings for diuers considerations and causes that may happen: which seruants and apprentises, we will and command, by this our remembrance, to be obedient vnto you as vnto vs, not onely to goe with you and to doe such things as you command them in your presence, but also to goe vnto such countreys or places as you shall appoint them vnto, either with wares or without wares and there to remaine and continue so long as you shall thinke good, and if they or any of them will refuse to do such things as you do appoint them, as aforesaid, or that any of them (be he hired seruant or apprentise) do misuse himselfe by any maner of disobedience or disorder, and will not by gentle and faire meanes be reformed, we will that you send him backe to the Mosco, with straight order that he may be sent from thence hither, aad let vs haue knowledge of his euill behauior, to the intent that if he be a hired seruant we may pay him his wages according to his seruice, and if he be an apprentise we may vse him according to his deserts.

We will also that you take with you such kersies, scarlet, and other clothes, or any other such wares of ours, as you shall thinke good, and so in the name of God to take your iourney towards Persia, either by the way of Astracan and Mare Caspium, or otherwise as you shall see cause: and when God sendeth you into Persia, our minde is, that you repaire vnto the great Sophy with the Queenes Maiesties letters, if he be not too farre from the Caspian sea for you to trauell, and that you make him such a present as you shall thinke meet, and if you passe by any other kings, princes, or gouernors, before or after you come to the presence of the Sophy, likewise to make them some present, as you see cause, according to their estate and dignitie, and withall to procure letters of priuilege or safeconduct of the sayd Sophy or other princes in as large and ample maner as you can, for the sure establishing of further trade in merchandise by vs heereafter to be made, frequented and continued in those parts, not onely that we may freely sell in all places within his dominions such wares as we cary thither, but also buy and bring away any maner of wares or merchandise whatsoeuer it be, that is for our purpose and commoditie within his dominions, with free passage also for vs at all times, to passe as often as we will with our goods and merchandise into any part of India or other countreys thereunto adioyning, and in like maner to returne thorow his dominions into Russia or elswhere.

And for the sale of our kersies or other wares that you shall haue with you, as our trust is that you will doe for our most profit and commoditie: euen so we referre all vnto your good discretion, as well in the sale of our sayd goods, as to make our returne in such things as you shall finde there, and thinke best for our profit. [Sidenote: The passage of Noua Zembla.] But if passage cannot be had into Persia by Astracan, or otherwise, the next Summer, which shalbe in the yere 1562, then our minde is, that you procure to sell our kersies, and other such wares as are appointed for Persia, in the Mosco, or other the Emperours dominions, if you may sell them for any reasonable price, and then to employ your selfe with such other of your seruants, as you shall thinke meet for the search of the passage by Noua Zembla, or els you to returne for England as you thinke good. Prouided alwayes, that if you do perceiue or vnderstand, that passage is like to be had into Persia the Summer folowing, which shalbe in the yeere 1563, and that you can not sell our kersies in the Emperours dominions, as aforesayd, at a reasonable price: then we will rather they may be kept till the said Summer in the yeere 1563, and then you to proceed forwards vpon your iourney towards Persia as aforesayd. If passage into Persia cannot be obteined the next yeere, neither good hope of passage in the yeere 1563, neither yet in the meane time good sale of our kersies in the Emperours dominions then we thinke good for you to see if you can practise to carry your said wares by safe conduct thorow Polonia or any other wayes vnto Constantinople, or els where you thinke beter sale may he had, then in Russia.

Thus haue we giuen you to vnderstand our meanings in this intended aduenture; but forasmuch as we do consider and know that if we should prescribe vnto you any certaine way, or direct order what you should doe, we might so worke cleane contrary to our purpose and intent: therefore knowing your approued wisedome with your experience, and also your carefull and diligent minde in the atchieuing and bringing to good successe (by the helpe of almighty God) all things that you take in hand, we doe commit our whole affaires concerning the said aduenture wholly vnto your good discretion, praying God so to prosper you as may be first for his glory, secondly for the honour and commoditie of this realme and next for our profit, with the increase of your good name for euer.

And yet further desiring, and also most earnestly requiring you, as you tender the state of our company, that you will haue a speciall regard vnto the order of our houses and our seruants as well at Colmogro and Vologda, as at Mosco and to see and consider if any misorder be amongst our seruants or apprentises wherby you thinke we might hereafter be put to hinderance or losse of any part of our goods or priuilege there, that you doe not onely see the same reformed, but also to certifie vs thereof by your letter at large, as our trust is in you.

[Sidenote: Weight and drugs deliuered to M. Ienkinson.] And for the better knowledge to be had in the prices and goodnes of such things as we do partly suppose you shall finde in the partes of Russia, we doe heerewith deliuer you a quantitie of certeine drugges, wherby you may perceiue how to know the best, and also there are noted the prices of such wares and drugges as be heere most vendible: also we deliuer you herewith one pound and one ounce weight in brasse, to the end, that you may therby, and with the bill of prices of wares, know what things be worth here. As for the knowledge of silks, we need not to giue you any instructions thereof, other than you know.

And if you vnderstand that any commoditie in Russia be profitable for vs to haue with you in Persia or other places, our minde is that our Agents shall either prouide it for you, or deliuer you money to make prouision your selfe. [Sidenote: The maine sea within thirtie days of Colmogro.] And because the Russes say that in traueiling Eastwardes from Colmogro thirty or forty dayes iourney, there is the maine sea to be found, we think that Richard Iohnson might imploy his time that way by land, and to be at Mosco time enough to goe with you into Persia: for if it be true that he may trauell to the sea that way, and that he may know how many miles it is towards the East from Colmogro, it will be a great helpe for vs to finde out the straight and passage that way, if any be there to be had.

William Gerard.
Thomas Lodge.
William Merike.
Blase Sanders.

Gouernors.

* * * * *

A compendious and briefe declaration of the iourney of M. Anth. Ienkinson, from the famous citie of London into the land of Persia, passing in this same iourney thorow Russia, Moscouia, and Mare Caspium, alias Hircanum, sent and imployed therein by the right worshipfull Societie of the Merchants Aduenturers, for discouerie of Lands, Islands, &c. Being begun the fourteenth day of May, Anno 1561, and in the third yere of the reigne of the Queenes Maiestie that now is: this present declaration being directed and written to the foresayd Societie.

First imbarking my selfe in a good shippe of yours, named the Swallow, at Grauesend, hauing a faire and good winde, our anker then weyed, and committing all to the protection of our God, hauing in our sailing diuersitie of windes, and thereby forced to direct and obserue sundry courses (not here rehearsed, because you haue bene thereof heretofore amply informed) on the fourteenth day of Iuly, the yere aforesayd I arriued the bay of S. Nicholas in Russia: and the sixe and twentieth day of the same moneth, after conference then had with your Agents there, concerning your worships affaires, I departed from thence, passing thorow the countrey of Vago, and on the eight day of August then following, I came to Vologda, which is distant from Colmogro, seuen hundred miles, where I remained foure dayes, attending the arriual of one of your boats, wherein was laden a chest of iewels with the present, by your worships appointed for the Emperors Maiesty: [Sidenote: The Queenes letters to the Emperour of Russia.] which being arriued, and the chest receiued, I therewith departed toward the city of Mosco, and came thither the twentieth day of the same moneth, where I immediately caused my comming to be signified vnto the Secretary of the Imperiall Maiesty, with the Queenes Highnesse letters address vnto the same his Maiestie, who informed the Emperour thereof. But his Highnesse hauing great affaires, and being at that present ready to be married vnto a Ladie of Chircassi, of the Mahometicall law, commanded that no stranger, Ambassadour, nor other, should come before him for a time with further streight charge, that during the space of three dayes that the same solemne feast was celebratine the gates of the citie should be shut, and that no person, stranger or natiue (certeine of his houshold reserued) should come out of their said houses during the said triumph, the cause thereof vnto this day not being knowen.

The sixt of September following, the Emperour made a great feast, whereunto were called all Ambassadours and strangers being of reputation, and hauing affaires: amongst whom I was one, but being willed by the Secretary first to come, and to shew him the Queenes Maiesties letters, I refused so to doe, saying I would deliuer the same vnto the Emperours owne hands: and not otherwise: which heard the Secretarie answered, that vnlesse he might first peruse the sayd letters, I should not come into the

Emperors presence, so that I was not at the feast. Neuerthelesse, I was aduertised by a noble man that I was inquired for by the Emperours Maiestie, although the cause of my absence was to his Maiestie vnknowen. The next day following, I caused a supplication to be made, and presented it to his Highnesse owne hands, and thereby declared the cause of my comming, signified by the Queenes Maiesties letters, and the answere of his sayd Secretary, most humbly beseeching his Grace that he would receiue and accept the same her Highnesse letters, with such honour and friendship, as his letters sent by Osep Napea were receiued by the hands of our late Souereigne Lady Queene Mary, or els that it would please his Highnes to dismisse me, saying that I would not deliuer the said letters but vnto his owne hands, for that it is so vsed in our countrey. Thus the matter being pondered, and the effect of my supplication well digested, I was foorthwith commaunded to come with the said letters before his Maiestie, and so deliuered the same into his owne hands (with such presents as by you were appointed) according to my request, which were gratefully accepted, and the same day I dined in his Grace's presence, with great entertainment. [Sidenote: Request to passe into Persia thorow Moscovie] Shortly after, I desired to know whether I should be licenced to passe thorow his Highnesse dominions into the land of Persia, according to the Queenes Maiesties request: hereunto it was answered, that I should not passe thither, for that his Maiestie meant to send an armie of men that way into the land of Chircassi, whereby my iourney should be both dangerous and troublesome, and that if I should perish therein, it would be much to his Graces dishonour, but he doubted other matters, although they were not expressed. Thus hauing received his answere, neither to my expectation, nor yet contentation, and there remaining a good part of the yere, hauing in that time solde the most part of your kerses and other wares appointed for Persia, when the time of the yeere required to returne for England, I desired passport, and post horses for money, which was granted, [Sidenote: Osep Napea, Ambassadour from the Emperor of Russia to Queen Mary.] but hauing received my passport, ready to depart, there came vnto our house there Osep Napea, who perswaded me that I should not depart that day, saying that the Emperor was not truely informed, imputing great fault to the frowardnesse of the Secretary, who was not my friend: before whom comming againe the next day, and finding the same Secretary and Osep Napea together, after many allegations and obiections of things, and perceiuing that I would depart, I was willed to remaine vntill the Emperours Maiestie were spoken with againe touching my passage: wherewith I was content, and within three dayes after sending for me, he declared that the Emperours pleasure was, that I should not onely passe thorow his dominions into Persia, but also haue his Graces letters of commendations to forren princes, with certaine his affaires committed to my charge, too long here to rehearse: [Sidenote: An Ambassador of Persia.] whereupon I appointed my selfe for the voyage, and the 15 day of March, the yeere aforesaid, I dined againe in his Maiesties presence in company of an Ambassadour of Persia and others, and receiuing a cup of drinke at his Maiesties hands, I tooke my leaue of his Highnesse, who did not only giue me letters, as aforesayd, but also committed matter of importance and charge vnto me, to be done when I should arrive in those countreys whither I intended to go, [Sidenote: Astracan.] and hauing all things in readinesse for the same voyage, I departed from the city of Mosco the 27 day of April 1561, downe by the great riuer of Volga, in company of the said Ambassadour of Persia, with whom I had great friendship and conference all the way downe the same riuer vnto Astracan, where we arriued all in health the 10 day of Iune.

And as touching the situations of the cities, townes, castles and countreys, aswell of Mahometans as also of Gentils adioyning to the same, whereby I passed from Mosco vnto Astracan, I omit in this breuiat to rehearse, for that I heretofore haue declared the same most amply vnto you in my voyage to Boghar. [Sidenote: M. Ienkinsons voyage to Boghar.] Thus being arriued at Astracan, as is aforesayd, I repaired vnto the captaine there, vnto whom I was commended from the Emperours Maiesty, with great charge that he not only should ayd and succor me with all things needfull during my abode there, but also to safeconduct me with 50 gunners well appointed in two stroogs or brigantines into the Caspian sea, vntill I had passed certaine dangerous places which pirats and rouers accustome to haunt, and hauing prepared my barke for the sea, the Ambassador of Persia being before departed in a barke of his owne the 15 day of Iuly, the yeere aforesayd, I and my company tooke our voyage from the sayd Astracan, [Sidenote: He passeth the Caspian Sea.] and the next day at a West sunne, passed the mouth of the said riuer being twenty miles distant, lying next Southeast. The 18 at a Southwest Sunne, we passed by three Islands being distant nine miles from the said mouth of Volga, and Southsouthwest from thence, sailing Southsouthwest the next day, at a West and by North sun we fel with the land called Challica Ostriua, being foure round Islands together, distant from the said three Islands forty miles. [Sidenote: The countrey of Tumen.] From thence sailing the said course the next day, we had sight of a land called Tuke, in the countrey of Tumen, where pirats and rouers do vse: for feare of whom we haled off into the sea due East forty miles, and fell vpon shallowes out of the sight of land, and there were like to haue perished, escaping most hardly: [Sidenote: The Island of Chatelet.] then the 22 day we had sight of a goodly Island called Chatalet, distant from the said Challica Ostriua an hundred miles, the wind being contrary, and a stiffe gale, we were not able to seize it: but were forced to come to an anker to the leeward of the same six miles off in three or foure fathom water, being distant from the maine land to the Westward of vs, which was called Skafcayl or Connyk a countrey of Mahometans, about miles, and so riding at two ankers a head, hauing no other prouision, we lost one of them, the storme and sea being growen very sore, and thereby our barke was so full of leaks, that with continuall pumping we had much adoe to keepe her aboue water, although we threw much of our goods ouerboord, with losse of our boat, and our selues thereby in great danger like to haue perished either in the sea or els vpon the lee shore, where we should haue fallen into the hands of those wicked infidels, who attended our shipwracke and surely it was very vnlike that we should haue escaped both the extremities, but onely by the power and mercy of God, for the storme continued seuen dayes, to wit, vntill the thirtieth day of the same moneth: [Sidenote: The Island of Shiruansha.] and then the winde comming vp at the West with faire weather, our anker weyed, and our saile displayed, lying South, the next day haling to the shore with a West sunne, we were nie a land called by the inhabitants Shryuansha, and there we came againe to an anker, hauing the winde contrary, being distant from the said Chatalet 150 miles, and there we continued untill the third day of August, [Sidenote: Derbent.] then hauing a faire winde, winding Southsoutheast, and sailing threescore miles, the next day at a Southeast sunne we arriued at a city called Derbent in the king of Hircans dominion, where comming to land, and saluting the captaine there with a present, he made to me and my company a dinner, and there taking fresh water I departed.

[Sidenote: A mighty wall.] This city of Derbent is an ancient towne hauing an olde castle therein, being situated vpon an hill called Castow, builded all of free stone much after our building, the walles very high and thicke, and was first erected by king Alexander the great, when he warred against the Persians and Medians, and then hee made a wall of a woonderfull height and thicknesse, extending from the same city to the Georgians, yea vnto the principall city thereof named Tewflish, [Marginal note: Or, Tiphlis.] which wall though it now be rased, or otherwise decayed, yet the foundation remaineth, and the wall was made to the intent that the inhabitants of that countrey then newly conquered by the said Alexander should not lightly flee, nor his enemies easily inuade. [Sidenote: Fortie one degrees] This city of Derbent being now vnder the power of the Sophy of Persia, bordereth vpon the sea, adioyning to the foresaid land of Shalfcall, in the latitude of 41 degrees. [Sidenote: Shabran.] From thence sailing Southeast and Southsoutheast about 80 miles, the sixt day of August, the yere aforesaid, we arriued at our landing place called Shabran, where my barke discharged: the goods layd on shore, and there being in my tent keeping great watch for feare of rouers, [Sidenote: Alean Murey the gouernour.] whereof there is great plenty, being field people, the gouernor of the said countrey named Alean Murey, comming vnto me, entertained me very gently, vnto whom giuing a present, he appointed for my safegard forty armed men to watch and ward me, vntill he might haue newes from the king of Shiruan. The 12 day of the same moneth newes did come from the king, with order that I should repaire vnto him with all speed: and for expedition, aswell camels to the number of fiue and forty to cary my goods, as also horses for me and my company were in readinesse, so that the goods laden, and taking my iourney from thence the said twelft day, on the 18 of the same moneth I came to a city called Shamaky, in the said countrey of Hircan, otherwise called Shiruan, and there the king hath a faire place, where my lodging being appointed, the goods were discharged: [Sidenote: King Obdolowcan.] the next day being the 19 day, I was sent for to come to the king, named Obdolowcan, who kept his court at that time in the high mountaines in tents, distant from the said Shamaki twentie miles, to auoyd the iniury of the heat: and the 20 day I came before his presence, who gently interteined me, and hauing kissed his hands, he bad me to dinner, and commanded me to sit downe not farre from him. [Sidenote: The maiestie and attire of King Obdolowcan.] This king did sit in a very rich pauillion, wrought with silke and golde, placed very pleasantly, vpon a hill side, of sixteene fathom long, and sixe fathom broad, hauing before him a goodly fountaine of faire water; whereof he and his nobility did drinke, he being a prince of a meane stature, and of a fierce countenance, richly apparrelled with long garments of silke, and cloth of gold, imbrodred with pearles and stone: vpon his head was a tolipane with a sharpe ende standing vpwards halfe a yard long, of rich cloth of golde, wrapped about with a piece of India silke of twentie yards long, wrought with golde, and on the left side of his tolipane stood a plume of fethers, set in a trunke of golde richly inameled, and set with precious stones: his earerings had pendants of golde a handfull long, with two great rubies of great value, set in the ends thereof: all the ground within his pauilion was couered with rich carpets, and vnder himselfe was spred a square carpet wrought with siluer and golde, and thereupon was layd two suitable cushions. Thus the king with his nobility sitting in his pauilion with his legs acrosse, and perceiuing that it was painfull for me so to sit, his highnesse caused a stoole to be brought in, and did will me to sit thereupon, after my fashion. Dinner time then approching, diuers clothes were spred upon the ground, and sundry dishes serued, and set in a ranke with diuers kindes of meats, to the number of 140 dishes, as I numbred them, which being taken away with the table clothes, and others spred, a banket of fruits of sundry kindes, with other banketting meates, to the number of 150 dishes, were brought in: so that two seruices occupied 290 dishes, and at the end of the sayd dinner and banket, the king said vnto me, Quoshe quelde, that is to say, Welcome: and called for a cup of water to be drawen at a fountaine, and tasting thereof, did deliuer me the rest, demanding how I did like the same, and whether there were so good in our countrey or not: vnto whom I answered in such sort, that he was therewith contented: then he proponed vnto me sundry questions, both touching religion, and also the state of our countreys, and further questioned whether the Emperor of Almaine, the Emperor of Russia, or the great Turke, were of most power, with many other things too long here to rehearse, to whom I answered as I thought most meet. [Sidenote: The Queenes letters to Sophy.] Then he demanded whether I intended to goe any further, and the cause of my comming: vnto that I answered that I was sent with letters from the Queenes most excellent Maiesty of England into the great Sophy, to intreat friendship and free passage, and for his safeconduct to be granted vnto English merchants to trade into his Segniories, with the like also to be granted to his subiects, when they should come into our countreys, to the honour and wealth of both realmes, and commodity of both their subiects, with diuers other words, which I omit to rehearse. [Sidenote: Casbin.] This sayd king much allowing this declaration sayd, that he would not onely giue me passage, but also men to safeconduct me vnto the sayd Sophy, lying from the foresayd citie of Shamaki thirty dayes iourney, vp into the land of Persia, at a castle called Casbin: so departing from the king at that time, within three dayes after, being the foure and twentieth day of August the yere aforesayd, he sent for me againe: vnto whom I repaired in the morning, [Sidenote: Multitude of concubines.] and the king not being risen out of his bed (for his maner is, that watching in the night, and then banketting with his women, being an hundred and forty in number, he sleepeth most in the day) did giue one commandement that I should ride on hawking with many Gentlemen of his Court, and that they should shew me so much game and pastime as might be: which was done, and many cranes killed. We returned from hawking about three of the clocke at the afternoone: the king then risen, and ready to dinner, I was inuited thereunto, and approaching nigh to the entring in of his tent, and being in his sight, two gentlemen incountered me with two garments of that countrey fashion, side, downe to the ground, the one of silke, and the other of silke and golde, sent vnto me from the king, and after that they caused me to put off my vpper garment, being a gowne of blacke veluet furred with Sables, they put the sayd two garments vpon my backe, and so conducted me vnto the king, before whom doing reuerence, and kissing his hand, he commanded me to sit not farre from him, and so I dined in his presence, he at the time being very mery, and demanding of me many questions, and amongst other, how I like the maner of their hawking. Dinner so ended, I required his highnesse safeconduct for to depart towards the Sophy, who dismissing me with great fauour, and appointing his Ambassadour (which returned out of Russia) and others, to safeconduct me, he gaue me at my departure a faire horse with all furniture, and custome free from thence with all my goods. So I returned to Shamaki againe, where I remained vntill the sixt of October, to prouide camels, horses, and other necessaries for my sayd intended iourney.

[Sidenote: The description of Hircania.] But now before I proceed further, I purpose to write something of this countrey of Hircan, now called Shiruan, with the townes and commodities of the same. This countrey of Hircan in times past was of great renowne, hauing many cities, townes, and castles in it: and the kings thereof in time of antiquity were of great power, able to make wars with the Sophies of Persia: but now it is not onely otherwise (for that the cities, townes, and castles be decayed) but also the king is subiect to the sayd Sophie (although they haue their proper king) and be at the commandement of the sayd Sophy, who conquered them not many yeres passed, [Sidenote: Diversity in religion.] for their diuersity in religion, and caused not onely all the nobility and gentlemen of that countrey to be put to death, but also ouer and besides, rased the walles of the cities, townes, and castles of the said realme, to the intent that there should be no rebellion, [Sidenote: Barbarous cruelty.] and for their great terror, caused a turret of free stone and flints to be erected in the sayd city called Shamaki, and in a ranke of flints of the said turret, did set the heads of the sayd nobility and gentlemen, then executed. [Sidenote: The citie of Arrash or Erex.] This city is distant from the sea side, with camels seuen dayes iourney, but now the same being much decayed, and chiefly inhabited with Armenians, another city called Arrash, bordering vpon the Georgians, is the chiefest and most opulent in the trade of merchandise, and thereabouts is nourished the most abundant growth of raw silke, and thither the Turks, Syrians, and other strangers do resort and trafficke. [Sidenote: The commodities of this countrey.] There be also diuers good and necessary commodities to be prouided and had in this sayd realme: viz. galles rough and smooth, cotton wooll, allome, and raw silke of the naturall growth of that countrey: besides, nere all kinde of spices and drugges, and some other commodities, which are brought thither from out of East India, but in the lesse quantity, for that they be not assured to haue vent or vtterance of the same: but the chiefest commodities be there, raw silks of all sorts, whereof there is great plenty. [Sidenote: The strong castle of Gullistone defaced.] Not farre from the sayd city of Shamaki, there was an olde castle called Gullistone, now beaten downe by this Sophy, which was esteemed to be one of the strongest castles in the world, and was besieged by Alexander the great, long time before he could win it. And not farre from the sayd castle was a Nunry of sumptuous building, wherein was buried a kings daughter, named Ameleck Channa, who slew herselfe with a knife, for that her father would haue forced her (she professing chastity) to haue married with a king of Tartarie: vpon which occasion the maidens of that countrey do resort thither once euery yere to lament her death.

Also in the sayd countrey there is an high hill called Quiquifs, vpon the toppe whereof (as it is commonly reported) did dwell a great Giant, named Arneoste, hauing vpon his head two great hornes, and eares, and eyes like a Horse, and a taile like a Cow. It is further sayd that this monster kept a passage thereby, vntill there came an holy man, termed Haucoir Hamshe, a kinseman to one of the Sophies, who mounted the sayd hill, and combating with the sayd Giant, did binde not onely him in chaines, but also his woman called Lamisache with his sonne named After: for which victory they of that countrey haue this holy man in great reputation, and the hill at this day (as it is bruited) sauoureth so ill, that no person may come nigh vnto it: but whether it be true or not, I referre it to further knowledge.

[Sidenote: The towne of Yauate.] Now to returne to the discourse of the proceeding in my voyage, towards the great Sophie. The 6 of October in the yeere aforesayd, I with my company departed from Shamachi aforesaid, and hauing iourneyed threescore miles, came to a towne called Yauate, wherein the king hath a faire house with orchards and gardens well replenished with fruits of all sorts. By this towne passeth a great riuer called Cor, which springeth in the mountaines of the Georgians, and passing thorow the countrey of Hircania aforesayd, falleth into the Caspian or Hircan sea, at a place betweene two ancient townes called Shabran and Bachu, situate within the realme of Hircane, and from thence issueth further, passing thorow a fruitful countrey, inhabited with pasturing people, which dwell in the Summer season vpon mountaines, and in Winter they remooue into the valleyes without resorting to townes or any other habitation: and when they remooue, they doe iourney in carrauans or troops of people and cattell, carrying all their wiues, children and baggage vpon bullocks. [Sidenote: The city of Ardouil] Now passing this wilde people ten dayes iourney, comming into no towne or house, the sixteenth day of October we arriued at a citie called Ardouill, where we were lodged in an hospitall builded with faire stone, and erected by this Sophies father named Ismael, onely for the succour and lodging of strangers and other trauellers, wherein all men haue victuals and feeding for man and horse, for three dayes and no longer. This foresayd late prince Ismael lieth buried in a faire Meskit, with a sumptuous sepulchre in the same, which he caused to be made in his life time. This towne Ardouill is in the latitude of eight and thirtie degrees, an ancient citie in the prouince of Aderraugan, wherein the Princes of Persia are commonly buried: and there Alexander the great did keepe his Court when he inuaded the Persians. [Sidenote: The citie Tebris or Tauris] Foure dayes iourney to the Westward is the citie Tebris in olde time called Tauris, the greatest citie in Persia, but not of such trade of merchandise as it hath bene, or as others be at this time, by meane of the great inuasion of the Turke, who hath conquered from the Sophie almost to the sayd citie of Tauris, which the said Turke once sacked, and thereby caused the Sophie to forsake the same, and to keepe his court ten dayes iourney from thence, at the sayd citie of Casbin.

The 21 day we departed from Ordowil aforesayd, trauelling for the most part ouer mountaines all in the night season, and resting in the day, being destitute of wood, and therefore were forced to vse for fewell the dung of horses and camels, which we bought deare of the pasturing people. [Sidenote: M. Ienkinsons arriuall at the Sophies court 2. Nouember, 1562.] Thus passing ten dayes iourney the yere aforesayd, the second day of Nouember we arriued at the foresaid citie of Casbin, where the saide Sophie keepeth his court, and were appointed to a lodging not farre from the kings pallace, and within two dayes after the Sophie commanded a prince called Shalli Murzy, sonne to Obdolowcan king of Shiruan aforesayd, to send for me to his house, who asked me in the name of the said Sophy how I did, and whether I were in health, and after did welcome me, and inuited me to dinner, whereat I had great enterteinment, and so from thence I returned to my lodging. The next day after I sent my interpreter vnto the Sophies Secretarie, declaring that I had letters directed from our most gracious Souereigne ladie the Queenes most excellent Maiestie of the Realme of England, vnto the sayd Sophy, and that the cause of my comming was expressed in the same letters, desiring that at conuenient time I might come into his Maiesties presence, who aduertising the Sophy thereof, shortly after answered me that there were great affaires in hand: which being finished, I should come before his presence, willing me in the meane time to make ready my present if I had any to deliuer.

[Sidenote: The Turkes Ambassadour to the Sophie.] At this time the great Turkes Ambassadour arriued foure dayes before my comming, who was sent thither to conclude a perpetuall peace betwixt the same great Turke and the Sophie, and brought with him a present in golde, and faire horses with rich furnitures, and other gifts, esteemed to bee woorth forty thousand pound. And thereupon a peace was concluded with ioyfull feasts, triumphs and solemnities, corroborated with strong othes, by their law of Alkaron, for either to obserue the same, and to liue alwayes after as sworne brethren, ayding the one the other against all princes that should warre against them, or either of them. And upon this conclusion the Sophy caused the great Turkes sonne named Baiset Soltan, a valiant Prince (who being fled from his father vnto the Sophie, had remained in his Court the space of foure yeeres) to be put to death. In which time the said Turkes sonne had caused mortall warres betwixt the sayd princes, and much preuailed therein: the Turke demanded therefore his sonne to be sent vnto him; and the Sophy refused thereunto to consent. But now being slaine according to the Turks will, the Sophy sent him his head for a present, not a little desired, and acceptable to the vnnaturall father. Discoursing at my first arriuall with the king of Shiruan of sundry matters, and being interteined as hath bene before declared, the sayd King named Obdolocan, demaunding whether we of England had friendship with the Turks or not: I answered, that we neuer had friendship with them, and that therefore they would not suffer vs to passe thorow their countrey into the Sophy his dominions, and that there is a nation named the Venetians, not farre distant from vs, which are in great league with the sayd Turks, who trade into his dominions with our commodities, chiefly to barter the same for raw silks, which (as we vnderstand) come from thence: and that if it would please the said Sophy and other Princes of that countrey, to suffer our merchants to trade into those dominions, and to give vs pasport and safe conduct for the same, as the said Turke hath granted to the sayd Venetians, I doubted not but that it should grow to such a trade to the profit of them as neuer before had beene the like, and that they should be both furnished with our commodities, and also haue vtterance of theirs, although there neuer came Turke into their land, perswading with many other words for a trade to be had. This king vnderstanding the matter liked it marueilously, saying, that he would write vnto the Sophy concerning the same: as he did in very deed, assuring me that the Sophy would graunt my request, and that at my returne vnto him he would giue me letters of safe conduct, and priuiledges. The Turkes Ambassadour was not then come into the land, neither any peace hoped to be concluded, but great preparation was made for warre, which was like much to have furthered my purpose, but it chanced otherwise. [Sidenote: The Turkes merchaunts withstand M. Ienkinson.] For the Turks Ambassadour being arriued, and the peace concluded, the Turkish merchants there at that time present, declared to the same Ambassadour, that my comming thither (naming me by the name of Franke) would in great part destroy their trade, and that it should be good for him to perswade the Sophy not to fauour me, as his Highnesse meant to obserue the league and friendship with the great Turke his master, which request of the Turkish merchants the same Ambassadour earnestly preferred, and being afterwards dismissed with great honour, he departed out of the Realme with the Turks sonnes head as aforesayd, and other presents.

[Sidenote: Shaw Thomas the Sophies name.] The 20 day of Nouember aforesayd, I was sent for to come before the said Sophy, otherwise called Shaw Thomas, and about three of the clocke at afternoone I came to the Court, and in lighting from my horse at the Court gate, before my feet touched the ground, a paire of the Sophies owne shoes termed in the Persian tongue Basmackes, such as hee himselfe weareth when he ariseth in the night to pray (as his maner is) were put vpon my feet, for without the same shoes I might not be suffred to tread vpon his holy ground, being a Christian, and called amongst them Gower, that is, vnbeleeuer, and vncleane: esteeming all to be infidels and Pagans which do not beleeue as they do, in their false filthie prophets, Mahomet and Murtezalli. At the sayd Court gate the things that I brought to present his Maiestie with, were deuided by sundry parcels to sundry seruitors of the Court, to cary before me, for none of my company or seruants might be suffered to enter into the Court with me, my interpreter onely excepted. [Sidenote: The Queenes letters deliuered.] Thus commihg before his Maiestie with such reuerence as I thought meete to be vsed, I deliuered the Queenes Maiesties letters with my present, which hee accepting, demaunded of mee of what countrey of Franks I was, and what affaires I had there to doe: Vnto whom I answered that I was of the famous Citie of London within the noble Realme of England, and that I was sent thither from the most excellent and gracious soueraigne Lady Elizabeth Queene of the saide Realme for to treate of friendship, and free passage of our Merchants and people, to repaire and traffique within his dominions, for to bring in our commodities, and to carry away theirs, to the honour of both princes, the mutuall commoditie of both Realmes, and wealth of the Subiects, with other wordes here omitted. He then demaunded me in what language the letters were written, I answered, in the Latine, Italian and Hebrew: well said he, we haue none within our Realme that vnderstand those tongues. Whereupon I answered that such a famous and worthy prince (as hee was) wanted not people of all nations within his large dominions to interprete the same. [Sidenote: The Sophies questions.] Then he questioned with me of the state of our Countreys, and of the power of the Emperour of Almaine, king Philip, and the great Turke, and which of them was of most power: whom I answered to his contentation, not dispraysing the great Turke, their late concluded friendship considered. Then he reasoned with mee much of Religion, demaunding whether I were a Gower, that is to say, an vnbeleeuer, or a Muselman, that is, of Mahomets lawe. Vnto whom I answered, that I was neither vnbeleeuer nor Mahometan, but a Christian. What is that, said he vnto the king of the Georgians sonne, who being a Christian was fled vnto the said Sophie, and he answered that a Christian was he that beleeueth in Iesus Christus, affirming him to be the Sonne of God, and the greatest Prophet. Doest thou beleeue so, said the Sophie vnto me: Yea that I do, said I: Oh thou vnbeleeuer, said he, we haue no neede to haue friendship with the vnbeleeuers, and so willed me to depart. I being glad thereof, did reuerence and went my way, being accompanied with many of his gentlemen and others, and after me followed a man with a Basinet of sand, sifting all the way that I had gone within the said pallace, euen from the said Sophies sight vnto the court gate.

[Sidenote: The curtesie of Shalley Murzey.] Thus I repaired againe vnto my lodging, and the said night Shally Murzey sonne to the king of Hircan aforesaid, who fauoured me very much for that I was commended vnto him from his father, willed mee not to doubt of any thing, putting mee in hope that I should haue good successe with the Sophie, and good intertainment.

Thus I continued for a time, dayly resorting vnto me diuers gentlemen sent by the Sophie to conferre with me, especially touching the affaires of the Emperour of Russia, and to know by what way I intended to returne into my countrey, either by the way that I came, or by the way of Ormus, and so with the Portingals ships. [Sidenote: Warres intended against the portingals.] Vnto whom I answered, that I durst not returne by the way of Ormus, the Portingals and wee not being friendes, fully perceiuing their meaning: for I was aduertised that the saide Sophie meant to haue warres with the Portingals, and would haue charged mee that I had bene come for a spie to passe through his dominions vnto the saide Portingals, thinking them and us to be all one people, and calling all by the name of Franks, but by the prouidence of God this was preuented.

After this the saide Sophie conferred with his nobilitie and counsel concerning me, who perswaded that he should not enterteine me wel, neither dismisse me with letters or gifts, considering that I was a Franke, and of that nation that was an enemie to the great Turke his brother, perswading that if he did otherwise, and that the newes thereof should come to the knowledge of the Turke, it should be a meane to breake their new league and friendship lately concluded: disswading further because he had no neede, neither that it was requisite for him to haue friendship with vnbeleeuers, whose Countreys lay farre from him, and that it was best for him to send me with my letters vnto the said great Turke for a present, which he was fully determined to haue done at some meet time, meaning to send his Ambassadour vnto the said great Turke very shortly after.

[Sidenote: The king of Hircans second letters in Mr Ienkinson's behalfe.] But the king of Hircanes sonne aforesaide, vnderstanding this deliberation, sent a man in post vnto his father, for to declare and impart the purpose vnto him, who as a gracious prince, considering that I had passed through his dominions, and that I had iourneyed for a good intent, did write to the Sophie al that which he vnderstood of his said determination, and that it should not stand with his Maiesties honour to doe mee any harme or displeasure, but rather to giue mee good entertainment, seeing I was come into his land of my free will, and not by constraint, and that if hee vsed me euill, there would few strangers resort into his country, which would bee greatly vnto his hinderance, with many other perswasions: which after that the saide Sophie had well and throughly pondered and digested (much esteeming the same king of Hircane, being one of the valiantest princes vnder him and his nigh kinseman) changed his determined purpose, and the twentieth of March 1562. he sent to me a rich garment of cloth of golde, and so dismissed me without any harme.

[Sidenote: Conference with Indian Merchants.] During the time that I soiourned at the sayde City of Casbin, diuers merchants out of India came thither vnto mee, with whom I conferred for a trade of spices: whereunto they answered that they would bring of all sorts so much as we would haue, if they were sure of vent, whereof I did promise to assure them, so that I doubt not but that great abundance thereof may from time to time be there prouided and had.

[Sidenote: Mr Ienkinsons returne.] The same twentieth day of March I returned from the saide Citie of Casbin where I remayned all the Winter, hauing sent away all my Camels before, and the thirtieth day I came to the saide Citie of Ardouil, and the fifteenth of April vnto Zauat aforesayd, where king Obdolowcan was at that present, who immediately sent for me, and demaunding of me many questions, declared that if it had not bene for him, I had bene vtterly cast away, and sent to the great Turke for a present by the Sophie, through the euill perswasion of his wicked counsell, that the Zieties and holy men were the chiefe and principal procurers and moouers thereof: but the Sophie himselfe ment mee much good at the first, and thought to haue giuen me good entertainement, and so had done, had not the peace and league fortuned to haue bene concluded betweene them and the great Turke. [Sidenote: Priviledges obtained of Obdowlocan, which are hereafter annexed.] Neuerthelesse, sayd he, the Sophie hath written vnto me to enterteine you well, and you are welcome into my Countrey, and so he intreated me very gently, in whose Court I remained seuen dayes, and obteined of him letters of safe conductes and priuiledges in your names to bee free from paying custome, which I deliuered vnto your seruants Thomas Alcocke and George Wrenne, at their departure towards Persia for your affaires: and his highnesse did giue mee two garments of silke, and so dismissed me with great fauour, sending with me his Ambassadour againe vnto the Emperour of Russia, and committed the chiefest secret of his affaires vnto me, to declare the same vnto the Emperours Maiestie at my returne: and thus departing the tenth day of April, I came to the City of Shamachi, and there remayning certeine dayes for prouision of Camels downe to the Sea side, I sent from thence before men to repaire my Barke, and to make her in a readinesse. [Sidenote: An Armenian sent to M. Ienkinson from the king of Georgia] And during my abode in Shammachi, there came vnto me an Armenian sent from the king of Georgia, who declared the lamentable estate of the same king, that being enclosed betwixt those two cruell tyrants and mightie princes, the said great Turke and the Sophie, hee had continuall warres with them, requiring for the loue of Christ and as I was a Christian, that I would send him comfort by the said Armenian, and aduise how he might send his Ambassadour to the sayd Emperour of Russia, and whether I thought that he would support him or no: and with many other wordes required me to declare his necessitie vnto the same Emperour at my returne: adding further that the said king would haue written vnto me his minde, but that hee doubted the safe passage of his messenger. Vnto whom I did likewise answere by word of mouth, not onely perswading him to send his Ambassadour to Russia, not doubting but that hee should finde him most honourable and inclined to helpe him, [Sidenote: Teneruk king of Chircassi.] but also I directed him his way how the sayde king might send by the Countrey of Chircassi, through the fauour of Teneruk king of the said country, whose daughter the said king had lately married. And thus dismissing the saide Armenian, within two dayes after I sent Edward Cleark your seruaunt vnto the Citie of Arrash, where the most store of Silkes is to be had, giuing him Commission to haue passed further into the saide Countrey of Georgia, and there to haue repaired vnto the sayde king. And after my commendations premised, and my minde declared to haue pursued for safeconduct of the same Prince for our Merchants to trade into his dominions, and that obtained to haue returned againe with speede. The same your seruaunt iourneying to the sayd Citie of Arrash, and there finding certaine Merchants Armenians, which promised to goe to the sayd City of Georgia, comming to the borders thereof, was perceiued by a Captaine there, that he was a Christian, and thereupon demaunded whither he went, and vnderstanding that he could not passe further without great suspition, answered that he came thither to buy Silkes, and shewed the king of Hircanes letters which he had with him, and so returned backe againe, and the fifteenth of April came to Shamachi: from whence I departed the sixteene of the same moneth, and the one and twentie therof comming to the Sea side, and finding my barke in a readinesse, I caused your goods to be laden, and there attended a faire winde.

But before I proceede any further to speake of my returne, I intend with your fauours somewhat to treate of the countrey of Persia, of the great Sophie, and of his countrey, lawes and religion.

[Sidenote: The description of Persia.] This land of Persia is great and ample, deuided into many kingdomes and prouinces, as Gillan, Corasan, Shiruan, and many others hauing diuers Cities, townes and castles in the same. Euery prouince hath his seuerall King, or Sultan, all in obedience to the great Sophie. [Sidenote: The chiefe Cities of Persia.] The names of the chiefest Cities be these: Teueris, Casbin, Keshan, Yesse, Meskit, Heirin, Ardouill, Shamachi, Arrash with many others. The countrey for the most part toward the sea side is plaine and full of pasture, but into the land, high, full of mountaines, and sharpe. To the South it bordereth vpon Arabia and the East Ocean. To the North vpon the Caspian sea and the lands of Tartaria. To the East vpon the prouinces of India, and to the West vpon the confines of Chaldea, Syria, and other the Turkes lands. All within these dominions be of the Sophies, named Shaw Thamas, sonne to Ismael

Sophie. This Sophie that now raigneth is nothing valiant, although his power be great, and his people martiall: and through his pusillanimitie the Turke hath much inuaded his countreys, euen nigh vnto the Citie of Teueris, wherein hee was wont to keepe his chiefe court. And now hauing forsaken the same, is chiefly resident at Casbin aforesaide, and alwayes as the said Turke pursueth him, he not being able to withstand the Turke in the fielde, trusting rather to the mountaines for his safegard, then to his fortes and castles, hath caused the same to bee rased within his dominions, and his ordinance to be molten, to the intent that his enemies pursuing him, they should not strengthen themselues with the same.

This prince is of the age of fiftie yeeres, and of a reasonable stature, hauing fiue children. His eldest sonne he keepeth captiue in prison, for that he feareth him for his valiantnesse and actiuitie: he professeth a kinde of holynesse, and saith that hee is descended of the Blood of Mahomet and Murtezalli: [Sidenote: The difference of religion.] and although these Persians bee Mahometans, as the Turkes and Tartars bee, yet honour they this false fained Murtezalli, saying that hee was the chiefest disciple that Mahomet had, cursing and chiding dayly three other disciples that Mahomet had called Ouear, Vsiran, and Abebeck, and these three did slay the saide Murtezalli, for which cause and other differences of holy men and lawes, they haue had and haue with the Turkes and Tartars mortall warres. To intreat of their religion at large, being more or lesse Mahomets lawe and Alkaron, I shall not heed at this present. These persons are comely and of good complexion, proude and of good courage, esteeming themselues to bee best of all nations, both for their religion and holinesse, which is most erroneous, and also for all other their fashions. They be martial, delighting in faire horses and good harnesse, soone angrie, craftie and hard people. Thus much have I haue thought good to treate of this nation, and nowe I returne to discourse the proceeding of the rest of my voyage.

[Sidenote: The 30. of May 1563.] My barke being ready at the Caspian sea as aforesaide, hauing a faire winde, and committing our selues vnto God the 30. day of May 1563. we arriued at Astracan, hauing passed no lesse dangers vpon the Sea in our returne, then wee sustained in our going foorth, and remayning at the said Astracan, vntill the tenth day of Iune, one hundred gunners being there admitted vnto mee for my safegard vp the riuer Volga; the fifteenth of Iuly I arriued at the Citie of Cazan, where the Captaine entertained me well, and so dismissing mee, I was conducted from place to place vnto the Citie of Mosco, where I arriued the twentieth day of August 1563. in safetie, thankes bee to God, with all such goods, merchandizes, and iewels, as I had prouided as well for the Emperours stocke and accompt, as also of yours, all which goods I was commaunded to bring into the Emperours treasurie before it was opened, which I did, and deliuered those parcels of wares which were for his Maiesties accompt, videlicit, precious stones, and wrought silkes of sundry colours and sortes, much to his Highnesse contentation, and the residue belonging to you, viz. Crasko, and rawe silkes, with other merchandizes, (as by accompt appeareth) were brought vnto your house, whereof part there remained, and the rest was laden in your shippes lately returned.

Shortly after my comming to the Mosco, I came before the Emperours Maiestie, and presented vnto him the apparell giuen vnto me by the Sophie, whose highnesse conferred with mee touching the princes affaires which he had committed to my charge: and my proceedings therein it pleased him so to accept, that they were much to his contentation, saying vnto mee, I haue perceiued your good seruice, for the which I doe thanke you, and will recompence you for the same, wishing that I would trauell againe in such his other affaires, wherein hee was minded to employ mee: to whom I answered, that it was to my heartie reioycing that my seruice was so acceptable vnto his highnesse, acknowledging all that I had done to bee but of duetie, humbly beseeching his grace to continue his goodnesse vnto your worships, and euen at that instant I humbly requested his Maiestie to vouchsafe to graunt vnto you a new priuiledge more ample then the first, which imntediately was graunted, and so I departed. [Sidenote: New privileges obtained hereafter following.] And afterwards having penned a briefe note howe I meant to haue the same priuiledges made, I repaired dayly to the Secretary for the perfecting of the same, and obtained it vnder his Maiesties broade seale, which at my departure from thence, I deliuered vnto the custody of Thomas Glouer your Agent there. The copy whereof, and also of the other priuiledges graunted and giuen by the king of Hircan, I haue already deliuered vnto you. Soiourning all that winter at Mosco, and in the meane time hauing bargained with the Emperours Maiestie, I sent away your seruant Edward Clarke hither ouerland with aduise, and also made preparation for sending againe into Persia in meete time of the yeere. [Sidenote: 28 Septemb. 1564.] And committing the charge thereof vnto your seruants Thomas Alcocke, George Wrenne, and Richard Cheinie, the 28. of Iune last, I departed in poste from the said Mosco, and comming to Colmogro and so downe to the Sea Side, I found your ships laden and ready to depart, where I embarked my selfe in your good ship called the Swallow, the 9. of Iuly, one thousand fiue hundred sixtie foure, and hauing passed the Seas with great and extreme dangers of losse of shippe, goods and life, the 28. of September last (God be praised) we arriued here at London in safetie.

Thus knowing that the couragious and valiant souldier, which aduentureth both fame, member and life, to serue faithfully his soueraigne, esteemeth not the perils and dangers passed (the victorie once obtained) neither for his guerdon desireth any thing more, then that his seruice bee well taken of him for whom he enterprised it: So I perceiuing your fauourable beneuolence to me extended in accepting my trauels in good part to your contentations, do thinke my selfe therewith in great part recompensed: beseeching Almightie God so to prosper your aduentures, from time to time hereafter to be made for reaping the fruits of my trauels (at your great charges, and to my no small dangers) that ye may plentifully gather in and enioy the same, to the illustrating of the Queenes most excellent Maiestie, the honour and commoditie of this her highnesse Realme, and to the ample benefit and abundant enriching of you and your succession, and posteritie for euer.

* * * * *

A copie of the priviledges giuen by Obdolowcan King of Hircania, to the company of English merchants Aduenturers for Russia, Persia, and Mare Caspium, with all the lands and countreys adioyning to the same, obtained by M. Anthonie Ienkinson at his being there about the affaires of the said company, April 14. Anno 1563.

We Obdolowcan by the mightie power of God maker of heauen and of earth, appointed and now raigning king of Shiruan and Hircan, of our meere motion and great goodnes, at the earnest sute and request of our fauoured and welbeloued Anthonie Ienkinson Ambassadour, haue giuen and graunted vnto the right worshipfull Sir William Garret, sir William Chester, sir Thomas Lodge, M. Richard Mallarie, and M. Richard Chamberlaine, with all their company of merchants Aduenturers of the Citie of London in England, free libertie, safe conduct, and licence to come or sende their factors in trade of merchandize into our countreys, and to buy and sell with our merchants and others, either for ready money or barter, and to tary and abide in our countrey, so long as they will, and to goe away when they list, without impediment, let, or hinderance, either of body or goods.

And further our commaundement and pleasure is, that the said English merchants with their company, shall pay no maner of custome for wares, which they or their factors shal buy or sel within our dominions. And if at any time our customers or other officers, or any of them, doe disturbe, misuse, force or constraine the said English merchants or any of them, or their factors, to pay any maner of custome or duetie for any wares they bring in or cary out of our dominions contrary to this our commaundement, and the same be knowen vnto vs, then we will that the saide customers and officers shall loose and be put out of their said offices, with our further displeasure, and the saide English merchants to haue restored all such money and wares as our customers haue taken of them for our said custome. And whensoeuer the saide English merchants or their factors shall bring any maner of wares meete for our treasurie, then our treasurer shall take the said wares into our treasurie, and shall giue vnto the said English merchants, either ready money or raw silkes, to the value of their saide wares. And wheresoeuer this our letter of priuiledges shall bee seene and read within our dominion, we straightly wil and command that it take effect, and be obeyed in al points.

Dated at our place of Iauat, the day and yere aboue written, and sealed with our princely seale, and firmed by our Secretarie in the 12. yere of our raigne.

* * * * *

The second voiage into Persia made by Tho. Alcock, who was slaine there, and by George Wrenne, and Ric. Cheinie seruants to the worshipfull companie of Moscouie merchants in Anno 1563. written by the said Richard Cheinie.

It may please your worships to vnderstand, that in the yere 1563. I was appointed by M. Antho. Ienkinson, and M. Thomas Glouer your Agent in Russia, to goe for Persia in your worships affaires, one Thomas Alcock hauing the charge of the voyage committed to him, and I one of your worships seruants being ioyned with him in your busines, hauing with vs, as they said 1500. rubbles. [Sidenote: A rubble is a marke English.] And if it shall please you I cannot tell certainly what summe of money we had then of the Emperors: for I received none, nor disbursed any of it in wares for the voyage. Also, God I take to record, I could not tell what stocke your worships had there, for the bookes were kept so priuily that a man could neuer see them. The 10. of May anno 1563, we departed from a towne called Yeraslaue vpon our voyage toward Persia. The 24. of Iuly we arriued at Astracan: and the second of August wee departed from Astracan, and the 4. of the same moneth we came to the Caspian sea, and the 11. day of the said moneth we arriued at our port in Media: and the 21. of the said August wee arriued at Shammaki, whereas the king Obdolocan lay in the fielde. We were wel entertained of heathen people, for the thirde day after our arriuall at Shammaki we were called before the king: we gaue him a present, and he entertained vs very well.

At our comming to the Court wee were commaunded to come before the king, who sate in his tent vpon the ground with his legs a crosse, and all his dukes round about his tent, the ground being couered with carpets: wee were commaunded to sit downe, the King appointing euery man his place to sit. And the king commaunded the Emperour of Russelands Merchants to rise vp, and to giue vs the vpper hande. [Sidenote: Casbin.] The 20. of October Thomas Alcock departed from Shammaki towards Casbin, leauing mee at Shammaki to recouer such debts as the dukes of Shammaki ought for wares which thay tooke of him at his going to Casbin. In the time I lay there I could recouer but little. [Sidenote: Leuuacta.] And at Thomas Alcocks comming from Casbin, who arriued at a towne called Leuuacta, whereas the king Obdolocan lay, a day and a halfes iourney from the towne whereas I lay, I hearing of his arriuing there, departed from Shammaki, finding him there in safetie with all such goods as he had with him. During his abode there for seuen dayes he made suite to the king for such money as the dukes ought him. But the king was displeased for that the Emperour of Russelands merchants had slaine a Boserman at his going to Casbin. [Sidenote: A Boserman is a Renegado.] Thomas Alcocke seeing the King would shewe vs no fauour, and also hearing from Shammaki, that the Russes sent their goods to the sea side, for that they feared that the king of Persia should haue knowledge of the death of the Boserman, willed mee to depart to Shammaki with all such goods as he had brought with him from Casbin, I leauing him at the Court.

[Sidenote: Thomas Alcocke slaine in the way betweene Leuuacta and Shammaki.] The thirde day after mine arriuall at Shammaki, I had newes that Thomas Alcocke was slaine comming on his way towards me. Then the king Obdolocan vnderstanding of his death, demaunded whether he had euer a brother. Some said I was, some saide I was not his brother. When this fell out, your worships had no other seruant there but mee among those heathen people. Who hauing such a summe of goods lying vnder my handes, and seeing howe the Russes sent their goods with as much hast as they might to the sea side, and hauing but foure men to sende our wares to the sea side, I vsed such diligence, that within two dayes after Thomas Alcocke was slaine, I sent in company with the Russes goods, all your worships goods with a Mariner, William August, and a Swethen, for that they might the safer arriue at the seaside, being safely layd in. All which goods afterwards arriued in Russeland in good condition, Master Glouer hauing the receipt of all things which I sent then out of those parties into Russeland. [Sidenote: Keselbash, or Ieselbash.] Concerning my selfe, I remained after I had sent the goods into Russeland sixe weekes in Shammaki, for the recouery of such debts as were owing, and at last with much trouble recouered to the summe of fiftene hundreth rubbles or there about, which M. Glouer receiued of me at my comming to Mosco, and all such goods as I brought with me out of Keselbash, as by a note of my hand that hee hath shall appeare. Also he hauing the receipt of all such goods as I sent into Russeland by these two aboue named, he then had that voyage in venter of his owne better then an hundreth rubbles, one Richard Iohnson twentie rubles, one Thomas Pette fiftie rubles, one Euan Chermisin a Tartar seuentie rubles. All these had their returne: M. Glouer allowed himselfe God knoweth howe, I then being in Persia in your worships affaires.

And whereas he saith, the Emperour had but for his part a dobble, as farre as I can see, knowing what the wares cost in those partes, hee had treble. If they gaue him so much wares, all charges turned to your worships, as well of the Emperours as of their owne returnes. I haue sowen the seede, and other men haue gathered the haruest: I haue trauailed both by lande and by water full many a time with a sorrowfull heart, aswell for the safegarde of their goods as yours, how to frame all things to the best, and they haue reaped the fruites of my trauaile. But euer my prayer was to God, to deliuer mee out of those miseries which I suffered for your seruice among those heathen people. Therefore knowing my duetie which I haue done, as a true seruant ought to do, I beseech your worships (although I haue but small recompence for my seruice,) yet let me haue no wrong, and God will prosper you the better.

Also, to informe your worships of your Persian voyage what I iudge: it is a voyage to bee followed. [Sidenote: Gillan in Persia.] The king of Gillan, whereas yet you haue had no traffique, liueth al by marchandise: and it is neere Casbin, and not past six weekes trauaile from Ormus, whither all the spices be brought: and here, (I meane at Gillan) a trade may be established: But your worships must send such men as are no riotous liuers, nor drunkards. For if such men goe, it wil be to your dishonour and great hinderance, as appeared by experience the yeere 1565. when as Richard Iohnson went to Persia, whose iourney had bene better stayed then set forward. For whereas before wee had the name among those heathen people to be such marchants as they thought none like in all respects, his vicious liuing there hath made vs to be compted worse then the Russes.

Againe, if such men trauaile in your affaires in such a voyage, you shall neuer know what gaine is to be gotten. For how can such men imploy themselues to seeke the trade, that are inclined to such vices? or howe can God prosper them in your affaires? But when a trade is established by wise and discreet men, then wil it be for your worships to traffique there, and not before: for a voiage or market made euil at the first, is the occasion that your worships shal neuer vnderstand what gaine is to be gotten thereby hereafter.

* * * * *

The thirde voyage into Persia, begun in the yeere 1565. by Richard Iohnson,
  Alexander Kitchin, and Arthur Edwards.

A letter of Arthur Edwards to M. Thomas Nicols, Secretarie to the worshipful company trading into Russia and other the North parts, concerning the preparation of their voyage into Persia.

Master Nicols, my bounden duetie remembred, with desire of God for the preseruation of you and yours: you shall vnderstand that the second of March I was sent by M. Thomas Glouer (your Agent) vnto Ieraslaue, [Sidenote: Ieraslaue a towne vpon the riuer of Volga.] appointed to receiue such goods as should come from Vologhda, as also such kinde of wares as should be bought and sent from Mosco by your Agent, and M. Edward Clarke, thought meete for your voyage of Persia. And further, I was to prouide for biscuit, beere, and beefe, and other victuals, and things otherwayes needful according to aduise. [Sidenote: Richard Iohnson chiefe of the third voyage into Persia.] Thus I remained here vntil the comming of your Agent, which was the 12. of May, who taried here three dayes, to see vs set forwards on our voyage, and then he departed towards Colmogro, hauing appointed (as chiefe for your voyage of Persia) Richard Iohnson. For my part I am willing, as also haue bene and shalbe content to submit my selfe vnder him, whom the Agent shall appoint, although he were such a one as you should thinke in some respects vnmeete. Thirtie two packes of carseis are all of that kinde of cloth that we shall haue with vs. The other 18. packs that should haue gone, were sold in Mosco. What other goods are shipped for our voyage, you shall vnderstand by your Agents letters. Whereas Edward Clarke (being an honest man) was appointed Agent for Persia, as one for those parts more fit then any I do know here, God hath taken him vnto his mercie, who departed this present life the 16. of March last past. I wished for God for my part he had liued: for my desire was in his company to haue traueiled into Persia. [Sidenote: A barke of 30. tunnes made at Ieraslaue 1564. to passe the Caspian seas.] Your barke or craer made here for the riuer of Volga and the Caspian sea is very litle, of the burthen of 30. tunnes at the most. It is handsomly made after the English fashion: but I thinke it too litle for your goods and prouision of victuals. If the worshipful company would send hither a Shipwright, being skilfull to make one of the burden of 60. tunnes or more, drawing but sixe foote water at the most when it is laden, I thinke it should be profitable. For if your owne goods would not lade the same, here be Marchants that would bee glad and faine to giue great fraight to lade their goods with vs, whereby your charges would be much lessened: And so it may happen, the wages of your men hired here may be saued, and your seruants and goods in farre greater assurance: for their boates here are dangerous to saile with and to passe the Caspian sea. There be Carpenters here that will doe well ynough hauing one to instruct them. Your wares bought here, and orders taken for those that goe for your voyage of Persia are yet vnknowen vnto me: wherefore I cannot (as I would at this present) write to you thereof. Yet, (as you do know) it was the Gouernors mind I should be acquainted with greater affaires then these. Howbeit I doubt not but I shall be informed of them that are appointed, and all things shall be bought when they shall see time and haue more laisure. Thus in hast (as appeareth) I commit you and yours into the hands of almightie God; who preserue you in perfect health with increase of worship.

From Ieraslaue the 15. of May 1565.

By yours to command here or elsewhere during life. Arthur Edwards.

* * * * *

Another letter of the said M. Arthur Edwards, written the 26. of, April 1566. in Shamaki in Media, to the right worshipful Sir Thomas Lodge Knight and Alderman: and in his absence to M. Thomas Nicols, Secretarie to the right worshipfull companie trading into Russia, Persia, and other the North and East partes, touching the successe of Richard Iohnson in the third voiage into Persia.

Worshipfull Sir, my bounden duetie remembred, with heartie prayer vnto God for the preseruation of you and yours in perfect health with increase of worship. It may please you that my last letter I sent you was from Astracan the 26 of Iuly 1565. [Sidenote: They departed from Astracan the 30. of Iuly 1565.] From whence Richard Iohnson, my selfe, and Alexander Kitchin, departed as the 30 of the same. And by meanes of contrary windes, it was the 23 of August before we came to our desired port named Nazauoe. There, after we had gotten your goods on land, with much labour and strength of men, as also windlesses deuised and made, we haled your barke ouer a barre of beach or peeble stones into a small Riuer, sending your ships apparell with other things to an house hired in a village thereby. And as soone as we might get camels, being the fift of September we departed thence, and came to this towne of Shamaki the 11. of the same: [Sidenote: Presents to the King Obdolowcan.] and the 17. day following, we presented vnto Abdollocan the king of this countrey, one timber of Sables, one tunne or nest of siluer cups parsill gilt, three Morses teeth, 4. Arshines of scarlet, 3. pieces of karseis, with 40. red foxes.

He receiued our presents with giuing vs thanks for our good wils, demanding if M. Ienkinson were in good-health, and whether he would returne into these parts againe. He willed vs also himselfe to sit downe before him the distance of a quoits cast from his tent, where he sate with diuers of his counsaile and nobilitie, sending vs from his table such meate as was before him: [Sidenote: A house giuen our men in Shamaki by the king.] And after certaine talke had with vs, he sayd, if he might perceiue or know any maner of person to doe vs any wrong, he would punish them in example of others, whereby we should liue in quietnesse, and haue no cause to complaine, giuing vs a little house for the time, vntill a better might be prouided in such place as we should thinke most meete, neuer willing vs to rise or depart, vntill such time as we of our selues thought it conuenient. At the taking of our leaue, hee willed vs to put our whole minds and requests in writing, that he might further vnderstand our desires. [Sidenote: The death of Abdollocan the 2. of October 1565.] But while we were about to doe so, God tooke this good king our friend out of this present life the 2. of October past. The want of him hath bene the cause that as yet wee cannot receiue certaine debts. Howbeit, we doubt not but we shall recouer all such summes of money as are owing vs for this voyage. As for Thomas Alcocks debts they are past hope of recouerie, which had not bene lost if the king had liued. [Sidenote: Mursay the new king of Media.] We trust in the place of him, God will send as friendly a king towards vs, which [Transcriber's note: 'towardswvsoh :' in original.] by report (and as we be credibly informed,) shall bee his sonne named the Mursay: who since the death of his father, at our being with him, promised to shew vs more friendship then ever we found. God grant the same.

Great troubles haue chanced in these parts. Of those which were of the old kings counsell or bare any rule about him in these quarters, some are in prison, some are pinched by the purse, and other sent for vnto the Shaugh. These troubles haue partly bene the let that wares were not sold as they might, to more profite. [Sidenote: The death of Alexander Kitchin the 23. of October 1565.] Your Agent Richard Iohnson bought foure horses, minding to haue sent to Casbin Alexander Kitchin, whom God tooke to his mercy the 23. of October last: and before him departed Richard Dauis one of your Mariners, whose soules I trust the Lord hath receiued to his mercy. We are now destitute of others to supply their roumes. Foure Mariners were few enough to saile your barke, whereof at this present we haue but one, whose name is William Smith, an honest yong man, and one that doeth good seruice here. For want and lacke of Mariners that should know their labours, we all were like to be cast away in a storme. For all the broad side of our barke lay in the water, and we had much adoe to recouer it, but God of his mercy deliuered vs. Mariners here may doe you good seruice all the winter otherwayes: and merchants here will be gladder to ship their goods in vs giuing good fraight. One merchant at this present is content to pay 20. rubbles for twentie camels lading fraight to Astracan. [Sidenote: The Caspian sea very shoald in diuers places.] Such barkes as must passe these seas, may not draw aboue fiue foote of water, because that in many places are very shallow waters. Wee mind hereafter to make the Russian boates more strong, and they shall serue our turnes very well.

And whereas some in time past tooke great paines, trauell and care, and could not haue their desire in the getting of the Shaughs letters or priuiledge: Now, I trust (with Gods helpe) they may be obtained: which being had, will be beneficiall to the company, and great quietnes to those that shal remaine here, although heretofore things haue chanced ill, as the like in other countries hath bene. But I doubt not, this priuiledge once gotten and obtained, we shall liue in quietnesse and rest, and shall shortly grow into a great trade for silkes both raw and wrought, with all kind of spices and drugs, and other commodities here, as to M. Anthonie Ienkinson is well knowen, who (I doubt not) hath long agoe throughly aduertised the Companie thereof.

[Sidenote: The murthering of Thomas Alcock.] The trueth of the slaughter of Thomas Alcock your seruant, is not certainly knowen. Some thinke it was by the meanes of a noble man, with whom your sayd seruant was earnest in demanding of your debts: vpon whose words he was so offended, that he procured his death. But other doe thinke verily, that in riding from the Court without companie, false knaues lay in waite, thinking he had much about him, and so slew him. I doubt not though this misfortune hath chanced, that things shall come well to passe, and that we shall be better beloued when we shall be more knowen.

Honest merchants are glad of our being here, and seeke to grow in acquaintance with vs, being glad to further vs in that they may, and haue spoken in our fauours to the chiefest of this Countrey: one being a noble man, with whom your Agent and I are entred into friendship, who is at this time in great fauour with the Shaugh. [Sidenote: Cozamomet a noble man that fauoured our nation.] He hath here and in other places of these parts set a good stay in things since the kings death: he is well knowen to M. Ienkinson, his name is Cozamomet. Also another Duke named Ameddin-beck is our great friend. And his sister is the Shaughes wife. These two haue promised your Agent by their lawe, not onely to procure to get the Shaughes priuiledge but also that I shall haue the debts paied me of those that went from hence to Casbin, if we would send one with them. In consideration whereof, I was vpon short warning (for want of a better) appointed by your agent, M. Richard Iohnson, all excuses laied apart, presently to put my selfe in readinesse, and to depart in company with these noblemen: with charge, when God should send me to Casbin, to vse my discretion with their aduise, for the recouering of your debts and priuiledge. I shall haue with mee one interpreter and two bought seruants: one of which partly vnderstandeth this tongue, and may be put in trust whatsoeuer should become of me. [Sidenote: The value of a tumen.] I, haue receuied 6. tumens in ready money, 200. shaughs is a tumen, reckoning euery shaugh for sixe pence Russe. I haue further receiued two timbers of Sables, one to be sold, the other to bee giuen to Thomas the Shaugh: and haue order further to giue as I shall see good to those that shall further my suite, and as occasion serueth. And forasmuch as I am commanded to go, I shall willingly do my best, putting my trust in God that he will send me well to speed in this iourney.

For all kind of wares bought or sold, you shal throughly be aduertised by your Agent Richard Iohnson, whose reckonings or accompts at no hands I might see or be priuie vnto. Your karseis were good and well sorted, they are and will be sold from 150. shaughs, to 160. the piece. Two hundred pieces were sold vnder, that needed not: one 100. pieces at 146. and 147. the piece but more would haue bene giuen, if circumspection had bene vsed. They were sold to those noble men aforesayd, which as yet it was not knowen that I should haue gone with them. They may stand vs much in stead, as they haue promised vs their good wils in that they may doe. [Sidenote: What a batman is.] Here is at this time bought for England 11. packes of rawe silke, 25. and 26. batmans being in euery packe: The batman being 7. pound, which may be 6. pound and a halfe of English waight, being bought here from 66. to 70. shaughes the batman. It is fine and good, litle course at this time was to be had. And where course silke might be had being at Grosin, we could not send thither: for that time was neglected at the first. When wee shall haue lidgers here to remaine in Sommer, we may buy it at the first hand of the countrey people that bring it to sell hither, and to other places. I would to God the Companie could find the meanes to haue a vent to make sales for the one halfe that we may buy here. The Companie may haue for 30. or 40. thousand pounds yeerely. [Sidenote: Varas a great mart for silke.] And as appeareth by your Agents wordes being at Varas, he and others sawe there so great abundance, that by report of diuers, you may bestow (if it were not for the Turkes) for a two hundred thousand pounds: besides silke of all colours died in graine, bound vp in pound waights, I thinke 15. of our ounces to their pound waight, and here sold for 23. shaughs, at 6. d. the shaugh, may be 11. s. 6. pence.

[Sidenote: Gilan 7. dayes sailing from Astracan.] From Astracan in 7. or 8. dayes, wee may saile with our barke to a place named Gilan: the which place in time to come, (I thinke) shall serue our purpose best to goe vnto. Alom is there good cheape, being brought from thence hither to Shamaki, and sold here for two bists their batman, which may be 5. pence in our money: and so I haue bought to bee sent home 223. batmans for example. And at Gilan there is rawe silke enough for the companies stocke. [Sidenote: Gilan 4. dayes iourney from Casbin.] I beleeue, if any great store of wares be sent from you, that must be the place: and from thence a man may trauell in 4. dayes to Casbin, and there make quicke and better sales, at which place your commodities are to be sold. For there the chiefe and best merchants, and diuers other cities round about, to wit, Teueris, Ardouil, and Caishan, being the heart of the countrey, where there is more ciuilitie and merchants are better vsed. Concerning this point I haue inquired of diuers merchants both Russes and others that haue bene in those parts and found them all agreeing in one tale, and perceiue the same to be true, and that all kind of wares come from thence into these parts. [Sidenote: From Casbin to Ormus a moneths trauel with camels.] And from Casbin to Ormus is about 30. daies trauelling with camels. I haue written the prices of wares in my letter to the gouernour both for spices and some drugs which I do know.

Also you shall vnderstand here is plentie of yew for bowstaues. I caused three horse loades to be bought vs for to know the trueth: but they were cut out of season this moneth of April, the sap being in them. Three moneths I neuer left speaking to the Countrey men to bring some. Your Agent will send some home for example.

This day being the 26. of Aprill I departed towards Casbin: God giue me a good houre and well to speed, with a mery heart in returning againe, as my hope is I shall. I haue written my mind to M. Glouer your Agent, what Russian wares I thinke best to be brought for this Countrey, and to send some one hither that hath the Russe tongue, for we haue need. [Sidenote: The secret doings of the Moscouie company.] And the companie shall do well hereafter in taking of seruants to be sent hither, to see that they be such as haue discretion, and be something broken in the world, and seene in the trade of merchandise, and one (if they can get some such) as can speake the Portingall tongue, may do them as good seruice, as those that shall be here two yeeres before him: for then we may buy a slaue that can speake this language and the Portingal tongue also, which shall then interprete vnto vs in all your secret doings, not making the Russes priuy: for they are sory that we doe trade into these partes for we are better beloued then they are: because they are giuen to be drunkards, they are much hated of these people. It is to be wished that none should serue your worships in these parts that be giuen to that kind of vice: And that your chiefe Agent and Factor should be able to rule and gouerne himselfe, that no dishonestie should be imputed to him and vs. By his euill vsage he paied here 24 rubbles, being in this Countrey 4. tumens for a boy, that he was charged to haue conueied away from a Tesicke one of this countrey men, who willed him to sweare that he knew not where the boy was become, and he should not pay it. If he were honest he might do your worships good seruice because of his Russian tongue.

Your London reds are not to be sent hither, for they will not giue aboue 18. shaughes their arshine. [Sidenote: Orient reds of Venice die.] Here be reds of more orient colour, being Venice die. The people are giuen much to weare cloth: the common peoples pecially weare karseis, and the merchants of more wealth weare broad cloth. You shall doe well to send fiue or sixe broad clothes, some blackes, pukes, or other sad colours, that maybe affoorded at 20. shaughes the arshine, and not aboue. It is here reported that King Philip hath giuen the Turkes a great ouerthrow at Malta, and taken 70. or 80. of his chiefe captains.

Thus wishing I had more time to write, I pray you to beare with this my scribled letter, and after you haue red it, that M. Nicols may haue a sight thereof,

By your seruant to command,

Arthur Edwards.

* * * * *

Commodities to be caried out of England into Persia, with their prizes there.

1 Karseis are sold there for 180. Shaughes: [Sidenote: A shaugh is 6d. English.] so that a karsey is sold there in Persia for foure pound ten shillings: for euery shaugh is sixe pence English, and euery Bist is two pence halfepeny English, and in Russe money three pence. 2 Tinne is sold in Persia for 14. and 18. shaughes the batman. The batman containing as I haue mentioned before. 3 Brasil is at 10. and 12. shaughes the batman. 4 Red cloth fine, at 25. and 30. shaughes the yard. 5 Copper at 20. and 25. shaughes the batman.

Commodities to be brought out of Persia for England.

1 Raw silke at 60 shaughs the batman. 2 Pepper at 32. shaughs the batman, 3 Ginger at 18. and 20. shaughs the batman. 4 Nutmegs at 30. shaughs the batman. 5 Brimstone at 4. shaughs the great batman.

The great batman is 12. li. English.

6 Allom at 2. bists and a halfe the batman and lesse. 7 Rice at halfe a bist the batman. 8 Gals at halfe a bist the batman, 9 Cloues at 40. shaughs the batman 10 Yew for bow staues, at [Transcriber's note: blank in original.]

* * * * *

A letter of M. Arthur Edwards, written the 8. of August 1566. from the towne of Shamaki in Media, to the right worshipfull the Gouernours, Consuls, Assistants and generalitie of the Companie of Russia, &c. Shewing his accesse vnto the Emperour of Persia, his conference with him, his obtaining of a priuiledge, with diuers other good obseruations.

Right worshipfull Sirs, my bounden dutie remembered, with most humble commendations and like request to God for the preseruation of your good healths, with the rest of the companie, &c. [Sidenote: His arrival at Casbin the 25. of May.] It may please you to vnderstand, that the last letter which I sent you from hence was of the 26. of April of this present yeere by Richard Iohnson at my departure towards Casbin: to which citie I came the 25. of May folowing, not slacking any day, houre, nor moment, to procure and make friends for the speedie bringing me before the presence of the Shaugh, being the 29. day of the same moneth brought before him, with, whose maiestie I was in talke (as 1 thinke) two houres. He willed me twise to come neerer him, demanding what were my requests: and hauing heard them, he promised me his gracious letters. [Sidenote: Conference and demands of the Shaugh.] Afterwards he called me twise againe to come neerer him, and talked with me of our Queenes maiestie and Countrey, and what commodities we had, and what other commodities we desired: and then of other countries adioining to vs and their commodities, as also of king Philip, what ouerthrow he gaue the Turks at the siege of Malta. And how long we had traded into Russeland and Moscouia, and in what space we might saile out of England into Russeland, and how many weekes trauell it is from Comolgro to Astracan: and then came to discourse of Russeland, and what townes the Emperour had wonne, declaring vnto me himselfe most of our commodities. [Sidenote: All sorts of cloth to be spent, specially Westerne dozens died into scarlet.] In the end he willed that your worships should send him of all sorts of clothes, but of one especially which maidens do make (as he sayd:) He named it Karengi, I thinke it is Westerne dozens died into scarlets. Time will not permit mee to write at large the conference which I had with his maiesty. It was strange to his people (knowing our religion) to see me so long in talke with him, willing his Secretarie before mee to write what he was desirous of: to wit, of London clothes, three or foure of all sorts for example, being well shorne and drest. Violets in graine and fine reds be most worne, but other good colours will away, when they shall see them. I wore a garment of London russet, being much esteemed. You shall doe well lo send such sorts as be liuely to the sight, and some blacks for womens garments, with some Orenge colours and tawneis. Here is much broad cloth worne. [Sidenote: London clothes much talked of in Persia.] They talke much of London clothes, and they that know the wearing, are desirous of them before the cloth of the womens making, for they find it nothing durable. For when it commeth to weare on the threed, it renteth like paper. [Sidenote: Much Venice clothe worn in Persia.] Here is much Venice cloth worne, being cromplisted a yard and a halfe broad, and sold here from 24. to 30. shaughes their arshine, being longer by two inches then the Russe arshine is; I wish also that you send some good chamlets and veluets died in graine, with purple colours and fine reds: because these are most worne. Also some blacks with other colours: some cloth of gold, tissue and bocky, some veluets wrought with gold, with sattins and damaskes, most purple, and reds of all sorts. You may not forget to send some Western karseis, to wit, dozens, which be thicked well, and close shut in the weauing, being died into fine reds, and some skarlets: for I thinke there is no such cloth for their caps.

[Sidenote: The second admission to the Shaughs presence, the 29. of Iune 1566. at which time he reciued the priuiledge. The Shaughs promise to increase the priuiledge.] Your worships shall vnderstand, that after my first departure from the presence of the Prince, I neglected no time in daily attendance on them, who had my priuiledge in writing, that I might haue it in readinesse at such time as I should againe bee called before the presence of the Shaugh, which was the 29. of Iune last. I was in apparell that he gaue vnto me, with other garments to mine interpreter, and one of your seruants, and then I receiued your letters or privilege, according to my desire, sealed and firmed with the Shaughs owne hand. Praysed bee God who hath wrought with me, and for me, in all my doings.

The 29. of Iune is one of their chiefe festiuall daies, so that all his nobilitie was there present, with two Ambassadors in companie with his maiestie, who sayd vnto me that if my letters were not to my mind, in time to come they should be mended. Whereupon I made my reuerence, and gaue his highnesse most humble and heartie thanks, saying, that with as much speed as might bee, our Queenes Maiestie should vnderstand of his goodnesse towardes her Merchants, which I thought would write their letters of request vnto his Highnes, in such forme and order as by them should be thought meete and requisite for their good assurance in the trade of merchandizes: who replied with these wordes: when wee shall see their reasonable requests, we will shew them our farther good will, and so I departed.

Since the receiuing of the Shaughs letters, I haue eaten in company of good Dukes and others, who before would not come neere me. And euery day some would come to my Shop, and eate and drinke with me out of mine owne dish. Likewise in riding from Casbin hither, on the way when I sate downe to dinner, they would come and eate with mee vnbidden, when I wished them further off: for I spared them that, which gladly I would haue eaten my selfe. I doubt not but we shall liue here from hencefoorth in quietnes: for now in all places where I come, I am friendly vsed with the best.

I was asked by the Shaugh if you were able to bring him yeerly one hundred thousand pieces of kersies, and clothes. And I answered him, saying, your worships were able to furnish his countrey with two hundred thousand. Whereat his Highnesse reioyced: for the Turkes Ambassador the last yere, as diuers haue told me, did put the Shaugh in despaire, saying, that the, Turke would not permit any cloth to be brought into his countrey.

[Sidenote: Aleppo a citie of great trade.] There is a citie in Syria named Aleppo, wherein coninually are many Venetians dwelling, besides other that come yeerely and there buy wools, gals, tallow, saffron, skins, cotton wooll, and other wares, and great store of spices. [Sidenote: Armenians barter with the Venetians.] Also the Armenians yeerly receeiue at the Venetians hands, karsies in barter for rawe silks, giuing sometimes 60. pieces of karsies for 70. batmans of silke of this countrey, and 40. pieces for Grosin silke. And karsies sold commonly for ready money in Aleppo, at 11. and 12. duckets the piece, (the ducket being here woorth 12. shillings) may cost the first peny 132. and 144. Shaughs a karsie. [Sidenote: The distance from Shamaky to Alappo.] By report it is one moneths trauel from this towne of Shamaky to Aleppo, and from thence to Tripolis, six dayes iourney: and from Tripolis to Venice by water, a moneth or fiue weekes sailing. As I learne, from hence to Venice may easily be trauelled in lesse then three moneths. Therefore I wish your worships to procure some trustie and assured friend there, to whom from hence letters may be sent For I can haue them here to put in suerties to deliuer my letters, and to bring answere. If I had any other here with me, I would nothing haue doubted to haue brought you the Shaughs letters that way.

[Sidenote: Armenians and others desirous to barter silke and spices for karsies.] The Armenians and other are desirous to barter with vs, giuing silke for katsies, and also will seme vs of all kind of Spices, we giuing them sufficient warning to fetch it in the Indies, and will deliuer it vs in Shamaky at these prizes.

Pepper this townes batman for 18. Shaughs, euery Shaugh is sixepence.

Maces large for 40. Shaughs, and 45. the batman.

Cloues for 40. Shaughs the batman.

Nutmegs for 16. and 18. Shaughs the batman.

Sinamon for 40. Shaughs the batman. I doubt not but there will be profile and good done in spices, with drugs and other like in time.

From Casbin to Ormus is six weeks trauel, and from hence to Casbin is 16. dayes with camels laden: but if one trauell with a good Mule vnladen, it may be gone in seuen or eight dayes. And I thinke to Ormus and other places, may be trauelled in like order and proportion, with cattel vnladen. But here in all places as men may trauel, they must carie their owne prouision on horses, which they are to buy, and thus they, uauel but a footepasse.

[Sidenote: The Shaugh desirous to bargaine for our commodities.] The Shaugh himselfe is desirous to bargaine with you who will giue money, silke, and other wares as we will, and take our wares as we may affoord them, willing me himselfe to bring such wares as we might gaine by him. The Armenians by report, and as I perceiue, bring from Aleppo yeerely, foure, fiue, and six thousand pieces of karsies, and clothes, besides those which other men bring. If your Worships might procure and find vent or sales for rawe silke, and silke died in graine, besides other silkes wrought and made here, by which, profile may be made: then you might send a great substance of wares hither. But I feare you shall be hindered by the Venetians if they may: for I know it will grieue them that you doe trade into these partes: for in short time it shall cleane alter their trade, and hinder the sales of their clothes in Aleppo and other places adioyning. You shall understand that 60. batmans of silke is a Mules lading: and as it is reported, one village of the Armenians yerely carieth 400. and 500. Mules lading of silke to Aleppo, and bringeth thence 800. or a thousand Mules laden with karsies and Venice clothes. And 18. pieces of karsies are a Mules lading. [Sidenote: 2000. pieces of karsies to be sent into Persia.] But I wish you not to send aboue 2000. pieces of karseis, although I haue bene willed to write for more. If I might haue had any vnderstanding what your Worships had written for in your letters sent this yeere, I should in this my letter haue bene better able to haue answered you. They which be now in Astracan, might haue written some thing vnto me hither, if it had pleased them, or else haue sent me such letters of mine, as I hope some of my friends haue written to me: for here are arriued eight weekes past, two boates with wares and Russes, by whom they might haue written, had it bene but 3. or 4. lines. They promised the Russes to write, but promise was not kept. I would be sory that any boat should depart out of these partes, and not write vnto them, waying how all things stand. I heare they haue bought a boat, which coast 40. rubbles, and shipped certaine wares to come hither. God send them in safetie. I do tarie their comming, or els I had thought to haue come to Astraean in those boates which departed hence lately.

[Sidenote: He departed from Casbin the 15 of Iuly.] The fifteenth of Iuly last, I departed from Casbin, and came to this towne the 29. of the same. And the fourth of August I found means to arrest the falsest knaue in this countrey, to wit, the Customer for 22. tumens, and 100. shaughs, (200. shaughs is a tumen.) I haue caused him to put in suerties for his foorth comming at all times, what ende I shall haue with him, God knoweth, the debt will be recouered, but not yet, for he must pay the Shaugh 1000. rubbles. These partes as yet are in no stay for lacke of a Gouernour or head to rule, which I thinke shall bee the Mursey. Within 5. or 6. dayes we shall know, for it is time, because men are in feare to trauell for being robbed. If there were a prince placed, I should soone get in your debts, for they dare not disobey the Shaughs letters or priuiledge: wherein he hath not onely written that our debts shall be paied, but also that we shall be taken heed to, so as we need not to doubt (God willing) in time to come, to be here as wel vsed as we are in Russeland. [Sidenote: Rich. Iohnsons great negligence.] The bils of debt that Rich. Iohnson left with me, had neither the parties name nor summe of money in two of them, and in other bils but his owne name. If I had not used discretion in causing to be written in our priuiledge, that such debtes as are owing, should be paied any of vs in the absence of the other, some men would not haue paied one penie, but onely to Richard Iohnson, who hath written but his owne name onely in the bils. I receiued in Casbin of Forackan in part of 29. tumens, 300. shaughs in money: the rest he will deliuer me here in silke, and this is all that I haue receiued to this day. And as for Hawrambecks twelue tumens, I make accompt, that if I could ride to speake with him, I should be paid in money and wares. Touching Ackons money, by meanes of Duke Ameddinbeck, who first owed the debt, because they meant not to pay a penie, he did rather seeke to hinder my sute then to further mee, but I found out a present remedie: for God sent me friends that were alwayes about the Shaugh, and daily put on his apparell, who opened all my sute, and brought mee to the presence of the Shaugh before that Cozomomet sawe the Shaughs eyes. [Sidenote: Cozomomet was Arthur Edwards friend to the Shaugh.] But Cozomomet in the end was my friend: for he was sent for, and declared vnto the Shaugh what good merchants we were, vsing trueth in all our doings, and how we were in great fauour with the Emperour of Russia, and what good commodities wee might bring into his Countrey, with other talke. And daily he was sent for to the Shaugh about the affaires in those partes, for no man was able to aduise the Shaugh of the state and affaires of those Countreys so much as hee was. He owed your Worships seuen tumens and 48. shaughs, which was not all this time to be gotten at his hands: for hee was at great charges in riding to Casbin, and giuing great gifts since his comming, which he twise declared vnto mee. I feeling his griefe became Physicion to ease his pain, and forgaue him his debt abouesayd, in recompence of ten pieces of karsies, that were promised him by Richard Iohnson and me, to giue him at the comming of our goods, in consideration that he should with speed doe what lay in him, to dispatch me away: for I perceiue hee procured other that did helpe me in my sute to delay me of, till time he had his purpose. [Sidenote: Victuals and all things dear at Casbin.] I neuer was in quiet, till I had the Princes priuiledge, and had got mee out of Casbin: for victuals, and all other things are very deare there, because they are brought thither from farre off. As for all other smal debts (which may be about 7. tumens) when our Merchants are come hither, we shall seeke, to get them in as we may. I wish your Worships to send some bullion to bee coyned here, it will please the prince there, and be profitable to you. Silke is better cheape by two or three shaughs the batman, then it was the last yeere. You shall vnderstand that I haue written two letters of all my proceedings, which I sent from Casbin long since: to wit, the 24. and 29. of Iune last, by one of your seruants to Gilan, there to take ship and to goe to Astracan, and to deliuer the same vnto your Factors, which might haue bene to their quietnes and mine, long agoe. But I am right sorie to heare since my comming hither, that he hath plaied the loitering merchant in Gilan, not going in those boats that went first, but taried for the last boats. But I will teach him, to the example of other, how he shall make haste hereafter in such affaires. The karsies which you sent last, being bought of M. Quarles, were good and full lengths and well sorted. [Sidenote: The Ambassador of the prince of Gilan.] The Ambassador of Gilan was in Casbin, at my being there. I hope in God, if I remaine here, and may goe to Gilan to obtaine for your worships the like priuiledge at the kings hand there also. [Sidenote: Gilan but five dayes riding from Casbin.] For I haue something moued the matter, being put in such comfort, that I doubt not the getting thereof with small charges, which I had done at this time if I had had other here with me to put in trust: for from Casbin to Gilan is but 5. dayes riding, which Countrey may be profitable to your Worships. There is in that Prouince good store of silke, better cheape, and better in goodnesse then this countrey silke is. Also great store of Alom, being there sold this townes batman, for one bist and a halfe. I haue made reckoning, al charges borne from hence to Colmogro, and from thence fraight into England at three pounds the tunne, al charges accounted, will not stand you in aboue 18. and 20. shillings the hundreth. You haue yeerly by report two or three hundred tunnes lading. Other commodities there for England I heare not of. [Sidenote: Gals.] As for gals here to bee bought, there is no profit to be done by them. They be brought from Aleppo, and sold here not vnder 3. or 4. shaughs their batman, being six pounds English waight. [Sidenote: Graine.] Graine that you die scarlet withall is worth the batman ready mony, 200 shaughs, reckoning the shaugh for 6. pence Russe, it may be 6. rubbles their batman. Your worships may send some portion of mony, if you may buy, as I thinke you may, for 12. and 13. s. a pound the berries, so you shall gaine both in the price and waight. [Sidenote: Ormus Aleppo.] If one Englishman more had bene here with me, to whom I might haue deliueied our bils of debts and other things, whatsoeuer should haue chanced of me, I would then haue become seruant to mine Interpreter, and so haue gone to Ormus and Aleppo, which both ioyne on the borders of this countrey, being the chiefe Marte townes, whereunto from all places merchants resort. And thus would I haue spent 4. or 5. months in trauelling for further knowledge of things for to haue certified your worships of. I hope in God to vse things in such order, that yeerly you shall haue returne of your goods from hence, as you haue forth of Russeland, and in those ships. For if we may, as I doubt not with diligence, prouide to make sales in time, and with speed receiue silke at the Shaughs hand, and other mens, that it may be sent from hence to be in

Astracan at the beginning of Aprill, from whence it may be sent to Colmogro in three moneths and lesse, and there to be ready with the rest of your goods by the end of Iune for your ships to receiue, that will be time inough. This I doubt, not to bring to passe within a yeere or two, when we are throughly setled in these parts, and better knowen. [Sidenote: M. Anthonie Ienkinsons offer to the Persain.] Moreouer you shall vnderstand, that at my last being in the presence of the Shaugh, it was sayd to mee that M. Anthonie Ienkinson did proffer to take all the rawe silke in those parties, delivering cloth and other commodities for the same. I assure you there is in those parts to be had three or foure thousand horses, lading, euery horse load being 50. or 60. batmans, beside silke of Grosin. Great abundance of silke at times is sent out of these parts, to wit. 4. or 5. hundred horse lodes at a time by the Turkes, who bring great store of siluer to be coined, to wit, Dollars at ten shaughs the piece. The Hungarie Ducket is at 12. shaughs. And hauing money in readines at the time of the yeere, they buy silke the better cheape, when the countrey men bring it first to be sold. If your worships may bargaine with the Venetians to take silke at your hands, or otherwise deale with them, I doe not mistrust but to haue at the Shaughs hand sixe batmans of silke for two pieces and a halfe of karsies. Your good aduise herein, and in other matters, I trust you will write with conuenient speed. [Sidenote: M. Anthonie Ienkinson commended.] Master Anthonie Ienkinson hath deserued great commendation at all your worships hands: for the good report of his well and wise doings in those parts, was oftentimes a comfort to me to heare thereof, and some good helpe to me in my proceedings. To this day I neuer heard from any of our merchants. God graunt me in health to see your worships, for I haue had a carefull trauell, with many a sorowfull day and vnquiet sleepes. Neither had I the company of one English person, to whom sometimes I might haue eased my pensiue heart, as God well knoweth, who hath deliuered me from mine enemies. Thus almightie God graunt you in health and wealth long to liue.

Your humble seruant at commandement during life,

Arthur Edwards.

* * * * *

Another letter of Arthur Edwards written in Astracan the 16. of Iune 1567. at his returne in his first voiage out of Persia, to the right worshipfull Companie trading into Russia, Persia, and other the North and Northeast partes.

It may please your Worships that herein I haue written not onely certaine articles of your priuiledge, but also the Gouernours names, with the Consuls, Assistants and generalitie. [Sidenote: The Shaughs letters to the Moscouy companie.] Also such commodities as the Prince or Emperour of the Countrey hath written in one of his letters directed to your Worships to be sent him, with other notes which I thought good to be remembered, as may appeare hereafter following. Your priuiledge is written, graunted, and giuen in the names of these sixe persons following: to wit, sir William Garrard, sir William Chester, gouernours, sir Thomas Lodge, master Anthony Ienkinson, master Thomas Nicols and Arthur Edwards.

1 First, it is granted that you shall pay no maner of customes or tols, any kinde of wayes now, nor in time comming, vnto his heires after him. And that all English merchants, such as you shall appoint now and hereafter, shall and may passe and repasse into all places of his dominions and other countries adioining in the trade of merchandise, to buy and sell all maner of commodities, with all maner of persons.

2 Item, that in all places where any of our merchants shall haue their resort, or abiding, his chiefe Gouernours, Rulers and. Iustices shall take heed vnto vs, being our aide and defence against all euil persons, punishing those that shall do vs any wrong.

3 Item, that for all such debts as shall be owing by any maner of person, iustice shal be done on the partie, and we paid at the day.

4 Item, that no maner of persons whatsoever estate or degree they be of, shall be so hardie as to take any kind of wares, or any gifts, without any leaue and good will.

5 Item, if by chance medley any of our merchants or seruants, as God forbid, should kill any of his subiects, that no part of your goods shall be touched or medled withall, neither any partie but the offendour, and true iustice to bee ministred, and being any of vs, not to suffer without the Princes knowledge and aduise.

6 Item, that all such debts as are now owing, or hereafter shall be, are to be paied vnto any of vs, in the absence of the other, be the partie dead, or aliue.

7 Item, that no person returne any kind of wares backe againe, being once bought or sold.

8 Item, that when God shall send your goods to shore, presently his people shall helpe vs on land with them.

These articles before written, I trust in God wil content your minds, vntil your farther letters be hitherto written vnto the Prince, who I am assured will graunt your farther reasonable requests, which his maiestie hath promised. For I moued the question, declaring vnto him that I thought your worships would write your letters of requests, to craue his farther good will, as should be thought meet for your better assurance in the trade of merchandise: you will hardly beleeue what long and gracious, talke he had with mee, which I assure you continued two houres, which was strange vnto the people and other merchant strangers. For betwixt euery question that his maiestie moued, when I had answered him, hee would talke with his Nobles and other his seruants hauing some knowledge of our Westerne parts and commodities, and then againe would demaund other questions. He caused his Secretarie to write the articles before named, in all of his foure letters giuen me (whereof two as I required, are in the Turkish tongue to be sent you.) On the, backe side of the one, hee hath written what wares his Maiestie would haue you to send him. He held me one houre within night before I departed from him.

These bee the names of the wares or commodities, which on the backe side of
  one of his letters the Shaugh hath written to you to be sent him.

First, some cloth of Gold, with cloth of Tissue, and cloth of Botky, as Veluets wrought with gold.

Item, good veluets, to wit, crimosins, purples, reds, greenes and blackes. Those colours his maiestie requireth, for they are most worne. And though there be some of these wares made in his citie of Cassan, yet nothing like in goodnes, to those that you may procure for him. Small profite I thinke will be in these wares: yet for diuers considerations, as also to satisfie the Princes mind, I wish you to send some, and those that be especiall good.

Item, good damasks and sattins of all sortes, with an hundred pieces of good chamlets, which are woorth here 80. shaughs the piece, at sixe pence the shaugh, and those silkes to bee of those colours aboue written, to wit, crimosins, purples, reds, greenes, blackes, with some light watchet colours.

Item, three or foure complete harnesses that wil abide the shot of a handgun with 10. or 12. targets of steele, being good.

Item, ten or twelue good shirts of male being very good or els none, that may abide the shot of an arrow, and two buffe ierkins.

Item, ten or twelue pieces of Westerne karsies, being thicked well and close shut in the weauing, and died into scarlets and fine reds. I thinke there wil be no such cloth for noblemens caps. The prince named them karangies [Marginal note: By the word Karangies, I thinke they meane Karsies.], saying, that maidens did make them, and is desirous of them.

Item, six pieces of fine Holland cloth for the Prince, with some other for Noblemen, of a lower price.

Item, twentie handguns being good, some of them with fire lockes, and also six good dags, with locks to trauell withall.

Item 100. brusshes for garments (none made of swines haire,) for gifts, and otherwise to be sold.

Item, six stone bowes that shoot lead pellets.

Item, a mill to grind corne in the field as they goe, finely deuised: for Cozomomet willed me to write for one to be sent, to giue the Prince.

Item, the Prince requireth of all sortes and colours of London clothes. I wish you to send no lesse then 40. or 50. for I know they will be sold to profit, especially such cloth as may be affoorded for 20. shaughs the arshine, which is longer by two of mine inches then Russia arshine is. Let there be fine skarlets, violets in graine, fine reds, blacks, browne blewes, foure or fiue of euery sort, for the Prince and other lords: the rest of other colours liuely to the sight, as London russets, tawnies, lion colours, good liuely greenes, with other, as you shall thinke good: for the prince desireth to see of all sorts, which will be an occasion that the Venetians and Turkes shall bee in lesse estimation then they are: for they themselues do feare, and secretly say the same. And truely the Princes subiects intend to enter into trade with vs for spices and other commodities that they were woont to sell vnto the Venetians and Turkes.

Thus I commit you all to God, who send you health with increase of worship.
Written in Astracan the 16. of Iune, 1567.

By your seruant during life to command,

Arthur Edwards.

* * * * *

Distances of certaine places in Russia.

The way from Saint Nicholas Baie to Mosco.

versts
To Colmogro 100
To Vstiug 500
To Totma 250
To Vologhda 250
All by the riuer of Dwina 1100

To Yenslaue 180
To Rostoue 60
To Pecaslaue 60
To Mosko 120
By land East and West 440

The way from Mosko to Smolensko.

To Moram 300
To Smolensko 200

The way from Mosko to Nouogrod.

To Ottuer 180
To Torzhoke 60
To Wisnouolloko 60
To Nouogrod 150
Southeast and Northwest 450

The way from Nouogrod to Narue

To Teseua 50
To the Friers 60
To Yria Niagorod 40
To Narue 15
Southwest and Northeast 165

From Nouogrod to Vobsky, is 180. versts by East.

The way from Vobski to Ry in Liefland.

                    versts
To Newhouse 50
To Gouen on the borders |
To Wenden |
To Trecado | Al is 200
To Newslot | versts.
To Rie |

The way from Mosco to Astracan.
To Costrom
To Nisnoaogrod
To Cazan
To Astracan in all is 2800 versts

The way from Vologhda to Narue.

To Belozerco 140
To Batag 80
To Witergen 40
To Ladiski 60
To Onega lake 80
To Oher 90
To Narue 180
Southwest and Northeast 770 versts

To go with a small boat within the land from S. Nicholas to Wardhouse.

To Newnox riuer |
To Ousca Gouba |
To Lobshanga |
To Oust Nauelocki | To Wardhouse
To Orlouanos | in
To Solusca Monasterie | all 800.
To Candelox | versts
To Oust Colla | Northwest
To Zhemaker | and Southeast
To Poganna Volocki |
To Chibe Nanolocke |
To Kegor |

The way from Colmogro to Mixemske Sloboda, where the Samoeds keep their
  Mart.

To Vst Pinnego |
To Palango |
To Vescom |
To Soyaua | Al is 230 versts
To Coula |
To Nendega |
To Lampas |
To Sloboda |

The way to Vromo from Mazemske Sloboda, where the Losh hides are gotten.

To Lampas | All is 115. versts
To Pogorel | Northeast and
To Zapolle | Southwest.
To Vromo |

The way and distances from Saint Nicholas, to the Caspian Sea.

If you goe straight from Saint Nicholas, to the Caspian Sea, you must goe to Vologhda by water, as by the easiest passage, and that is accomplished, passing day and night, in fourteene dayes and fourteene nights, in boates cut out of a tree: (the boates are called Stroogs) 1100. versts it is.

By horse and sleds in 8. dayes you may passe it in Winter. In Summer the way is dangerous by meanes of marishes and bogs, and not safely then to be passed. Then from Vologhda to Yeraslaue 180. versts ouer land. This

Yeraslaue standeth vpon the riuer of Volga, 180. versts I say distant from Vologhda.

To the Caspian sea are 2700. versts from Yeraslaue.

So from S. Nicholas to the Caspian sea, are 3800. 80. versts.

The iourney from S. Nicholas to Yeraslaue is accomplished in foureteene dayes by water, and two dayes by land. 16. dayes.

From thence to Astracan men trauell by water in 30. dayes and 30. nights.

So between S. Nicholas and the Caspian sea, are 46. dayes iourney.

There passe downe Volga euery Summer, 500. boats great and smal, from all the vpper parts of the riuer, whereof some be of 500. tunne. They go for Minerall salt and for Sturgeon.

The salt lieth in rocks (and is whitish red, and in fine sand) as it were 30. miles from Astracan toward the Caspian sea. They dig it themselues and pay nothing for it, but to the prince a peny a pood, viz. 40. pound waight.

[Sidenote: Fishing for Sturgeon for 3 moneths.] The Sturgeon which they call Ocetera is taken fiftie miles on this side Astracan. Along the riuer the space of 20. miles, they make their booties in plaine grounds, and fish for the space of three moneths, viz. from the end of May till, the end of August, and hauing salt they vse to salt them.

The riuer is there 5. or 6. miles broad, but with some Islands. The riuer below Yeraslaue, where it is most narrow, is a mile broad from side to side.

The riuer runneth vpon red clay, all woods of birch and oke on the riuer sides, saue about the townes of the fishing places.

Dwina from S. Nicholas to Vstiug runneth all on chalke and sand: the fish are sweete and fat The Mene a fish with a great head a foot long breedeth about Vologda, and is fat and delicate.

Between Vobsko and Nouogrod, the space of an 180. miles, groweth flax: the whole soile in length is so imploied, and as much in breadth: this is vpon a flat soile.

The hempe groweth about Smolensko vpon the Polish border, 300. miles in compasse: much of the soile is so imploied.

[Sidenote: The Englishmen in making of cables set on worke 100 men in Russia.] Of this hempe they bring in Winter to Vologda and Colmogro, and we set in worke in making of cables aboue 100 men.

The Russians do spin and hachell it, and the English tarre it in threed and lay the cable. And one cable of those is woorth two of Danzick, because the

Danzickers put in old cable and rotten stuffe, which in fowle weather is found of no strength.

[Sidenote: Sosnoua tree excellent for the cure of the wolfe.] Sosnoua, a tree that cureth the wolfe with the shauings of the wood, groweth in these parts, and of the barks they make ropes as big as a mans arme for their boats.

The Samoeds lacking linnen make handkerchiefs and towels of the very wood of this tree. The wood of this tree is as heauie as hollie, and the shauings tough.

[Sidenote: The description of Rose Island.] Rose Island in S. Nicholas Baie is full of Roses damaske and red, of violets and wild Rosemarie: This Island is neere 7. or 8. miles about, and good pasture, and hath the name of the roses.

The snow here about the midst of May is cleared, hauing bin two moneths in melting, then the ground is made dry within 14. dayes after, and then the grasse is knee high within a moneth. Then after September the frost commeth in, the snow is a yard deepe vpon plaine ground. The Island hath Firre and Birch, and a faire fresh spring neere the house built there by the English.

* * * * *

The way discouered by water by vs Thomas Southam and Iohn Sparke, from the towne of Colmogro, by the Westerne bottome of the Baie of S. Nicholas, vnto the citie of Nouogrod in Russia, containing many particulars of the way, and distance of miles, as hereafter foloweth. Anno 1566.

We departed from Colmogro about 10. of the clocke afore noone in a Lodia or Barke, which we hired to bring vs along the coast to a place called Soroka, and in the sayd barke we hired 6. mariners, and a boy to conduct vs to the place before rehearsed.

The Lodia or barke was of the burden of 25. tunnes or thereabout, wherewith we valed downe the riuer of Dwina, the winde being then calme, vnto a monasterie, called S. Michael where we were, constrained to anker because of a contrary wind which there met vs.

[Sidenote: A verst is but 3 quarters of an english mile.] From Colmogro to this monasterie are 50. versts or miles of Russia, at which place we taried till the 21. day in the morning, and then hauing the wind somewhat faire, we set saile and departed thence.

21 We departed, from the monasterie of S. Michael, hauing the wind somewhat faire, and arriued at Rose Island, ouer and against the monasterie of S. Nicholas, the 22. day at 2. of the clocke in the morning, which is 35.

miles distant from the monasterie of S. Michael. By reason of contrary wind and tide we were constrained to tary there all that day.

23 We departed from the monasterie of S. Nicholas at 7. of the clocke in the euening, and came to an anker at the Beacons, and continued there vntil halfe an houre past 10. of the clocke, and then set from thence, the wind being South: our course was West vntil 5. of the clock in the morning, when as we came to an anker against Newnox towne, where we continued vntil the 25. day.

[Sidenote: At this towne Newnox Richard Chanceller in his first voyage, with his companie ashipboard were relieued.] The sayd towne of Newnox is from the monasterie of S. Nicholas 35. miles.

25 We departed from Newnox hauen at one of the clocke in the after noone, the wind at South and Southeast, and our course Northwest and by West.

The point of Tolstick which is the headland before the entrance of Newnox hauen, and the headland of Seusemski lie next Southeast and by South, Northwest and by North. We came to an anker there this day at 4. of the clock in the afternoone being from Newnox hauen 15. miles, where we continued in harbour til the 27, day of the moneth, by reason of contrary winds.

27 We departed from Seusemski in the morning at 5. of the clocke, the wind next at East and by North, and our course Northwest and by West.

The said land of Seusemski and the headland going into Owna riuer lieth East and by South, west and by North, and between them is 25. miles.

This day at Sunne set we came to an Island called Sogisney passing betwixt it and the maine, with the wind at South and by East, our course was West and by South, being 85. miles from Owna riuer.

Being past the said Island 10. miles, the wind came contrary, whereupon we returned to the Island of Sogisney, where we remained vntil the 29. day.

29 The 29. day we departed from Sogisney aforesayd, at 5. of the clocke in the afternoone, the wind at East northeast, and our course was Southwest and by west, passing by an Island called Anger, being 30. miles from Sogisney, and keeping on our course, we came by the headland of an Island called Abdon, being from the Island of Anger 15. miles, where we found many rocks: and if the great prouidence of God had not preserued vs, wee had there perished, being fallen amongst them in the night time, and our pilot none of the perfectest, which was contrary to his profession as we found it.

But whosoeuer will trauell that way must either keepe hard aboord the shore, for that there is a chanell which goeth along the coast within the rocks, or els giue the headland a birth of 6. miles at the least, and so goe a seaboord all: for there are ledges of rocks that lie fiue miles from the headland.

We gaue the headland a birth of 3. miles, notwithstanding there lay two rockes two miles to sea boord of vs, so that we were inclosed with them, and sate vpon the highest of them: but it pleased God to make it calme, and giue vs the day also, or els we had miscaried.

30 We departed from the headland of the Island of Abdon, at 4. of the clocke in the morning, directing our course West, and at 10. of the clocke before noone, we arriued at a monasterie named Solofky, which is 15. miles from Abdon.

At this monasterie we continued vntill the 31. day of this moneth. We had here detracted vs by the chiefe monkes of the monasterie, their letter and house seale, and a seruant of theirs to conduct vs safely through the dangerous riuer of Owiga.

The people of all those parts are wild, and speake another kind of language, and are for the most part all tenants to the monasterie. The effect of the letter was, that they should be ready to helpe and assist vs in all dangerous places, and carie our boats and goods ouer land in places needfull, as in deed they did, as hereafter shall appeare.

Note, that at our being at the monasterie, there was no Abbot for the place as then chosen: for 15. dayes before our arriual there, the Abbot was sent for by the Emperour, and made Metropolitane of the realme, as he now is. The number of monkes belonging to the monasterie are at the least 200.

31 Wee departed from the monasterie of Solofky, as is aforesayde, to a faire stone house of theirs, which is 5. miles from the monasterie, lying from it South and by West.

[Sidenote: August] 1 We departed from the Stone house at 3. of the clocke in the morning: our course was West for 60. versts, and then passing betwixt diuers and sundry rocks, with many small Islands round about vs for the space of 20 miles, keeping most commonly the same course still, we then shaped a new course, and yet sundry times shifting, [Sidenote: The riuer Owiga.] but we alwayes kept the Southwest, and neerest of all South southwest vntill we came within two miles of the entrance of the riuer Owiga where we were to beare in, West and by North.

From the riuer Owiga, to the Islands and rocks before mentioned, are 20. miles.

We arriued about 4. of the clocke in the after noone within the riuer of Owiga, at a place named Soroka, at which place we forsooke our barke or Lodia, and continued there in making prouision for small boates to carie vs vp the riuer vntill the 3. day of the same.

3 We departed from Soroka at two of the clocke in the afternoone, with 3. boats and 12. men to rowe, and set the foresaid boates vp the riuer of Owiga, which we hired.

[Sidenote: The fall of a riuer.] We went this day 7. miles to a place called Ostroue, where we lay all night, but in the way 4. miles from Soroka, at a place where the water falleth from the rocks, as if it came steepe downe from a mountain, we were constrained to take out our goods and wares out of the said boats, and caused them to be caried a mile ouer land, and afterwards also had our boates in like sort caried or drawen ouer land by force of men which there dwelled, being tenants to the monasterie aforesaid.

And when our boats were come to the place where our wares were laid, we lanched our boats and laded our wares againe, and went to the place before named, where we continued and remained that night.

We departed from Ostroue in the morning before Sunne rising, rowing and setting vp the riuer 5. miles, where we came to a place whereas we were againe constrained to take out our wares, and to carie them and our boats three miles ouer land, so that with rowing, drawing and setting, we went this day 7. miles more to a place called Sloboday, where we lay all night.

5 We departed from Sloboday in the morning at Sunne rising, and at sixe of the clocke in the aftemoone, we came to a village called Paranda, which is from Sloboday 30. miles, where wee remained all that night.

6 We departed from Paranda at 6. of the clocke in the morning, and all that day what with setting and drawing our boats, we went but 11. miles, for we twise vnladed our wares, and drew our boats ouerland, in one place a mile and an halfe, in another place as it were the eight part of a mile, and so we came to a place called Voyets, where we taried all that night.

7 We departed from Voyets at 4. of the clocke in the morning, and so came to an Ozera or lake, called after the name of the riuer, and vnto a place called Quequenich, wee rowed all this day, and came thither by one of the clock in the afternoone, which is 25. miles from Voyets, and there we remained all night to hire men and boats to carie vs forward on our iourney.

Here departed backe from vs the seruant which we had at the Monasterie, being sent by the monkes to go thus far with vs. And after that he had hired the boats and taken the mens names that should conduct vs, and giuen them charge to deliuer vs with all things in safetie, at a place being a litle towne called Pouensa, then hee departed from vs without taking any reward for his paines, for so he was charged and commanded by the monkes.

[Sidenote: A lake very full of Islands.] 8 We departed from Quequenich at sunne rising, and all that day rowed vpon the lake amongst many Islands. The inhabitants doe there report that there are as many Islands in their lake, as there are dayes in the yeere. In the euening we came to a village named Tellekina, which is 60. miles from Quequenich.

9 We departed from Tellekina in the morning at 5. of the clocke, and so entring into a riuer, we went that day 13. miles. In one place we caried our boates and goods ouerland 3. miles. At euening we came to a place called Oreiche na maelay, where we lay all night.

10 Wee departed thence at 5. of the clocke in the morning, and so rowing, came to a place where the riuer ended, being 20 miles distant from the place where wee lay all night, at which place wee forsooke our boates and vnladed our wares, and sent a man to the towne of Pouensa, which was seuen mile ony for horses to cary vs and our wares to the said place. The horses came, and we laded our goods, and at sixe of the clocke in the afternoone wee arriued at the towne of Pouensa, with all things in safetie.

[Sidenote: The famous lake of Onega.] This towne of Pouensa standeth within one mile lake of of the famous lake or Ozera of Onega, which is 320. miles long and in some places 70. miles ouer. But where it is narrowest it is 25. miles ouer, being fed with many goodly riuers which fall into it. Hard aboord the shore within 6. miles, you shall haue 40. and 45. fathoms of depth.

Here it is to bee noted that from this place of Pouensa vnto the village of Soroka downe those dangerous riuers which wee came through, at no time of the yeere can or may any man cary or transport any goods that come from Nouogrod, or the Narue, and such other places: for in the Sommer it is impossible to cary downe any wares by reason of the great fals of water that doe descend from the rockes. Likewise in the Winter by reason of the great force and fall of waters which make so terrible raises, that in those places it neuer freezeth, but all such wares as come from Nouogrod to Pouensa, are transported by land to a place called Some in the Winter, which Some standeth on the sea side, as doth Soroka. The ready way from Pouensa by land to this place of Some, with the distance of miles I will shew hereafter.

12 We departed from Pouensa at 9. of the clocke in the morning, with 2. smal boats which we hired to cary vs to a place called Toluo vpon the lake of Onega, being 50 miles from Pouensa, where we arriued the 13. day in the

morning, where wee bought a boate that caried vs and all our wares from thence to the Citie of Nouogrod.

14 We departed from Toluo at 3. of the clocke in the afternoone, and at the euening arriued at a certaine Island named Salasalma, vpon the said lake 7. miles from Toluo, and by reason of contrary windes we there taried vntill the 16. day of this moneth.

16 We departed from Salasalma, at 8. of the clocke in the morning, and came to an Island the 17. day in the morning, named Vorronia, where wee continued by reason of contrary winds, vntill the 21. day of the said moneth, and it is 60. miles from Salasalma.

[Sidenote: S. Clement his Monasterie.] 21 We departed from Vorronia Island two houres before day, and arriued at S. Clements Monasterie at 2. of the clocke in the after noone, being from Vorronia 48. miles.

22 We departed from S. Clements Monasterie at the breake of the day, hauing a faire wind all a long the lake: we sailed without striking of saile vntil two houres within night, and then entred into a riuer called Swire, at a Monasterie called Vosnessino Christo, fiue miles from the entrance of the riuer, where we taried al night. It is from S. Clements Monastery 160. miles: the streame of that riuer went with vs.

23 Wee departed from Vosnessino Christo before Sunne rising, and valed downe the riuer sometime sailing, and sometime rowing, so that this day wee went 90. miles and lay at night at a place called Vassian.

24 Wee departed from Vassian at the breake of the day, and came to a place called Selucax [Marginal note: Or Sermaxe.], where we lay all night, and is 10. miles from Vassian.

[Sidenote: The riuer of Volhuski. The lake of Ladeskai.] 25 We departed from Selucaxe at 4 of the clocke in the morning, and entred vpon the Lake of Ladiskaie, the winde being calme al that day sauing 3. hours, and then it was with vs, so that we sailed and rowed that day 10. miles, along vpon the said lake, and entred into the riuer of Volhuski, which riuer hath his beginning 20. miles aboue Nouogrod, and runneth through the midst of the Citie, and so falleth into this lake, which is farre longer then the lake of Onega, but it is not so broad. This lake falleth into the sea that commeth from the Sound: where any vessel or boat, hauing a good pilot, may goe through the Sound into England.

As soone as we were entred into the riuer, we came to a Monasterie called S. Nicholas Medued, where we lay all that night.

[Sidenote: The Monasterie of Gosnopoli.] 26 Wee departed from S. Nicholas Medued, at fiue of the clocke in the morning, rowing and drawing our boates all day, and came at night to another Monasterie called Gosnopoli, which is 30 miles from S. Nicholas Medued, where we lay all that night.

27 We departed from Gosnopoli at 6. of the clocke in the morning, and at euening came to a place called Moislaue, where we lay all night, being 46. miles from the Monasterie of Gosnopoli.

28 We departed from Moislaue, and the saide day at night came to a place called Grussina, 35. miles from Moislaue where we lodged.

29 Wee departed from Grussina in the morning, and the same day at euening came to a place called Petroe Suetoe, where we lay all night, being 40 miles from Grussina.

[Sidenote: The citie of Nouogrod.] 30 We departed from Petroe Suetoe in the morning, and at two of the clock in the afternoone we arriued at the Citie of Nouogrod, being twentie miles from Petroe Suetoe. Here we found William Rowlie Agent to the company, who was there stayed with all his company, and was not licenced to depart thence for the Mosco, by reason that the plague was then in the Citie of Nouogrod. Vnto him we deliuered all the wares that wee brought from Colmogro, for by the way we sold not a peny worth, the people of the countrey euery where be so miserable.

The right way to bring and transport wares from Nouogrod to Rose Island into S. Nicholas bay, where our Ships yeerely lade, with the distance of miles from place to place, is as followeth:

20 Miles from Nouogrod to Petroe Suetoe.

40 Miles from thence to Grusina.

35 Miles from thence to Moislaue.

46 Miles from thence to the Monasterie Gosnopoli.

15 Miles from thence to Ladega towne.

15 Miles from thence to Selunaz ouer the lake of Ladega, albeit there be many villages all along the lake.

180 Miles from Ladega towne vp the riuer of Swire, vnto the Monasterie of Vosnessino Christo, albeit there are many villages vpon the riuer: for within euery fiue or six miles you shall haue villages or small townes.

160 Miles from Vosnessino Christo to S. Clements Monastery, albeit there be many villages all along the lake of Onega.

48 Miles from thence to Voronia.

67 Miles from thence to Toluo towne: and there are diuers villages al along the lake where the carriers may lie, and haue meate for man and horse.

50 Miles from thence to Pouensa, where Onega lake endeth.

The way from Pouensa to Some towne is this:

> 30 Miles from Pouensa to Mastlelina. 10 Miles from thence to Tellekina. 30 Miles from thence to Toluich. 35 Miles from thence to Carraich. 20 Miles from thence to Varnich. 10 Miles from thence to Ostrouo. 15 Miles from thence to Lapina. 20 Miles from thence to Some it selfe.

Note, that from the Citie of Nouogrod vnto the towne of Some is 936. miles, and from the towne of Some vnto the Monasterie of S. Nicholas or Rose Island, ouer and against where our Ships do ride, is iust as many miles as is Soroka village from S. Nicholas, as the Russes doe accompt it, as also we do iudge it, namely 325. miles. So that from Nouogrod to S. Nicholas road, is by our accompt 1261. miles or versts.

[Sidenote: Trauel by Sleds.] Furthermore it is to be noted that all such wares as shall be bought at Nouogrod, and sent to Some towne, must be sent by sled way in the Winter: for if any ware should be sent from Nouogrod by water in the spring of the yeere after the yce is gone, then must the said wares remaine at Pouensa towne al that Summer, by reason that in the Summer there is no way to goe from Pouensa vnto Some towne.

At Pouensa there are many warehouses to be hired, so that if there were as much goods as ten ships could cary away, you might haue warehouses to put it in: but if there should remaine much ware all the Summer, to be caried in the Winter to Some towne, then horses are not easily to be gotten at that place to cary it thither: [Sidenote: 2000. Sleds belonging to one towne.] so that your wares once bought at Nouogrod, you musthaue cariers there to cary it to the towne of Some by Sleds, whereof you may there haue 2000. if you will, by the report of the Russes.

For from Nouogrod yerely there go many Sleds in the Winter to fetche salt from Some, with carriers and emptie Sleds there to buy it, and to bring it to Nouogrod to sell it in the market or otherwise.

[Sidenote: A good caueat for seasonable trauell.] From Nouogrod vnto Some towne you may haue a pood of wares carted for eight pence or nine pence: but in any wise your wares must bee sent from Nouogrod by the sixt of Ianuary, so that the wares may bee at Some by Candlemas, or soone after: for if your wares should tary by the way vntill the 15. of February, when the Sunne is of some power, then is it dangerous: for the heate of the Sunne in the day causeth the deepe lakes of Ladega, and specially of Onega to cleaue: and if there should come then a sudden thaw, as oftentimes in that time of the yeere doeth, then doe these lakes open and breake, whereby many men are lost, and both men and horse drowned, although other riuers do remaine frozen a long time after.

In the towne of Some also there are many warehouses, whereof we cannot be destitute for the reposing of our wares, as also as many barkes as you wil to transport your wares from thence to S. Nicholas road, and that for three pence a poods caryage: so that from the Citie of Nouogrod vnto S. Nicholas road you may haue wares caried for two altines. The pood commeth vnto 23. altines the tunne.

[Sidenote: Nouogrod within 180 miles of the Narue.] Prouided alwayes, that you buy your wares there your selfe, and send it thence: for there is no hope that the natiues will bring their wares from Nouogrod to Some, in hope to sell vnto vs, considering the great trade that they haue at the Narue, which is within 180. miles off them.

Written by Thomas Southam a seruant to the company.

* * * * *

An Act for the corporation of Merchants aduenturers for the discouering of new trades, made in the eight yere of Queene Elizabeth. Anno 1566.

Whereas diuers very good Subiects of this Realme of England in the latter end of the reigne of the late right high and mightie prince our Soueraigne Lord king Edward the sixt, at the gracious incouragement, and right good liking of the said king, and by his Maiesties liberall example, did at their aduenture, and to their exceeding great charges, for the glory of God, the honor and increase of the reuenues of the Crowne, and the common vtilitie of the whole Realme of England, set forth three ships for the discouery by Sea, of Isles, lands, territories, dominions, and Seigniories vnknowen, and by the Subiects of the sayd late king not commonly by seas frequented: and after that Almightie God had called to his mercie the said king, who died before the finishing and sealing of his most ample and gracious letters of priuiledges promised to the said Subiects, as wel in consideration of the said enterprise, as for diuers other respects it pleased our late soueraigne Q. Mary, at the humble suites of the same subiects, to graunt by her letters Patents vnder the great Seale of England, bearing date at Westminster the 26. day of February, in the second yeere of her raigne, for the considerations mentioned in the said letters Patents, to the saide subiects being specially named in the saide letters Patents, and to their successors, that they by the name of Merchants aduenturers of England, for the discouerie of lands, territories, Isles, dominions, and Seigniores vnknowen, and not before their late aduenture or enterprise, by seas or Nauigations commonly frequented, should be from thenceforth one body, and perpetual felowship and communalitie of themselues, both in deed and in name, and that same felowship and communaltie from thenceforth should and might haue one or two gouernours, foure Consuls, and 24. assistants, of the said fellowship and comminaltie of Merchants aduenturers, and that they by the name of the Gouernour, Consuls, assistants, felowship, and comminaltie of Merchants aduenturers, for the discouery of lands, territories, Isles, dominions, and Seigniories vnknowen by the seas and Nauigations, and not before their said late aduenture or enterprise, by Seas frequented, should or might be able in the lawe to implead and to be impleaded, to answere and to be answered, to defend, and to be defended, before whatsoeuer Iudge or Iustice temporall or spiritual, or other persons whatsoeuer, in whatsoeuer court or courts, and in all actions, real, personal, and mixt, and in euery of them, and in all plaints of Nouel descision, and also in all plaints, suites, quarrels, affaires, businesse, and demaunds whatsoeuer they be, touching and concerning the said felowship and comminaltie, and the affaires and businesse of the same only in as ample maner and forme, as any other corporation of this Realme might doe, giuing also, and granting vnto them by the said letters Patents, diners authorities, powers, iurisdictions, prehemmences, franchises, liberties and priuiledges, as by the same letters Patents more at large will appeare. And among other things mentioned in the said letters Patents, whereas one of the three ships, by the said fellowship before that time set foorth for the voyage of discouery aforesaid, named the Edward Bonauenture, had arriued within the Empire and dominion of the high and mightie Prince Lord Iohn Vasiliwich, Emperour of all Russia, Vlodimersky, great duke of Musky, &c. who receiued the Captaine and Merchants of the saide shippe very graciously, granting vnto them freely to traffique with his subiects in all kinde of Merchandizes, with diuers other gracious priuiledges and liberties: therefore the said late Queene by the same letters Patents, for her, her heires and successors, did graunt that all the maine lands, Isles, ports, hauens, creeks, and riuers of the said mighty Emperour of all Russia, and great duke of Mosco, &c. and all and singular other lands, dominions, territories, Isles, ports, hauens, creeks, riuers, armes of the seas, of al and euery other Emperour, king, prince, ruler, or gouernour whatsoeuer he or they be, before the said late aduenture or enterprise not knowen, or by the aforesaid merchants and subiects of the said king and Queene, by, the seas not commonly frequented, nor any part or parcel thereof, and lying Northwards, Northeastwards, or Northwestwards, as in the said letters patents is mentioned, should not be visited, frequented nor haunted by any the subiects of the said late Queene, other then of the said company and fellowship, and their successors, without expresse licence, agreement, and consent of the Gouerner, Consuls, and Assistants of the said felowship, and communaltie or the more part of them, in maner and forme, as is expressed in the saide letters patents, vpon paine of forfeiture and losse aswell of the ship and ships, with the appurtenances, as also of the goods, merchandizes, and things whatsoeuer they be, of those the subiects of the said late Queene not being of the saide fellowship and communaltie, which should attempt or presume to saile to any of those places, which then were, or after should happen to be found and traffiqued vnto, the one halfe of the same forfeiture to be to the vse of the said late Queene, her heires and successors, and the other halfe to be to the vse of the said felowship and communaltie, as by the same letters patents more plainly will appeare.

Since the making of which letters patents, the said fellowship haue, to their exceeding great costes, losses and expences, not onely by their trading into the said dominions of the saide mightie prince of Russia, &c. found out conuenient way to saile into the saide dominions: but also passing thorow the same, and ouer the Caspian sea, haue discouered very commodious trades into Armenia, Media, Hyrcania, Persia, and other dominions in Asia minor, hoping by Gods grace to discouer also the countrey of Cathaia, and other regions very conuenient to be traded into by merchants of this realme, for the great benefite and commodities of the same.

[Sidenote: This is meant for Alderman Bond the elder.] And forasmuch as diuers subiects of this realme, vnderstanding the premises, and perceiuing that now after the charge and trauel aforesaid, diuers wares and merchandizes are brought by the saide fellowship into this Realme, out of the dominions already discouered, which bee within this realme of good estimation, minding for their peculiar gaine, vtterly to decay the trade of the sayde fellowship, haue contrary to the tenor of the same letters patents, in great disorder traded into the dominions of the said mightie prince of Russia, &c. to the great detriment of this common wealth: And for that the name by which the saide felowship is incorporated by the letters patents aforesaid, is long, and consisteth of very many words: [Sidenote: English Merchants for discouery of new trades.] Therfore be it enacted by the Queenes most excellent Maiestie, the Lords spiritual and temporal, and the commons in this present parliament assembled, and by authoritie of the same, that the said felowship, company, society and corporation made or created by the said letters patents, shal at al time and times from henceforth be incorporated, named and called only by the name of the fellowship of English merchants, for disouery of new trades, and by the same name for euer shall and may continue a perpetuall body incorporate in deede and name, and onely by the same name from henceforth, shall implead, and be impleaded, answere and be answered, defend and be defended, sue and bee sued, in whatsoeuer courts and places, and shall and may by the same name bee inabled to purchase, haue, holde, possesse, reteine, and enioy whatsoeuer manors, landes, tenements, rents, reuersions, seruices, and hereditaments not exceeding a hundred marks yeerly, not being holden of the Queenes matestie, her heires, or successors by knights seruice in Capite, and all goods, merchandizes, chattels, and other things whatsoeuer, and shall and may by the same name make and do all things as any other corporation may do, and also shall haue and enioy all and singular the liberties, priuiledges, iurisdictions, franchises, preheminences, powers, authorities, and things, and may doe and execute all other matters and things in the sayd letters patents mentioned, or in any wise conteined. And that no part nor parcell of the maine lands, Isles, ports, hauens, roades, creekes, riuers, armes of the seas of any Emperour, king, prince, ruler or gouernor whatsoeuer he or they be, before the said first enterprise made by the merchants, of the saide corporation, not knowen by the merchants and subiects of this Realme, or by them not commonly by seas frequented, and lying from the City of London Northwards, Northwestwards, or Northeastwards, nor any part or parcel of the maine lands, dominions, isles, ports, roades, hauens, creeks, armes of the Seas, that now be subiect to the said high and mightie prince Lord Iohn Vasiliwich, his heires, or successours, or to the Emperour, chiefe gouernour or ruler of the said country of Russia for the time being, his heires or successors, nor the countries of Armenia maior or minor, Media, Hyrcania, Persia, or the Caspian sea, nor any part of them shall be sailed or traffiqued vnto, visited, frequented, or haunted by any person being or that shalbe a subiect or denizen of this realme, by themselues, their factor or factors, or any other to their vse or commoditie, by any wayes or meanes, directly or indirectly, other then by the order, agreement, consent, or ratification of the gouernour, Consuls and assistants of the saide fellowship and comminaltie, or the more part of them, and their successors for the time being: vpon paine that euery person and persons offending in this behalfe, shall forfeit and loose, Ipso facto, euery such ship and ships, with the appurtenances, and all such goods, Merchandizes, and things whatsoeuer, as by any such person or persons shalbe by any wayes or meanes, directly or indirectly, prouided, caried, conducted, brought, or exchanged, in, at, to, through or from any of the places prohibited, as is aforesiade, contrary to the true intent of this statute: the one moietie of all which forfeitures to bee to our said souereigne Lady the Queenes Maiestie, her heires and successors, and the other moietie thereof to the sayde fellowship of English Merchants for discouery of newe trades, and their successors, to be seized and taken wheresoeuer they may be found, by any person or persons, to the vse of our said Souereigne Lady, her heires and successors, and of the said fellowship of English Merchants for discouery of newe trades, and of their successors, or the same or the value thereof to bee demaunded or sued for by the Queenes highnesse, her heires and successors, or by the saide fellowship of English Merchants for the discouery of newe trades, or their successors, or their atturney or atturneis, or by any person or persons being of the same fellowship of English Merchants for discouery of newe trades, or their successors in any court of Record, or in any other Court or courtes within this Realme, or els where, by Action of debt, action of detinue, bill, plaint, information, or otherwise: in which suite no essoine, protection, wager of lawe, or iniunction shal be allowed, for, or on the behalfe of the partie or parties defendant.

Prouided alwayes, that whereas diuers Subiects of this Realme being not of the fellowship aforesaid, haue heretofore made aduentures to and from some of the places prohibited by the said letters patents, that the said subiects, their heires, executors, administrators and assignees, or any of them shall not be impeached, impleaded, troubled, sued, nor molested for the same in their goods or persons in any maner of wise, either by our saide souereigne Lady, her heires or successors, or the said fellowship, or their successors.

Prouided also, that it shall be lawfull for any subiect of this Realme, hauing presently any shipping, goods, wares, or ready money, remayning at or in any place, of or within the dominion of the said mighty prince of Russia, or in any other of the places prohibited to be visited or traffiqued vnto by this statute or the said letters Patent, to fetch, brings and conuey the same, or cause the same to be brought or conueyed from thence by sea or otherwise, before the feast of S. Iohn Baptist, which shalbe in the yeere of our Lord God 1568. any thing, conteined in this statute, or in the said letters Patents to the contrary notwithstanding.

Prouided also, that it shall be lawfull for any of the subiects of this Realme, to saile to the port, towne, territorie, or castle of Wardhouse, or to any of the coastes, townes, hauens, creekes, riuers, Islands, and land of Norway for trade of fishing or any other trade there vsed by the subiects of this Realme, any thing in this statute to the contrary notwithstanding.

And for the better maintenance of the Nauie and Mariners of this Realme, be it prouided and inacted that it shall not be lawfull to the saide fellowship and company, nor to any of them to cary and transport, or cause to be caried any commodie of this Realme to their newe trade, but only in English ships, and to be sailed for the most part with English Mariners, nor also to bring into this Realme nor into Flanders from their saide new trade, any merchandizes, or other commodities but in English ships, and sailed for the most part by the English Mariners, on paine to forfeit for euery such offence two hundred pounds, whereof the one moietie shall be to the Queenes Maiestie, her heires and successors, the other moietie to the head officers of any port towne, hauing any hauen or harborough decayed, by what name soeuer they bee incorporate, to the reparation of such harborough, that will sue for the same in any Court of Record, by action, bill, plaint or information, wherein no essoine, protection, wager of lawe for the defendant shall be admitted or allowed.

Prouided also, and be it enacted, that no maner of person or persons shall from henceforth carrie or transport, or cause to be carried or transported out of this Realme of England, any maner of clothes or karsies into any of the partes where the said fellowship and societie is priuiledged to trade by this Act, before the same clothes and karsies shall be all dressed, and for the most part died within this Realme vpon paine of forfeiture for euery such cloth and karsie, otherwise caried and transported, fiue pounds: the one halfe thereof to the Queenes Maiestie, her heires and successors, the other halfe to the Master and Wardens of the Cloth-workers in the Citie of London for the time being, by what name soeuer they be incorporate that will sue for the same.

Prouided also that whensoeuer the said societie of company shall willingly withdraw, and discontinue wholy by the space of three yeeres in time of peace, the discharging of their merchandizes at the road of S. Nicholas bay in Russia, and doe not discharge their said merchandizes at some other port or roade lying on that North coast of Russia, or other territofie nowe subiect to the saide mightie prince of Russia, &c. hitherto by the subiects of this realme not commonly frequented, that then during the time of any such discontinuance and withdrawing, as is aforesaid, it shalbe lawful to all the subiects of this realme to trade to the Narue onely in English bottoms, any thing in this Act to the contrary notwithstanding.

Prouided also, that euery of the Queenes Maiesties Subiects inhabiting within the Citie of Yorke, the townes of Newcastle vpon Tine, Hull and of Boston, hauing continually traded the course of merchandize by the space of ten yeeres, and which before 25. of December that shalbe in Anno D. 1567. shal contribute, ioyne, and put in stocke, to, with, and amongst the said company, such summe and summes of money, as any of the said company, which hath throughly continued and contributed to the saide newe trade, from the yeere 1552. hath done, and before the saide 25. of December 1567. shall do for the furniture of one ordinary, full and intire portion, or share, and do in all things behaue himselfe as others of the said societie be bound to doe, and hereafter shall bee bound to do by the priuiledges, ordinances and statutes of the saide company, shall from the same 25. day of December 1567. be, and be accompted free, and as one of the said societie and company, and subiect to the priuiledges, ordinances and statutes of the saide company, reasonably made and to be made, any thing in this present Act to the contrary notwithstanding.

* * * * *

A very briefe remembrance of a voyage made by M. Anthony Ienkinson, from London in Moscouia, sent from the Queenes Maiestie to the Emperour, in the yeere 1566.

The fourth day of May in the yere aforesaid, I imbarked my selfe at Grauesend in the good ship called the Harry of London, and hauing had a prosperous voyage arriued at the bay of S. Nicholas in Russia the 10. day of Iuly following, and immediately I sent in post to the Emperor to aduertise of my comming, and traueiling then thorowe the countrey, I with my company came to the Mosco where the Emperour kept his court, the 23. of August and foorthwith gaue the Secretarie to vnderstand of my arriuall, who aduertised the Emperours Maiestie of it, and the first day of September, being a solemne feast among the Russes, I came before the Emperours Maiestie, sitting in his seate of honour, and hauing kissed his hand and done the Queenes Maiesties commendations, and deliuered her graces letters and present, he bad me to dinner, which I accepted, and had much honour done vnto me both then and all the time of my abode in Russia.

END OF VOL III.

Milton Keynes UK
Ingram Content Group UK Ltd.
UKHW040818051024
449151UK00004B/308

9 789362 510112